Literature Links

Thematic Units Linking Read-Alouds and Computer Activities

Linda D. Labbo • Mary Susan Love • Miri Park Prior
Betty P. Hubbard • Tammy Ryan

INTERNATIONAL
Reading Association
800 BARKSDALE ROAD, PO BOX 8139
NEWARK, DE 19714-8139, USA
www.reading.org

The International Reading Association attempts, through its publications, to provide a forum for a wide spectrum of opinions on reading. This policy permits divergent viewpoints without implying the endorsement of the Association.

Director of Publications Dan Mangan
Editorial Director, Books and Special Projects Teresa Curto
Managing Editor, Books Shannon T. Fortner
Acquisitions and Developmental Editor Corinne M. Mooney
Associate Editor Charlene M. Nichols
Associate Editor Elizabeth C. Hunt
Production Editor Amy Messick
Books and Inventory Assistant Rebecca A. Fetterolf
Permissions Editor Janet S. Parrack
Assistant Permissions Editor Tyanna L. Collins
Production Department Manager Iona Muscella
Supervisor, Electronic Publishing Anette Schütz
Senior Electronic Publishing Specialist R. Lynn Harrison
Electronic Publishing Specialist Lisa M. Kochel
Proofreader Stacey Lynn Sharp

Project Editors Elizabeth C. Hunt and Amy Messick

Art cover design, Linda Steere; cover and part page illustrations (pp. 13, 107, and 185): © Images.com, Inc.; images from Figures 5, 21, 30, 34, and 37 (pp. 26, 114, 181, 210, and 220): © Clipart.com; image from Figure 16 (p. 82): Linda Steere

Web addresses in this book were correct as of the publication date but may have become inactive or otherwise modified since that time. If you notice a deactivated or changed Web address, please e-mail books@reading.org with the words "Website Update" in the subject line. In your message, specify the Web link, the book title, and the page number on which the link appears.

Library of Congress Cataloging-in-Publication Data

Literature links : thematic units linking read-alouds and computer activities / Linda D. Labbo ... [et al.].
    p. cm.
  Includes bibliographical references and indexes.
  ISBN 0-87207-562-1
  1. Language arts (Primary)--Computer-assisted instruction. 2. English language--Composition and exercises--Study and teaching (Primary) 3. Education, Primary--Activity programs--Computer-assisted instruction.
  I. Labbo, Linda D. II. International Reading Association.
    LB1528.L57 2006
    372.64078'5--dc22
                                                                    2006000526

We dedicate this book to family members near and far who offer encouragement and support.
We especially thank David, Don, Steven, and Barry.

CONTENTS

PART 1: LITERARY CONCEPTS AND LANGUAGE ARTS CONNECTIONS

PART 2: SOCIAL AND MULTICULTURAL CONNECTIONS

PART 3: CONTENT AREAS AND MULTIDISCIPLINARY CONNECTIONS

ACKNOWLEDGMENTS

We owe a debt of gratitude to the students and teachers in early childhood classrooms at Whit Davis Elementary School, Fowler Drive Elementary School, and Benton Elementary School, all in Georgia, USA, who took the time to field-test many of the ideas we crafted for linking literature and computer activities. We thank them for being our colleagues and helping us to think through many of the issues.

We also acknowledge the support of other colleagues who provided feedback on the original idea, read first drafts of our work, or supported the idea from the start of the project. We recognize William Teale, University of Illinois–Chicago, Illinois; Charles Kinzer, Teachers College, Columbia University, New York; Nancy Roser, University of Texas at Austin, Texas; and Miriam Martinez, University of Texas at San Antonio, Texas, for their time and encouragement. We make note of the special contribution of Achariya Tanya Rezak, doctoral student at the University of Georgia, Athens, who devoted her time and talents to help us complete this project. We especially wish to thank our editors, Elizabeth Hunt and Amy Messick, for their tireless devotion to this project.

Effective primary-grade teachers, those who make a difference in the literacy development of their prekindergarten through second-grade students, are able to create literacy-rich learning environments that make the best use of classroom resources, time, and materials (Morrow, 1989). Teachers and students in primary grades routinely have access to an ample supply of two valuable resources—children's literature and computers (Ansell & Park, 2003; National Center for Educational Statistics [NCES], 1999). Teachers read well-loved books aloud; guide grand conversations (Eeds & Wells, 1989); use books as a springboard for literacy instruction; and provide cozy reading nooks where students joyfully explore books of all genres in reading lofts, beanbag chairs, bathtubs, and rocking chairs. In many classrooms, primary-grade students also eagerly play literacy learning games in computer centers; create word-processing documents; engage in keypal exchanges, an e-mail version of pen pals; publish work on class webpages; conduct Internet searches; and ultimately become computer literate (Clements & Nastasi, 1993; Labbo, Kinzer, Leu, & Teale, 2003).

Rationale for Linking Read-Alouds With Computer Activities

There is little doubt that literature-based and computer-related learning opportunities are important for primary-grade students' literacy development (Clements & Nastasi, 1993; Labbo & Reinking, 2003); however, it is our belief that teachers and students miss out on powerful learning events because storybook time and computer time frequently stand alone in the classroom curriculum and daily schedule (Labbo, Love, Park, & Hubbard, 2004). In fact, it is not unusual for the computer games young students play, word-processing documents they create, or information they acquire through Internet explorations to be completely unrelated to stories and story-related literacy activities (Labbo et al., 2003).

Indeed, the idea to write a book linking children's books to computer activities came about when we, the authors, realized that this theme had continued to surface in presentations that we gave at professional conferences, undergraduate courses that we taught, doctoral seminars that we participated in, and inservice staff development that we conducted. In contrast, we observed that although many prekindergarten through second-grade teachers enthusiastically embrace children's literature and computer applications separately to support literacy development, story time rarely links with computer time. In addition, we noticed that many of the prekindergarten through second-grade teachers we know enthusiastically use children's literature during story time as a springboard for literacy instruction. We knew that these same teachers enthusiastically use computer applications during computer-center time to support young children's literacy development. After discussing our observations, we decided to collect the ideas for story-time and computer-time links we had been sharing in so many other venues, field-test the ideas in primary-grade classrooms, and arrange them into a practical book of ideas.

While many possible underlying reasons for the disjuncture between literature and computer resources exist, we have focused on the lack of practical guidance in the form of constructive staff development, effective preservice teacher development, useful curriculum guides, or insightful teacher resources for crafting literature–literacy–computer connections in ways that enhance students' learning (Ansell & Park, 2003). We hope that this book will serve as a missing link—a practical guidebook of ideas in this area. It is worth noting that the purpose of this book is not to provide a technical manual on how to use specific computer applications. We believe that each software program or computer application includes adequate operating instructions that are beyond the scope of this book to address. Instead, we address how to work with programs and applications for optimal literacy learning.

Students in primary grades have opportunities to learn about literacy while they work in classroom computer centers or in computer labs playing varied interactive games; conducting focused informational searches on the Internet; creating multimedia documents, such as slide shows that include music and photographs to accompany text; writing with word-processing programs; or engaging in authentic online communication exchanges through e-mail (International Reading Association [IRA], 2001). Features of interactive multimedia computer applications make computers an especially valuable tool for primary-grade students' literacy learning. Components of these computer applications, such as animation, speech on demand, oral narration of directions, and feedback on the correctness of choices during games, are ideal for supporting primary-grade students' literacy development through computer-related activities (Cochran-Smith, Paris, & Kahn, 1991; International Society for Technology in Education [ISTE], 2002; National Association for the Education of Young Children [NAEYC], 1998). For example, students who cannot yet read independently are able to read a CD-ROM talking book because they can click on any word they do not know and hear it pronounced (McKenna, 1998). Animations that bring story text to life and music or sound effects that add artistic drama to plot twists can motivate the most reluctant young reader (de Jong & Bus, 2002). We hope that this book will make teachers want to use children's books we present in thematic unit collections as a springboard for many of the practical, timely, motivating, and developmentally appropriate computer activities we recommend.

Many ideas and activities presented in this book have been field-tested in prekindergarten through second-grade classrooms. As part of the field testing, we conducted a seven-month qualitative study during the 2003–2004 academic year of teachers' use of the computer-related thematic units to sort out their perceptions and enactments of the units (Labbo et al., 2004). Fifteen prekindergarten through second-grade teachers in three school districts volunteered to try out the units and invited us into their classrooms to observe how the computer activities within specific units were being used. We selected a subsample of one teacher from each grade level to observe at least four times. The observations consisted of one hour each, which we deemed sufficient to revise unit activities during the course of the field-testing. Data consisted of field notes in selected classrooms. We also conducted open-ended interviews with all the teachers about their perceptions of their students' opportunities for literacy learning through computer activities. We analyzed the data (Lincoln & Guba, 1985) with predetermined categories for instances of teachers' perceptions for what works, what does not work, and what should be changed and why in order to fulfill teachers' views for computer use. In this way, we could determine which parts of the units that were field-tested needed tweaking or revising.

Results indicate that teachers' perceptions of the units were clearly positive. For example, teachers reported that they noticed students using more unit-related vocabulary words at the computer when computer time was linked to story time. They seemed to use their language to guide their thinking processes and computer-related work. For example, one teacher noted that during the transportation unit, two prekindergarten children referred to a booklet that came with Tonka Construction, a software program that invites children to build construction equipment and use it to build a park, a house, or a castle:

> These two boys used vocabulary they learned from book read-alouds and from initial interactions with the Tonka program to problem solve. They talked about excavation equipment, earth movers, seeking the foreman for directions, etc. This is a type of oral language and vocabulary use I've never witnessed before when kids were working at the computer. I'm thrilled. (L. Sprauge, personal communication, April 15, 2005).

Teachers also noted students were highly motivated to participate with digital camera activities. Teachers stated that students wrote more sentences and more complex sentences when they had a photograph to support their memories of events. Teachers further reported students' more ample use of adjectives and descriptive sentences in dictating or writing in response to Digital Language Experience Approaches (D-LEAs; Labbo, Eakle, & Montero, 2002). Thus, while the purpose of this book is not to report on the research study, we want readers to know that suggestions we provide have been shaped and revised in response to intensive feedback from classroom teachers. Where appropriate, we have included quotes from teachers at various grade levels to capture the nature of their perceptions of suggested activities.

Presentation of the Book

This book is appropriate for beginning and veteran primary-grade teachers. Beginning teachers, especially those who are developing a knowledge base about children's literature but who already possess extensive computer knowledge, will benefit from learning about literature–computer connections. In other words, beginning teachers will connect what they need to learn more about (literature) with their knowledge base (computers). Veteran teachers, those who may be developing a knowledge base about computers in classrooms but already possess extensive knowledge about children's literature, will benefit from learning about computer–literature connections by connecting what they need to learn more about (computers) with their knowledge base (literature). Instructors of preservice teacher education classes may use the book to provide a general overview of ways to link literature–literacy–computer activities successfully. Students in preservice education classes may also use the book as a resource for trying activities during field placements when they write lesson plans and prepare learning activities. Finally, students in graduate classes and inservice teachers in staff development training may benefit from discussing the underlying theories behind literature–literacy–computer links or from writing and implementing literature–computer units that follow our organizational framework.

It is important to note that while we believe that most of the activities we suggest are appropriate for students of all literacy ability levels, we have made a point to address issues related to differentiating the curriculum when particular activities or computer applications lend themselves to doing so. As stated in Hall (2002),

> Differentiated instruction is a process to approach teaching and learning for students of differing abilities in the same class. The intent of differentiating instruction is to maximize each student's growth and individual success by meeting each student where he or she is, and assisting in the learning process. (n.p.)

As a result, we do not arrange units by grade level because each primary-grade classroom will consist of students of varying ability levels. We do, however, highlight generic literacy skills that are included in various computer-related activities. In addition, when appropriate, we provide ideas for activities suitable for a range of readers—emerging, developing, and fluent.

We define *emerging readers* as those students who are not yet able to break the sound–symbol code but who are learning foundational concepts about how meaning making with print works. *Developing readers* have broken the sound–symbol code but are in the process of accumulating sight words, learning vocabulary, practicing fluency, and becoming confident in their ability to decode unknown words. *Fluent readers* are confident in their abilities and can read connected text with few or no hesitations but will benefit from spending time reading various genres; writing on challenging topics; and speaking, listening, viewing, and representing ideas symbolically in electronic formats that may not be available in the reading curriculum.

In keeping with the purpose of this book, which is to serve as an inspirational and informative resource idea book, we organized it into 19 units, plus two appendixes: Appendix A, Steps for Conducting a D-LEA, and Appendix B, Steps for Conducting Author's Computer Chair. We began with 100 children's books, most of them published between 2000 and 2005, that we believe align especially well with a primary-grade curriculum. We also began with an assortment of 100 children's software applications, programs, and DVD animated big books. These animated big books, which are animated recreations of children's storybooks, can be played on DVD players and displayed on television monitors because they are frequently larger than computer monitors. Ultimately, after receiving feedback on the preferences of teachers who field-tested the units, we selected a subsection of the books and computer programs to include in units. Each unit is based on a collection of three books and computer activities that relate to a theme or topic. We adapted our framework for unit components from an analysis of guidelines for thematic-unit writing provided by experts in the field (Galda & Cullinan, 1991; Hoffman, Roser, & Battle, 1993; Moss, 1984). Thus, our units are intended to integrate the language arts of reading, writing, speaking, and listening with the digital and computer-related arts of reading on screen; writing on screen; speaking through audio capabilities (e.g., narrating text that others may listen to); listening by clicking on narration, sound effects, or music that is available on screen; viewing graphic illustrations, animations, video, or photographs on screen; and interacting with multimedia (IRA, 2001). We suggest cross-curricular activities when particular books or unit focuses lend themselves to a traditional subject area such as social studies, science, or mathematics. In addition, we address how specific features of individual books lend themselves to computer technologies, widely adopted approaches to instruction, and literacy objectives that range from foundational knowledge, such as ABC order and concepts about print, to higher order thinking skills, such as comparing and contrasting and distinguishing between real and make believe. We offer teachers a range of possibilities for how much preparation it takes for implementing units. Some of the units (e.g., art, music, poetry) suggest that a teacher take the time to create an extensive classroom learning environment. Other units (e.g., ABC order, fantasy, and writing) suggest less complex ways of implementing units—ways that do not require, for example, teachers to totally construct a new classroom learning environment. Thus, we believe that the units present various approaches to implementation and will help teachers develop a repertoire of approaches and become flexible and adapted to local contexts.

Units in our book consist of eight easy-to-implement components: (1) unit title and list of books, (2) thematic connection, (3) matrix of literacy skills and strategies, (4) unit introduction, (5) book reviews, (6) read-aloud and book discussion ideas, (7) computer activities, and (8) unit conclusion.

1. Unit title and list of books: Units consist of three books that may include narrative fiction or informational text in the form of picture books, easy readers (we define easy readers as short books that use limited vocabulary), or reference books. The annotation for the list of books, included for teachers' easy reference, includes the names of authors and illustrators. Most of the books included are picture books because primary-grade students find them engaging, they span wide topic areas, and they are developmentally appropriate both for whole-group read-alouds across primary-grade levels and for students' individual literacy levels (Galda & Cullinan, 1991). We anticipate that each teacher will adapt units by adding books that seem to fit the unit focus or by including favorite books—perhaps some in their library collections that are no longer in print—that are just too good to leave out.

2. Thematic connection: Because of our discussions with prekindergarten through second-grade teachers about the units they routinely teach throughout an academic year, we aimed to create collections of books that teachers indicated align with a general primary-grade curriculum. Thus, the book is divided into three parts that represent different primary-grade focuses. Part 1, Literary Concepts and Language Arts Connections, includes six units that delve into various ways to learn about and appreciate literacy. Part 2, Social and Multicultural Connections, consists of five units that deal with issues that are often important to primary-grade students, such as taking care of pets and gaining a positive self-concept. Part 3, Content Areas and Multidisciplinary Connections, presents eight units with topics that relate to social studies, science, or mathematics. The balance of topics related to content areas results from preliminary feedback from teachers who field-tested units. For example, teachers told us that they did not want to have separate units related to specific mathematical concepts. It is also worth noting that we could not locate children's literature selections for every mathematical concept. Thus, across the three parts of the book, we organize units by topics (e.g., jobs and careers, holidays, school and family life), themes (e.g., learning to like ourselves, appreciating differences), and genre studies (e.g., ABC books, fables and tall tales, poetry). When deciding on the focus for each unit, we first sorted books into collections by reading book abstracts and book jacket summaries. Next, we read every book that might potentially fit in a collection, determined a general unit focus, and asked ourselves a series of foundational questions:

- What thread or idea runs through all the books in this collection that will support teachers' efforts to help students make intertextual connections across books?

- Are the books related in ways that will provide occasions for students to learn more about the specific focus or topic?

- Are the books connected by a thematic link that delves into larger issues that allow students to explore their feelings and insights into humankind or make connections to their own lives?

- Are the books linked by a genre focus that gives students occasions for learning from concept books or gaining insights about aspects of a particular genre?

- Does the subject of particular books in a collection align with social studies, mathematics, or science content?

- Do specific features of individual books lend themselves to literary or literacy skills?

- What computer resources and activities align with unit themes and enhance literacy skills?

The overview at the beginning of each unit provides the rationale for linking the collection of books. Ultimately, we expect that each teacher who uses the units will refine the themes or topics to meet the needs of the students he or she teaches.

3. Matrix of literacy skills and strategies: Primary-grade classroom teachers who conducted field tests of the activities all indicated that it would be helpful if we included lists of the literacy skills and strategies that are addressed in each unit. They reminded us that in this age of teacher accountability—a time when documenting skills instruction is frequently expected by many stakeholders, such as parents, or even required by district literacy coordinators, school administrators, or instructional lead teachers—a list of skills is needed. Therefore, we include a matrix of literacy skills and strategies at the beginning of each unit. We spent a great deal of time looking at various curricular and instructional resources (e.g., supplementary, primary, standards based) for ideas about separating skills and strategies (that was a suggestion made by one reviewer). As a result of our informal review of these curricular and instructional resources, we have decided not to separate skills from strategies for several reasons. First, skills and strategies are not listed separately in two widely adopted teacher reading methods manuals (e.g., Leu & Kinzer, 2003; Vacca et al., 2003). Second, main sources we located that attempted any separation of skills and strategies were basal readers; however, for the most part the overall title of "skills and strategies" is employed in almost all basal reader scopes and sequences. Our book, which we wrote on a smaller scale than a basal series, is not intended to represent the range or the scope and sequence of a basal reader. Instead, we focus on what particular books and response activities lend themselves to within and across our units. Finally, in following up with three prekindergarten teachers we are currently working with, none indicated that it would be helpful to them to have skills and strategies sorted out separately.

In this way, teachers may make note of skills included in computer activities in their written lesson plans, through conversations with or in written notes to parents, or in discussions with other teachers and administrators. Unit activities were drawn from curricular scope and sequence guidelines followed in classrooms of teachers who field-tested the units; however, it is worth noting that the literacy skills we identify align well with our informal sampling of early literacy, curricular scope, and sequence guidelines on district and state Internet websites across the United States. Skills we include focus on both conventional literacies (e.g., phonics, comprehension, predictions, context clues, visualization) and many new literacies—which include the ability to understand and use information in multiple formats from a wide range of sources when it is presented via computers (Gilster, 1997)—that are explicitly identified (e.g., multimedia composition, hyperlink navigation) and embedded in units (e.g., using a digital camera, manipulating the computer mouse, reading multimedia text on screen, assembling knowledge from Internet sources, using creativity and presentation software).

4. Unit introduction: Collections of books we include should be introduced in simple but imaginative ways that excite students' interest and motivate them to want to learn more about focus themes or topics (Hoffman et al., 1993). Consequently, we include practical ideas for accomplishing this goal. Thus, for some units, the introduction suggestion may be as simple as posing a question for students to ponder before reading the first book in the collection. Doing so may help students activate relevant background knowledge and be drawn into learning more about a topic. Some units begin with a display of books and an invitation for students to predict what the books all have in common (Hoffman et al., 1993). Other suggestions may be more specific to a unit focus; for example, a unit on emotions might begin with a wrapped gift with no label sitting on a classroom table. Teachers might then ask students how they are feeling about the gift and explain that the emotion they are feeling is curiosity. Opening up the gift and finding the first book in the unit to read aloud would be a sure way to add to students' interest and excitement. The ideas for introducing units vary, but we in no way attempt to provide an exhaustive list of all possible ways to introduce units; we expect that teachers will tap into their own creativity.

5. Book reviews: We review three books for each unit by first noting the title, author and illustrator, date of publication, publisher information, price, and page count. We include this information so teachers will have enough information to locate copies of books. Next, we describe different aspects of the books that may integrate various elements such as story content, comments about literary language, delightful twists in the plot, an author's development of characters, richness of settings, aesthetic features, and so forth. We also briefly discuss the illustration style or artistic media employed by the illustrators of picture books. For informational texts, we discuss the organization, instructional features, design, and style of writing. The purpose of reviews is to help teachers get a sense of the nature of the books. However, we believe that it is important for teachers to read each book and get to know its content and tone before sharing it with students (Moss, 1984).

6. Read-aloud and book discussion ideas: Goals for read-aloud and book discussion time include modeling fluent reading, engaging students in higher-level thinking, helping them make intertextual connections, fostering life-to-text connections, and sharing a heartfelt love of reading through grand conversations (Eeds & Wells, 1989). We know that some teachers prefer to read straight through a story without stopping so that students can enjoy the entire story without interruption. Other teachers prefer to conduct interactive readings that involve students in affective and cognitive engagements such as predicting upcoming events, reflecting on cause–effect sequences, or connecting moments from their own lives with lives of story characters. Thus, the purpose of book discussion ideas we share is not to dictate the way teachers share books. The purpose is to highlight various aspects of the book that we find to be unique, interesting, or related to the unit focus. We do not attempt to provide an exhaustive list of all possible discussion ideas but merely provide a springboard to support teachers' and students' creative thinking as they enjoy books together. After books have been read aloud, discussed, loved, and shared, the time is right for teachers to introduce selected computer activities that are designed to enhance students' engagement with the story, provide occasions for extended literature-related literacy learning, and foster students' abilities to utilize computer technologies.

7. Computer activities: We organize computer activities that we suggest by means of what we call a *boutique collection* (Labbo & Teale, 2001). In other words, we do not present an entire department store or warehouse of computer applications (e.g., all of the thousands of possible computer software programs and online resources that are available) because we believe that doing so would be overwhelming to us as writers and to readers of this book. Rather, we focus on small, boutique collections of specific types of computer applications and activities that may be used effectively to support primary-grade students' literary and literacy development.

The boutique collection of computer activities we recommend consists of (a) creativity and presentation software (e.g., KidPix Studio Deluxe, 1998; PowerPoint, Microsoft Office 2003, 2003; Microsoft Paint, 1981–2001); (b) a D-LEA; (c) computer software activities (e.g., interactive CD-ROM games, talking books); and (d) Internet resources and ideas (e.g., resources for teaching ideas, student informational resources, online games, e-mail or keypal exchanges, online publishing). Within the boutique are many suggestions for author's computer chair, which is based on a fairly common print-based practice for students to participate in author's chair, a time for students to share final copies of stories or elicit feedback from peers on drafts of their works in progress. We recommend that teachers build upon this common practice with a similar literature–literacy–computer activity link. When students are figuring out how to play a computer game; trying to access information on the Internet; and composing stories, slide shows, or multimedia projects with computer technologies, we believe that they should have time and invitations to participate in an author's computer chair (Labbo, 2004) in order to receive feedback from peers or showcase their completed work.

The key difference from routines involved in author's chair and author's computer chair is that during author's computer chair, students discuss their computer-related processes of meaning making as they work to accomplish various tasks. Providing sanctioned time for students to talk about how they make meaning with computers is critical if teachers are to provide students with opportunities to develop print-based and multimedia literacies (Flood & Lapp, 1997–1998) in ways that prepare them for their literacy futures (IRA, 2001). By inviting others in the classroom to view their works in progress at the computer, young children will have unique occasions to use computer-related vocabulary, demonstrate how to use computer application tools, and discover the value of collaboration and feedback. By having occasions to showcase their computer work during author's computer chair, students will value their own and others' work. Thus, author's computer chair includes a physical place, sanctioned time, and social routine for sharing with peers during any phase of computer-related activities. Appendix B outlines key procedures in successfully integrating author's computer chair as part of the literacy curriculum.

The following paragraphs explain each component of the boutique collection of computer activities.

(a) Creativity and presentation software ideas: Creativity and presentation software that is well designed allows students to draw, paint, stamp, write, listen, view, compose, and craft their ideas on a malleable computer screen through multimedia symbol systems and interactive tools. Primary-grade students often enjoy expressing their ideas and make meaning by selecting from various symbol systems that include print, pictures, animations, sound, music, or computer screen special effects (Labbo, 1996). When students are motivated to spend quality time on task through their interactions with playful components of creativity and presentation software features, they have unique occasions to develop as literate computer users. Indeed, they gain multimedia literacy, a skill that will enable them to perform academically throughout their school careers.

(b) Digital Language Experience Approach (Labbo et al., 2002): D-LEA is a computer-enhanced version of a traditional language experience approach (Stauffer, 1970). (See Appendix A for a step-by-step description of D-LEA routines.) Language experiences, occasions for students to participate in classroom experiences and then dictate stories about them, are enhanced when digital photographs are used to create a tangible record of the experience. For example, when teachers take digital photos of students' activities, students have a visual resource that elicits rich oral language and serves as a memory link. In addition, multimedia features of creativity and presentation software—applications that include tools for drawing, selecting graphics, importing photographs, adding sound, using speech synthesis, and writing in the same computer screen—offer unique support for primary-grade students' efforts to compose stories (Labbo, 1996; Lomangino, Nicholson, & Sulzby, 1999).

Teachers can use a D-LEA to suit the literacy learning needs of students of various literacy abilities. For example, some students will benefit if they serve as a photographer for their own experience (Turbill, 2003). In these instances, students determine the focus of their D-LEA project; take selected photographs; and organize and compose their thoughts with creativity and presentation software (e.g., KidPix Studio Deluxe, 1998), presentation applications (e.g., PowerPoint, Microsoft Office 2003, 2003), or word-processing programs (e.g., Microsoft Word). Thus, teachers may adapt procedures to meet the literacy learning needs of emerging, developing, or fluent readers.

(c) Computer software activities: Well-designed interactive games or talking books allow students to work independently at computer centers with little intervention from teachers (Labbo, 2000; McKenna, Reinking, & Bradley, 2001). Of course, students will need initial support, directions, demonstrations, or one-on-one cross-age buddies. Children from the upper grades may serve as cross-age computer buddies for younger students for the first time or two they try out a program. See Figure 1 for cross-age computer buddy guidelines to post in the classroom. The chart lists activities cross-age computer buddies should follow to be effective when working with younger students at the computer.

Effective computer programs that we recommend in this part of the boutique collection give students appropriate feedback on choices they make while playing literacy games.

Furthermore, the programs use auditory prompts to support screen illustrations and directions.

(d) Internet resources and ideas: The Internet is a powerful resource for teachers and students (IRA, 2001; Leu & Leu, 1999). In identifying Internet resources for boutique collections, we suggest a wide variety of possibilities that include teacher resources such as lesson plans online (see, e.g., http://school.discovery.com/lessonplans/k-5.html), informational resources for students such as a link to a live camera at an aquarium to complement and extend learning related to sea creatures (see, e.g., http://waquarium.otted.hawaii.edu/vt/index.html), online books such as Story Book (see http://story.lg.co.kr:3000/english/story/index.jsp), and websites supporting e-mail or keypal exchanges such as KIDLINK (see www.kidlink.org).

Please note that we do not expect teachers to select every suggested computer activity that is listed for every unit. Indeed, we believe that teachers would be wise to select only those activities that meet the needs of their students and fit with their circumstances. Also, keep in mind that students may enjoy and benefit from having some choice in the selection of two or three possible computer activities related to stories they have heard in class.

8. Unit conclusion: We also offer suggestions for how to bring units to a conclusion in ways that invite students to celebrate and represent things they have learned through book discussions and computer activities (Hoffman et al., 1993). Ideas in this area range from computer slide shows to shared readings of class or individual books students have created with word-processing programs. Taking time to reflect on what was learned, how it was learned, and how the computer played a role in the learning can help students make valuable links between print-based and computer-based learning. Some units lend themselves to displays of students' computer printouts, students' individual books or onscreen slide shows, books written by the entire class or small groups of students, author's computer chair (see Appendix B on page 300) celebrations, or websites where children's work is published.

Conclusion

A word about Internet safety is in order because the Internet is a form of communication that is open to the public. In other words, people with varying agendas can post anything on the Web and make it accessible to anyone who has a computer and Internet connection. Many teachers limit students' potential access to inappropriate websites by bookmarking websites that they have selected. Thus, students do not surf the entire Web when seeking information. Rather, they scroll down their list of "favorites" to selected sites that have been previously screened for content and format. Yahooligans! (www.yahooligans.com) offers suggestions for guiding students to surf the Internet safely. In addition, most school districts and school campuses restrict access to inappropriate websites (Leu & Kinzer, 2003) by using blocking software programs such as Net Nanny 4 (www.netnanny.com). Programs that filter websites do so by listing keywords or websites that are inaccessible on computer systems on which the software has been installed. Finally, many schools require that teachers, parents, and students read or listen to and sign an acceptable-use policy contract. School district technology and curriculum directors or campus administrators should have information about acceptable Internet and computer-use policies.

We believe that teachers and students in prekindergarten through second grade have an exciting time in store for them when they begin to link children's literature with computer activities. It is our hope and expectation that students will benefit in many ways from this connection. Many teachers may want to begin slowly by selecting one book to read aloud and one related computer activity to assign to all students who may need an entire week to cycle through a one-computer classroom. Other teachers will want to focus on making connections between children's literature and computer experiences that allow all of the students to have Internet access to games or informational resources.

Over time, it is our hope that teachers will embrace the notion of a boutique collection of children's literature and children's computer-related activity resources. In those classrooms, students will be e-mailing keypals by sending attachments of their artwork (done in the artistic style of a favorite illustrator). They will be conducting Internet searches to complete scavenger hunts at developmentally appropriate websites. They will be composing multimedia projects on a computer screen. They will be sharing their computer works in progress during author's computer chair. They will be learning through play as they engage in meaningful game-playing activities that focus on literacy learning. And they will be utilizing the power of digital photography to innovate on text or capture ideas and make meaning with multiple symbol systems. In classrooms where these types of rich activities occur, students will find that their love of literature and their enhanced learning through computers will result in enriched literacy development.

About the Authors

Linda D. Labbo, PhD, professor and lead author, drew upon her experiences teaching prekindergarten through grade 5 in San Antonio, Texas, USA, for 6 years before serving as an instructor in reading methods courses at the University of Texas at San Antonio for 5 years. She has taught and conducted research at the University of Georgia, Athens, Georgia, USA, for 13 years. She serves as a coprimary investigator on a National Science Foundation grant to explore the impact of multimedia anchor cases on preservice teachers' effectiveness as first-year teachers. She also conducts research in primary-grade classrooms on young children's opportunities for development of literacies during computer-center activities.

Mary Susan Love, MEd, taught kindergarten, first grade, and second grade for 11 years in Wisconsin, USA, and taught courses in educational technology and design for grades K–4 and 5–8 at Middle Tennessee State University, Murfreesboro, Tennessee, USA. She is currently pursuing her PhD in the Department of Language and Literacy Education at the University of Georgia. Mary wrote several units for this book.

Miri Park Prior, MS, is currently pursuing her PhD in the Department of Language and Literacy Education at the University of Georgia where she serves as a research assistant for various projects that explore the role of computers in literacy. She is interested in using computer technologies with English as a second language students with a particular focus on vocabulary development. Miri wrote several units for this book.

Betty P. Hubbard, MA, is currently pursuing her PhD in the Department of Language and Literacy Education at the University of Georgia where she serves as a research assistant for projects that explore the role of computer technologies in teacher professional development. Betty wrote several units for this book.

Tammy Ryan, MS, has 16 years of teaching experience ranging from first through seventh grades in remedial reading, Chapter One, and Title One programs. She has taught in inner-city, urban, and research schools. Presently, she is pursuing her PhD in the Department of Language and Literacy Education at the University of Georgia where she serves as a research assistant for research projects investigating the role of computer technologies in the primary grades. She is interested in the use of various computer technologies to create an engaging, inviting, and effective whole-class learning environment. Most recently, she focuses her work on the use of interactive white boards to support young children's literacy learning. Tammy wrote several units for this book.

PART 1

Literary Concepts and Language Arts Connections

"My second-grade students who were still developing readers learned so much from doing this unit. They really enjoyed creating their own alphabet concept books about the food the lunch ladies prepare for us to eat!"

—SECOND-GRADE TEACHER

ABC Books

UNIT BOOKS

Arf! Beg! Catch! Dogs From A to Z
By Henry Horenstein

Alphabet Adventure
By Audrey Wood
Illustrated by Bruce Wood

Into the A, B, Sea
By Deborah Lee Rose
Illustrated by Steve Jenkins

COMPUTER RESOURCES

Clifford Reading
Alphabet: Play With the ABCs
Dr. Seuss's ABC

Thematic Connection

Alphabet books come in many shapes and sizes and cover various topics that are intriguing to young learners. For example, two of the books in this collection, *Arf! Beg! Catch! Dogs From A to Z* (Horenstein, 1999) and *Into the A, B, Sea* (Rose, 2000), are concept books that exhibit letters, words, and illustrations that represent a topic. Cullinan (1989) defined a concept book as an informational text about a theme or topic that is organized in alphabetical order. In other words, the first letters of names of objects related to a specific topic are arranged in alphabetical order. The third book, *Alphabet Adventure* (Wood, 2001), employs narrative to weave together a mystery about letters of the alphabet. Emerging and developing readers will have numerous occasions to identify letters, learn ABC order, and acquire a foundational understanding of sound–symbol relationships as they explore why certain letters are accompanied by specific illustrations and words. By participating in read-alouds and computer-related activities, fluent readers will have opportunities to reinforce foundational knowledge. Finally, readers of all levels will benefit from innovating on text by creating their own concept books related to classroom social studies or science topics. Research suggests that alphabet knowledge is foundational to primary-grade students' successful literacy development (Adams, 1990). The purpose of this unit is to provide primary-grade students with opportunities to learn more about the alphabet and related concepts.

Matrix of Literacy Skills and Strategies in Unit 1

Literacy Skills and Strategies	Activities	Title of Book	Pages
Building background knowledge on the Internet*	I I	*Arf! Beg! Catch! Dogs From A to Z* *Into the A, B, Sea*	19–20 27
Composing in multimedia*	C, D C, D C, D	*Arf! Beg! Catch! Dogs From A to Z* *Alphabet Adventure* *Into the A, B, Sea*	18, 18–19 21–22, 23–24 25, 26
Developing a sense of beginnings, middles, and endings	C	*Alphabet Adventure*	21–22
Developing choral reading	R	*Into the A, B, Sea*	25
Developing comprehension	S	*Arf! Beg! Catch! Dogs From A to Z*	19
Developing context clues	R R	*Arf! Beg! Catch! Dogs From A to Z* *Alphabet Adventure*	17 21
Developing creative writing	C, I C, D	*Arf! Beg! Catch! Dogs From A to Z* *Alphabet Adventure*	18, 19–20 21–22, 23–24
Developing oral language	R C R, C, D	*Arf! Beg! Catch! Dogs From A to Z* *Alphabet Adventure* *Into the A, B, Sea*	17 21–22 25, 25, 26
Identifying letters	U, UC R, C, S R, D, S, I D, S	— *Arf! Beg! Catch! Dogs From A to Z* *Alphabet Adventure* *Into the A, B, Sea*	16, 27–28 17, 18, 19 21, 23–24, 24, 24 26, 27
Making predictions	R	*Arf! Beg! Catch! Dogs From A to Z*	17
Navigating hyperlinks*	I	*Arf! Beg! Catch! Dogs From A to Z*	19–20
Reading and listening for a purpose	R R	*Arf! Beg! Catch! Dogs From A to Z* *Alphabet Adventure*	17 21
Recognizing ABC order	U, UC C, D, S C, D, S, I S	— *Arf! Beg! Catch! Dogs From A to Z* *Alphabet Adventure* *Into the A, B, Sea*	16, 27–28 18, 18–19, 19 21–22, 23–24, 24, 24 27
Using adjectives	R, D	*Arf! Beg! Catch! Dogs From A to Z*	17, 18–19
Using nouns	R, D	*Arf! Beg! Catch! Dogs From A to Z*	17, 18–19
Using phonics: Rhyming words	R, S	*Into the A, B, Sea*	25, 27
Using verbs	R, D	*Arf! Beg! Catch! Dogs From A to Z*	17, 18–19
Writing descriptive sentences	D	*Arf! Beg! Catch! Dogs From A to Z*	18–19

* Indicates a new-literacy skill.
U = unit introduction; R = read-aloud and book discussion ideas; C = creativity and presentation software ideas; D = Digital Language Experience Approach; S = computer software activity, I = Internet resources and ideas; UC = unit conclusion

Unit Introduction

To start the unit, display a scrambled set of magnetic alphabet letters on a cookie sheet and ask students to tell you what the objects are. Point to an alphabet chart or a set of alphabet cards posted in the classroom. Ask students to tell you how the letters on the cookie sheet are the same or different from the letters on the chart. Direct students to notice that the letters on the cookie sheet are not in ABC order. Tell them that during the upcoming unit you will be reading books and doing activities on the computer that will help them learn more about the names of letters, the order of letters in the alphabet, and words that go with each letter. For a group of mostly fluent readers, display the three books in the unit and ask students to explain what all the books have in common. Bring particular attention to the books that focus on a concept, such as dogs. Tell students that by reading and studying the books, they will learn how to make their own alphabet books about a topic of study that is related to a social studies or science unit you will be studying. After making arrangements with another kindergarten or first-grade teacher at your school, announce that by the end of the unit each student, or small group of students, will have published a concept book that they will share with other students.

MATERIALS

- Alphabet chart or set of alphabet cards
- Magnetic alphabet letters
- Metal cookie sheet

Book 1: Arf! Beg! Catch! Dogs From A to Z

Horenstein, H. (1999). New York: Scholastic. $12.95. 40 pp.

BOOK REVIEW

Colorful, uncomplicated photographs capture the spirit of canine life in the pages of this winsome book. Throughout these delightful pages, traits about dogs of all sizes and breeds are presented in alphabetical order next to pictures of dogs. Dogs jump, get kissed, ride, sit, sleep—and even yawn. Photographs range from full-body shots to close-ups. For example, a full-length photograph of a beagle sitting up and begging for a treat from his master's outstretched hand represents the letter *B b* for *begs*. A close-up photograph of a curly, longhaired, blond dog's tail represents the letter *T t* for *tail*. Upper- and lowercase letters, displayed on the top outside margins of each page, allow for easy reference to letters of emphasis. The last two pages of the book offer a colorful display of the alphabet in upper- and lowercase. The starting and ending pages, which usually are blank pages that attach the pages of a book to the cover, of this book display a charming photograph album collage of dogs relaxing on outstretched bellies, playing in water, striking a pose, or chasing tails. This book is bound to elicit oral language as students discuss the details presented in the photographs and talk about the traits of their pets.

READ-ALOUD AND BOOK DISCUSSION IDEAS

Before reading the book aloud, tell students that this book is written in ABC order. Referring to an alphabet chart displayed in your room will remind emerging readers of the order of the letters. Show the cover of the book and ask students to predict what they think the book is going to be about. Be sure to follow up students' ideas by asking why they have made a prediction. Asking, "Why do you think so?" will encourage primary-grade students to provide a rationale that builds upon their ability to observe details and make a prediction based on

evidence. This foundational skill will foster students' future abilities to determine cause and effect, draw conclusions, and use details to solve mystery stories. After you read the title, students can confirm or change their predictions based on the new evidence they encounter in the story.

Please note as you read the book that most students love pets and either have one or want one. Dogs seem to be an especially popular pet choice for students of all ages. Thus, ask for a show of hands for students who own dogs and ask for an additional show of hands for those who would like to own a dog someday. If students are especially interested in sharing details about their dogs (e.g., names, ages, breeds, activities, tricks), ask them to think of one thing they would like to say and share it with a neighbor. Students' oral language development and comprehension will be enhanced when they make connections between the books they read and their out-of-school lives. Direct students to look back at you to show they are ready for you to begin reading the book. Tell them that they will be learning more about dogs and why each letter goes with each photograph and word.

During reading, ask students to predict what action word (e.g., things dogs do) or noun (e.g., parts of the dog) might be shown in the photograph to depict the next letter. For emerging readers, it may be wise to have an alphabet chart handy to point to the next letter in ABC order. For example, what word might go with the letter *F f*? Talk about how some words describe things and are called adjectives. Write examples of action words (i.e., verbs), things (i.e., nouns), and describing words (i.e., adjectives) on a chart for students to refer to as you conduct the read-aloud. Students might predict words such as *furry, fluffy*, and *fast*. Show the picture of dogs being friends and ask them to think about how dogs show they are friends with humans. Build on emerging readers' love of language play by inviting them to make the sound of "Arf" for the letter *A a* (and subsequent letter–sound relationships revealed on each page).

After reading, to extend this activity in subsequent rereadings, ask students to tell you what other letters go with other sounds a dog would make when speaking. For example, on the page that has "Arf" written at the bottom of the page for *A a*, students might also associate other letters and sounds such as *B b* for "bark," *W w* for "woof," or *B b* and *W w* for "bow-wow." Help developing readers learn to make sense of contextual information by asking them to notice details on pages that display action shots and action words. For example, on the page that lists "drink for the letter *D d*," ask students to figure out the source of the stream of water from which the dog is drinking. You also can elicit oral language by asking students to think about other sources of water a dog might find when he is thirsty. After you finish reading the book, announce, explain, or demonstrate computer-related story extension activities.

COMPUTER ACTIVITIES

Creativity and Presentation Software Ideas

Emerging, developing, and fluent readers will enjoy creating their own alphabet pages. For example, the "jump for J j" page shows a dog jumping through a hula hoop. Ask students to illustrate on the computer screen other things dogs can jump over or other ways dogs can move (e.g., *r* for run, *t* for tiptoe on hind legs). Students may utilize painting software (e.g., Microsoft Paint) for this assignment. If you have access to KidPix Studio Deluxe creativity and presentation software, ask each student to select a page of the book and create an animation that represents the action word depicted.

For example, for the "jump for J j" page, students might

> ### MATERIALS
>
> ■ KidPix Studio Deluxe (1998) software
> ■ Microsoft Paint (1981–2001) software

1. Select an icon or stamp of an object (e.g., a chair, a bicycle, an apple).

2. Select an icon or stamp of a dog.

3. Dynamically illustrate the way the dog is jumping over the object through the easy-to-use animation program (Stampimator). This program function is as simple as clicking on an icon or stamp and holding down and moving the mouse (or track pad) to drag the object across the screen in different types of movements. Releasing the mouse results in instant animation. The dog can leap, hop, jump, or skip across the screen.

4. Dictate or keyboard a sentence as text for the animation.

Celebrate students' work by allowing them to display and talk about their animations as an author's computer chair (Labbo et al., 2004) activity.

Digital Language Experience Approach

After students have discussed how and why photographs are framed as they are in the book, invite individuals or small groups of students to use a digital camera to illustrate an extreme focus on a letter and word of their choosing. For example, when discussing the book as a springboard for this activity, note that, for the word *kiss*, only the faces of the dog and the person who is kissing the head of the dog appear from an overhead shot. This narrow perspective allows the viewer to focus on the action of the keyword—*kiss*. Talk about different types of speech as appropriate. For example, discuss how much richer writing is when writers include action and describing words. The black clothing and shadows at the bottom of the photograph create a perfect backdrop to emphasize tones of the dog

> ### MATERIALS
>
> ■ Digital camera
> ■ KidPix Studio Deluxe (1998) or PowerPoint (Microsoft Office 2003, 2003) software

and human. Their close proximity also speaks to the emotion of the moment. You may also discuss the perspective taken for the word *jump*. The photograph of the dog jumping is taken from a dog's-eye view. Getting the shot from this angle allows the viewer to feel the movement by seeing the front legs and head of the black dog leaping through a red hoop that is poised above the unfocused green grass of the background. The following list provides suggested steps for completing this activity.

1. Brainstorm a list of objects or activities in the school environment to illustrate with close-up photographs (e.g., playground equipment or play, cafeteria food or actions, library items or events, school personnel or activities).

2. Take close-up photographs of the objects on the list. (Hint: Keep a list of photos as they are taken along with names of group members.)

3. Import the photos into creativity and presentation software of your choice, such as KidPix Studio Deluxe or PowerPoint.

4. Have small-group members dictate a sentence that follows the pattern from the book, for example, "S is for slipping and sliding" to accompany a close-up picture of a child going down a slide or "T is for talking on the phone" to accompany a close-up photograph of a school secretary talking on the phone.

5. Allow students to display their work in a photography exhibit displayed on hallway or classroom walls, or as a slide show on a classroom computer screen during author's computer chair sharing time. Students will enjoy talking about the artistic aspects of their close-up photographs. Students may also take home printouts of their D-LEA pages or books to share with family members.

Computer Software Activity

Clifford and friends experience adventures that invite students to note ABC order, letter identification, and letter–sound recognition in the Clifford Reading CD-ROM.

> **MATERIALS**
>
> ■ Clifford Reading (2004) CD-ROM

Differentiate the assignment of the menu of activities to meet the different ability levels of the students. The following list highlights activities for readers of differing ability levels.

- Emerging readers will enjoy listening to text read aloud.

- Developing readers will reinforce letter names and initial letter–sound recognition through games.

- Fluent readers will benefit from serving as a cross-age tutor for younger students who are just learning the program or basic letter concepts. When fluent readers work with a younger student, they will need specific guidelines in order to be successful tutors. For example, posting a chart of expected behaviors and tasks will help older students stay on task and accomplish learning tasks with younger students.

Internet Resources and Ideas

How to Love Your Dog—A Kid's Guide to Dog Care: www.loveyourdog.com
This website is appropriate for use as a teacher resource, for guided Internet activities, or for computer-center activities. How to Love Your Dog, a fun and interactive website for students who

love dogs, has garnered numerous awards including recognition from the Internet Kids and Family Yellow Pages and Pet Talk America With Bob Vella 2001. It also won a Canadian Kennel Club Web Award for Dog Site of the Year for 1998 and a Lightspan Academic Excellence Award. The website is based on thematic curricula designed and developed by Janet Wall, a teacher for 23 years. The content, originally intended for elementary grade levels, has been expanded to include secondary grade levels. This website features over 80 topics and 200 pages; thus, students will need support in navigating through the links. The stated focus is on kindness, commitment, and responsible dog care. Teachers can use this website to build background knowledge about dogs and pet ownership.

There is also a place for students from around the world to publish "Your Dog Stories." Wall extends an invitation, which follows, and provides basic directions for students who want to write a story but do not wish to publish online.

> Did you have fun reading about other kids' dogs? You can write about your dog, too. Get some paper, sit down, and write about your dog. When you write, use complete sentences that are interesting and descriptive. Give your paper a title and share it with your parents. Show your friends or your teacher. Put it on the refrigerator or on the wall of your bedroom. Call your grandparents on the phone and read it to them. Be proud of what you wrote. (n.p.)

By following the guidelines, with adult support, primary-grade students may dictate a short, three-sentence story. This website also includes resources to build students' background knowledge or supplement the unit with additional information—an online quiz, dog poetry, photographs of dogs, safety tips, training dogs to do tricks, and overcoming behavior problems. When teachers demonstrate how to use selected online resources, students gain computer skills such as navigating through hyperlinks, enhancing learning, and accessing information related to a topic.

Book 2:   Alphabet Adventure

Wood, A. (2001). Ill. B. Wood. New York: Blue Sky Press. $15.95. 40 pp.

BOOK REVIEW

Audrey and Bruce Wood have created an interesting mystery adventure that is sure to delight students. Illustrations, rendered in bright primary colors, were digitally mastered with three-dimensional modeling software packages. This artistic process gives the letters the distinctive look of magnetic letters that are frequently displayed on refrigerator doors in students' homes. The story begins with an explanation that the little, or lowercase, letters have worked all summer to learn how to be a good team by lining up in proper order. On the first day of school, the lowercase letters are ready to cast off from Alphabet Island to help a little child learn the alphabet. As they disembark, Little i tumbles into the water. By quickly forming a chain, the letters are able to save her; however, as the letters scramble to rearrange themselves in correct order (some are backward or upside down), it becomes clear that Little i has lost her dot. Hopping on a boat the letters look for a floating dot in the water. Next, they join the uppercase letters, who are having a party filled with streamers and confetti dots. Capital I, wiser and older than the little letters, announces, "Dots love to hide, and they're difficult to find. But I have a plan." The lowercase letters then scramble down many streets on a scavenger hunt for objects. They quickly reassemble in alphabetical order. A finds an anchor. B finds a bug. K finds a kite, etc. Capital I announces that Little i can choose something from the assembled objects to put in place of the missing dot. Students are bound to giggle as Little i tries on S's star, H's heart, and C's cherry. When the dot thinks she will be replaced, she jumps from hiding into the proper spot above Little i. Where has the little dot been hiding?

READ-ALOUD AND BOOK DISCUSSION IDEAS

Before reading, begin the discussion by displaying the lowercase letters from a magnetic alphabet set. Ask students to name letters they know. Then tell the students that they are going to hear a story about an adventure that the little, or lowercase, letters had a long time ago because one of the little letters had a big problem. Talk about characteristics of adventures and mystery stories (e.g., there is a strange problem to be solved, there are attempts to solve the problem, the problem is solved by looking for clues and details).

MATERIALS

■ Chart paper
■ Lowercase letters from a magnetic alphabet set
■ Markers

During reading, when sharing the pages of the alphabet letters, students can identify the objects they found during the scavenger hunt and state why each letter selected a particular object (e.g., A finds an anchor. B finds a bug. K finds a kite.). Use markers to keep a list of the letters and their objects on a chart paper. These activities not only help students learn to recognize letters but also build vocabulary knowledge that can serve as a keyword for each letter.

After reading, or during a rereading of the story, invite students to scour each page for a careful look at the illustrations. A little detective work of their own will reveal where Little i's dot was hiding. Little i's dot was actually following her around, playing hide-and-seek.

COMPUTER ACTIVITIES

Creativity and Presentation Software Ideas

Ask students to create a "before and after" digital illustration (see Figure 2) to help them gain insights into beginnings and ends of stories. The before picture should display the ABCs in disarray. The after picture should display the ABCs in correct order. The following section provides steps for completing the activity.

MATERIALS

■ KidPix Activity Kits Volume 1 (1998) or PowerPoint (Microsoft Office 2003, 2003) software

1. Tell students they may either type or use a stamp pad function to randomly place letters on the screen for the before picture and after picture.

2. Remind each student to place his or her name and the date on the screen pages. If the computer monitor does not display the date in the upper portion of the screen, tape a spiral notepad with the current date on the wall and slightly above the computer monitor. Demonstrate for students how to enter the date on their computer screen.

3. If you assign two students to work together at the computer center on this assignment, be sure that you provide them with turn-taking ideas. For example, emerging readers may need to be reminded to share the mouse or keyboard by doing one or two letters at a time and then switching.

4. Invite students to orally share their work, explaining what they have learned about ABC order and the concepts "before and after" during author's computer chair (see Appendix B on p. 300).

5. Students may take printouts of their work home to read with family members. Parents and caregivers will appreciate a brief note that suggests different ways to interact with their children about their work (see Figure 3).

Figure 2
Before and After ABCs

ABCs Before   **ABCs After**

Figure 3
Family Letter Example

Dear Parents and Caregivers,

Your child worked hard at the classroom computer today to create a before-and-after picture. Please take a few minutes to ask your child to tell you about his or her picture. You could ask the following questions: Which is the before picture? Why? Which is the after picture? Why? Can you read the ABCs in order with me? How did you make this? How did you use the computer? Take a moment to praise your child's efforts.

Sincerely,
Your Child's Teacher

Digital Language Experience Approach

MATERIALS

- Chart paper
- Digital camera
- KidPix Studio Deluxe (1998) or PowerPoint (Microsoft Office 2003, 2003) software
- Magnetic set of letters
- Markers
- Metal cookie sheet

Invite students to create a class alphabet mystery by writing a D-LEA story that is based on *Alphabet Adventure* (Wood, 2001). Small groups of students or individuals can create one page of a mystery book as a computer screen slide show or as a paper publication. The activity focuses on selecting a missing letter and providing clues about which letter is missing. A possible title for the story might be, "Which Letter is Missing? How Do You Know?" The following section outlines steps to follow to complete this activity.

1. Display the magnetic set of lowercase letters on a metal cookie sheet.

2. Tell each small group of students to select one letter from the display.

3. Have each student or the adult working with the small group take an overhead photograph of the a group of letters (minus one). Each student will select a different "missing" letter.

4. Ask each student to draw a cookie sheet–sized picture that gives clues about where the missing letter might be hiding. For example, if the letter is *h*, students might draw green hedges, a hippopotamus, a game of hopscotch, etc. The letter *b* might be hiding in a batch of cookies, on a bicycle, or on a baby rattle, etc. Adults will need to help students brainstorm possible hiding places that can provide clues for the missing letter.

5. A student or an adult working with the small group will take overhead digital photographs of the missing letter arranged (and hidden) on each of the students' pictures.

6. Create a cover for the book.

7. Create a title page.

8. Write the first page of the story. Students may innovate on the *Alphabet Adventure* story or create a new premise and setting for their story. A good story beginning might consist of a few simple sentences such as the following:

   > Once upon a time, all the lowercase letters of the alphabet were getting ready to go on a picnic in the park. The letter *n* noticed that someone was missing, but he just couldn't figure out which letter wasn't there. There were so many letters. All the letters decided to help *n* look around for the missing letter. Which letter was missing? Where could it be?

9. Assemble students' photograph pages in order of the story sequence.

10. Create a final page that describes the places the missing letter was hiding before it was found and rejoined the alphabet. For example, a good story might end with a few simple sentences (see Figure 4).

11. Share a printout of the books during whole-group time. Then make the book available in the class library. A digital version of the book may be presented by students or the teacher by following the directions for creating a slide show in creativity and presentation software such as KidPix Studio Deluxe or PowerPoint.

All of the letters were so happy. The missing letter *h* had been found.

She'd been hiding in the hedges, hiding on the hippopotamus, and hiding in the game of hopscotch on the sidewalk. Now that *h* was back where she belonged, the letters could enjoy their picnic, at last. The End.

Computer Software Activity

MATERIALS

- Alphabet: Play With the ABCs (2002) CD-ROM

Letters presented in an acrobatic circus theme change to sound through students' interactions.

The setting of the *Alphabet Adventure* (Wood, 2001) story begins on Alphabet Island and ends at an elementary school. Invite students to think about the type of mystery adventure the lowercase letters might have if they were in a circus. Thus, as students interact with the CD-ROM game Alphabet: Play With the ABCs, which occurs in a circus setting, they will have occasions to make connections between the story and the games they play. After students have played with the game, ask them to show you at least one thing they learned about the alphabet.

Internet Resources and Ideas

Literacy Center.net—The Early Childhood Education Network: www.literacycenter.net
Enter the website and click on "English" link in the left-hand corner. The link offers nine games. Five of the games focus on letters or words. Click on the "Uppercase Letters" hyperlink and find five games related to recognizing letters. Game 2 presents a split screen with a gray alphabet letter on the top portion and bright blue puzzle pieces of the letter at the bottom. Demonstrate how to build each letter of the alphabet by clicking and dragging the letter pieces to cover the gray letter. Tell students that after they have built letters on the screen, they should explain how they built one of them. The website is especially supportive of students' explorations about the alphabet because the name of each letter is spoken aloud during their interactions.

Book 3: Into the A, B, Sea

Rose, D.L. (2000). Ill. S. Jenkins. New York: Scholastic. $15.95. 40 pp.

BOOK REVIEW

Rhyming text and vibrant collage illustrations join together in pages arranged in alphabetical order to create in young readers an awareness of the unique textures and movements of sea life. The focus letter for each page, embedded within a short block of text, is capitalized for emphasis. Dolphins spin through white torn-paper waves splashing onto blue rag-paper seas. Wrinkled, mossy-green kelp forests sway where yellow-and-black spotted crepe-paper leopard sharks prey. A glossary provides information about the sea creatures presented in the words and pictures of the book. For example, for the text about crabs, the accompanying explanation informs readers that hermit crabs carry their home, which is an empty shell of other sea creatures, on their backs. Thus, as they grow larger, they are looking for new and bigger houses. Students will learn many important facts about sea life in this informational text that uses the alphabet to organize and present factual information.

READ-ALOUD AND BOOK DISCUSSION IDEAS

Help students enjoy and identify the rhyming words in the story. Expressively read the text in ways that help students feel the swaying of the seawaters. Have students chorally read parts of the text to enjoy the swaying rhythm. Enjoy the rhyming words during the first read-aloud. During subsequent read-alouds, invite students to identify rhyming words. Draw attention to the textures and tones of the collage illustrations. To build vocabulary, ask students to describe the textures (e.g., crunchy, scrunchy, slick, smooth, soft) they see. This is a unique experience because textures are usually felt. Students will have unique occasions to develop oral language when they use their powers of observation and words to articulate textures.

COMPUTER ACTIVITIES

Creativity and Presentation Software Ideas

Using artistic tools in creativity and presentation software (e.g., KidPix Studio Deluxe, Microsoft Paint), invite students to create collage illustrations of the sea that are similar to those displayed in the book *Into the A, B, Sea* (Rose, 2000). The following list provides steps for completing this activity.

> **MATERIALS**
>
> ■ KidPix Studio Deluxe (1998) or Microsoft Paint (1981–2001) software

1. Ask students what texturizing tools or combinations of paint colors they can devise to capture moving sea kelp or the armor of crawling crabs.

2. Tell students they will be using artistic tools in the computer program to make a picture of the sea.

3. Provide a demonstration or a cross-age computer buddy (see Figure 1 on page 10) to support the efforts of students who do not know how to use the software. Tell students as they use clip art, paintbrushes, and special effects, they are learning how to use a range of multimedia artistic composing tools and techniques.

4. Create a slide show of students' sea art and display on a class computer monitor during class transition times (e.g., when children begin to gather on the rug for group time).

5. During author's computer chair, invite students to explain which digital tools they utilized to create their works of art.

This D-LEA begins with these intriguing questions: What textured objects in the room or school, when a close-up photograph is taken, might result in a picture that looks like something else? For example, can a close-up photograph of a chain-link fence be made to look like the scales of a fish? Can green felt be made to look like the shaggy green of seaweed? The following list offers suggested steps for completing this activity.

1. Make a list and take pictures of objects (far away and close up).

2. Create a T-chart by drawing a large capital letter *T* in the middle of chart paper. Write the title "Things That Look Different Up Close" (see Figure 5, at the top of the chart).

3. Instruct small groups or individual students to take close-up and far-away photographs to include on the chart.

4. Ask students to create a title for each picture related to a letter of the alphabet. For example, if they take a photo of a fence, they would dictate or keyboard "*F* is for fence." for the far-away shot. For the close-up photograph, the title might be "*F* is for fish scales." Print out photographs for a class bulletin board display or create a digital slide show for an on-screen display.

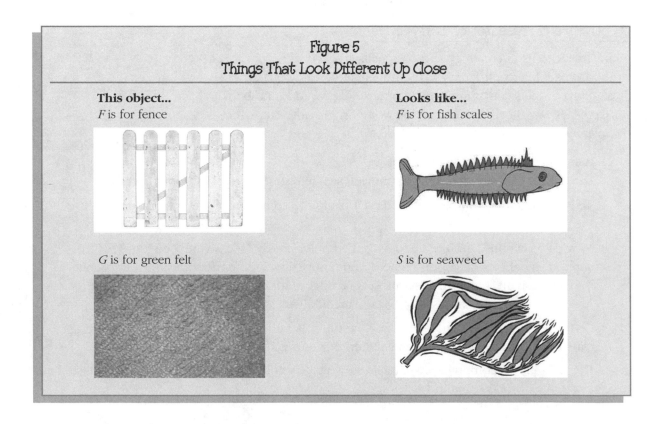

Figure 5
Things That Look Different Up Close

This object...	**Looks like...**
F is for fence	*F* is for fish scales
G is for green felt	*S* is for seaweed

Computer Software Activity

MATERIALS

■ Dr. Seuss's ABC (1999) CD-ROM

Students wander through the pages of the CD-ROM book Dr. Seuss's ABC exploring letters and rhyming words through interactive, game-like pages.

Tell students that the book focuses on a special part of the world, the sea. The CD-ROM is set in a special world created by Dr. Seuss. Tell them they will learn more about rhyming words as they interact with the story on screen. Remind them that they can click on specific words to hear them pronounced.

Demonstrate how to click on words and navigate through the story during whole-group time. Tell students that you would like them to be able to point out, or remember, at least two rhyming words (vary the number of rhyming pairs based on the abilities of students) when they are finished. Providing students with specific learning objectives will help ensure that they focus their attention while simultaneously enjoying free exploration.

Internet Resources and Ideas

Waikiki Aquarium Virtual Tour: http://waquarium.otted.hawaii.edu/vt/index.html

The Waikiki Aquarium Virtual Tour website is appropriate for a teacher resource or a guided Internet activity. Visiting this website as a whole group will enhance concepts about the sea that are included in the book *Into the A, B, Sea* (Rose, 2000). This website offers four galleries that present vibrant photographs of aquarium features. Gallery 1 presents marine communities of the South and West Pacific. Gallery 2 offers an overview of the diversity of marine habitats in Hawaii, USA, that range from shallow lagoons to deeper levels of darkness. Gallery 3 demonstrates diversity of animal life in the sea through protective adaptations (e.g., armor, deception and camouflage, venom). Gallery 4 examines the role humans play in protecting marine life through fisheries and conservation. Students may also enjoy viewing the monk seal pool and coral farm. Fluent readers can learn some interesting facts about sea life in Hawaii. Emerging readers will enjoy locating and viewing various photographs of jellyfish, sharks, and coral reefs.

This website also offers live cameras that allow visitors to get real-time images of sharks, seals, and coral reef research. Furthermore, the website provides guidelines for using the web cameras. For example, it states, "The live cameras at the Waikiki Aquarium allow you to get a look at some fascinating marine life, 24 hours a day, seven days a week, from anywhere. We have three cameras now and are adding more. As seen on TV! The Shark Cam at the Waikiki Aquarium stares unflinchingly into the Hunters on the Reef Exhibit. See sharks, rays, jacks, snappers and groupers and get some background on these amazing hunters of the coral reef, maybe even catch feeding time! The sharks are fed three times a week—Tuesday, Thursday, and Saturday, but at varying times" (n.p.).

Unit Conclusion

MATERIALS

■ ABC concept books
■ Alpha-Bits cereal
■ Plastic bowls

For a group of mostly emerging and developing readers, celebrate students' knowledge of the alphabet by having an ABCs snack time. For example, give each student a small bowl of Alpha-Bits cereal. Ask everyone who can find a specific letter of the alphabet to hold it up for all to see. Next, ask who can think of one of the words they learned in the alphabet books that go with the letter. For example, students might remember the word *arf* from the book *Arf! Beg! Catch! Dogs From A to Z* (Horenstein, 1999). Continue through the alphabet and finish up with letter munching. For a group of mostly fluent readers in upper primary grades, share copies of ABC concept books they have published during the unit with younger students either in person or by giving the books to kindergarten and first-grade classroom teachers to share.

"My first-grade students read and wrote more poetry during this unit than in any other poetry activities I've taught in previous years. The class-created poetry books we wrote, poems we created using digital cameras and creativity software, became the most treasured books in our classroom library."

—FIRST-GRADE TEACHER

Poetry—Rhyme Time and More

UNIT BOOKS

I Love You: A Rebus Poem
By Jean Marzollo
Illustrated by Suse MacDonald

Farmer's Garden: Rhymes for Two Voices
By David L. Harrison
Illustrated by Arden Johnson-Petrov

Color Me a Rhyme: Nature Poems for Young People
By Jane Yolen
Photographs by Jason Stemple

COMPUTER RESOURCES

I Spy: School Days
Jump Start First Grade
Blue's Clues ABC Time Activities

Thematic Connection

The purpose of the books and activities in this unit is to call attention to the beauty of words, to the pleasures of rhythm and cadence, and to the ability of words to evoke visual imagery, an essential element for comprehension. The books embrace a variety of poetic forms. *I Love You: A Rebus Poem* (Marzollo, 2000) stresses visual clues in a rebus form. *Farmer's Garden: Rhymes for Two Voices* (Harrison, 2000) first captures attention with its loveable farm animal characters, and then through its alternating, rhythmic voices. *Color Me a Rhyme: Nature Poems for Young People* (Yolen, 2000) uses photographs and poems to isolate and emphasize colors found in nature. The activities we suggest involve students using auditory discrimination skills and having the ability to discriminate between the smallest units of sounds in spoken words when reading, listening to, and learning from rhymed text. In addition, reading and listening to poetry helps to strengthen phonemic awareness and sound–symbol relations when students use the rhymed text patterns to predict upcoming words. Attention to similes and colorful language will bring poetry to life, evoking images to help students appreciate their surrounding world.

Matrix of Literacy Skills and Strategies in Unit 2

Literacy Skills and Strategies	Activities	Title of Book	Pages
Composing in multimedia*	C, D	*Farmer's Garden: Rhymes for Two Voices*	37–38, 38–39
	C, I	*Color Me a Rhyme: Nature Poems for Young People*	41–42, 44
Developing choral reading	R	*I Love You: A Rebus Poem*	33
	C, S, I	*Farmer's Garden: Rhymes for Two Voices*	37–38, 39, 39–40
Developing comprehension	UC	—	44
	R, I	*I Love You: A Rebus Poem*	33, 36
	R	*Color Me a Rhyme: Nature Poems for Young People*	40–41
Developing creative writing	R, C, S	*I Love You: A Rebus Poem*	33, 33–34, 35–36
	C, D	*Farmer's Garden: Rhymes for Two Voices*	37–38, 38–39
	C, D, I	*Color Me a Rhyme: Nature Poems for Young People*	41–42, 42–43, 44
Developing phonemic awareness	R	*I Love You: A Rebus Poem*	33
Developing vocabulary	R	*Color Me a Rhyme: Nature Poems for Young People*	40–41
Distinguishing between real and make-believe content	I	*Farmer's Garden: Rhymes for Two Voices*	39–40
Following directions	I	*Farmer's Garden: Rhymes for Two Voices*	39–40
	C, I	*Color Me a Rhyme: Nature Poems for Young People*	41–42, 44
Identifying letters	S	*Color Me a Rhyme: Nature Poems for Young People*	43
Making predictions	R	*I Love You: A Rebus Poem*	33
	R	*Farmer's Garden: Rhymes for Two Voices*	37
Navigating hyperlinks*	I	*I Love You: A Rebus Poem*	36
Presenting work on a computer*	C, D	*I Love You: A Rebus Poem*	33–34, 34–35
	C, D	*Farmer's Garden: Rhymes for Two Voices*	37–38, 38–39
	D	*Color Me a Rhyme: Nature Poems for Young People*	42–43
Reading aloud	UC	—	44
	C, D, I	*Farmer's Garden: Rhymes for Two Voices*	37–38, 38–39, 39–40
	D, I	*Color Me a Rhyme: Nature Poems for Young People*	42–43, 44
Reading and listening for a purpose	R	*I Love You: A Rebus Poem*	33
	R, I	*Farmer's Garden: Rhymes for Two Voices*	37, 39–40
	R, I	*Color Me a Rhyme: Nature Poems for Young People*	40–41, 44
Retelling	C	*Farmer's Garden: Rhymes for Two Voices*	37–38
Sequencing	I	*I Love You: A Rebus Poem*	36
Using adjectives	R	*Color Me a Rhyme: Nature Poems for Young People*	40–41
Using nouns	R	*I Love You: A Rebus Poem*	33
Using phonics: Letter–sound correspondence	U	—	31–32
	R	*I Love You: A Rebus Poem*	33
	D, I	*Farmer's Garden: Rhymes for Two Voices*	38–39, 39–40
	S, I	*Color Me a Rhyme: Nature Poems for Young People*	43, 44

(continued)

Literacy Skills and Strategies	Activities	Title of Book	Pages
Using phonics: Onsets and rimes	R, S, I I	*I Love You: A Rebus Poem* *Color Me a Rhyme: Nature Poems for Young People*	33, 35–36, 36 44
Using phonics: Rhyming words	U R, C, D, S, I R, C, D, S, I S, I	— *I Love You: A Rebus Poem* *Farmer's Garden: Rhymes for Two Voices* *Color Me a Rhyme: Nature Poems for Young People*	31–32 33, 33–34, 34–35, 35–36, 36 37, 37–38, 38–39, 39, 39–40 43, 44
Using similes	R, C, D	*Color Me a Rhyme: Nature Poems for Young People*	40–41, 41–42, 42–43
Visualizing	U R, I R, I	— *I Love You: A Rebus Poem* *Color Me a Rhyme: Nature Poems for Young People*	31–32 33, 36 40–41, 44
Writing descriptive sentences	C, D C, D C, D	*I Love You: A Rebus Poem* *Farmer's Garden: Rhymes for Two Voices* *Color Me a Rhyme: Nature Poems for Young People*	33–34, 34–35 37–38, 38–39 41–42, 42–43

* Indicates a new-literacy skill.
U = unit introduction; R = read-aloud and book discussion ideas; C = creativity and presentation software ideas; D = Digital Language Experience Approach; S = computer software activity; I = Internet resources and ideas; UC = unit conclusion

Unit Introduction

To benefit fully from a unit on poetry, students need an environment that is rich in visual representations of poetic forms, writing materials, and books. Gather and display a rhyming dictionary for yourself and a bounty of poems from books in the classroom library. Copy several of your favorite poems onto chart paper and display them around the room for studying and for rereading. To enrich the learning experience even further for students, have a variety of pointers (e.g., a yardstick, a dowel stick painted the colors of the rainbow) to track text. Tracking text will help emerging readers learn about concepts about print, such as left-to-right directionality, return sweep, and the concept of words. Also, to encourage reluctant readers and make reading chart poems a special event, have sunglasses (remove the lenses) in a variety of shapes, sizes, and colors for students to wear when rereading displayed poems. Place poems on tape or CDs in a listening center or poems on CD-ROMs in the computer center so students of all literacy ability levels can enjoy hearing the sounds of poetry read aloud.

Create a poem center by filling baskets with an assortment of poetry books. Be sure to include a sack full of magnetic letters and a large metal cookie sheet so students can try manipulating

MATERIALS

- Assortment of poetry books
- Baskets
- Bulletin boards to display poems of the week
- CDs of poems for students
- Colored pencils
- Construction paper in various colors
- Dry-erase boards
- Glittery pens
- KidPix Activity Kits Volume 1 (1998)

(continued)

31

- Magnetic letters
- Markers
- Metal cookie sheets
- Notebooks
- Overhead projector
- Poems on chart paper
- Pointers—yardsticks or dowel sticks painted in different rainbow colors
- Posters of poetry
- Rhyming dictionary
- Sparkly markers
- Stationery in various shapes and designs
- Sunglasses
- Tapes of poetry and a tape recorder and player
- Transparency sheets

rhyming word patterns. To inspire young poets, include unique writing materials, such as an assortment of shaped and designed stationery, colored pencils, sparkly markers, and glittery pens in the center. You may want to use the toolbar option to demonstrate for the students how they can change fonts, colors, sizes of letters, and placement of text when using a creativity and presentation software during multimedia compositions at the computer center. For example, use KidPix Activity Kits Volume 1 software to type the morning message. Highlight one word and demonstrate using the toolbar options how to select and change the font, size, and color of the morning message text. Dry-erase boards with bold markers will entice students to practice writing sound–symbol relationships. Prepare and have available for whole-class discussions letters of the alphabet printed on and cut from transparency sheets. Demonstrate how to make rhyming words by exploring word families and manipulating the transparency letters into words and patterns, projecting them onto the board with an overhead projector. Students also may want to share favorite poems from home, so design a poem-of-the-week bulletin board area to showcase those poems along with rhythmic patterns and sensory vocabulary words.

Start the unit by copying poems to chart paper and displaying them around the room. The website CBeebies (www.bbc.co.uk/cbeebies/tweenies/songtime) contains a list of poems and songs that begin with different letters of the alphabet. Tell students that during the upcoming unit you will be reading poetry books and doing activities on the computer that will help them learn more about rhyming words, patterned sentences, and words that create mental movies. Start each day with a song or poem read from a chart. Briefly discuss the meaning of the poem or the feelings and images evoked by the words. Invite students to illustrate the poems on construction paper. Students may then store their favorite poems in a student-designed poetry notebook.

Book 1: I Love You: A Rebus Poem

Marzollo, J. (2000). Ill. S. MacDonald. New York: Scholastic. $7.95. 40 pp.

BOOK REVIEW

Smooth, rhythmic text and bold, colorful illustrations create this quick-to-read, but highly entertaining, four-stanza poem. With double-page spreads, one line of the stanza is centered on the left page, the accompanying illustration is displayed on the right page, and a rebus format is used to replace particular words in the text. The predictable, repeated-pattern text will automatically invite students to chant portions of the phrase "Every ____ loves a _____ and I love you." Text soon becomes supplementary to the comprehension process as the rebuses tempt students into making visual and textual connections. For example, ask students how the pictures of a bird and bee, flower and tree, or lock and key relate and how they contribute to the uniqueness of this rebus poem. As you read the book and emphasize the rhyming words and patterned text, students are sure to practice sound discrimination as they listen for words that have similar endings, identify sound–symbol relationships, and visualize text.

READ-ALOUD AND BOOK DISCUSSION IDEAS

Before reading the book, review onset and rimes, which are word endings, showing how and why some words rhyme. Read a short poem displayed on chart paper to students, stopping before the final rhyming pair to ask a volunteer to predict the rhyming word. Point out and circle similar sounds and rhythmic text to help develop and strengthen auditory discrimination skills. The CBeebies Tweenies website (www.bbc.co.uk/cbeebies/tweenies/songtime) offers many familiar songs and poems that are printable and that may be used for this purpose. Tell students to listen carefully to the words because they can paint pictures and make movies about the words in their minds. Read aloud a short poem of your choice and describe to the students the visual images you create in your own mental movie to help you understand the poem. After reading, give students a copy of the poem and ask them to illustrate on construction paper their mental movie. Tell students how important it is to use imagery when reading. These images help good readers understand and remember story events. Explain to students that a rebus poem uses pictures instead of words, and that this book has lots of picture pairs that go together. Tell students to listen to the rhyming words and to study the pictures because they will be helpful in predicting upcoming words.

MATERIALS
■ Blackboard
■ Chalk
■ Construction paper
■ Copy of the poem for each student
■ Markers
■ Poem on chart paper

During reading, encourage students to chant along with the repeated text "Every ___ loves a _____and I love you."

After reading, read the book a second time and ask students to listen for three rhyming word pairs and list these pairs on the board. For example, students will hear *tree, bee,* and *key*. List these words and write an *e* above the list because all the words rhyme with the long *e* sound. Ask students to suggest additional rhyming pairs. Invite selected students to find and circle the words on the chart that are nouns (i.e., people, places, or things).

Use the book's patterned text and create a one-stanza poem with the students, using the rhyming lists and circled nouns only. For example, an *e* list might include the nouns *flea, knee, pea,* and so forth. Ask students to suggest associated words that go with these nouns. For example, a dog goes with a flea, a leg with a knee, and a pod with a pea. Then, complete a text pattern similar to the following: "Every dog loves a flea, every leg loves a knee, every pod loves a pea, and I love you." Create additional stanzas with other word pairs. Post the stanzas around the room for referencing and rereading.

COMPUTER ACTIVITIES

Creativity and Presentation Software Ideas

Invite students to create their own rebus poems.

1. Use creativity and presentation software rich in stamp icons and design three different rhyming picture templates before assigning the activity. Kidspiration 2.1 software is especially helpful for this activity. It offers a text-to-speech option to assist students of various reading ability levels to hear and track text as they create their rebus stanza. If using Kidspiration 2.1, on the first template

MATERIALS
■ Kidspiration 2.1 (2005) software

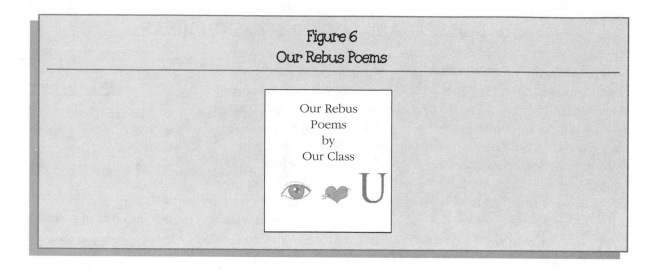

Figure 6
Our Rebus Poems

Our Rebus
Poems
by
Our Class

you might select a dog, fog, and frog; on the second template you might select a tree, manatee, and monkey; and on the third template you might select a buffalo, window, and hippo. On each template, include the phrase *loves a*; the words *every* and *and*; and the icons of an eye, heart, and the letter *u*.

2. Using the patterned text from *I Love You: A Rebus Poem* (Marzollo, 2000) as a guide, students work individually or with partners to arrange text and pictures into sentences.

3. Tell students to view all the icons and select picture partners for each template's icon. For example, a picture of a man might partner with a dog and complete the sentence "Every man loves a dog."

4. Instruct students to select pictures and use the mouse to arrange text and a picture to create four different sentences and the rebus stanza. However, caution students to leave lots of space between the sentences to ease readability.

5. Print pictures and bind into a class book titled *Our Rebus Poems* (see Figure 6).

Digital Language Experience Approach

Invite students to create rebus name poems.

MATERIALS

- Digital camera
- KidPix Studio Deluxe (1998) software

1. Take a digital photograph of each student.

2. Import the photos into creativity and presentation software, such as KidPix Studio Deluxe.

3. Ask students to write a rebus name poem (see Figure 7) below their imported picture by including stamps for at least two words that rhyme with their name. For example, a student named Jake might select the stamp icons of a rake and a cake. If a student has an unusual name or a name that does not easily rhyme, suggest that he or she use initials (e.g., Bartholomew Carroll = B.C., which could rhyme with bee, knee, key, sea, etc.).

Figure 7
Rebus Name Poem

Every gardener loves a

Every baker loves a
and of course everybody loves me, Jake.

4. Collect the rebus name poems into a slide show to view on the computer screen, or display the printed versions on a bulletin board or in a class book for subsequent readings.

Computer Software Activity

I Spy books consistently invite students to solve picture and rhyming riddles through the display of objects that are connected by a theme. I Spy: School Days software is an appropriate software program for primary-grade students because it consists of a user-friendly interface and it displays many familiar objects that are related to schooling. Support and challenge students to create and solve their own rhyming riddles.

MATERIALS

■ I Spy: School Days (1995) software

1. Begin by reading and discussing rhyming riddles from the pages of an I Spy book or from the introductory screens of the software program. You may want to demonstrate how to use the software to design an I Spy riddle of your own.

2. Ask students to solve a rhyming poem as they search for rhyming objects. Students may also work with a cross-age computer buddy (see page 10) to explore various creative thinking aspects of this software.

3. Invite students who have interacted with the I Spy: School Days software game to demonstrate some of the things they have learned or to share some of the rhyming riddles they created. At the end of the unit, invite students to sit in the author's computer chair in order to share the final copies of their rebus poems. As they read and display the rebus

poems, ask them to emphasize the rhyming words they included. Students may discuss their composition processes. During discussions, you may want to ask students to identify the words that rhyme or contribute additional rhyming words. List the word pairs on chart paper, continually add to the list, and use the list for reviewing and referencing throughout the unit.

Internet Resources and Ideas

Magnetic Poetry: http://home.freeuk.net/elloughton13/scramble.htm
On this interactive website, students unscramble favorite nursery rhymes by clicking on and dragging words around a computer-screen version of a magnetic board. There is an area below the board to type the poem when it is finished.

Rebus Rhymes: Paint a Rhyme Online: Mother Goose and Other Rhymes: www.enchanted learning.com/rhymes/painting
This website contains a large selection of rebus poems, organized from A to Z, to read with students or use as examples. For additional fun, the website includes a Paint a Rhyme activity where students add colors to the images of a rebus poem.

Rebus Rhymes: Tongue Twister Rebus Rhymes:
www.enchantedlearning.com/rhymes/Twisters.shtml
This website offers many tongue-twister rebus rhymes to read with students, and it is an excellent website for developing readers to practice reading strategies, especially when using visual and context clues.

Favorite Poem Project Video Collection: www.favoritepoem.org/thevideos
This website offers 50 videos of people, such as Hillary Clinton, reading poems.

WIL's Thirty Featured Rimes and Rhymes: http://curry.edschool.virginia.edu/go/wil/rimes_and_rhymes.htm#Thirty_Featured_Rhymes
This website, titled WIL's Thirty Featured Rimes and Rhymes, contains practice for both rimes and rhymes. This is an excellent website for teaching about word patterns and picture clues. A link lists several rimes, ranging from *-ack* to *-ump*.

Book 2:   Farmer's Garden: Rhymes for Two Voices

Harrison, D.L. (2000). Ill. A. Johnson-Petrov. Honesdale, PA: Boyds Mills Press. $9.95. 32 pp.

BOOK REVIEW

In *Farmer's Garden: Rhymes for Two Voices*, the dog asks his garden friends, which include an ear of corn, a strawberry, a redbird, a bunny, and a cow, what they do in the farmer's vegetable garden. Students' curiosity and imaginations will spark, as they too will ponder over and predict the animals' and plants' answers. For example, when the dog asks, "Worm, worm, what do you eat?" the worm responds, "Delicious dirt is such a treat!" Fifteen short, two-verse rhythmic poems are arranged in two four-line stanzas. Two different fonts indicate alternating speakers, and each conversation consists of more than one question and answer. Brightly colored illustrations capture how the dog interacts with his friends in the garden. This book is an excellent introduction to poetry because it orchestrates rhythmic elements, lines, and stanzas in a somewhat narrative form.

READ-ALOUD AND BOOK DISCUSSION IDEAS

Introduce students to rhyming words and patterned text by accessing Grandpa Tucker's Rhymes & Tales at www.grandpatucker.com and reading the short poems aloud with students. Copy some of the students' favorite poems onto chart paper for additional activities. After discussing the meaning of the poems, the feelings they evoke, and the parts of the poems the students enjoyed most, turn their attention to skills practice. For example, as you point to the words on the chart, instruct students to listen for rhyming words. After reading, draw lines under the rhyming words and reread them as a group.

> **MATERIALS**
> - Chart paper
> - Markers
> - Pointer

Before reading *Farmer's Garden: Rhymes for Two Voices* (Harrison, 2000), show the book jacket and ask students to predict what the story will be about. Ask students to share what they know about farm environments. Tell students that the dog on the front cover is part of the farm family and has lots of farm friends. The story is about the curious dog who wonders what his garden friends do. Ask students to think about what answers the dog might hear from the corn, strawberry, redbird, bunny, cow, cricket, and others. List predictions on the board or chart paper.

During reading, stress patterned text and rhyming words with an exaggerated voice and point out how the questions' and answers' last words rhyme.

After reading, return to students' predictions and compare them to the responses in the poem.

COMPUTER ACTIVITIES

Creativity and Presentation Software Ideas

Invite students to retell the story for a slide show presentation, or they may create their own two-voices poems. To create individual or whole-class poems, use creativity and presentation software, such as KidPix Studio Deluxe, that is rich in nature backgrounds and stamp icons and that offers a recording option.

Either on chart paper or on index cards, you may want to print the questions from the story or generate additional questions for students to ask of an animal and plant stamp icon they will paste on the screen. For example, questions might include the following:

> **MATERIALS**
> - Chart paper
> - Computer microphone
> - *Farmer's Garden: Rhymes for Two Voices* (Harrison, 2000)
> - Index cards
> - KidPix Studio Deluxe (1998) software

What do you eat?
Why did you do it?
How do you grow?
When did you do it?
Why do you ___?
What do you see?
Where have you been?

Generate a list of words that rhyme with the questions' ending words and write them on the board or chart paper. For example, *meat* and *seat* rhyme with *eat*. Instruct students to work with a partner or as a whole class to create sets of question-and-response dialogues that rhyme. For example, the previously mentioned dialogue set includes *meat*, *seat*, and *eat*. After discussing and listing rhyming words with the students, demonstrate to them how to use the creativity and presentation software to complete the following activity.

1. Ask students to select a background scene; for example, a mountain scene.

2. Have them select nature stamp icons such as a rabbit, fox, flower, snake, and an owl.

3. Instruct them to type or dictate questions and responses on the background in two alternating fonts. For example, a student question might be "Rabbit, Rabbit, what do you eat?" and a response, "I eat leaves without any meat."

4. Have students use a computer microphone to record themselves reading each question and response. Students can select background scenes and stamp icons before typing question-and-answer dialogues.

5. Save pictures and follow software directions to import them into a slide show. Print pages and bind into a book titled "Two-Voices Poems."

6. Invite students to share their created two-voices poems in one of two modes: (1) taking turns reading the questions and responses or (2) listening to a recorded version of the poems in two voices. Students are expected to share their work, solve creativity problems, give suggestions, and offer positive feedback. Students who need support with reading aloud will enjoy chorally reading the two-voices poems.

Digital Language Experience Approach

Invite students to create a class two-voices book that is patterned after the book *Brown Bear, Brown Bear, What Do You See?*

MATERIALS

- *Brown Bear, Brown Bear, What Do You See?* (Martin, 1992)
- Chart paper
- Digital camera
- KidPix Studio Deluxe (1998) software
- Markers
- Students' favorite objects from home

1. Ask students to bring from home their favorite objects such as a teddy bear, Barbie doll, army man, etc.

2. Take a digital picture of each student holding his or her object.

3. Use creativity and presentation software, such as KidPix Studio Deluxe, and import each picture. Size each picture to one side of the page.

4. On the opposite side, type a question and response with the second and fourth lines rhyming. Type the question and response in two different fonts to indicate alternating voices, as in the following example:

Barbie, Barbie
What do you see?

I see you
looking at me.

Teddy Bear, Teddy Bear
Where have you been?

Out to the kitchen
And back again.

Other dialogue ideas for questions might include What do you eat? Why did you do it? How do you grow? When did you do it? Why do you ____? To help students create rhyming dialogues, generate a list of words that rhyme with the questions' ending words on chart paper for students to refer to as they are composing.

Print pages and bind into a class book titled "Our Two-Voices Poems of Our Favorite Things" or combine computer-screen pages into a slide show that can be viewed during free time or whole-group story time.

Computer Software Activity

Invite students to read along (e.g., echo read, chorally read) with Frankie, an on-screen character, in his virtual classroom in the JumpStart First Grade software. Several different types of books are available on the JumpStart First Grade program. Students will enjoy reading along with the narrator, who reads aloud several favorite Mother Goose rhyme classics such "Humpty Dumpty" and "Jack Be Nimble." Many of the book titles contain stories with rhyming text. The program highlights text and each screen page has an accompanying picture. The stories are useful for reinforcing beginning reading skills. For instance,

> ### MATERIALS
>
> - Crayons
> - JumpStart First Grade (1995) software
> - Paper
> - Pencils

1. Tell emerging readers to notice how the text is highlighted from left to right. Doing so will help them gain awareness of concepts about print, such as directionality.

2. After reading along with the stories, invite students to search for rhyming word pairs. Developing or fluent readers will enjoy hunting for and writing down rhyming word pairs or patterns they find in a poem. For example, students who are developing readers may hunt for and list words that rhyme with long *i*.

Internet Resources and Ideas

The Little Animals Activity Centre: www.bbc.co.uk/schools/laac/music/fd2.shtml
Tell students to listen to and interact with the Little Critter's Animal Muddle rhyming story. Text, presented in a white box, is highlighted and read slowly as characters move around the sides of the box. During repeated readings, students can chorally read the text. Ask young readers to see if they can identify some rhyming words.

Grandpa Tucker's Rhymes & Tales: Short Stuff: www.grandpatucker.com/index.html-ssi#short
This website presents a selection of short poems in a familiar book format. Poems are short and entertaining. Emerging and developing readers may need assistance to read them, so set up cross-age buddies or parent volunteers. Ask them to tell you their favorite poems and why.

Grandpa Tucker's Rhymes & Tales: Lots of Silly Poems! www.grandpatucker.com/index.html-ssi#table
Grandpa Tucker's Rhymes & Tales contains a selection of silly poems. Ask students to read the poems to find out why they are silly. For instance, the poems contain real and make-believe statements. You might ask students to listen for and discuss the pretend elements used to make the poems silly. Fluent readers may enjoy reading text independently. Emerging and developing readers may need assistance to read them.

Book 3: Color Me a Rhyme: Nature Poems for Young People

Yolen, J. (2000). Photos. J. Stemple. Honesdale, PA: Wordsong/Boyds Mills Press. $19.95. 31 pp.

BOOK REVIEW

Dazzling photographs capture a variety of colors found in nature, and the text is used to paint colorful expressions with words. Thirteen poems highlight different colors. One page of each spread displays the poem and the other displays the photograph. Some pages also include an appropriate quotation such as the one that appears on a layout devoted to the color white (e.g., Mother Goose's "Its fleece was white as snow," p. 16). Many poems include synonyms for a color word. For example, white is referred to as alabaster, bone, snow, or chalk. Some poems have rhythmic appeal, while others achieve their vividness through free verse or haiku. Many of the following activities capitalize on the book's visual imagery by providing ideas for how to use similes to create mind pictures.

READ-ALOUD AND BOOK DISCUSSION IDEAS

MATERIALS

- Chart paper
- Markers

Before reading the book, design a color-word examples chart (see Table 1) with columns, leaving spaces at the top for five student-suggested color words on chart paper. Tell students to close their eyes and to imagine themselves walking through a forest. What types of colors surround them? Write these suggested colors as headings on the chart and list the items visualized. Next, tell students to name other colored items seen in their daily environments. For example, students might suggest shamrocks, pencils, and plants because they see these items in their classroom environment. Add these items to the chart. Continue in this manner with several colors. Display the book's cover and ask students to describe what they see. Inform students that the poems in this book are all about colors, and that the book not only helps them learn what colors are, but it also helps them learn many things about colors and how to make mind pictures to help enjoy what they read.

Table 1
Color-Word Examples Chart

Green	Brown	Yellow	Grey	Blue
Leaves	Sticks	Sun	Rocks	Water
Trees	Tree trunks	Daisies	Boulders	Streams
Grass	Soil	Flowers	Dirt	Books
Plants	Pebbles	Crayons	Walls	Crayons
Shamrocks	Tables	Markers	Floor tiles	Bulletin board
Pencils	Chairs	Paint	Bunny	Rug

During reading, without first showing the pictures to the students, select a poem to read aloud. Tell students to close their eyes and use the poem's words to form mental movies. Slowly read the poem, accentuating important sensory and color words and pointing out other names for the color words. After reading a poem, ask students to tell what they saw in their mind before showing the book's picture. Briefly discuss the fact that each person was able to "see" many of the same things, but that some of the details were different than the picture in the book. Tell them that good readers always make mind pictures about what they are reading about. Continue in this manner for the other poems.

After reading, extend the discussion to a brief chat about similes. Using the color green as an example, hold up a green bean. Hold up a leaf from a plant. Tell students that one way to describe the green bean is to say that it is as green as a blade of grass. Ask students to close their eyes and try to describe what a green bean might look like when compared to something else. Tell the students to compare using the words *like* or *as*. For example, the bean is as green as an alligator. The leaf is a green as an apple. Extend their thinking to realize that another way to describe the green bean is to say that it was like a blade of grass. Continue playing with descriptions so that students become familiar with and understand the importance of similes.

COMPUTER ACTIVITIES

Creativity and Presentation Software Ideas

Invite students to create similes at the computer center. Kidspiration 2.1 creativity and presentation software is suggested for this activity because it offers a text-to-speech option that enables students to hear and track the text when creating similes. Additionally, the writing option offers fluent readers a chance to compose sentences with similes.

MATERIALS

■ Kidspiration 2.1 (2005) software

1. Use Kidspiration 2.1 to create a simile template for students to use. For example, a template might include the statements "as big as a ____," "small like a ____," "quiet as a ____," "loud as a ____," "smelly as a ____," "red like a ____," "blue like a ____," and so forth. Using the user-friendly software tools and directions, type each phrase in an oval, fill each oval with the same background color, and place the ovals in a row across the top of the page.

2. Show students how to select an icon from the program display to complete the similes. For example, below the oval "as big as," a student might drop pictures of a whale, tree, or Styracosaurus; under the oval "small like," a student might drop pictures of a mouse and cupcake; and under the oval "as green as," a student might drop the pictures of a broccoli and shamrock.

3. Invite students to create and then share original simile sentences using their similes activity on Kidspiration 2.1. For example, a student might share, "Grandpa's heart is as big as a whale" or "Grandpa's tree is as big as a Styracosaurus."

Digital Language Experience Approach

Invite students to participate in a Color-Me Day.

> **MATERIALS**
>
> ■ KidPix Studio Deluxe (1998) software
> ■ Letter for parents announcing Color-Me Day
> ■ Selected color for bulletin boards and objects

1. Send a letter home (see Figure 8) asking parents to help students dress mostly in one color of their choosing on a particular day. For example, on Tuesday one student might wear a blue shirt, blue jeans, blue socks, blue hair bows, and so forth, and bring in a blue-colored object such as a blue stuffed monkey. Locate a blue wall, bulletin board, or something to use as a blue background and take the student's picture as he or she stands in front of the board. For another student, who dresses in green, walk outside and have the student stand near green bushes or trees for their picture.

2. Use creativity and presentation software such as KidPix Studio Deluxe and import the pictures onto a coordinating colored or textured background. Size the pictures to a full page and leave enough room for the background to act as a frame.

3. In the center of each picture, ask students, cross-age computer buddies, or volunteers to type a student-created simile about the color. For example, the sentence of a student in blue holding a blue stuffed monkey might read, "My favorite stuffed monkey is as a blue as the ocean."

4. Share students' color simile pages in a slide show and ask the students to read aloud their sentences.

As an alternative activity, have students create a My Favorite Color Is poem (see the following Blue poem for an example) using the following instructions as a guide.

Blue

Blue looks like
Blue sounds like
Blue smells like
Blue tastes like
Blue feels like

1. Instruct students to type the text on their pictures using contrasting type colors and font sizes.

Dear Parents and Caregivers,

We are learning about the importance of colors and how colors are represented in poetry through similes. During this unit, students will have an opportunity to dress in their favorite color and participate in a Color-Me Day. For example, on our blue day, your child might choose to wear a blue shirt, blue jeans, blue socks, blue hair bows, and so forth, and bring in a blue-colored object such as a blue stuffed monkey. During that school day, our class will take a journey around the school searching for objects and places of the same color. After having his or her picture taken standing with the discoveries, each student will then create a simile sentence telling about his or her favorite color. Please look over the color-day schedule below and select a day for your child to dress in his or her favorite color. We look forward to sharing our simile sentences with you soon.

Sincerely,
Your Child's Teacher

Our Color-Me Day Schedule
Monday: Dress in blue or brown
Tuesday: Dress in green or orange
Wednesday: Dress in yellow or pink
Thursday: Dress in purple or red
Friday: Dress in black or white

2. Encourage students to read their poems if they are using software that has a record option.

3. Print pages and bind into a class book titled *Colors, Colors, Everywhere Colors.*

4. Import the pictures into a slide show and enjoy.

Computer Software Activity

Blue's Clues ABC Time Activities software offers students a variety of activities to practice phonics, letter identification, and rhyming skills. Visual and auditory reinforcements help students as they play games, answer questions, and use words to create their own stories. Invite students to interact with the slippery soap activity. Four bubbles appear with pictures and text. Students select a picture to complete the first line of a rhyme. Students then select a second picture that rhymes with the first to complete the rhyme. Students use their growing awareness of letter–sound correspondence as they see text, listen to it read, and select words to complete the rhyme.

MATERIALS

- Blue's Clues ABC Time Activities (1998) software
- Ongoing chart of rhyming words

1. Instruct students to create an ongoing chart of rhyming words.

2. Tell students that as they work with the program, they will listen for and write rhyming words that they find while playing the program's various games on a chart placed next to the computer.

Internet Resources and Ideas

The Magic Key: The Cream Cake Mystery: www.bbc.co.uk/schools/magickey/adventures/creamcake.shtml
This website offers an interactive opportunity for students to use rhyming words to complete poems and rhymes. Below a poem or rhyme, word patterns are displayed. Students click on and drag individual words to complete a poem or rhyme. Options are available to click on phrases and word selections to see them highlighted and read aloud.

Tongue Twisters: www.starfall.com/n/level-b/twisters/load.htm
This Tongue Twisters website offers four different tongue twisters for students to make associations to beginning letter–sound correspondences and to onsets and rimes. Options are available to click on individual words or on entire tongue twister to hear them read aloud. Text highlights as sound is played.

Color Poems: http://adifferentplace.org/color.htm
Scroll to the end of this website for several links to color poems written by students. Select several poems as models to read with the students; then use the website's poem templates to create color poems.

A to Z: www.k111.k12.il.us/lafayette/a_to_z/atoz.htm
This A to Z website reinforces beginning sounds through alliterations and offers students a chance to read free verse poems from a first-grade created and illustrated alliterative alphabet class book.

The Tongue Twister Database: www.geocities.com/Athens/8136/tonguetwisters.html
This website offers students several tongue twisters for additional practice in alliteration and reinforces beginning letter–sound correspondence.

KidzPage: http://gardenofsong.com/kidzpage
The KidzPage website offers pages of poetry to read aloud to students. Poems use visually rich words so students can practice visual imagery.

Unit Conclusion

MATERIALS

- Cookies
- Fruit
- Invitations to high tea
- Milk
- Poems written by students
- Tea

Conclude the unit by sharing students' poems with family members or peers in other classrooms by offering a "high tea" poetry-reading event on a designated day. Students compose and decorate invitations that include a short rhythmic or free verse poem and invite guests to come to listen and enjoy the poetry or to join in the fun by bringing a favorite poem to read aloud. Students share their created class books, slide shows, and their new appreciation for poetry during the poetry high tea. Conclude the event with tea, milk, and cookies or fruit.

"My students loved this unit, and we hated to see it end. One of the most powerful components was connecting the activity of listening to music to help my students better understand how the main characters in stories feel."

—KINDERGARTEN TEACHER

Music–Learning With a Beat

UNIT BOOKS

Ah, Music!
By Aliki

Music Is
By Lloyd Moss
Illustrated by Philippe Petit-Roulet

Rap a Tap Tap: Here's Bojangles—Think of That!
By Leo and Diane Dillon

COMPUTER RESOURCES

Music Ace or Music Ace 2
JumpStart Music
Clifford's Musical Memory Games

Thematic Connection

For early learners, music is a natural way to learn auditory awareness and discrimination skills, concepts that help to improve phonemic awareness and understanding of phonics elements. But what is music? The purpose of this unit is to highlight aspects of music, rhythm, melody, tone, pitch, volume, and sound, which are concepts that enable the mind to use imagery to describe, soothe, and enlighten how we feel. Furthermore, the objective is to use music to invite students to learn the rhythm and beat of language. The book *Ah, Music!* (Aliki, 2003) presents musical concepts ranging from prehistoric to present-day styles. Topics include what music is and how to create and demonstrate it. The book *Music Is* (Moss, 2003) complements these concepts further by bringing awareness of how music exists in our everyday lives. Students will learn to appreciate a variety of music styles and forms of expression. *Rap a Tap Tap: Here's Bojangles—Think of That!* (Dillon & Dillon, 2002) taps students into a time when a man was recognized and known for using music by talking with his feet.

Matrix of Literacy Skills and Strategies in Unit 3

Literacy Skills and Strategies	Activities	Title of Book	Pages
Building background knowledge on the Internet*	U	—	47–48
	I	*Ah, Music!*	50–51
Comparing and contrasting	R	*Rap a Tap Tap: Here's Bojangles—Think of That!*	54–55
Composing in multimedia*	C, D	*Ah, Music!*	49, 50
	C, D	*Music Is*	52, 52–53
	C	*Rap a Tap Tap: Here's Bojangles—Think of That!*	55
Creating and using charts	U, UC	—	47–48, 57
	R	*Ah, Music!*	48–49
	R	*Music Is*	51–52
Developing comprehension	R	*Ah, Music!*	48–49
	R, I	*Music Is*	51–52, 54
	R, S	*Rap a Tap Tap: Here's Bojangles—Think of That!*	54–55, 56
Developing oral language	U	—	47–48
	R	*Music Is*	51–52
	R, D	*Rap a Tap Tap: Here's Bojangles—Think of That!*	54–55, 55–56
Developing vocabulary	R, D, S, I	*Ah, Music!*	48–49, 50, 50, 50–51
	R, S, I	*Music Is*	51–52, 53, 54
	R, D, S	*Rap a Tap Tap: Here's Bojangles—Think of That!*	54–55, 55–56, 56
Distinguishing sounds	C, D, S	*Ah, Music!*	49, 50, 50
	C, S, I	*Music Is*	52, 53, 54
Following directions	S, I	*Ah, Music!*	50, 50–51
	C, S	*Music Is*	52, 53
	C, D, S, I	*Rap a Tap Tap: Here's Bojangles—Think of That!*	55, 55–56, 56, 56–57
Inferring	R, D	*Ah, Music!*	48–49, 50
Navigating hyperlinks*	I	*Ah, Music!*	50–51
	I	*Music Is*	54
	I	*Rap a Tap Tap: Here's Bojangles—Think of That!*	56–57
Predicting	R	*Rap a Tap Tap: Here's Bojangles—Think of That!*	54–55
Presenting work on a computer*	C, D	*Ah, Music!*	49, 50
	C, D	*Music Is*	52, 52–53
	C	*Rap a Tap Tap: Here's Bojangles—Think of That!*	55
Reading and listening for a purpose	C, S, I	*Ah, Music!*	49, 50, 50–51
	I	*Music Is*	54
	R, I	*Rap a Tap Tap: Here's Bojangles—Think of That!*	54–55, 56–57
Understanding story structure and events	R, S	*Rap a Tap Tap: Here's Bojangles—Think of That!*	54–55, 56
Understanding syllables	C, S, I	*Ah, Music!*	49, 50, 50–51

(continued)

Literacy Skills and Strategies	Activities	Title of Book	Pages
Using phonics: Rhyming words	R, D	*Rap a Tap Tap: Here's Bojangles—Think of That!*	54–55, 55–56
Using verbs	R, D	*Ah, Music!*	48–49, 50
	C, D	*Music Is*	52, 52–53
	D, S	*Rap a Tap Tap: Here's Bojangles—Think of That!*	55–56, 56
Writing descriptive sentences	D	*Ah, Music!*	50
	C, D	*Music Is*	52, 52–53
	D	*Rap a Tap Tap: Here's Bojangles—Think of That!*	55–56

* Indicates a new-literacy skill.
U = unit introduction; R = read-aloud and book discussion ideas; C = creativity and presentation software ideas; D = Digital Language Experience Approach; S = computer software activity; I = Internet resources and ideas; UC = unit conclusion

Unit Introduction

Plan to play music daily so students will learn to hear, express, create, and appreciate its various forms and styles. Collect, display, and label pictures of musical instruments—woodwind, brass, strings, percussion—to display around the room for vocabulary exposure, and create a music center equipped with materials and directions to make simple instruments. The Dallas Symphony Orchestra (DSO) website offers instructions for making a variety of simple instruments (see www.dsokids.com/2001/hactivities.asp?Action=Search&Title=&Inst="2"&Type="3").

For example, the DSO website offers the following directions for how to make shakin' maracas: Collect paper towel and toilet paper tubes, dried beans, paper plates, masking tape, staplers, markers, and stickers. Put beans inside the paper tubes, covering the ends of the tubes with masking tape. Or place beans on a paper plate, cover the plate with a second plate, and staple together. Use markers and stickers to decorate the shakers.

Also gather a variety of CDs, songbooks, versions of familiar songs, and a selection of different types of music, such as classical, jazz, waltz, and rap, and highlight a different era of music each day during whole-group time. Play CDs that have singing rounds, such as "Row, Row, Row Your Boat," so that students can participate in the music. Copy a variety of songs on chart paper for independent reading and for group sharing. Provide a pointer so students can track print or follow along as you track the words of a song. If possible, display words of songs on large computer monitors and use a cursor as a pointer. Throughout the unit, help students hear and express how various forms of music make them feel. For example, play a style of music on the playground and invite students to march, sway, or stroll to its melody and beat.

Before starting the unit, complete a musical K-W-L (what I <u>K</u>now, what I <u>W</u>ant to know, what I <u>L</u>earned; Ogle, 1986) chart (see Figure 9) with the students. Ask students what they know and what they would like to learn about music. Tell them that during the upcoming unit on music, you will read books and complete computer activities that will help them learn more about melody, rhythm, how music paints pictures in the mind, and how music plays an important role in our lives.

MATERIALS

- CD player
- CDs of various types of music
- Chart paper
- Copies of songs
- K-W-L chart
- Markers
- Pictures of musical instruments
- Pointer
- Songbooks

Figure 9
Musical K-W-L Chart

What We **K**now About Music	What We **W**ant to Learn About Music	What We **L**earned About Music

Book 1:   Ah, Music!

Aliki. (2003). New York: HarperCollins. $16.99. 48 pp.

BOOK REVIEW

From prehistoric origins to today's popular music, *Ah Music!* covers it all. It is perfect for all ages, for learning about music for the first time, or for revisiting musical elements that students have already learned. The first pages of this informational text explain through text and pictures that music is sound, rhythm, melody, pitch, tone, and volume and that it represents feelings. Subsequent pages tell how music is created with notes, lines, spaces, feelings, words, and instruments. The ending pages conclude by describing conductors, dance, voice, harmony, and the history of music from prehistory to today's diverse popular sounds. All elements are presented in a child-friendly manner. Even the youngest student can enjoy learning from the multicultural images of students demonstrating musical concepts. For example, a young boy swings in a hammock with his dog as he hums a tune that expresses his mood. Additionally, students learn about volume as they relate to the illustrations of people singing "Happy Birthday" loudly at a party and to the quiet of Grandpa's "shhhh" as he rocks a baby to sleep. With a format similar to an encyclopedia, this book can be read in any order and is sure to enlighten students to musical sounds and elements encompassing them in their everyday worlds.

READ-ALOUD AND BOOK DISCUSSION IDEAS

Before reading the book, play short excerpts from a variety of musical styles. Invite students to move according to how the music makes them feel. For example, when listening to a marching band, students will want to march; to lullaby music, lay their heads down; and to waltzing music, sway. Verbally label for students the actions they are doing and write a list of the terms on a vocabulary chart to foster vocabulary development. Tell them that "doing words" are called verbs. To help manage the activity, remind students that as soon as the music stops they need to stop moving around and look at you. Students can express music through facial expressions as you play scary, melancholy, or "happy birthday" music. Learning to express how the music makes them feel will help students learn how to make inferences while reading. Tell students that when they read a good book, they also should be thinking about how the words and pictures make them feel. Show the book's jacket and complete a picture walk that highlights informational book features. Picture walks involve looking at the illustrations to predict the content of the page or book.

During reading, make note of how the encyclopedia format of the book allows you to select particular concepts to read about and discuss. For emerging readers, point to the illustrations, asking the students to describe what they see before you paraphrase the text. Write on a poster board or blackboard or type using a computer all the verbs the students heard in the book.

After reading, discuss new musical elements and concepts learned. Which were the most interesting and why? List responses on the K-W-L chart under "What We Learned About Music."

MATERIALS
■ Blackboard
■ CD player
■ CDs of various styles of music
■ Chart paper
■ Computer
■ K-W-L chart
■ Microphone
■ Poster board
■ Vocabulary chart

COMPUTER ACTIVITIES

Creativity and Presentation Software Ideas

Ah, Music (Aliki, 2003) is fun because it has rhythm and a beat, but so do words. Help students hear the 1, 1-2, 1-2-3, 1-2-3-4 beats (syllables) in words by clapping and singing to pictures and words they select from creativity and presentation software.

MATERIALS
■ KidPix Activity Kits Volume 1 (1998) or KidPix Studio Deluxe (1998) software
■ Microphone

1. Use KidPix Activity Kits Volume 1 or another creativity and presentation software program, such as KidPix Studio Deluxe, that includes stamps or icons to make a beats picture, which is a picture for exploring the number of syllables in a word. Model for the students how to select an icon, say the word, and count the number of syllables.

2. Ask each student to select a stamp to place on the computer screen.

3. Instruct students to use the microphone to pronounce the word clearly.

4. Instruct fluent readers and writers to type in the word. Emerging and developing readers and writers may use invented spelling or dictate the word while a classroom helper types it on the screen.

5. Ask students to say the word and clap their hands every time they hear a musical beat in the word. *Butterfly* (but-ter-fly) has three syllables and would thus have three hand claps. Creative students may enjoy spontaneously singing their word repeatedly to a musical beat.

6. Encourage students to share the beats pictures they created at the computer center with creativity and presentation software and during author's computer chair (see Appendix B). Guide the class in a game with the pictures. For example, one student can share his or her screen-picture slide (e.g., a butterfly). Students listen to the student's recorded voice say the word and then echo read while clapping the number of beats they hear. Invite students to clap as they sing each of the words aloud, as they would clap along with a song.

Digital Language Experience Approach

MATERIALS

- Digital camera
- KidPix Studio Deluxe (1998) software

Take students on a musical walk around the school to listen for various forms of music.

1. Ask students to listen for music. Where is rhythm, pitch, or volume heard? When music is located, take a digital picture of the item or person creating the music. For example, someone might play the piano in the music room; a cook might make "music" when mixing batter, a gardener when raking leaves, a secretary when typing forms, and so on.

2. Import the pictures into KidPix Studio Deluxe software and type captions below the pictures such as "Mr. _____ plays a smooth rhythm on the piano." Other examples might include "Mrs. _____ makes soft music in the cafeteria with mixers"; "First graders produce a loud volume while eating lunch in the cafeteria"; or "The sink drips a steady rhythm of drops."

3. Print and bind the pictures into a class book titled "Ah, Music in Our School." Another option is to create a slide show that includes sound effects to accompany each photograph and sentence. Each student may also highlight the verb word in his or her sentence by highlighting it in a different font color.

Computer Software Activity

MATERIALS

- Music Ace: Makes Learning Fun (2000) or Music Ace 2 (2003) software

Music Ace and Music Ace 2 software teach musical concepts such as rhythm, melody, harmony, pitch, volume, musical staffs, notes, scales, keyboard use, and much more. Students listen to a maestro as he provides information on each topic before students complete the topic's lessons on a doodle pad, play games, and practice creating and using musical concepts on their own. Music Ace introduces basic concepts while Music Ace 2 continues the experience through a higher level program. Choose the lessons most appropriate for your students.

1. Demonstrate and model the lesson's routine and activities before inviting students to explore and learn from the animation, sound, and visual effects; for example, view the lesson about beats with the class.

2. Students listen to the maestro explain the sense of beats. When they click on a box to hear the beat, a ball bounces to show the rhythm of the beat visually.

3. Assign students to repeat the lesson, play the games, and use the doodle pad to practice creating and using beats independently. Learning to distinguish beats in music may help some students become more sensitive to hearing beats or syllables in words.

Internet Resources and Ideas

Dallas Symphony Orchestra: Composer's Keyboard: www.dsokids.com/games/notegame/default.htm
On this website, students drop quarter notes anywhere on a musical staff, listen to individual notes, and then listen to the song they create.

Music Education at Datadragon: Learn About Instruments: http://datadragon.com/education/instruments

This website teaches about the families of instruments. Learn about different strings, woodwinds, brass, and percussions. A picture of each instrument is displayed along with a short description and an audio example. QuickTime is required for audio.

Dallas Symphony Orchestra: Music Room: www.dsokids.com/2001/rooms/musicroom.asp

The DSO Music Room website is filled with activities. Learn about orchestra musical seating arrangements, hear various instruments, and learn how to make a variety of instruments at home. Several activities can be printed. Younger students may need assistance from a cross-age computer buddy to read challenging text and to navigate the website.

Dallas Symphony Orchestra: Families of the Orchestra: www.dsokids.com/2001/instrument chart.htm

On this DSO website, hear a variety of instruments played, such as strings, percussions, brass, woodwinds, or keyboards. Students can listen to the instrument played alone, playing a familiar song, or as it plays in the orchestra.

Book 2: Music Is

Moss, L. (2003). Ill. P. Petit-Roulet. New York: Putnam. $14.95. 32 pp.

BOOK REVIEW

Whether fast or slow, loud or soft, haunting or uplifting, music enriches our world. *Music Is* shows how people use music when they dance, write, play, or sing. This delightful book shows how the power of music touches everyone in different ways: People enjoy music in crowds or alone; music marks grand occasions and bedtime. Cleverly designed text demonstrates the fun in music as it dances, rolls, and taps across each page as it reinforces and captures the mood of the concepts being discussed. Pastel-colored cartoons illustrate where music is found daily: in elevators, on phones, and in the brass and strings heard at a concert. The rhyming text adds to the fun of reading and learning about the magic and beauty of music as it adds a beat and rhythm to words read.

READ-ALOUD AND BOOK DISCUSSION IDEAS

Before reading the book, display a collection of items that play or produce music, such as a radio, drum, conch shell, and flute. Ask students open-ended questions to foster oral language development and to provide a set of questions for the book. Where might the students hear these sounds? What other instruments and objects produce sounds? List responses on chart paper under the headings Where Music Is Heard and Items or Objects That Produce Music.

During reading, use music vocabulary when referring to and describing sounds, such as volume (the loud and soft sounds), pitch

MATERIALS

- Chart paper
- Conch shell
- Drum
- Flute
- Markers
- Radio

(the high and low sounds), melody (the feelings you get from music), and rhythm (the beat). Write these vocabulary words on the chart.

After reading, continue listing and revising responses on the chart. Add a section for Our Favorite Types and Sounds of Music and list students' responses such as "Joe likes rap. Mark loves country."

COMPUTER ACTIVITIES

Creativity and Presentation Software Ideas

Invite students to create melody movies, movies that students create that capture and reflect how music influences their thinking. Because music is personal, we each create slightly different mental images when listening to the sounds of music. For example, one person might visualize a parade when listening to marching melodies while another person might see a band performing at a football game. Scary music might evoke images of a dark, rainy night for one person while producing images of a black cat walking down a dark sidewalk for another.

MATERIALS

■ KidPix Studio Deluxe (1998) software

Moopies and Stampinator in KidPix Studio Deluxe creativity and presentation software are excellent ways to practice making mental images. In either activity, students follow these directions:

1. Instruct students to preview a variety of sounds and music (located under Goodies on the toolbar) before making a selection.

2. Encourage students to listen to the melody again, thinking about the mental picture created in their mind.

3. Instruct students to select a background picture or use the drawing tools to create a picture to represent this mental image.

4. Tell students to scroll through stamp icons to select additional items to accessorize their picture. Stampinator's option for animated stamp icons will enrich and enhance the melody movies as they add movement to the pictures created.

5. Instruct students to dictate or write a sentence that describes the action or emotions expressed in the animation.

Save pictures from the melody movies for a slide show to be shared during author's computer chair (see Appendix B).

Digital Language Experience Approach

MATERIALS

■ Disposable cameras
■ KidPix Studio Deluxe (1998) software

Music is often referred to as a universal language. To help students make connections to the music that surrounds them in their daily lives, design a home–school connection with digital photography.

1. Send a letter (see Figure 10) home to each student's parent or guardian explaining the assignment.

Figure 10
Letter to Parents and Caregivers

Dear Parents and Caregivers,

We are learning all about the ways that music is present in our lives. Please help your child use the enclosed disposable camera to take pictures of the music that is found in your child's life outside of school. Does someone hum while preparing supper? Does anyone listen to music on the radio? On CDs? In the car? Does anyone sing songs before bedtime?

Please return the camera to me within two days. Thank you for helping your child learn more about the magic of music in our lives.

Sincerely,
Your Child's Teacher

2. Send home a disposable or digital camera to take pictures of where music is found in each student's home. For example, Dad hums when cooking dinner; Grandma listens to her records; an older sibling listens to MTV; a younger brother plays the violin.

3. Import photographs into a creativity and presentation software such as KidPix Studio Deluxe.

4. Instruct students to select a background color or texture.

5. Import the pictures one to a page, and adjust the background size as needed. If using KidPix Studio Deluxe, stamp icons can be dropped around the picture on the background to create a frame.

6. Instruct students to dictate or type captions below each picture about the music found in their homes; for example, "Caitlin's dad hums while cooking dinner."

7. Print and bind pictures into a class book titled "Music Is Found Everywhere." Invite students to share their melody movies made with creativity and presentation software during author's computer chair (see Appendix B). Encourage students to describe the creative process and tell why they selected the music, why they selected certain stamp icons, how the music made them feel, and what it reminds them of. Instruct the class then to share and describe the images the music evokes for them.

Computer Software Activity

The JumpStart Music software program teaches students about melody, harmony, notation, and musical scales in the Land of Music. Animation and sounds will entertain students as they join Hopsalot the bunny to find sour notes while learning about musical concepts. Students play games that involve them repeating rhythms and melodies and identifying sounds of different musical instruments. You may want to post a musical question of the day or week near the computer, and as students uncover the answer while playing, they illustrate or leave the answer in a secret, musical container placed next to the computer. Depending on the question, you can create bar graphs to compare answers.

MATERIALS

■ JumpStart Music (1998) software

iKnowthat.com: Music Maker: www.iknowthat.com/com/L3?Area=Music
iKnowthat.com offers an interactive music website. Students select from various instruments and either create their own music or listen to different songs. Students can save, print, and submit their compositions to the website.

CBeebies—Tweenies: Song Time: www.bbc.co.uk/cbeebies/tweenies/songtime
On this website, students can sing along with a variety of songs. Songs are listed from A to Z and include such favorites as "The Wheels on the Bus," "This Old Man," and "Twinkle, Twinkle Little Star." Songs are printable for students to read along and to practice reading skills.

New York Philharmonic Kidzone! www.nyphilkids.org/main.phtml
With the help of a cross-age computer buddy, students can navigate through this website and select activities that involve them in composing music, watching short videos about various instruments, playing instruments, and playing games and puzzles that quiz and extend musical knowledge reinforced on the site. Java, QuickTime, and Macromedia Shockwave are required and downloadable through the website.

Book 3:   Rap a Tap Tap: Here's Bojangles—Think of That!

Dillon, L., & Dillon, D. (2002). New York: Blue Sky Press. $15.95. 32 pp.

BOOK REVIEW

Meet a man who "didn't just dance, he made art with his feet" (n.p.). Mr. Bill "Bojangles" Robinson was an African American tap dancer. His talents and influences on the world of music are showcased in this captivating, rhythmic book. Mr. Bojangles is known for tapping past doors, some that opened while others closed. He tapped through busy city neighborhoods; subway trains; and throughout Manhattan, New York, USA. These settings are recreated through paintings that resemble collages. Shadows and silhouettes capture his tapping feet across each page. Pages on the left display a variety of audiences he tapped for while the pages on the right highlight his performances. Not only will the energy and rhythm of these pages excite the students, but also the repeated text "Rap a tap tap—think of that!" will have them up on their feet tapping in no time.

MATERIALS

■ Cane
■ CD player
■ Tap-dancing music
■ Tapping shoes
■ Top hat

READ-ALOUD AND BOOK DISCUSSION IDEAS

If possible, gather tap-dancing equipment to share with the students. For example, bring in a top hat, a cane, tapping shoes, and tap-dancing music. Play tap music and demonstrate how the taps work on the shoes. Ask students to tell you what the different items are used for. Elicit oral language by asking students to describe the objects. If possible, invite a tap dancer to perform and demonstrate his or her musical talent and this wonderful musical concept. If any students take tap lessons, ask them to share their skill by demonstrating various moves.

Before reading the book, complete a picture walk by asking students to view the pictures' details and describe what they see. Ask students to predict the story's settings and character.

During reading, encourage students to chant the refrain "Rap a tap tap—think of that."

After reading, share the biographical information about Mr. Bojangles on the last page and compare this writing style to fiction writing styles. How is this biography similar to yet different from the story of *Rap a Tap Tap: Here's Bojangles—Think of That!* Point out the words that rhyme and ask students to supply additional rhyming words that go with the *-ap* and *-at* word families.

COMPUTER ACTIVITIES

Creativity and Presentation Software Ideas

Students will enjoy using the Digital Puppets feature in KidPix Studio Deluxe creativity and presentation software to make a puppet dance. Certain music inspires us to tap our fingers, clap our hands, or shake a leg, but what about the Digital Puppets? How might they move to various sounds? Help students "feel" music and get a sense for movement by having a digital puppet move to the sounds of music.

> **MATERIALS**
>
> ■ KidPix Studio Deluxe (1998) software

1. Ask students to preview a variety of sounds (sounds are located under the Goodies heading on the toolbar).

2. Ask students to select a sound and return to the Goodies option to locate a matching background picture and puppet.

3. After students import selections to the working screen, ask students to strike different keyboard buttons to make the puppet dance. Instruct students to practice the movements.

4. Ask students to use the record option to record their puppet's movements.

5. Save as a slide show and enjoy watching the dancing puppet shows during author's computer chair (see Appendix B) as students develop oral language skills, sharing steps in designing their puppet movie using toolbar and other software options.

Digital Language Experience Approach

An important aspect of music is movement. Students will practice learning about verbs while making connections to how music enables people to express themselves.

> **MATERIALS**
>
> ■ Digital camera
> ■ KidPix Studio Deluxe (1998) software

1. Use a digital camera and capture students moving to music by dancing, rapping, jumping rope, or bouncing balls to a musical beat.

2. Discuss with the students the verbs represented in their movements.

Figure 11
Moving to Music

Once there was a class that danced all around the school. Rap a tap tap—think of that!
Tom rapped in the ____. Rap a tap tap—think of that!
Sue danced past ____. Rap a tap tap—think of that!
Molly danced while bouncing balls. Rap a tap tap—think of that!
Mike danced as he jumped rope. Rap a tap tap—think of that!

3. Instruct students to import the pictures onto their own screens using creativity and presentation software such as KidPix Studio Deluxe.

4. Create a text template similar to the one shown in Figure 11 and type text below the pictures.

5. Print pictures and bind into a class book titled "We Are Bojangles, Too!"

6. As students reread the book in the whole group, in small groups, or individually, ask them to point out to you the words that rhyme as well as the action words.

Computer Software Activity

MATERIALS

■ Clifford's Musical Memory Games (2002) software

After a storm breaks Birdwell Island's radio tower, Clifford and his friends need help to restore music back to the island. Nineteen activities and songs involve students in problem solving and challenging thinking. Use the program and invite students to create an instrument and compose and play jazz music. They can also play along with Clifford, Cleo, and T-Bone, and learn to dance like Mac by arranging his dance steps and watching him dance. These games extend vocabulary and help students notice movement and verbs.

Internet Resources and Ideas

The Little Animals Activity Centre: www.bbc.co.uk/schools/laac/music/fdi.shtml
Students practice reading, sequencing, and listening for a purpose to observe musical patterns in order to repeat the same patterns that make the little animals dance. This website is very useful for students to develop comprehension skills as well as to reinforce the order they hear as they repeat sounds in a sequencing activity.

Build a Band and Hit the Charts: www.bbc.co.uk/cbbc/music/index.shtml
This website offers students an opportunity to build a band, make tunes with various instruments, link to radio sites, play games, learn dance steps, or just sing songs.

CBeebies: Sing a Song: www.bbc.co.uk/cbeebies/singasong/
Several types of songs are presented for students to sing along with. Several activities are interactive, such as Karoake and Animal ABC, which require students to listen and follow directions. Other selections involve students listening to, reading along with, and singing a song. A print option is available to print song sheets.

Students will enjoy sharing some of the things they have learned from their Internet explorations during author's computer chair. This is an important precursor to being able to assemble knowledge and conduct research reports with Internet resources.

Unit Conclusion

Complete the K-W-L chart you began at the beginning of the unit so students will have an opportunity to list all the things they have learned about music. Invite parents or students from another class to a musical extravaganza. Set up a variety of musical centers for exploration. For example, one musical center houses shakers students have made during the unit (see example provided in unit introduction on page 47). Provide a tape player, headphones, and various styles of music and another musical center becomes a musical listening station. Display pictures students have created that represent the visual imagery that various types of music evoked. If possible, students and parents can share musical talents by playing instruments, singing, or dancing; remember to share the unit's slide shows, the ongoing K-W-L chart, and class-produced books.

MATERIALS

- Headphones
- Invitations to a musical extravaganza
- K-W-L chart
- Markers
- Musical center
- Musical shakers
- Student-created work from the unit
- Tape player

Writing—Getting "Write" to the Heart of the Matter

UNIT BOOKS

Diary of a Wombat
By Jackie French
Illustrated by Bruce Whatley

The Princess's Secret Letters
By Hilary Robinson
Illustrated by Mandy Stanley

Mrs. Goodstory
By Joy Crowley
Illustrated by Erica Dornbusch

COMPUTER RESOURCES

Curious George Downtown Adventure
Bailey's Book House
The Jolly Postman's Party
Arthur's Reading Games

Thematic Connection

Knowing how to write well helps primary-grade students develop ownership and authority over their writing skills. Moreover, students who know how to record their private thoughts in a diary are more likely to be reflective thinkers. Likewise, students who know how to share their ideas in letter format are more likely to be writers who correspond with others for personal and professional reasons. Thus, the purpose of this unit is to introduce primary-grade students to various purposes and forms of writing by integrating reading and writing experiences in ways that support their early literacy development (Yaden, Rowe, & MacGillivray, 2000). Characters in the books in this unit write for a variety of delightful reasons. Wombat in *Diary of a Wombat* (French,

2002) keeps a daily diary that describes his activities and provides an account of a close encounter with his human neighbors. The girls in *The Princess's Secret Letters* (Robinson, 2002) exchange a series of letters that not only reveal things they have in common but also result in an unexpected face-to-face meeting. *Mrs. Goodstory* (Crowley, 2001), an expert on story writing, gives advice about how to write exciting stories. Suggested activities in this unit offer students many supported occasions for learning how to keep a classroom diary, send e-mail messages, write letters, and craft exciting stories.

Matrix of Literacy Skills and Strategies in Unit 4

Literacy Skills and Strategies	Activities	Title of Book	Pages
Brainstorming	U	—	61
	C	*Diary of a Wombat*	62–63
	R, I	*The Princess's Secret Letters*	64–65, 66–67
	D, S, I	*Mrs. Goodstory*	68–69, 69, 69–70
Building fluency	C	*Diary of a Wombat*	62–63
	I	*The Princess's Secret Letters*	66–67
Comparing and contrasting	S	*Diary of a Wombat*	63
Composing in multimedia*	C, D, I	*Diary of a Wombat*	62–63, 63, 64
	C, D, I	*The Princess's Secret Letters*	65, 65–66, 66–67
	C, D, S, I	*Mrs. Goodstory*	68, 68–69, 69, 69–70
Creating and using charts	R, C	*Diary of a Wombat*	61–62, 62–63
Determining cause and effect	I	*Mrs. Goodstory*	69–70
Determining chronological order	D	*Diary of a Wombat*	63
	D	*Mrs. Goodstory*	68–69
Developing comprehension	R, S	*Diary of a Wombat*	61–62, 63
	R, D	*The Princess's Secret Letters*	64–65, 65–66
	R, C, S, I	*Mrs. Goodstory*	67, 68, 69, 69–70
Developing creative writing	C, I	*Diary of a Wombat*	62–63, 64
	I	*The Princess's Secret Letters*	66–67
	C, D, S, I	*Mrs. Goodstory*	68, 68–69, 69, 69–70
Developing oral language	U, UC	—	61, 70
	D, S	*Diary of a Wombat*	63
	R, C, D, I	*The Princess's Secret Letters*	64–65, 65, 65–66, 66–67
	R, C, D, S	*Mrs. Goodstory*	67, 68, 68–69, 69
Developing vocabulary	R, C, D, S, I	*Diary of a Wombat*	61–62, 62–63, 63, 63, 64
	R, C	*The Princess's Secret Letters*	64–65, 65
	R, C, S, I	*Mrs. Goodstory*	67, 68, 69, 69–70
E-mailing*	I	*Diary of a Wombat*	64
	I	*Mrs. Goodstory*	69–70

(continued)

Literacy Skills and Strategies	Activities	Title of Book	Pages
Following directions	S	*Diary of a Wombat*	63
	S, I	*The Princess's Secret Letters*	66, 66–67
	C, D, S	*Mrs. Goodstory*	68, 68–69, 69
Making predictions	U	—	61
	R	*Diary of a Wombat*	61–62
	I	*The Princess's Secret Letters*	66–67
Presenting work on a computer*	D	*Diary of a Wombat*	63
	I	*The Princess's Secret Letters*	66–67
	C, D, S	*Mrs. Goodstory*	68, 68–69, 69
Reading aloud	U, UC	—	61, 70
	R, C	*Diary of a Wombat*	61–62, 62–63
	R, C, I	*The Princess's Secret Letters*	64–65, 65, 66–67
	R, C	*Mrs. Goodstory*	67, 68
Reading and listening for a purpose	UC	—	70
	R	*Diary of a Wombat*	61–62
	R	*The Princess's Secret Letters*	64–65
	R, C, S	*Mrs. Goodstory*	67, 68, 69
Reading informational text	S	*The Princess's Secret Letters*	66
Retelling	C	*Diary of a Wombat*	62–63
	R, S	*Mrs. Goodstory*	67, 69
Sequencing	D	*Diary of a Wombat*	63
	I	*Mrs. Goodstory*	69–70
Summarizing	C	*Diary of a Wombat*	62–63
	D, I	*The Princess's Secret Letters*	65–66, 66–67
Understanding a main idea	S	*Diary of a Wombat*	63
Understanding story structure and events	I	*Diary of a Wombat*	64
	R, D, S, I	*Mrs. Goodstory*	67, 68–69, 69, 69–70
Using adjectives	C, D, I	*Diary of a Wombat*	62–63, 63, 64
	D, I	*The Princess's Secret Letters*	65–66, 66–67
	R, C, D, S	*Mrs. Goodstory*	67, 68, 68–69, 69
Using English as a second language	I	*Mrs. Goodstory*	69–70
Writing descriptive sentences	C, D, I	*Diary of a Wombat*	62–63, 63, 64
	C, I	*The Princess's Secret Letters*	65, 66–67
	C, D, S, I	*Mrs. Goodstory*	68, 68–69, 69, 69–70
Writing letters	R, I	*The Princess's Secret Letters*	64–65, 66–67

* Indicates a new-literacy skill.
U = unit introduction; R = read-aloud and book discussion ideas; C = creativity and presentation software ideas; D = Digital Language Experience Approach; S = computer software activity; I = Internet resources and ideas; UC = unit conclusion

Unit Introduction

To encourage students to try their hands at various styles and forms of writing, set up an inviting writing center in a corner of the classroom. Place a sign labeled "Writing Center" over a table that is filled with a variety of writing instruments, such as pencils, pens, magic markers, crayons, stamps, and ink pads, and writing materials, such as stationery, construction paper, lined paper stapled in diary format, and greeting cards. Remind students that the computer center is also a place for composing and writing.

During whole-group time, display the covers of the three books in the unit, read the titles, and ask students to predict what they think the books will be about. Draw attention to the details of the book covers (e.g., hints that point to writing as a theme). Tell students that all the stories in this unit have something to do with writing and that by the end of the unit, they will have had a chance to try many different types of writing.

MATERIALS

- Construction paper
- Crayons
- Greeting cards
- Ink pads
- Lined paper stapled in diary format
- Markers
- Pencils
- Pens
- Stamps
- Stationery
- Writing center sign

Book 1:   Diary of a Wombat

French, J. (2002). Ill. B. Whatley. New York: Clarion Books. $24.95. 32 pp.

BOOK REVIEW

What is a wombat? Where do they live? What kind of lives do these creatures lead? Readers of *Diary of a Wombat* have a unique opportunity to answer these questions and more through a charming diary written, of course, from a wombat's perspective. Wombats, native to Australia, look like very small bears. The first entry of the wombat's diary begins with all the activities for morning, afternoon, and evening. On Tuesday, when the wombat's taste for grass changes, so do his efforts to find tastier food from a human family. Following the wombat's daily diary entries shows readers how humans endeavor to happily coexist with this intriguing creature.

READ-ALOUD AND BOOK DISCUSSION IDEAS

Before reading, display a diary or journal, complete with a little lock and key. Explain to students that sometimes people write down their thoughts every day and that some people keep their diary entries under lock and key so no one else can read their private thoughts. However, in *Diary of a Wombat* (French, 2002), we see what a unique little character has written about his daily life. Display the cover of the book and take a quick picture walk by paging through the pictures and asking students to comment on things they notice. Direct students to

MATERIALS

- Chart paper
- Diary or journal
- Markers

listen in order to learn what the wombat wrote about. For example, the wombat wrote about the same events for several days because the routine did not change. Students might speculate why things might change in the wombat's life. During reading, point out characteristics of the wombat's diary. Discuss the main character's close encounter with human beings. Record on chart paper any words that the students find especially meaningful or interesting.

After reading, ask students what they learned about the little creature by reading about his daily life. Discuss and write on the chart paper why people like to keep diaries. Review the simple form of diary writing: the date, and the thoughts about the day. Discuss why it is important to record the date on each entry—because including the date is a feature of writing in journals or diaries. Doing so reminds writers of things that happened on a particular day.

COMPUTER ACTIVITIES

Creativity and Presentation Software Ideas

MATERIALS

- Chart paper
- KidPix Studio Deluxe 3 (2000) or PowerPoint (Microsoft Office 2003, 2003) software
- Markers

Innovating on a story helps students understand how to take a character's point of view, invites them to explore the structure of a genre, and allows them to try out an author's writing style. Ask students to think about how the story of the wombat would be different if an animal from their own neighborhood was involved. What would a stray cat write about in a diary? A stray dog? A squirrel or raccoon?

1. Invite students to write a story similar to the little Wombat's story in the book by creating entries for a few days, written from the perspective of another hungry or lost little animal.

2. Brainstorm characteristics of two or three animals to help students get started. For example, ask students what they know about cats. Write on the chart paper:

   1. Cats like to catnap.

   2. Cats eat several small meals a day.

   3. Cats take lots of cat baths.

   4. Cats meow.

   5. Cats are curious (and so forth).

3. Refer students to the classroom calendar, review the days of the week, and demonstrate how to write diary entries for a character such as Scamp the Spotted Cat in Figure 12. Emerging readers may need the support of a cross-age computer buddy to make diary entries.

4. Set up the computer center with creativity and presentation software, such as Kidpix Studio Deluxe 3 or PowerPoint, that allows students to record and illustrate their animal diaries.

Students using a writing process or multimedia composition process approach to writing an animal diary story may want peer feedback to help them solve writing problems. Be sure to allow students time for giving and receiving feedback on computer-related activities during author's computer chair (see Appendix B).

Figure 12
Scamp the Spotted Cat's Diary

Monday morning—ate a bowl of cat food at home
Monday midmorning—catnapped on window seat
Monday noon—meowed to my boy for more cat food from the bowl at home
Monday afternoon—gave myself a good cat bath with my rough tongue
Monday night—curled up to sleep at the foot of my boy's bed
Tuesday morning—the kitchen door was open and I wondered what was outside, so I scampered out
Tuesday midmorning—wanted a catnap but I was too hungry
Tuesday noon—tried some food from a garbage can but nothing smelled good
Tuesday midafternoon—a nice lady gave me a bowl of milk on her back porch. Note to self—meow on her back step more often

Digital Language Experience Approach

Invite students to start a class photograph diary.

1. Take digital photographs of daily events throughout the day for three days.

2. Import the photographs into creativity and presentation software such as KidPix Studio Deluxe 3 or PowerPoint.

MATERIALS

- Digital camera
- KidPix Studio Deluxe 3 (2000) or PowerPoint (Microsoft Office 2003, 2003) software

3. Ask students who are in the photographs to comment about the activity. Record students' comments through dictation or allow them to keyboard their comments. Follow the wombat's format by listing the day of the week, the time of day, and a photograph of and comment about the activity. Taking photographs of daily events, such as what students do when they arrive at school, participate in calendar time, line up for recess, go to lunch, participate in center time, and read during reading group time, will allow students to sort the pictures in chronological order.

4. Print out and display on a bulletin board titled "Our Wombat Diary of School," or save for a slide show presentation.

Computer Software Activity

Curious George, the little monkey who has had many grand adventures with the man in the yellow hat, is alone in the city. The Curious George Downtown Adventure CD-ROM begins with an electronic book introduction to set the stage. Students follow the directions to help George solve problems he has created. After participating in various scenarios, students can think about what George's problems were mostly about (main idea) and orally share events during author's computer chair (see Appendix B) that they would include in a Curious George Diary. Students can also compare the little wombat's day with Curious George's day.

MATERIALS

- Curious George Downtown Adventure (2002) CD-ROM

Animal Diaries: Travel Buddies: www.tesan.vuurwerk.nl/diaries/t2/index.htm
Go to this website to learn how to have a Travel Buddy exchange. Students in two different classroom locations agree to exchange a stuffed animal. Students receive the stuffed animal and write daily diaries about its adventures. If a long-distance exchange is not feasible, invite students in another classroom to exchange a class mascot (e.g., stuffed animal) and keep a diary of major daily events for a week. After the stuffed animal and diary have been returned, read aloud the adventures during whole-group time.

Book 2:   The Princess's Secret Letters

Robinson, H. (2002). Ill. M. Stanley. New York: Harcourt. $12.95. 32 pp.

BOOK REVIEW

Lucy, a young girl who admires Her Royal Highness Isabella, the princess in her country, sent a letter to the princess on her birthday because they shared the same birth date. Because she asked a question about what princesses eat at birthday parties, the princess writes back. Thus begins a delightful exchange about the secret life of the princess that culminates in a secret visit from the princess to Lucy's birthday party. A box, attached to the back cover of the book, contains six small notecards and envelopes so that young readers can write their own special secret letters.

READ-ALOUD AND BOOK DISCUSSION IDEAS

MATERIALS

- Business letters and bills
- Cards in envelopes
- Catalogs
- Chart paper
- Friendly letters
- Junk mail
- Markers
- Postcards
- Prepared letter to the class

Before reading, display and discuss various types of mail such as junk mail, postcards, catalogs, business letters and bills, cards in envelopes, and friendly letters. Ask students what the items are and how they are used. Open one of the envelopes and read the pretend letter (see Figure 13) from Lucy, the main character in the story. Address the envelope from Lucy, 38 Orange Grove Road, Townsville. Address the envelope to the teacher's name, class, school address, or room number. Draw a stamp.

During reading, ask students to identify the questions being asked in one of the letters written by a main character. Next, ask students to predict the answer that the princess or Lucy might include in their letters. Confirm the answers that students shared during the letter exchanges by reading them aloud.

After reading, show students the contents of the box of stationery that is attached to the book's back cover and ask them to think about other things Lucy and the princess could write about. Write their suggestions on chart paper for use in a computer activity that follows.

COMPUTER ACTIVITIES

Creativity and Presentation Software Ideas

From the main menu of the software, students or teachers may click on the stationery and envelopes on the table in the lower left corner. Teach students how to design a card they would like to send to the princess.

MATERIALS

- Bailey's Book House (1994) software
- Envelope
- Markers
- Shoebox

1. Show students how the toolbar at the top of the screen allows them to select a theme.

2. Explain how a list down the left side of the screen allows them to select a particular type of card.

3. Point out how they can use stamps, which are appropriate for various themes, holidays, and other events, to design their cards.

4. Print out cards and ask students to write or dictate a question for the princess. For example, ask them to think about what would they like to learn about the princess? Why?

5. Address an envelope, if time permits, and "mail" the cards in a shoe box mailbox. Open and read the cards during whole-group time. Another option is for students to pretend to be the princess and answer questions.

Digital Language Experience Approach

Invite the mailperson who delivers mail to your school to visit your classroom for a brief interview. Seek his or her permission to take photographs of the interview.

MATERIALS

- Chart paper
- Digital camera
- KidPix Studio Deluxe 3 (2000) or PowerPoint (Microsoft Office 2003, 2003) software
- Markers

1. Brainstorm three to five questions about the mailperson's job before the mailperson visits the classroom. Write students'

questions on an interview chart. For example, students may want to know why the mailperson wears a uniform or how a mailperson knows where to go to deliver the mail. Supplement the interview chart with additional questions as needed.

2. Take digital photographs of the mailperson displaying and explaining the uniform, the mailbag, different types of mail, and so forth.

3. Record his or her answers to questions.

4. Import photographs into creativity and presentation software such as KidPix Studio Deluxe 3 or PowerPoint.

5. Invite small groups of students to reread and summarize answers to the key questions so you can write captions for each photograph.

6. Print out photographs for a class book and bind or save into a slide show to share during group time.

Computer Software Activity

MATERIALS

■ The Jolly Postman's Party (1997) software

Effective responses to literature activities extend students' thinking about the story. In fact, engaging in activities that are similar to those encountered in the original story will enhance students' opportunities to learn more about story content and vocabulary. Just like the main character, Lucy, planned a birthday party in *The Princess's Secret Letters* (Robinson, 2002), the Jolly Postman is having a party and students are invited to participate in a variety of party activities.

Students can create and send a card by using various tools such as an on-screen typewriter tool; a drawing and painting tool; or a collection of stamps about characters, objects, and food. The Make and Do activity allows students to create their own party stationery and design hats that can be printed, cut out, and worn for story reenactments or used as props for retelling the story. Students will enjoy sharing their work during author's computer chair (see Appendix B). Elaborate on their oral language by eliciting descriptive words that enrich their vocabulary development.

Internet Resources and Ideas

KeyPals Club International: www.teaching.com/keypals
With the help of an adult, such as a teaching assistant or parent volunteer, and with parent permission, invite students to exchange a message with a keypal online. Go to www.teaching.com and register for free. Click on the link KeyPals Club and then About KeyPals to learn why the club is important. For example, one reason the website is important is because "it lets people who are from different countries get acquainted and that is very important. It is important because one day WE will be the grownups who run the countries and because we were friends when we were little we won't have any more wars!" (n.p.). The website has over 50,000 registered users from 76 countries and is updated consistently. Follow the format of the letters Lucy and the princess exchanged in *The Princess's Secret Letters* (Robinson, 2002) by brainstorming questions to ask in a

friendly letter. Follow safety guidelines and remind students not to give out any personal information (e.g., telephone number, address) when communicating online.

Students who are connecting with a keypal will enjoy getting feedback from peers during author's computer chair (see Appendix B) on a draft of their letters before they are sent. Students who created items for *The Jolly Postman's Party* (1997) will enjoy displaying and describing their work.

Book 3:   Mrs. Goodstory

Crowley, J. (2001). Ill. E. Dornbusch. Honesdale, PA: Boyds Mills Press. $15.95. 32 pp.

BOOK REVIEW

A young boy joins Mrs. Goodstory on a series of adventures that relate to qualities of good story writing. Descriptive language that helps stories come alive is captured on a page of pink clouds of flamingos fly over a river. When a cowboy appears on the African scene, Mrs. Goodstory tells him he is in the wrong story; however, he simply smiles and reminds her that stories should be full of surprises. Other pages remind readers that good writers are not boring. If good writers "get lost" in the story they can always go back to the beginning. If readers do not know where to go next in a story, just think and make it up. Using your imagination can change a biplane into a space shuttle blasting off for the stars and a perfect ending. In her final words, Mrs. Goodstory reminds readers that sometimes stories just go their own way, but at other times, stories follow a clear path.

READ-ALOUD AND BOOK DISCUSSION IDEAS

Before reading, tell students that the book is about a woman named Mrs. Goodstory because she loves reading, telling, and writing good stories. Ask them to help you figure out what makes a story good. For example, ask students what a writer should do to help a reader understand who the main character is. How can a writer help a reader understand how a main character feels about a problem? Write students' comments on chart paper.

MATERIALS

- Chart paper
- Markers

During reading, tell students while they are reading to point out what Mrs. Goodstory thinks makes up a good story. Write their observations on the board.

After reading, review the pages of the book (in an after-reading picture walk) and summarize, writing on chart paper, characteristics of good stories. Include other ideas for good stories. For example, specifically point out the elements of good story structure for narratives (e.g., for developing and fluent readers discuss setting, initiating an event or problem, episodes, resolution; for emerging readers, focus on beginning, middle, and end). Tell students that they will have many opportunities to practice writing good stories during the unit.

COMPUTER ACTIVITIES

Creativity and Presentation Software Ideas

MATERIALS

■ KidPix Studio Deluxe 3 (2000) or PowerPoint (Microsoft Office 2003, 2003) software

One of the characteristics of good story writing mentioned by Mrs. Goodstory is the ability to use verbs and adjectives—rich language (e.g., a *trumpeting* elephant, a flamingo *rises*). The following is a list of steps to complete this activity.

1. Tell students to draw on screen a picture or use stamped icons using KidPix Studio Deluxe 3 or PowerPoint creativity and presentation software to create a picture. Explain the concept of adjectives as describing words and provide examples from the book. Tell them that good writers will write sentences, ask someone to give them feedback, and then change words in the sentences to make them more descriptive. Demonstrate by keyboarding in a sentence with no adjectives, for example, "My dog likes food." Next, talk about how using describing words will help readers paint a picture in their minds and will equip them to better understand the meaning. Demonstrate multimedia composition by using editing tools such as moving the cursor to the point in the sentence to add words, as in the sentence "My big, black dog likes juicy, brown dog food."

2. Tell students to dictate or write a sentence that describes the picture they create on screen. Extend and elaborate on the sentences by focusing on adjectives to make their sentences richer. Help students use editing tools to compose and revise their sentences.

3. During author's computer chair (see Appendix B), instruct students to read their descriptive sentences and ask peers to paint a picture in their minds. Then, instruct students to display their pictures on the computer monitor. Ask peers to explain how very descriptive words helped them make a mental picture and suggest other descriptive words students can use in a revision that would help paint a better word picture.

4. Instruct students to revise their sentences, adding more descriptive words and using multimedia tools.

5. Print out and bind work in a class book titled "Mrs. Goodstory Would Like Our Words."

Digital Language Experience Approach

MATERIALS

■ Digital camera
■ KidPix Studio Deluxe 3 (2000) or PowerPoint (Microsoft Office 2003, 2003) software

Using a digital photograph of each student will motivate him or her to engage in multimedia composition and step into a story. Additionally, students will gain new literacy skills as they learn to revise text (e.g., add descriptive words to original text) on screen. The following section includes steps to complete this activity.

1. Take a digital snapshot of each student and import into creativity and presentation software such as KidPix Studio Deluxe 3 or PowerPoint.

2. Tell students to use multimedia artistic tools and stamp icons to place themselves in an imaginary setting for a story. For example, the boy and Mrs. Goodstory found themselves in Africa in a stampede of African animals, on a ship in the Arctic, in a circus tent, and on a space shuttle.

3. After they have created a story setting, invite students to use their imaginations and story structure to tell a fantasy story about an adventure. Remind students that a good story also has a beginning, middle, and end. Recall some of the beginnings, middles, and endings of stories they know.

4. Instruct students to dictate or keyboard a first draft of their stories. Ask them to confer with you at the computer center to add adjectives for a second draft. On-the-spot revision helps students understand the ease of on-screen revising and multimedia composing.

5. During author's computer chair (see Appendix B), instruct students to seek feedback from peers or showcase their work and invite comments.

Computer Software Activity

After students have listened to the Arthur's Reading Games CD-ROM story about Arthur's love for reading and the challenge he gives to his little sister, D.W., to prove that she can read, they will enjoy being coauthors of the story. The Write It option allows even the youngest students to participate. Demonstrate how to interact with the screen tools and explain the assignment before students enter the computer center.

> ### MATERIALS
>
> ■ Arthur's Reading Games (1999) CD-ROM

A sentence stem appears at the top of one of the story scenes on each screen. Students select an object by clicking the mouse and dragging the object to the sentence. Tool features allow students to hear text read aloud. For example, the blank in the sentence stem in the family room setting "Arthur likes _____" can be filled in with a toy sitting on the floor; however, the sentence stem "Arthur loves _____" should be filled in with the name of a book, his puppy, or his sister. This tool feature allows emerging and developing readers to participate in an activity that is usually reserved for students who are already reading. Students will enjoy figuring out the nuances of vocabulary word meanings. Insightful discussions will help students learn that authors are careful to select words that express the meaning they intend to convey, which is an important insight that fosters active reading and comprehension.

Internet Resources and Ideas

Animal Diaries: Students All Over the World Writing Together Online Books: www.tesan. vuurwerk.nl/diaries/t8/progressivestory.htm

On this website, students are invited to use their most adventurous and creative writing to write a progressive story with others online. One group of students in a classroom writes a chapter of the story. Afterward, another classroom agrees to pick up the story line and write the next chapter. Students will eagerly await each new installment. Teachers can register online.

Kidscribe: A Bilingual Site for Kid Authors: www.brightinvisiblegreen.com/kidscribe
This bilingual website for student authors provides directions, prompts, stories, poetry, jokes, and links in English and Spanish. The homepage shows students' thoughts about the meaning of peace, as expressed in one of the subtitles: "What does 'peace' mean to you? ¿Qué significa 'la paz' para ti?" (n.p.). Directions for adults to help students submit work online are provided.

Columbia Education Center: Creative Writing: www.col-ed.org/cur/lang/lang03.txt
The purpose of this activity is to encourage creativity and analytical and critical skills through multiauthor story writing. Directions explain how students begin a story that is finished by classmates.

Columbia Education Center: A Photo Essay: www.col-ed.org/cur/lang/lang20.txt
This website provides instructions to create photograph essays. Explain that photograph essays are stories told in pictures. This activity will help students see that the world can be read in multiple ways and that everything can be readable text.

Literacy Center: Chain of Events: www.abcteach.com/samples/language_arts.pdf
Teachers can use this resource to help students learn sequencing. Students recall and retell events in the story in their original order and rewrite those events to consider how the conclusion would be changed. Instructions and printable worksheets are available here. This resource is appropriate for all reader levels.

Unit Conclusion

Display all the types of writing the students have created throughout the unit. Discuss the forms, content, and intent of each type of writing. Have a read-aloud jamboree in which students read aloud their choice of diary entries, keypal correspondence, computer compositions, slide shows, and stories. Ask students to share how they feel about being good writers and authors. Other students may share something they learned about writing during the unit.

"One of the most powerful things we did in this unit was to use the chart that helped us compare and contrast stories. My students couldn't wait to talk about the story components. Most importantly, they began to look for those components in other fairy tales we read in class. I'll use this idea in many other units."

—KINDERGARTEN TEACHER

Fun, Fantasy, and Fairy Tales

UNIT BOOKS

Three Tales of Three:
Goldilocks and the Three Bears, The Three Billy Goats Gruff, The Three Little Pigs
By Marilyn Helmer
Illustrated by Chris Jackson

Rufferella
By Vanessa Gill-Brown and Mandy Stanley

Leola and the Honeybears: An African-American Retelling of Goldilocks and the Three Bears
By Melodye Benson Rosales

COMPUTER RESOURCES

Snow White and the Seven Hansels
Cinderella: The Original Fairy Tale
Storybook Weaver Deluxe
Flossie and the Fox

Thematic Connection

Fairy tales and fantasies simply delight young minds with a type of literary engagement that has lasted from an oral to a written tradition. Discourse knowledge—understanding various genre styles and structures—supports students' comprehension (Spiegel & Fitzgerald, 1986). For example, knowing narrative structures helps students form logical predictions about upcoming events and helps them make inferences about story details that authors may not include. Classics such as Cinderella and Goldilocks and the Three Bears become the foundations for new learning as the unit's selections of *Rufferella* (Gill-Brown & Stanley, 2000) and *Leola and the Honeybears: An African-American Retelling of Goldilocks and the Three Bears* (Rosales, 1999) add twists and turns to these favorites. *Rufferella*, a modern-day version of Cinderella, will charm listeners as Diamante turns her dog, Ruff, into Rufferella. *Leola and the Honeybears: An African-American Retelling of Goldilocks and the Three Bears* will inspire an appreciation for and an acceptance of differing interpretations and perspectives. No fairy tale unit is complete without the beloved The

Three Little Pigs from *Three Tales of Three: Goldilocks and the Three Bears, The Three Billy Goats Gruff, The Three Little Pigs* (Helmer, 2000). This version adds yet another creative ending to the third little pig's historical adventures, and it is accompanied by two additional favorites: Goldilocks and the Three Bears and The Three Billy Goats Gruff. The purpose of this unit is to introduce and broaden students' exposure to and understandings of particular categories of literature such as the genres folk tales, fairy tales, and fantasies.

Matrix of Literacy Skills and Strategies in Unit 5

Literacy Skills and Strategies	Activities	Title of Book	Pages
Brainstorming	D	*Rufferella*	83–84
Building background knowledge on the Internet*	R, C, I	*Rufferella*	81–82, 82–83, 84–85
	I	*Leola and the Honeybears*	88
Building fluency	I	*Three Tales of Three: Goldilocks and the Three Bears, The Three Billy Goats Gruff, The Three Little Pigs*	79–81
	D, S	*Rufferella*	83–84, 84
Comparing and contrasting	I	*Three Tales of Three: Goldilocks and the Three Bears, The Three Billy Goats Gruff, The Three Little Pigs*	79–81
	R, C	*Rufferella*	81–82, 82–83
	R	*Leola and the Honeybears*	85–86
Composing in multimedia*	C, D, I	*Three Tales of Three: Goldilocks and the Three Bears, The Three Billy Goats Gruff, The Three Little Pigs*	78–79, 79, 79–81
	C, D	*Rufferella*	82–83, 83–84
	D, I	*Leola and the Honeybears*	86–87, 88
Creating and using charts	U, UC	—	75–77, 88–89
	R	*Three Tales of Three: Goldilocks and the Three Bears, The Three Billy Goats Gruff, The Three Little Pigs*	77–78
	R, C	*Rufferella*	81–82, 82–83
	R	*Leola and the Honeybears*	85–86
Determining story details	U, UC	—	75–77, 88–89
	R, C, S	*Three Tales of Three: Goldilocks and the Three Bears, The Three Billy Goats Gruff, The Three Little Pigs*	77–78, 78–79, 79
	R	*Rufferella*	81–82
	C	*Leola and the Honeybears*	86
Developing a sense of beginnings, middles, and endings	UC	—	88–89
	R	*Three Tales of Three: Goldilocks and the Three Bears, The Three Billy Goats Gruff, The Three Little Pigs*	77–78
	R	*Rufferella*	81–82
	R, S	*Leola and the Honeybears*	85–86, 87–88

(continued)

Literacy Skills and Strategies	Activities	Title of Book	Pages
Developing choral reading	D, S	*Rufferella*	83–84, 84
	S	*Leola and the Honeybears*	87–88
Developing comprehension	UC	—	88–89
	R, S, I	*Three Tales of Three: Goldilocks and the Three Bears, The Three Billy Goats Gruff, The Three Little Pigs*	77–78, 79, 79–81
	R, S	*Rufferella*	81–82, 84
	R, C, I	*Leola and the Honeybears*	85–86, 86, 88
Developing creative writing	D, S, I	*Three Tales of Three: Goldilocks and the Three Bears, The Three Billy Goats Gruff, The Three Little Pigs*	79, 79, 79–81
	D	*Rufferella*	83–84
	C, D	*Leola and the Honeybears*	86, 86–87
Developing critical reading and thinking	R, D	*Three Tales of Three: Goldilocks and the Three Bears, The Three Billy Goats Gruff, The Three Little Pigs*	77–78, 79
Developing oral language	U, UC	—	75–77, 88–89
	R, D	*Three Tales of Three: Goldilocks and the Three Bears, The Three Billy Goats Gruff, The Three Little Pigs*	77–78, 79
	R, D	*Rufferella*	81–82, 83–84
	R, D	*Leola and the Honeybears*	85–86, 86–87
Developing vocabulary	U, UC	—	75–77, 88–89
	R, D	*Three Tales of Three: Goldilocks and the Three Bears, The Three Billy Goats Gruff, The Three Little Pigs*	77–78, 79
	R, D	*Rufferella*	81–82, 83–84
	R	*Leola and the Honeybears*	85–86
Distinguishing between real and make-believe content	U, UC	—	75–77, 88–89
	R, C	*Rufferella*	81–82, 82–83
Drawing conclusions	U	—	75–77
	R	*Rufferella*	81–82
Following directions	UC	—	88–89
	C, D, S, I	*Three Tales of Three: Goldilocks and the Three Bears, The Three Billy Goats Gruff, The Three Little Pigs*	78–79, 79, 79 79–81
	C, D, I	*Rufferella*	82–83, 83–84, 84–85
	D, I	*Leola and the Honeybears*	86–87, 88
Making multicultural connections	I	*Three Tales of Three: Goldilocks and the Three Bears, The Three Billy Goats Gruff, The Three Little Pigs*	79–81
	R	*Leola and the Honeybears*	85–86

(continued)

Matrix of Literacy Skills and Strategies in Unit 5 (continued)

Literacy Skills and Strategies	Activities	Title of Book	Pages
Making predictions	U	—	75–77
	R	*Three Tales of Three: Goldilocks and the Three Bears, The Three Billy Goats Gruff, The Three Little Pigs*	77–78
`	R	*Rufferella*	81–82
Navigating hyperlinks*	I	*Three Tales of Three: Goldilocks and the Three Bears, The Three Billy Goats Gruff, The Three Little Pigs*	79–81
	C, I	*Rufferella*	82–83, 84–85
	I	*Leola and the Honeybears*	88
Presenting work on a computer*	UC	—	88–89
	D	*Three Tales of Three: Goldilocks and the Three Bears, The Three Billy Goats Gruff, The Three Little Pigs*	79
	C, D	*Rufferella*	82–83, 83–84
	D	*Leola and the Honeybears*	86–87 ·
Reading aloud	R, I	*Three Tales of Three: Goldilocks and the Three Bears, The Three Billy Goats Gruff, The Three Little Pigs*	77–78, 79–81
	R, D	*Rufferella*	81–82, 83–84
Reading and listening for a purpose	R, S, I	*Three Tales of Three: Goldilocks and the Three Bears, The Three Billy Goats Gruff, The Three Little Pigs*	77–78, 79, 79–81
	R, S, I	*Rufferella*	81–82, 84, 84–85
	R, C, I	*Leola and the Honeybears*	85–86, 86, 88
Reading informational text	I	*Three Tales of Three: Goldilocks and the Three Bears, The Three Billy Goats Gruff, The Three Little Pigs*	79–81
Retelling	UC	—	88–89
	I	*Three Tales of Three: Goldilocks and the Three Bears, The Three Billy Goats Gruff, The Three Little Pigs*	79–81
	R	*Rufferella*	81–82
	S	*Leola and the Honeybears*	87–88
Sequencing	UC	—	88–89
	R	*Three Tales of Three: Goldilocks and the Three Bears, The Three Billy Goats Gruff, The Three Little Pigs*	77–78
	R	*Rufferella*	81–82
	D	*Leola and the Honeybears*	86–87
Understanding concepts about print	D, I	*Three Tales of Three: Goldilocks and the Three Bears, The Three Billy Goats Gruff, The Three Little Pigs*	79, 79–81
	D	*Rufferella*	83–84
	S	*Leola and the Honeybears*	87–88

(continued)

Literacy Skills and Strategies	Activities	Title of Book	Pages
Understanding story structure and events	U, UC	—	75–77, 88–89
	R, C, S, I	*Three Tales of Three: Goldilocks and the Three Bears, The Three Billy Goats Gruff, The Three Little Pigs*	77–78, 78–79, 79, 79–81
	R, C, S	*Rufferella*	81–82, 82–83, 84
	R, C, D, I	*Leola and the Honeybears*	85–86, 86, 86–87, 88
Using adjectives	U, UC	—	75–77, 88–89
	D	*Three Tales of Three: Goldilocks and the Three Bears, The Three Billy Goats Gruff, The Three Little Pigs*	79
	R, D	*Rufferella*	81–82, 83–84
Using English as a second language	I	*Three Tales of Three: Goldilocks and the Three Bears, The Three Billy Goats Gruff, The Three Little Pigs*	79–81
	D	*Rufferella*	83–84
Using phonics: Onsets and rimes	D	*Leola and the Honeybears*	86–87
Writing descriptive sentences	C, D, S, I	*Three Tales of Three: Goldilocks and the Three Bears, The Three Billy Goats Gruff, The Three Little Pigs*	78–79, 79, 79 79–81
	D	*Rufferella*	83–84
	D	*Leola and the Honeybears*	86–87

* Indicates a new-literacy skill.
U = unit introduction; R = read-aloud and book discussion ideas; C = creativity and presentation software ideas; D = Digital Language Experience Approach; S = computer software activity; I = Internet resources and ideas; UC = unit conclusion

Unit Introduction

Create a special folk and fairy tale reading area. Beanbag chairs, large pillows, and soft glowing lamps will invite students to focus on reading. Posters of castles, forests, and cottages displayed in the reading area will help students feel as if they are stepping into a fairy tale world. Several days before the unit, assemble a selection of fairy tale books and story props, including books on tape, CD-ROM, and DVD. Designate a section of the room as the Fairy Tale Corner and fill baskets with various versions of fairy tales. For example, label one basket "Tales of Three" and fill with tales based on the number three such as *The Three Pigs* (Weisner, 2001), *Goldilocks and the Three Bears* (Marshall, 1988), and *The Three Billy Goats Gruff* (Galdone, 1981). Label a second basket "Tales of Trickery" and fill with *Little Red Riding Hood* (Evertts-Secker, 2004), *Hansel and Gretel* (Lesser, 1999), and

MATERIALS

- Beanbag chairs
- Brick
- Butcher paper
- Cardboard theater
- Character props

(continued)

MATERIALS (continued)

- Crown (made from cardboard and glitter)
- Dress-up clothes
- Fairy tale books
- Fairy tale books on tape, CD-ROM, and DVD
- Fairy tales chart
- Hand puppets
- Lamps
- Large pillows
- Magic wands
- Markers
- Masks
- Medium-size gift bag
- Pictures
- Pictures or posters of fairy tale settings
- Plastic pigs
- Plastic wolf
- Props
- Slippers
- Stick puppets
- Sticks
- Story props
- Straw
- Stuffed toy mouse
- Turnip

Rumpelstiltskin (Gay, 1997). Label the third basket "Prince Charming Tales" and include favorites such as *Cinderella* (Lewis, 2004), *Snow White* (Copper, 2005), and *Rapunzel* (Zelinsky, 1997). To encourage retellings and reading with expression, create a prop center and include such items as slippers, magic wands, pictures, a cardboard theater, stick puppets, hand puppets, masks, and dress-up clothes. When students bring special fairy tale books and possessions from home, have a display area ready to showcase and celebrate these personal treasures.

Before reading the books, arouse students' interest by filling a medium-size gift bag with fairy tale props such as a slipper, magic wand, a small crown (made from cardboard and glitter), a fuzzy stuffed toy mouse, a turnip (used in one of the books), straw, sticks, a brick, and plastic pigs or a wolf. Students will have hands-on opportunities to learn vocabulary words related to fairy tales and folk tales as they play with the props. Next, during whole-group time, ask students to take turns peeking inside a box and selecting and describing a hidden object. Model for emerging and developing readers how to describe an object by using multiple, rich adjectives. For example, point to a student's shoe and say, "The object that I'm thinking of is black. It has white laces on it, it has a rubber sole, and it lights up if you walk on it." Tell students if they put all of those descriptions together, they can make a good guess about what the object is. Next, ask each student to take a turn looking in the bag and describing objects. Their classmates should guess what each described object is before the student displays it for all to see. Occasionally recap the key clues that helped students identify the objects. Last, after students remove and describe all objects, students suggest how the items are related. Prompt with directing questions until students make the fairy tale connection. For example, you might ask students, "What kind of story has a magic wand, a princess, or pigs and a wolf?"

Introduce a fairy tales chart, written on butcher paper (see Figure 14 for an example). As you go over the components of the chart, tell students that in fairy tales things can happen in threes, animals can talk and act like humans, and other make-believe things happen. Explain that during this unit you will be reading fairy tale books and filling out the chart for each story. Tell students that they will complete computer activities that will help them learn more about real and imaginary story elements and parts of fairy tales and that they will create their own fairy tales.

Book 1: Three Tales of Three: Goldilocks and the Three Bears, The Three Billy Goats Gruff, The Three Little Pigs

Helmer, M. (2000). Ill. C. Jackson. Niagara Falls, NY: Kids Can Press. $10.95. 32 pp.

Figure 14
Fairy Tales Chart

Title	Story Beginnings	Setting Place and Time	Good Characters	Bad Characters	Real	Fantasy	Problem	Story Middle	(Happy) Story Ending

BOOK REVIEW

Three Tales of Three: Goldilocks and the Three Bears, The Three Billy Goats Gruff, The Three Little Pigs contains The Three Little Pigs, which is the unit's fairy tale focus. Briefly tell the traditional version of the story so students will have a point of reference for comparing and contrasting with Helmer's version of the story. As you read Helmer's version, students will delight in and enjoy chanting along during choral reading with the popular refrains "Little pig, little pig, let me come in. Not by the hair on my chinny-chin-chin!" (p. 24). They will cheer with pleasure as they spontaneously repeat, "Then I'll huff and I'll puff and I'll blow your house in!" (p. 24). Students may know the tale, but they may not know this version's unexpected ending. Large outlined watercolor illustrations in red ink vividly capture story events. Text length, refrains, and illustrations are just right to captivate inquisitive young minds.

READ-ALOUD AND BOOK DISCUSSION IDEAS

Before reading the story, explain or review story parts: characters, settings, problems, and solutions. Tell students that as you read the story they will need to listen very carefully for these story parts.

During reading, to engage students in listening for and remembering specific story elements, you can tell students that when they recognize a story part, they should give you a big smile and tuck one finger into their hand to help them remember the part because after the story is read, the parts will be discussed and added to the story comparison chart (see Figure 15).

MATERIALS

- Markers
- Story comparison chart

After reading, model critical and evaluative thinking by saying, "I remember that the little pigs met the man outside on the road, but the pictures show all the pigs inside their houses, so I think the setting is in two places: outside and inside houses." Over time, with modeling, practicing, and thinking about story parts, students will learn to internalize this important comprehension concept. Fill in the chart and ask students to recap the beginning, middle, and ending of the story.

		Figure 15		
		Story Comparison Chart		
Title and Author of Story	**Characters**	**Settings**	**Problems**	**Solutions**

COMPUTER ACTIVITIES

Creativity and Presentation Software Ideas

Invite students to explore story grammar by creating a story concept map (a way to organize the story's setting, characters, events, and ending). Either individually or in small groups, students create a story concept map by using creativity and presentation software such as Kidspiration 2.1.

MATERIALS

■ Kidspiration 2.1 (2005) software

1. Select from the teacher menu one of the ready-made templates that includes the following questions: Where is the setting? Who are the characters? What are the three story events? How does the story end?

2. Model for students how to scroll through picture icons before they select and drag icons onto the screen.

3. Instruct students to select picture icons and create a story concept map by using their growing awareness of fairy tale elements.

Kidspiration 2.1 offers a text-to-speech option, which assists emerging and developing readers as they listen to and read letter–sound symbols. Fluent readers can use the writing option to construct sentences. Kidspiration 2.1 also includes character and story stamp categories to support students' fairy tale selections.

Share student work during an author's computer chair (see Appendix B) schedule on a Thursday (because it is the fourth day of the school week) and declare it "The Fourth Little Pig's Day." Ask students to share the computer slides of the house they designed for the fourth pig in the Digital Language Experience Approach and tell details about the inspiration behind the design, materials used, and what was easy and difficult.

On another day, invite students to share their created fairy tale concept maps from the creativity and presentation software ideas activity during author's computer chair. Encourage students to explain why they selected certain pictures and how the pictures help to build the story. Younger students are excellent at making up stories, so encourage them to orally tell a story as they point to their selected pictures. Invite a few students to share their mixed-up stories from Snow White and the Seven Hansels from the Internet resources and ideas activity during a special author's computer chair.

Digital Language Experience Approach ➤ – – – – – – – – – – ➤

Students create a digital photo essay about a fourth little pig's house. The house should be the size of a shoebox. Provide a variety of materials such as beads, ribbons, plastic flowers, twigs, rocks, toothpicks, and fabric scraps. If supplies are scarce, consider including them as a wish list in a class newsletter you send to parents.

1. Direct the students to select one type of material to create their houses. For instance, one little pig made his house of straw, so a student might choose to make his or her house out of buttons. Have students glue the materials onto their shoeboxes.

2. Use a digital camera to take pictures of each student with his or her house.

3. Import the pictures into creativity and presentation software such as KidPix Studio Deluxe. Students dictate or keyboard a sentence about what the Big Bad Wolf might say if he came upon a fourth little pig's house. For example, if the house was made of buttons, the wolf might say, "Little pig, little pig, let me come into your house of buttons or I'll huff and I'll puff and I'll blow your house down." Encourage students to use adjectives to help describe the decorations. For example, the wolf might say, "Little pig, little pig, let me come into your house of blue, red, and yellow plastic buttons." Doing so builds knowledge about adjectives and increases students' vocabulary. Assemble finished pictures into a slide show for sharing during author's computer chair (see Appendix B). In addition, print pictures and bind into a class book called "Our Ideas About the Fourth Little Pig's House."

Computer Software Activity ➤ – – – – – – – – – ➤

Snow White and the Seven Hansels software invites students to interact with several fairy tale character favorites such as Little Red Riding Hood, Snow White, and Hansel and Gretel. In these animated storybooks, students need to click on hidden arrows to make progress. If the wrong path is selected, the characters end up in the wrong stories. Because the possibilities for story creating are endless, you may want students to create a fairy tale diary to draw or list the exciting events that occur as they interact with the program. Invite a few students to share their mixed-up stories during author's computer chair (see Appendix B).

Internet Resources and Ideas

CBeebies: Build a House: www.bbc.co.uk/cbeebies/funandgames/buildahouse.shtml
This Build a House game involves selecting one of four character helpers. By using the mouse or the arrows, students travel through a maze collecting materials to build either a castle, treehouse, or tent. Students learn to navigate through hyperlinks as they respond to fairy tales.

CBeebies—Tweenies: The Three Little Pigs: www.bbc.co.uk/cbeebies/tweenies/storytime/stories/3littlepigs/index.shtml
This website offers an interactive Three Little Pigs e-book. When instructed, readers follow directions to locate and click on hiding characters. Teachers can lead a comparison and contrast of this version of the story with other versions.

Kiz Club: The Three Little Pigs: www.kizclub.com/pigstory/pig1.html
This printable version of The Three Little Pigs offers readers a chance to practice left-to-right directionality as text highlights individual words as text is read aloud. Teachers can print a copy to send home with students to read with their parents.

Kiz Club: The Three Billy Goats Gruff: www.kizclub.com/goatstory/goat1.html
This website offers an e-book of The Three Billy Goats Gruff. Text becomes highlighted when read, helping emerging readers to understand concepts about print (e.g., left-to-right directionality, concepts of words).

iKnowthat.com: Scrambled Stories: www.iknowthat.com/com/L3?Area=ScrambledStory
iKnowthat.com offers scrambled stories. Students change nouns and verbs to make a new story and choose words before or while reading the story. When readers select a word, it becomes highlighted, and the pictures change. You can print stories or save them to refer to during class discussions. Story selections include the Gingerbread Boy and the Tortoise and the Hare. A quick, free registration is required.

Korean Folk Tales: http://story.lg.co.kr:3000/eng.jsp
This website offers Korean fairy tales and other worldwide folk tales for developing multicultural awareness. You may want to select from the various tales to teach similarities and differences. An option is available to hear the stories in different languages.

Eurotales: www.eurotales.eril.net/pigsuk.htm
This website offers students an opportunity to explore creative writing as they read and learn from other students' composed versions of The Three Little Pigs. Student-composed illustrations also accompany the versions. Emerging readers may need reading assistance from a cross-age computer buddy.

Eurotales: www.eurotales.eril.net/pigsdiy.htm
This website encourages creative writing opportunities as students use the site's The Three Little Pig's illustrations to construct descriptive sentences that retell story events.

A Ladybird "Easy-Reading" Book—"Well-Loved Tales": The Three Little Pigs: http://math-www.uni-paderborn.de/~odenbach/pigs/pigs.html
This website offers the Three Little Pigs e-book to read with the class. Text is written on the left and full-color illustrations are displayed on the right. When viewing, cover the text and ask students to retell story events by looking at the illustrations only. You may want to ask students to use the illustrations to practice writing or saying descriptive sentences. After students use the illustrations to discuss the story event, uncover the text and compare with the e-book's version.

Pork 4 Kids: www.pork4kids.com
Several factual interactive activities are available; for example, students can read a photo essay about a pig farm, make a mask and print it, send an e-mail to a pig farmer, guess the season, and take a cyber tour of a pig farm.

Elementary Reader's Theatre: http://hometown.aol.com/rcswallow/TruePigs.html
This website includes the True Story of The Three Little Pigs theater script to use for role-playing and for fluency building.

Book 2: Rufferella

Gill-Brown, V., & Stanley, M. (2000). New York: Scholastic. $8.58. 32 pp.

BOOK REVIEW

Rufferella puts an amusing twist on the classic Cinderella tale. Diamante "desperately wanted to turn something into something" (p. 1) and then sets her sights on her dog, Ruff. Pretending to be a fairy godmother without a magic wand, Diamante turns Ruff into a girl by teaching her how to be human through various entertaining lessons. Wherever Ruff goes, from riding in a limousine wearing sunglasses to drying her new hairdo under a beauty parlor hairdryer, she captures attention. All of these events happen before Rufferella becomes famous, receiving an invitation to the Queen's ball. Light, pleasant watercolors will appeal to young listeners as they connect to their favorite household pet and learn lessons about remaining true to one's identity.

READ-ALOUD AND BOOK DISCUSSION IDEAS

Several days before reading the book, have on display in the reading center several versions of Cinderella and, from a Cinderella coloring book, select different pictures for story retellings. Color with markers and then cut and laminate these pictures. Depending on the storyboard used, affix Velcro, flannel, or magnetic tape to the back of the pieces to manipulate on a storyboard. You can make a simple storyboard from heavy poster board or foam board. Cover the board with approximately two yards of any colored flannel material, fold excess material to the back of the board, and hot glue it in place. Use Velcro- or flannel-backed pieces for flannel storyboards. You also can use metal cookie sheets or the side of a file cabinet to manipulate story parts backed with magnetic tape.

Before reading, place in a suitcase several different types of shoes: rain boots, hiking boots, dress shoes, tennis shoes, slippers, and so forth. Ask students to predict the suitcase's contents by playing a clue game. Students ask questions involving color, size, shape, smell, number of items, and texture. Provide clues as needed. For example, say, "They come in pairs." As you open the suitcase, ask students to

MATERIALS

- Chart paper
- Coloring book pictures of Cinderella
- Fairy Tales Chart
- Flannel
- Foam board
- Glue gun
- Laminate
- Magnetic tape
- Markers
- Metal cookie sheets
- Poster board
- Scissors
- Suitcase
- Various types of shoes
- Velcro

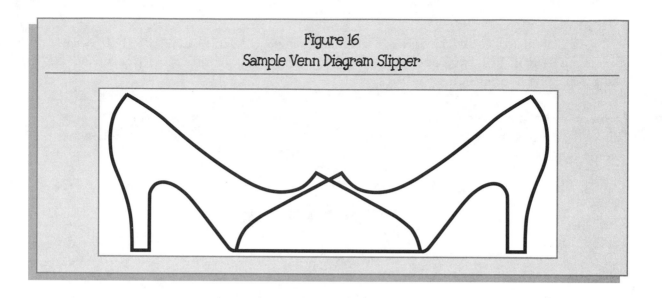

Figure 16
Sample Venn Diagram Slipper

observe the objects and think about a fairy tale that involves a special pair of shoes. After students have suggested Cinderella, use the laminated coloring book pieces and work from students' prior knowledge of Cinderella to create a class version of Cinderella. Discuss with the students and list on chart paper the story elements told in the student version.

If possible, access one of the following websites to listen to a traditional version of Cinderella: www.childrenstory.com/tales/1page/cinderella.html (a read-only version) or http://www.bbc.co. uk/cbeebies/storycircle/fairystories/cinderella/cinderella_s.shtml?fairy (an animated, interactive version). After listening, draw two slippers overlapping and use them as a Venn diagram (see Figure 16) to compare and contrast the class's version with the Internet version.

During reading, draw students' attention to what could be real in the story and what could be fantasy or make-believe.

After reading, fill in the ongoing Fairy Tales Chart (see Figure 14 on page 77) and ask students to recap the beginning, middle, and ending of the story.

Fairy tales are fun because of their pretend and fantasy elements. Animals talk and wear clothes, magical things happen, and fairy tales end happily. However, they are pretend. Draw students' attention to the chart to compare and contrast real and make-believe events and objects in the fairy tales they read.

MATERIALS

- KidPix Studio Deluxe (1998) software
- Teacher-prepared template

COMPUTER ACTIVITIES

Creativity and Presentation Software Ideas

This activity involves students distinguishing between real and make-believe. If possible, view this informative yet instructional website before completing the activity: Game Goo—Tina's World Real or Make-Believe? (www.cogcon.com/gamegoo/games/tina/tina.html). The short, interactive animated movie reinforces the difference between real and make-believe elements.

Use creativity and presentation software such as KidPix Studio Deluxe, which is rich with stamp icons that will be useful for this activity.

1. Prepare a template before assigning the activity. Enlarge two different shapes, fill with a background color, and label one make-believe and the other real.

2. Demonstrate for students how to accomplish the activity. For example, stamp an icon of a girl under "real," but place a stamp of a magic wand under "make-believe."

3. Depending on the program used, either preselect stamp icons and place around the shapes or challenge students to scroll through the icons to select real and make-believe icons before dragging and dropping them under the corresponding labeled shapes.

4. Print out students' comparison charts and share during author's computer chair (see Appendix B).

Digital Language Experience Approach

One of the key items in the original Cinderella story was the glass slipper. Help students make a life-to-text connection by writing descriptive sentences about their shoes.

> ### MATERIALS
> - Blackboard
> - Chalk
> - Digital camera
> - KidPix Studio Deluxe (1998) software
> - Pair of shoes
> - Picture of Cinderella's glass slipper

1. Tell students if Cinderella had not lost her glass slipper, the prince would have had to tell people what the slipper looked like in order to find Cinderella. Draw a picture of or have on hand a picture of the glass slipper and offer students an oral description such as "It was a shiny, small, clear, glass slipper." Tell students that they will be making a class slide show or book that includes how they describe their own shoes.

2. Demonstrate how to describe a pair of shoes and use the adjectives in a sentence. First, show students a pair of your shoes. Write a list of descriptive words or phrases on the blackboard. For example, the list might include the following:

> Green shoes
> High-heeled shoes
> Going-to-church shoes
> Dress-up shoes

3. Show students how you would use the phrases to complete a sentence (e.g., "Cinderella wore her shiny, clear, glass slippers to the ball. [Insert teacher's name] wears her green, high-heeled, going-to-church, dress-up shoes to dinner.").

4. Take one picture of each student's shoes. Focus on a knee-to-shoe close-up shot.

5. Import the pictures, one per screen page, into creativity and presentation software, preferably one with a slide show presentation such as KidPix Studio Deluxe.

6. Work with students to complete a descriptive sentence that highlights vocabulary words and adjectives that describe the shoes. Students begin by observing the details of their shoes and generating a list of words. Teachers elicit language by asking prompting questions such as the following: What color are the shoes? Where do you mostly wear them? What things do you do in your shoes? How do the shoes feel?

7. Ask students to refer to the brainstormed list of words to complete a pattern sentence: "Cinderella wore her shiny, clear, glass slippers to the ball. (Student's name) wears his or her (descriptive words) shoes to school and (other places)." For example a student might write the following sentence: "Cinderella wore her shiny, clear, glass slippers to the ball. Jawanza wears his brown, leather, laced-up, clunky shoes to school and to church." In KidPix Studio Deluxe, type each sentence below each student's picture.

8. Decorate a title page with shoe stamp icons and type the text, "Cinderella wore her shiny, clear, glass slippers to the ball. What type of shoes do we wear to school and other places?" Import the pictures to a slide show. If using KidPix Studio Deluxe, students can use the record option to narrate their sentences.

9. Share the slide show during author's computer chair (see Appendix B). After students listen to the text read aloud, students chorally read along with the text. Emerging readers will gain concepts about print, and developing and fluent readers will gain fluency.

Students for whom English is a second language may benefit from dictating or keyboarding their sentence in their first language and then adding a translated line of text below. Enlist the help of a native language speaker (e.g., parent volunteer, teaching assistant in the school, district volunteer, cross-age computer buddy who speaks the native language) to type the sentences in both languages. Students who reread text on the screen during subsequent viewings will have unique occasions to learn vocabulary words in English. For example, a student might generate the following brainstormed list of adjectives:

las botas	boots
demasiado grande	too big
oscuro	dark
rojo	red

Computer Software Activity

MATERIALS

■ Cinderella: The Original Fairy Tale (1990) CD-ROM

Cinderella: The Original Fairy Tale allows students to click on pictures or words to hear them read aloud. Soft music plays in the background as text highlights each sentence. To practice fluency, developing or fluent readers can read along with the text. Emerging readers can echo read the text. Because this is a lengthy story that is heavily text based, younger students will need support from a cross-age computer buddy to negotiate a multiday reading with small-group viewing and to discuss the story.

Internet Resources and Ideas

CBeebies—Story Circle Fairy Tales: Cinderella: www.bbc.co.uk/cbeebies/storycircle/fairystories/cinderella/cinderella_s.shtml?fairy
Students build fluency and practice following directions as they read along with an interactive Cinderella e-book online.

Disney Online: Cinderella's Sticker Story: http://disney.go.com/characters/activities/stickerstory/Cinderella/index.html
Students interact with a Disney Cinderella interactive Sticker Story as they follow directions and click on objects to help Cinderella dress for the ball. Younger students may need initial assistance with website use.

Cinderella Around the World: Cinderella's Slipper Matchup: www.northcanton.sparcc.org/~ptk1nc/cinderella/shoematch.html
This website offers an interactive concentration game. Students match pairs of shoes worn by people from around the world.

Childrenstory.com: Cinderella: www.childrenstory.com/tales/1page/cinderella.html
This website offers Cinderella and several other fairy tale stories to read to the students and to build fairy tale genre knowledge. Text is challenging for students to read independently; however, an audio option is available for some of the stories. RealPlayer is required for the audio option.

Book 3:   Leola and the Honeybears: An African-American Retelling of Goldilocks and the Three Bears

Rosales, M.B. (1999). New York: Scholastic. $15.95. 40 pp.

BOOK REVIEW

Leola, an African American girl, lives with her grandmother near Pine Hollow Woods. One day she decides to follow milkweed seeds into a meadow. Oil paintings bursting with color show Leola's emotions as she enters the chilly woods and becomes frightened by Ol' Mister Weasel before finding the Honeybears' cottage. In this country-folk style retelling, pastries replace porridge and a lovely blue bird escorts Leola safely back home. Traditional three-bears fairy tale characters mix and mingle in this modern-day version.

READ-ALOUD AND BOOK DISCUSSION IDEAS

Several days before reading the text, assemble a variety of Goldilocks and the Three Bears books. Use a Three Bears coloring book or the following webpages from the First-School Preschool Activities and Crafts website to create story props: www.first-school.ws/activities/fairytales/3bears.htm, www.first-school.ws/t/craft/3bears_puppets.htm, and www.first-school.ws/t/ac3bears_sizingc.htm. Color, cut, and laminate the pieces so students can practice retelling and sequencing a familiar story version. Before reading the story, display the story pieces and ask for a student volunteer to predict the title of the story and ask students to

MATERIALS

- Coloring book
- Markers
- Laminate
- Scissors
- Story props
- Various book versions of Goldilocks and the Three Bears

retell the beginning of Goldilocks and the Three Bears. Students take turns, using the story pieces to tell the beginning, middle, and ending events.

Before reading, also show students the book jacket and tell them that you are going to read a different version of Goldilocks and the Three Bears. Ask students to compare this version to the version they created.

During reading, when students hear story parts that are the same, they should smile, and when they hear parts that are different, they should frown.

After reading, fill out the Fairy Tales Chart (see Figure 14 on page 77) and discuss the parts of the story.

COMPUTER ACTIVITIES

Creativity and Presentation Software Ideas

MATERIALS

■ Storybook Weaver Deluxe (1994) software

Invite students to create their own fairy tales. Using their growing understanding of story elements and referring to the Fairy Tales Chart (see Figure 14 on page 77), students select from the many background scenes, stamp icons for story items, and characters before giving their story a problem and solution. A cross-age computer buddy may help students navigate through the various tools to create and write their own fairy tale during computer-center time.

Digital Language Experience Approach

To further enhance students' engagement with the Honeybears from the story, have a teddy bear picnic and document the event by taking pictures of each activity and using the pictures to create a photo essay. You may want to print the songs and rhymes (sites listed below) on chart paper and share them with the students a few days or weeks before the day of picnic. Send home a note (see Figure 17) asking parents to allow students to bring to school their favorite teddy bear, a beach towel or blanket, and a brown bag lunch. Be sure to have a few extra stuffed bears on hand for those who forget or who do not have a teddy bear at home.

MATERIALS

■ Blankets or towels
■ Brown bag lunches
■ Chart paper
■ Digital camera
■ KidPix Studio Deluxe (1998) software
■ Letter to parents
■ Teddy bears

1. Spread the blankets and towels outdoors. Students eat their lunches with their teddy bears and classmates.

2. Clean up lunch and arrange the students and teddy bears in a standing circle, alternating by student and teddy bear. Students hold hands, including the bears'. Sing songs and play games such as "Teddy Bear, Teddy Bear, Turn Around" (students chant this rhyme while jumping rope). You may want to access Literacy Connections (http://literacyconnections.com/AS TeddyBear.html) for a copy of the rhyme. Students also can play "Ring Around the Rosey" (see rules and a copy of the rhyme at www.geocities.com/toddlermoms/ring.html). Students may also enjoy playing the "Hokey Pokey" with their teddy bears.

Figure 17
Sample Teddy Bear Picnic Letter to Parents and Caregivers

Dear Parents and Caregivers,

We are busy learning about story elements found in fairy tales, folk tales, and fantasies. Recently we have studied such books as The Three Little Pigs, Cinderella, and Goldilocks and the Three Bears. To further enrich this wonderful learning experience, we are having a Teddy Bear Picnic. Please send to school with your child on [day and date] the following items: their favorite stuffed teddy bear, a brown bag lunch, and either a beach towel or blanket.

    To celebrate these wonderful stories, the day's events will include lunch, singing teddy bear songs, and playing teddy bear games. You are invited to extend this experience at home by joining in and sharing the songs and games learned and played during our picnic. Also, in the very near future, look for "Our Teddy Bear Picnic" photo essay class book to learn more about this wonderful day's events.

Sincerely,
Your Child's Teacher

---

3. Use a digital camera to document the events in chronological order.

4. Import the pictures into creativity and presentation software such as KidPix Studio Deluxe and print one copy of each picture.

5. Gather the students around you, telling them that together you will create a photo essay of their teddy bear picnic, but first you need to sequence the pictures according to the day's events. During computer-center time, students practice sequencing the pictures. Then, during whole-group time, they decide together on the order of the pictures.

6. Share the keyboard with the students, deciding on the text that best describes the pictures, and assist students in typing those sentences below the pictures. Work together to sound stretch words (students slowly pull their hands apart as they pronounce words that are challenging to spell) before typing. Teach students about the program's editing symbols and how to make corrections. Design and create a title page.

7. Create a slide show or print the pictures and bind into a class book titled "Our Teddy Bear Picnic." Make the book and slide show available for viewing during computer-center time and celebrate the publication during author's computer chair (see Appendix B).

Computer Software Activity

Read the *Flossie and the Fox* DVD animated big book during whole-group time. Select the extras link that allows you to see text on the screen as the animations unfold. In this animated big book, Flossie meets a clever fox that has a bad reputation around town. Ask students

---

MATERIALS

- DVD player
- *Flossie and the Fox* (Gagne & McDonald, 2004) DVD
- Pointer
- Television monitor

---

to predict if Flossie will be able to outfox a fox, even if she has never even seen a fox before. Point to text while the story is narrated to help emerging readers understand concepts about print such as directionality and speech-to-print matching. Subsequent viewings allow students to chorally read the text, echo read, or point to words they know.

Internet Resources and Ideas

CBeebies—Fun and Games: Fairy Footprints: www.bbc.co.uk/cbeebies/funandgames/fairyfootprints.shtml
This Fairy Footprints website takes you on a picnic with Barnaby Bear. Students listen for a purpose as they read along with text and follow directions to find a fairy. The website includes a fairy cake recipe.

Kiz Club—Stories: Three Little Bears: www.kizclub.com/storytime/goldistory/bear1.html
This website offers The Three Bears e-book for students to practice reading with fluency. Students can hear text read aloud while it is highlighted on screen. The e-book is also printable.

Jigzone: www.jigzone.com/ms/z.php?ui=67619i131456andz=6_piece_classic
Students select the number of pieces before assembling a Goldilocks and the Three Bears Puzzle.

CBeebies—Fimbles: The Three Bears: www.bbc.co.uk/cbeebies/fimbles/comfycorner/story8.shtml
Students build fluency while reading along with audio text. They also learn to read and listen for a purpose as they follow directions to interact with The Three Bears story. The story is printable.

First-School Preschool Activities and Crafts Sizing Worksheet Printable Activities:
www.first-school.ws/t/ac3bears_sizingc.htm
This website offers colored props for retelling and sequencing the Three Little Bears. Props include a bed, chair, and bowls.

First-School Preschool Activities and Crafts: Goldilocks and The Three Bears Puppets Craft: www.first-school.ws/t/craft/3bears_puppets.htm
This website offers printable bears and Goldilocks stand-up finger puppets for retelling, sequencing, and reinforcing oral language development.

MATERIALS

- Fairy tale dress-up props
- Fairy Tales Chart
- Masks
- Oatmeal
- Pigs in a blanket

Unit Conclusion

Ask students to tell about their fairy tale favorites. Survey the class and use the most popular tale to build a class retelling. Students sit in a circle and take turns going around the circle adding sequential story details, telling the beginning, middle, and ending events. Then, use this retelling to direct attention toward story elements. Refer to the Fairy Tales Chart (see Figure 14 on page 77) to identify and review elements.

Which parts of the stories were real and which parts were fantasy? Who were the good and bad characters? Where did the stories mostly take place? You may also conclude the unit with either a favorite fairy tale character dress-up day or allow the students to wear character props or create favorite character masks. Invite selected guests from the school (e.g., the principal, a secretary, a janitor) to read aloud a fairy tale favorite. For a special treat, serve refreshments such as pigs in a blanket (mini hot dogs baked in the middle of croissants) and a variety of oatmeal flavors to celebrate food items related to the stories. Be sure to save a little time for enjoying the slide shows and class-created books, highlighting the unit's unique learning experiences.

"Parents came for our art exhibit and were just blown away by the way we used computers in our art unit. They were so impressed with the amount of oral language and vocabulary the children used when talking about their masterpieces!"

—FIRST-GRADE TEACHER

Artrageous Art

UNIT BOOKS

David's Drawings
By Cathryn Falwell

Nature's Paintbrush: The Patterns and Colors Around You
By Susan Stockdale

The Magic Gourd
By Baba Wagué Diakité

COMPUTER RESOURCES

ArtRageous: The Amazing World of Art
IBM Crayola Magic 3-D Coloring Book Cool Critters
JumpStart Artist

Thematic Connection

The books and activities assembled in this unit will help students learn to see their world through artistic details, encourage an appreciation for art, and inspire a love for reading through the visual arts. Students are unique and so, too, are their thoughts, feelings, perceptions, and expressions toward their external world. When differences are encouraged and respected, students learn to accept and to appreciate one another's unique tastes. The world will come alive through the unit's books and multisensory activities. For example, *David's Drawings* (Falwell, 2001) heightens students' awareness of art techniques such as outlining, perspective, and depth. *Nature's Paintbrush: The Patterns and Colors Around You* (Stockdale, 1999) explores how colors, patterns, and shapes help to camouflage animals in their habitats. *The Magic Gourd* (Diakité, 2003), an African folk tale, uses photographs of colorful patterned ceramic plates, bowls, and tiles to illustrate story events. The unit's activities offer students an opportunity to transfer these artistic concepts to the landscapes found in their natural surroundings.

Matrix of Literacy Skills and Strategies in Unit 6

Literacy Skills and Strategies	Activities	Title of Book	Pages
Building background knowledge on the Internet*	U	—	93–94
	C, I	*David's Drawings*	95–96, 97–98
	R, C	*Nature's Paintbrush: The Patterns and Colors Around You*	99, 99–100
	C	*The Magic Gourd*	102–103
Building fluency	UC	—	104–105
	D, I	*David's Drawings*	96, 97–98
Comparing and contrasting	R, C, D	*The Magic Gourd*	102, 102–103, 103
Composing in multimedia*	C, D	*David's Drawings*	95–96, 96
	C, D, S	*Nature's Paintbrush: The Patterns and Colors Around You*	99–100, 100, 100–101
	C, D	*The Magic Gourd*	102–103, 103
Determining story details	R	*The Magic Gourd*	102
Developing creative writing	D	*David's Drawings*	96
	D	*Nature's Paintbrush: The Patterns and Colors Around You*	100
	D	*The Magic Gourd*	103
Developing critical reading and thinking	S	*David's Drawings*	97
	R	*Nature's Paintbrush: The Patterns and Colors Around You*	99
	D	*The Magic Gourd*	103
Developing oral language	UC	—	104–105
	D, S	*David's Drawings*	96–97, 97
	D, S	*Nature's Paintbrush: The Patterns and Colors Around You*	100, 100–101
Developing vocabulary	U, UC	—	93–94, 104–105
	R, C, D, S, I	*David's Drawings*	95, 95–96, 96, 97, 97–98
	R, C, D, S, I	*Nature's Paintbrush: The Patterns and Colors Around You*	99, 99–100, 100, 100–101
	R, C, D, I	*The Magic Gourd*	102, 102–103, 103, 104
Following directions	D, S, I	*David's Drawings*	96, 97, 97–98
	C, D	*Nature's Paintbrush: The Patterns and Colors Around You*	99–100, 100
	C, D	*The Magic Gourd*	102–103, 103
Making multicultural connections	R, C, S, I	*The Magic Gourd*	102, 102–103, 104, 104
Making predictions	R	*The Magic Gourd*	102
Navigating hyperlinks*	S	*David's Drawings*	97
	R, C, I	*Nature's Paintbrush: The Patterns and Colors Around You*	99, 99–100, 101
	S, I	*The Magic Gourd*	104

(continued)

Literacy Skills and Strategies	Activities	Title of Book	Pages
Presenting work on a computer*	UC	—	104–105
	C, D	*David's Drawings*	95–96, 96
	C, D	*Nature's Paintbrush: The Patterns and Colors Around You*	99–100, 100
	D	*The Magic Gourd*	103
Reading aloud	UC	—	104–105
	D, I	*David's Drawings*	96, 97–98
	R	*Nature's Paintbrush: The Patterns and Colors Around You*	99
Reading and listening for a purpose	U	—	93–94
	R, D, I	*David's Drawings*	95, 96, 97–98
	R, C, I	*Nature's Paintbrush: The Patterns and Colors Around You*	99, 99–100, 101
	R, C, S, I	*The Magic Gourd*	102, 102–103, 104, 104
Reading informational text	S, I	*David's Drawings*	97, 97–98
	R	*Nature's Paintbrush: The Patterns and Colors Around You*	99
	S, I	*The Magic Gourd*	104
Retelling	UC	—	104–105
Sequencing	D	*David's Drawings*	96
	D	*The Magic Gourd*	103
Summarizing	UC	—	104–105
	D, S	*David's Drawings*	96–97, 97
Understanding a main idea	C	*David's Drawings*	95–96
	S	*Nature's Paintbrush: The Patterns and Colors Around You*	100–101
	D	*The Magic Gourd*	103
Using phonics: Letter–sound correspondence	D, I	*David's Drawings*	96, 97–98
Writing biographies	D	*The Magic Gourd*	103
Writing descriptive sentences	D	*David's Drawing*	96
	D	*Nature's Paintbrush: The Patterns and Colors Around You*	100
	D	*The Magic Gourd*	103

* Indicates a new-literacy skill.
U = unit introduction; R = read-aloud and book discussion ideas; C = creativity and presentation software ideas; D = Digital Language Experience Approach; S = computer software activity; I = Internet resources and ideas; UC = unit conclusion

Unit Introduction

Before starting the unit, encourage home–school connections by sending a note (see Figure 18) home telling parents about the upcoming art unit that will be used to inspire students' love for reading through the visual arts. If appropriate, include a wish list, noting needed art supplies such as art reproductions in the forms of landscapes and impressionist art, photographs, posters, pictures, and colorful, richly patterned ceramic bowls and pottery. Also consider including additional items such as smocks, painter's caps, paint palettes, easels, disposable cameras, art books, colored pencils, markers, watercolors, and brushes.

Use art reproductions to transform the room into an art studio. For example, disassemble an art calendar and display the pictures on easels or bulletin boards. Students create a sign, such as "Welcome to the Art Gallery of Room 2B," to hang above the classroom door.

Use art centers and display areas to showcase the students' artwork that will be created throughout the unit. For example, one art center might contain an assortment of art materials such as crayons, markers, paints, and paper. A reading center with an abundance of art books will further encourage students' art explorations. An "Our Beautiful Things" art display area showcases student productions, highlighting their growing understanding and knowledge of artistic expression, media, forms, and techniques. An indispensable resource will be an art word wall list or poster (see Figure 19).

MATERIALS

- Art books
- Art reproduction prints
- Art word wall list
- Colored pencils
- Crayons
- Disposable cameras
- Easels
- Letter to parents
- Markers
- Paintbrushes
- Painter's caps
- Paint palettes
- Smocks
- Watercolor paints
- "Welcome to Our Art Gallery" sign

Figure 18
Sample Art Unit Note to Parents and Caregivers

Dear Parents and Caregivers,

Our next unit will focus on art as a way to inspire a love for reading through the visual arts. If you can donate one or two items on our "wish list" below, you will be helping the students have some hands-on experiences with art. Thanks in advance for your support.

Sincerely,
Your Child's Teacher

Wish List
Art reproduction prints
Photographs or posters
Pottery
Smocks (e.g., men's shirts)
Painter's caps
Disposable cameras
Art books
Colored pencils
Watercolor paints
Paintbrushes
Paint palettes
Easels
Markers

Figure 19
Sample Art Word Wall List

A, B, C, D, E	F, G, H, I, J	K, L, M, N, O	P, Q, R, S, T	U, V, W, X, Y, Z
Background	Foreground	Landscapes	Palette	Vertical
Bright colors	Geometric	Light	Pastels	Water colors
Camouflage	Shapes	Masterpiece	Patterns	Wavy lines
Composition	Horizon line	Oil painting	Perspective	Zigzag
Depth		Outlines	Portraits	
		Pottery		
		Silhouettes		
		Soft colors		
		Still life		
		Straight lines		
		Stripes		
		Textures		
		Thin lines		

Use the art word wall to increase students' vocabulary and background knowledge. You can display a collection of landscape reproductions in the art center and write art vocabulary words on cards such as *horizon line, foreground, background, wavy lines, straight lines*, and so on. During art center time and when reviewing art vocabulary and concepts, instruct students to match vocabulary cards to their corresponding meanings located on the landscape reproductions.

Visit the Artist's Toolkit, the animated website from the Walker Art Center (www.artsconnected. org/toolkit/watch_types_line.cfm), during whole-group time to introduce the unit and demonstrate how artists use various lines to create symbols, figures, shapes, and words. The website tells about straight, horizontal, vertical, thin, wavy, zigzag, and lively lines, as well as lines showing movement, anger, sadness, and happiness. Use the site's "paint palette" and "drawing a city" with straight or wavy lines activity to help students begin viewing and discussing artistic elements. Tell students that during the upcoming art unit, you will be reading and discussing books and completing computer activities that will help them learn more about art techniques such as patterns, colors, camouflage, various line types, and the natural location of art in their environments.

Book 1:   David's Drawings

Falwell, C. (2001). New York: Lee and Low Books. $16.95. 32 pp.

BOOK REVIEW

One winter morning as David, a shy African American boy, walks to school, he stops before a tree to admire its silhouette against a gray skyline. At school, he uses a black crayon to recreate the tree's outline on a horizon line. Classmates observe David as he draws, making suggestions such as "That tree needs leaves," "It needs a person—like me!" and "It needs a rainbow, too!" (n.p.).

David shares his crayons and permits his classmates to add their suggestions. When finished, he titles the drawing "Our Class Picture" and attaches it to the bulletin board. After school as David walks home, he again stops to observe the beauty of the tree. At home, he recreates his original vision for the picture and titles it "My Drawing" before hanging it over his bed.

Unit activities include using a variety of line forms to create silhouettes of beautiful things often gone unnoticed in our environments. Students learn to apply the art concepts of depth, horizon line, perspective, foreground, silhouettes, and background in their designs. *David's Drawings* illuminates artistic techniques and hints at the importance of cooperation, respect, and politeness when jointly constructing unique pieces of art. However, an important lesson involves learning to respect and explore one's unique vision and artistic techniques.

READ-ALOUD AND BOOK DISCUSSION IDEAS

Before reading *David's Drawings* (Falwell, 2001), use a 14-inch piece of black yarn to teach the concept of lines and outlines. Students silently observe your manipulations of the yarn as you form it into various shapes.

> ## MATERIALS
> - 14-inch piece of black yarn
> - Large white construction paper or poster board
> - Red and black markers

1. On white construction paper or on a piece of poster board, form a straight line and place a red circle one at a time at each end. Help students infer that the yarn formed a straight line and that the red circles indicate its beginning and end.

2. Shape the straight line into a circle and ask students to observe the classroom for objects with circular lines such as an apple, a doorknob, or a clock.

3. Use the yarn to trace around a student's hand, including his or her fingers. After the student lifts his or her hand, carefully trace around the yarn with a black marker. The black line forms an outline, or a silhouette, of the hand. Talk about how a black outline can draw attention to the overall shape and position of the hand or other objects outlined.

4. Add a horizon line (the line separating the sky from the land), coloring the area above the horizon line blue for the sky and below the horizon line green for land. Color the hand brown and use a darker green crayon to add leaves to the fingers. The hand is artistically transformed into a tree. Tell students they will be listening to a story about a little boy who decided to use the technique of outlining in a very special way.

During reading, draw attention to how the characters collaborated to create David's picture.

After reading, engage the students in an oral line exploration, a guided picture book walk with open discussion that focuses on the various line types used to create the book's illustrations.

COMPUTER ACTIVITIES

Creativity and Presentation Software Ideas

Land is the most important feature in landscapes. Use All Seasons North American Landscapes by Hanne Lore Koehler (www.koehlerart.com/ga01007.htm) to show how an artist uses horizon line, depth, and

> ## MATERIALS
> - KidPix Studio Deluxe (1998) software

perspective when painting. Point out how depth and perspective are created when larger items are painted in the foreground and smaller items are painted in the background.

Before starting the activity, demonstrate how to use the KidPix Studio Deluxe software drawing tool functions, paint color options, pencil widths, and so on.

1. Demonstrate how artists use perspective and depth in landscapes by first drawing a horizon line and adding a large outline (i.e., a silhouette) of a tree in the upper right corner. The background appears after an outline of a smaller tree is drawn on or near the horizon line. Use the Fill Can tool to add blue above the horizon line and green below it.

2. Instruct students to create their own landscapes. Help students understand the concept of main idea by having them type a title that best describes their landscape.

3. Print and bind landscapes into a class book titled "Our Class Knows Landscapes." Save and insert landscapes into a slide show presentation to share during the art exhibit.

Digital Language Experience Approach

Tell students they will be working together, just like David's friends worked with him, to make a drawing. In this activity, students create a photo essay that explains how they cooperated to make a large poster-sized landscape drawing.

MATERIALS

- Crayons
- Digital camera
- KidPix Studio Deluxe (1998) software
- Poster board

1. Take digital photographs of a small group of students drawing a poster-sized picture of a landscape. Start with a photograph of the students standing with an empty piece of posterboard and crayons.

2. Photograph the beginning, middle, and end of creating the landscape. Import photos into creativity and presentation software such as KidPix Studio Deluxe.

3. Ask students to put the pictures into sequential order and talk about what they were doing in each picture. Elicit oral language and incorporate artistic vocabulary terms you are learning in the unit.

4. Instruct students to dictate a photograph essay, explaining what they did on each photograph.

5. Assemble the digital photographs into a class-printed book or computer slide show.

6. On subsequent days, invite students to (a) point to letters or words they recognize and (b) read sentences they dictated or chorally read the story with you.

7. If possible, send a copy of the photo essay home for students to read to caregivers and siblings.

During author's computer chair (see Appendix B), invite students in small groups to share their Digital Language Experience Approach photograph essays. Encourage them to use artistic terms in their explanation of what they were doing. Support students' emerging, developing, or fluent readings of the text. Other students may want to explain how they designed landscape pictures or what they learned by interacting with the software ArtRageous: The Amazing World of Art (1995; see the following computer software activity).

Figure 20
Art Exploration Sheet

Student's Name:
Computer Buddy's Name:
Name of painting selected:
Name of artist:
1. Draw or list objects found in the foreground.
2. Draw or list objects found in the background.
3. Write a sentence about something you liked about the painting.

Computer Software Activity → - - - - - - - - - - - - - - →

MATERIALS

■ ArtRageous: The Amazing World of Art (1995) software

ArtRageous: The Amazing World of Art software offers six interactive, virtual three-dimensional worlds for students to explore. Experiment with color, light, perspective, and composition, and adjust, recolor, or distort favorite masterpieces. After you demonstrate and model program options, students will enjoy playing the various games in each art concept area. Use the software as a teacher resource and access the database for historical information about artists, their roles, and art movements. Audio and colorful screens will assist and scaffold the learning experiences for younger viewers.

Design an art exploration sheet (see Figure 20) and assign students to examine and select a favorite painting. With the help of a cross-age computer buddy, students draw, label, or list objects found in the foreground and background and include the painting's title and artist. Students share their work during author's computer chair (see Appendix B) and or group time.

Internet Resources and Ideas

CBeebies—Fimbles: The Painting Elves: www.bbc.co.uk/cbeebies/fimbles/comfycorner/story2.shtml
The Painting Elves is a BBC CBeebies interactive storybook that tells about painting the sun yellow, the grass green, and some flowers red. But a problem arises when the elf that needs to paint the sky blue is too grumpy to complete his job. A copy of the story is printable for building fluency by reading aloud. This website requires Flash 4 plug-in for audio, which is downloadable from the website.

ArtsConnectEd—The Artist's Toolkit: Visual Elements and Principles: www.artsconnected.org/toolkit/watch_space_overlap.cfm
Increase students' artistic background knowledge and enhance their vocabulary knowledge about depth, overlap, and perspective through the use of the interactive Artist's Toolkit. A short, animated video demonstrates depth and horizon lines. A painting palette is offered for practicing the techniques.

iKnowthat.com—The Arts: Paint: www.iknowthat.com/com/L3?Area=Paint
Help students transfer ongoing unit skills, such as artistic principles, concepts, and vocabulary, and continue to build artistic background knowledge by using iKnowthat.com. This website offers an online painting studio so students can practice painting techniques. Landscapes, still lifes, or portraits rest on a side easel as users attempt to duplicate the artwork. A variety of backgrounds, textures, and art materials are available. Paint with watercolors on dry or wet surfaces, use oil paints or markers, or select from six paint palettes to create designs. Print, save, open, and submit works options to an online gallery are available. Requires a free registration and Shockwave. Younger students may need assistance with a cross-age computer buddy.

Landscape Art—Constable, Monet, Grandma Moses: http://members.aol.com/Sabetour/Landscape.html
Three landscapes are displayed to demonstrate horizon lines, perspective, and line types. Surrounding paragraphs give minimal landscaping art history and information about Claude Monet. Teachers may need to paraphrase challenging vocabulary and phrases for younger students.

Louvre Museum Official Website: www.louvre.fr/llv/commun/home_flash.jsp?bmLocale=en
Take a virtual tour of the Louvre in France. Quick Time 5 plug-in is required for viewing images in the museum and is downloadable from the website. First click on the museum website map then on the virtual tour button to see paintings, prints, and drawings.

Kinderart: www.kinderart.com/drawing/perspective.shtml
This website offers teachers a lesson plan on teaching the concept of perspective and offers links to additional ideas and reference books to help you further design art lessons.

Book 2:   Nature's Paintbrush: The Patterns and Colors Around You

Stockdale, S. (1999). New York: Simon & Schuster Books for Young Readers. $16.95. 32 pp.

BOOK REVIEW

Nature's Paintbrush: The Patterns and Colors Around You uses easy-to-read text and dazzling illustrations to show how patterns and colors found in nature camouflage animals in their environments. For example, a tiger's wavy stripes blend nicely into the surrounding tall, green-striped grass, green katydids almost become invisible when mingling on shades of green leaves, and the arctic fox blends almost magically into winter's snowy landscapes and then into rocky backgrounds as his fur changes seasonally from white to brown. Each page opens with a question such as "Have you ever noticed the eyespot near the tail of a butterfly fish?" (n.p.) or "Have you ever been pricked by a cactus?" (n.p.). Questions are followed by short, informative explanations. Bright, colorful spreads illustrate the questions and answers. Art concepts are reinforced through illustrations and text and are sure to heighten students' awareness of the patterns and colors found in surroundings.

READ-ALOUD AND BOOK DISCUSSION IDEAS

Before reading the story, assemble collections of items of one color. For example, if you decide to focus on the color brown, you might assemble brown leaves, sticks, mulch, brown plastic animals, and brown paper. Tell students that when animals blend into their surroundings, it is called camouflage. Ask students to suggest animals that could camouflage into the color you selected and encourage them to give reasons for their suggestions.

> **MATERIALS**
>
> ■ Chart paper
> ■ Collection of items of one color
> ■ Markers

During reading, tell students that as they listen to the story, they should observe the illustrations and think about additional animals that blend into their environments.

After reading, ask students to describe these animals according to their patterns and colors and list responses on chart paper under various color names.

To reinforce the concept of camouflaging, access and discuss the following websites. Safety in Colors (www.lpzoo.com/education/zebra/stories/story_colors.htm) offers three pictures and short explanations for how a fawn, bee, and king snake use patterns and colors to blend into their environments.

Why Does Zebra Have Stripes? (www.lpzoo.com/education/zebra/student/formfunction/ h.html) is a website that allows you to demonstrate how to change the appearance of a zebra by clicking on one of four different patterns—eyespots, dark jackets, spots and speckles, and stripes—to see which pattern best camouflages the zebra into its environment. Share the keyboard with students so they can manipulate the mouse and interact with the website tools.

COMPUTER ACTIVITIES

Creativity and Presentation Software Ideas

Before starting the activity, access Bev Doolittle's gallery so students can analyze animal oil paintings for patterns, colors, and camouflaging techniques (www.bnr-art.com/doolitt/doolitt1.htm). To view the galleries, scroll to the bottom of the page and locate the 10 gallery buttons. Paraphrase the accompanying text for younger students.

> **MATERIALS**
>
> ■ KidPix Studio Deluxe (1998) software

Invite students to practice camouflaging techniques with patterns, textures, and colors using KidPix Studio Deluxe creativity and presentation software.

1. To create a camouflage picture, instruct students to first select a Color Me Natures picture from the Goodies toolbar option.

2. Instruct students to use similar shades of colors to create camouflage pictures using the Fill Can tool, patterns, textures, and paint palette. For example, a student might select a desert scene and use the Fill Can to add a sandy brown texture to the ground and brown shades from the paint palette to color other picture items.

3. Instruct students to select and drop matching colored nature stamp icons into their pictures.

4. Save as a slide show and show during the art exhibit (see unit conclusion on pages 104–105) or author's computer chair (see Appendix B).

5. Print pictures and bind into a class book titled "Our KidPix Nature's Paintbrush."

Digital Language Experience Approach

MATERIALS

- Digital camera
- KidPix Studio Deluxe (1998) software

Have a camouflage day and ask students to dress in one particular color. For example, everyone wears green, including hats, barrettes, socks, and possibly face paint.

1. Go outdoors and group students near things outside that match the color they have chosen to wear, for example, under trees, in bushes, and so on.

2. Take digital pictures of the groups.

3. Import the pictures into creativity and presentation software such as KidPix Studio Deluxe.

4. Instruct students to use paint tools to add additional shades of green and similar colored stamp icons.

5. Instruct students to type or dictate a sentence telling or asking something about their picture, for example, "Lizards are hiding in this picture. Can you find them?"

Another activity involves walking around the school and allowing the students to act as camouflage explorers.

1. Students search for and take pictures of animals or insects blending into their surroundings such as a yellow butterfly on a yellow flower or an ant on dirt.

2. Insert the pictures into a drawing program such as KidPix Studio Deluxe.

3. Using drawing tools, students add paint details. For example, students can add similar-colored stripes, shades of a color, and patterns to emphasize camouflaging.

4. Students add text or use the record option to narrate how each picture highlights the camouflaging experience; for example, "Tom found a butterfly camouflaged on a yellow daisy." Insert the pictures into a KidPix Studio Deluxe slide show and present during the art exhibit (see unit conclusion on pages 104–105).

5. Print pictures and bind into a class book titled "So This Is Camouflaging?"

Computer Software Activity

MATERIALS

- IBM Crayola Magic 3-D Coloring Book Cool Critters (2004) software

Using the IBM Crayola Majic 3-D Coloring Book Cool Critters software to explore camouflaging techniques will help students understand the main idea behind the book *Nature's Paintbrush: The Patterns and Colors Around You* (Stockdale, 1999). Selecting from bugs, teddy bears, or farm pictures, students practice camouflaging techniques by selecting from two different crayon sizes, pencil sizes, 42 glitter and classic crayons, and 13 different textures and patterns. The various coloring tools are easy to navigate, and students will enjoy hearing different sounds awarding their work. Pictures are printable in color and black and white. As students talk about their creations, they practice using vocabulary they have learned, develop oral language skills, and consider the main idea of the story.

Have students share their camouflage pictures and describe the techniques used to design their pictures during author's computer chair (see Appendix B). Encourage students to describe and tell which drawing tools worked best, how they solved design problems and used outlining, and why they selected particular colors. Use peer questions and responses to scaffold the learning experience.

Internet Resources and Ideas

CBBC—Wild: Build a Beast: www.bbc.co.uk/cbbc/wild/games
Build a Beast is an interactive website that reinforces the concept of camouflaging by showing how an animal uses color to adapt to its environment. Students select from a variety of animal parts. Then they click, drag, and drop the parts on a camouflaged background to build an animal.

Kendra's Coloring Book: www.isoverse.com/colorbook/KCBselect.html
Kendra's Coloring Book is an actual online coloring book. Students select from a variety of pictures: scenery, designs, shapes, or 28 animal pictures. Pictures are printable for adding artistic elements offline or can be colored online.

Crayons and Computers by Carol Sabbeth—Focus on Nature: http://members.aol.com/Art1234567/Npeacock.html
This website offers a pattern and color lesson plan using creativity and presentation software such as KidPix Studio Deluxe (1998). The lesson focuses on colors and patterns found in nature's masterpieces. Easy steps and illustrations are provided.

Crayons and Computers by Carol Sabbeth—Mother Nature's Cozy Quilt:
http://members.aol.com/Art1234567/Nquilt.html
This website offers a pattern and color lesson plan using creativity and presentation software such as KidPix Studio Deluxe (1998). Students select two things that go together in nature to design a Mother Nature quilt. Easy steps and illustrations are provided.

Book 3: The Magic Gourd

Diakité, B.W. (2003). New York: Scholastic. $16.95. 32 pp.

BOOK REVIEW

The Magic Gourd is a retelling of an oral African folk tale Diakité recalls from his childhood living in Mali, West Africa. The book leaps and jumps with patterns and bright-colored photographs, which highlight story events painted on ceramic plates, bowls, and tiles. Familiar story elements and favorite animal characters will engage the students as they learn how characters solve the story's conflicts. For example, after Brother Rabbit rescues Chameleon from the tangled bushes, Chameleon shows his gratitude to Brother Rabbit by giving him a magic gourd. However, after the evil king hears of this magic gourd, he selfishly takes it from Brother Rabbit. Suspense escalates when a rock is used to solve Brother Rabbit's problem. Bold colors, shapes, and a sprinkling of Bambara words, the national language of Mali, are sure to captivate students' visual and auditory attention.

READ-ALOUD AND BOOK DISCUSSION IDEAS

MATERIALS

- Chart paper
- Markers

Before reading the story, complete a picture walk by asking students to comment on the photographs of the painted bowls, tiles, and plates, pointing out and discussing various patterns, wavy and straight lines, border art, and the contrast of bright and soft colors. Tell students that the artwork illustrates the story's events. Ask students to predict the story's setting, characters, problems, and solutions and record these story predictions on chart paper.

During and after reading, confirm and alter students' predictions. After reading, complete a follow-up picture walk, closely examining and studying the photographs of the ceramic plates, tiles, and bowls. Engage students in an art think-aloud by discussing the patterns, colors, and geometric shapes used in their designs. Which elements do students prefer? You may want to compare and contrast the art techniques employed such as the intricate and detailed patterns on the edges of the artwork, the black-and-white line drawings, and the blending of colors. Where are patterns repeated? Help students understand that art is a personal expression and each person has unique tastes and preferences toward art; however, much art also reflects the culture and customs of an area.

COMPUTER ACTIVITIES

Creativity and Presentation Software Ideas

MATERIALS

- KidPix Studio Deluxe (1998) software

Before starting this activity, go to www.joannegoodwin.com/technology/2nd/indians/pottery.html for examples of student-designed pottery bowls. View and discuss the art techniques and patterns employed in the design of the bowls. Emphasize vocabulary that will help students understand the nuances of pattern, texture, and color. To build students' background knowledge about designing with patterns, compare and contrast the patterns of the pottery bowls to those of the book *The Magic Gourd* (Diakité, 2003). Using creativity and presentation software such as KidPix Studio Deluxe, students create their own art reproductions of patterned ceramic bowls or plates.

1. Model the use of various drawing options and tools.

2. Show students how to select a geometric shape and how to enlarge the shape.

3. Instruct students to select stamps icons and fill the shape with patterns under the Goodies toolbar option.

4. Instruct students to add background colors, use the Fill Can to add colored textures, and type a title for their artwork.

5. Print and bind student work into a class book or computer slide show titled "Our Pretty Pottery Patterns."

Digital Language Experience Approach

1. Invite students to use self-hardening clay to shape and form their own pottery bowls.

2. Once bowls have hardened, instruct students to use acrylic paints to add background colors and patterns. Ask students to compare their designs with the designs in the book *The Magic Gourd* (Diakité, 2003).

> **MATERIALS**
>
> - Acrylic paint
> - Digital camera
> - KidPix Studio Deluxe (1998) software
> - Self-hardening clay

3. Document students creating their bowls by taking photographs of each stage of the process. For example, take pictures of students forming and working their clay and adding paint and patterns. Also take pictures of each student's finished product.

4. Import pictures of each student with his or her finished bowl into creativity and presentation software such as KidPix Studio Deluxe and size pictures as needed. Instruct students to add background colors, textures, and patterned stamp icons to create a frame around their picture. At the top of each picture, help students understand and apply main ideas and instruct them to type a title for their bowl.

5. Import a picture of each student, size it to the bottom corner of the picture, and type the student's name next to the picture. Instruct students to add a sentence telling something interesting about each student artist.

6. View the pictures and agree as a class on their sequence before importing them into a slide show. Students work together and share the keyboard to type sentences describing each picture's stage of the creation process. Then, import each student artist's picture to the slide show.

Before printing the pictures and binding them into a class book, design and include a table of contents. The table of contents might include chapter titles such as materials used, steps followed, and either the names of each bowl or each artist's name, and a comments page. Include a title page such as "Our Pottery Masterpieces."

During author's computer chair (see Appendix B) students share their patterned creations, telling which software options worked best for patterning, which did not work, and why they selected certain patterns and icons for the design. Use student expertise to scaffold the learning experience further by asking students to describe and share how they used icons for design patterns, what program elements worked best, how they problem solved, and which toolbar options were their favorites.

Computer Software Activity

MATERIALS

■ JumpStart Artist (2000) software

Students will enjoy using the JumpStart Artist software to discover and explore the world of art when they create their own masterpieces at Kisha the Koala's Art Fair, play games, learn about artists and their art work, discover and learn about cultural crafts from around the world, and experiment with art concepts. Five different art activities are available along with three skill levels. Invite students to play along with CJ and Edison on their Amazing Art Expedition. Different items, each relating to different art projects, are loaded into a hot-air balloon. After items are loaded, students learn something about the item before finding out the destination of the trip. For example, students load a sheep, ball of yarn, and a rug and learn about Navajo rug making in New Mexico, USA. Animation and songs are sure to engage the students as they transfer and apply art concepts to their designs. Several printable arts and crafts activities are available for additional offline fun.

Internet Resources and Ideas

Lil' Fingers—Draw Me Shapes by David Lumerman: www.lil-fingers.com/shapes/index.html
"Draw Me Shapes," an animated Lil' Fingers e-book, teaches about color words and shapes. Animations and colors may assist students in figuring out unknown words and may reinforce reading skills such as reading by using context clues.

The Artist's Toolkit—See Artists in Action: Ta-Coumba Aiken: www.artsconnected.org/toolkit/tacoumba_video.html
This ArtsConnectEd website shows a video of an artist, Ta-Coumba Aiken, as he manipulates various geometric shapes to create a picture. While designing, he thinks aloud about the process.

The Artist's Toolkit—Explore the Toolkit: Shape: www.artsconnected.org/toolkit/create_shape_geometric.cfm
This ArtsConnectEd website extends students' artistic vocabulary through a short video that shows how to use organic and geometric shapes to create pictures. Organic shapes refer to the natural shapes found in plants and animals. Geometric shapes refer to shapes, such as circles and squares, that are uniform and even. A link is available to a drawing tools kit to reinforce designing with patterns, colors, and geometric shapes.

MATERIALS

■ Class-created art books
■ Iced tea
■ Invitations
■ KidPix Studio Deluxe (1998) software
■ Slide shows
■ Student artwork from unit
■ Student-baked cookies

Unit Conclusion

End the unit with an art exhibit. Students demonstrate using artistic vocabulary and their new knowledge and appreciation for art by designing invitations. You may want to design a class invitation using creativity and presentation software such as KidPix Studio Deluxe or import a class picture of the students involved in one of the unit's activities to invite students from another classroom or VIPs (very important people; e.g., the principal, secretary, media specialist, art teacher) to the upcoming "[Your classroom] Art Exhibit." Further enrich the experience by requesting that attendees wear black or white attire. During the exhibit students act as art studio docents, narrating student-created slide shows, reading class-created art books, and sharing their masterpieces. Conclude the exhibit with iced tea and student-baked and frosted (painted) cookies. To paint cookies, students spread frosting with a paint palette and use decorating tubes with thin tips and icing in various colors to draw a horizon line, stick trees, and so forth and, depending on the season, further decorate with pieces of candy, sprinkles, and edible items.

Social and Multicultural Connections

Learning to Like Ourselves: Lessons in Self-Concept

UNIT BOOKS

Miss Hunnicutt's Hat
By Jeff Brumbeau and Gail de Marcken

Suki's Kimono
By Chieri Uegaki
Illustrated by Stéphane Jorisch

Unique Monique
By Maria Rousaki
Illustrated by Polina Papanikolaou

COMPUTER RESOURCES

Neighborhood Map Machine
IBM Crayola Magic Princess Paper Doll Maker
Stellaluna

Thematic Connection

All the books in this unit deal with characters who go through the sometimes difficult process of learning to like themselves. At the outset of many of the stories, the authors present situations that reveal the main characters' problems with self-concept. The books in this collection address the issue of learning to like yourself from multiple perspectives. For example, several of the books are drawn from international cultures, which highlight that learning to like yourself is a universal condition. *Miss Hunnicutt's Hat* (Brumbeau & de Marcken, 2003) is set in a village in England. *Suki's Kimono* (Uegaki, 2003) draws upon the main character's Japanese heritage. *Unique Monique* (Rousaki, 2003) takes place in an urban setting in Greece. Through book discussions and extension activities (activities that extend students' engagement with stories), emerging, developing, and fluent readers will have many opportunities to appreciate their own strengths as individuals as they come to understand how story characters learn to identify their strengths and uniqueness. Suki learns to enjoy her individuality, Unique Monique learns that trying to be unique sometimes means ending up a trendsetter, and Miss Hunnicutt learns that being an individual sometimes involves being misunderstood by other people.

Matrix of Literacy Skills and Strategies in Unit 7

Literacy Skills and Strategies	Activities	Title of Book	Pages
Brainstorming	U	—	111
	D	*Miss Hunnicutt's Hat*	113–114
Building background knowledge on the Internet*	I	*Miss Hunnicutt's Hat*	115
	I	*Suki's Kimono*	118–119
	I	*Unique Monique*	121
Comparing and contrasting	C, S	*Unique Monique*	120, 121
Composing in multimedia*	C, D, S	*Miss Hunnicutt's Hat*	112–113, 113–114, 114–115
	C, D, S, I	*Suki's Kimono*	116–117, 117–118, 118, 118–119
	C, D	*Unique Monique*	120, 120–121
Determining cause and effect	C	*Miss Hunnicutt's Hat*	112–113
	R	*Unique Monique*	119–120
Developing comprehension	U	—	111
	R, I	*Miss Hunnicutt's Hat*	112, 115
	R, I	*Suki's Kimono*	116, 118–119
	R, C	*Unique Monique*	119–120, 120
Developing context clues	R	*Unique Monique*	119–120
Developing creative writing	C, D, S	*Miss Hunnicutt's Hat*	112–113, 113–114, 114–115
	C, D, S	*Suki's Kimono*	116–117, 117–118, 118
	D	*Unique Monique*	120–121
Developing critical reading and thinking	R, C	*Suki's Kimono*	116, 116–117
Developing oral language	U, UC	—	111, 122
	R, C, D, I	*Miss Hunnicutt's Hat*	112, 112–113, 113–114, 115
	R, S	*Suki's Kimono*	116, 118
	D	*Unique Monique*	120–121
Developing vocabulary	UC	—	122
	R, C, D, S, I	*Miss Hunnicutt's Hat*	112, 112–113, 113–114, 114–115, 115
	R, C, D, S, I	*Suki's Kimono*	116, 116–117, 117–118, 118, 118–119
Drawing conclusions	R, I	*Suki's Kimono*	116, 118–119
Following directions	C, D, S, I	*Miss Hunnicutt's Hat*	112–113, 113–114, 114–115, 115
	C, D, I	*Suki's Kimono*	116–117, 117–118, 118–119
	D, I	*Unique Monique*	120–121, 121

(continued)

Literacy Skills and Strategies	Activities	Title of Book	Pages
Inferring	UC	—	122
	R	*Miss Hunnicutt's Hat*	112
	R	*Unique Monique*	119–120
Making multicultural connections	S	*Miss Hunnicutt's Hat*	114–115
	R, C, S, I	*Suki's Kimono*	116, 116–117, 118, 118–119
	I	*Unique Monique*	121
Making predictions	R	*Miss Hunnicutt's Hat*	112
	R	*Unique Monique*	119–120
Navigating hyperlinks*	I	*Miss Hunnicutt's Hat*	115
	S, I	*Suki's Kimono*	118, 118–119
	I	*Unique Monique*	121
Presenting work on a computer*	D, I	*Miss Hunnicutt's Hat*	113–114, 115
	D, I	*Suki's Kimono*	117–118, 118–119
	D	*Unique Monique*	120–121
Reading aloud	R, D	*Miss Hunnicutt's Hat*	112, 113–114
	R, I	*Suki's Kimono*	116, 118–119
	R	*Unique Monique*	119–120
Reading and listening for a purpose	R, I	*Miss Hunnicutt's Hat*	112, 115
	R, S, I	*Suki's Kimono*	116, 118, 118–119
	R, C, I	*Unique Monique*	119–120, 120, 121
Reading and using map skills	S	*Miss Hunnicutt's Hat*	114–115
Reading informational text	S, I	*Miss Hunnicutt's Hat*	114–115, 115
	S, I	*Suki's Kimono*	118, 118–119
	I	*Unique Monique*	121
Recalling story details	R, C, S	*Miss Hunnicutt's Hat*	112, 112–113, 114–115
	R, C	*Suki's Kimono*	116, 116–117
	R, C, D	*Unique Monique*	119–120, 120, 120–121
Understanding a main idea	UC	—	122
	R, D, S	*Miss Hunnicutt's Hat*	112, 113–114, 114–115
	C, D, I	*Suki's Kimono*	116–117, 117–118, 118–119
	R, C, D, I	*Unique Monique*	119–120, 120, 120–121, 121
Understanding story structure and events	R	*Suki's Kimono*	116
	C	*Unique Monique*	120
Using adjectives	U	—	111
	R, C, D, S, I	*Miss Hunnicutt's Hat*	112, 112–113, 113–114, 114–115, 115
Using nouns	U	—	111
Visualizing	S	*Miss Hunnicutt's Hat*	114–115
Writing descriptive sentences	C, D	*Miss Hunnicutt's Hat*	112–113, 113–114
	C, D	*Suki's Kimono*	116–117, 117–118
	D	*Unique Monique*	120–121

* Indicates a new-literacy skill.

U = unit introduction; R = read-aloud and book discussion ideas; C = creativity and presentation software ideas; D = Digital Language Experience Approach; S = computer software activity; I = Internet resources and ideas; UC = unit conclusion

Unit Introduction

Display a collection of items: a woman's hat, a man's tie, a pair of glasses, a child's tennis shoe, and books from the unit. Each of the items relates to at least one of the characters from each of the books in the unit. Begin by asking students to name and then to describe the objects to reinforce their understanding of nouns and adjectives. Ask students to speculate about who might wear each of the items. Ask them to speculate further about why people might need or want to wear the items. Tell them that in the collection of books you will read together in this unit, they will be meeting many different types of characters who learned to like and express themselves in some very unusual ways, many of which involve the displayed objects.

MATERIALS

- Books from this unit
- Child's tennis shoe
- Man's tie
- Pair of glasses
- Woman's hat

Book 1:   Miss Hunnicutt's Hat

Brumbeau, J., & de Marcken, G. (2003). New York: Orchard Books. $20.00. 48 pp.

BOOK REVIEW

Teachers and students who open the book *Miss Hunnicutt's Hat* will enter a vibrant, detailed world that is filled with watercolor images and descriptive text that traces Miss Hunnicutt's exuberant journey of self-discovery. The story begins with a burst of energy as the townspeople of Littleton prepare for a visit from the queen. Miss Hunnicutt, a very timid person who always does her shopping on Tuesdays at 3:00, spends her life making everyone else happy instead of herself. But, on the day of the queen's visit, Miss Hunnicutt decides that she has the right to express her individuality by wearing a very unique hat. Her decision to wear a hat, one that boasts a live, clucking chicken, sets up a chain of events that involves all the townspeople in one disaster after another. At every turn, the townspeople challenge Miss Hunnicutt to take off her hat. And, at every turn, Miss Hunnicutt is able to stand her ground because she wants to be special on the special day of the queen's visit. Through a series of mishaps involving Miss Bisbee's 27 cats, Miss Whimple's overflowing bathtub, and a collision between Mrs. Coriander's 12-foot-high cake and a truck of raspberry soda, the town ends up in a real mess.

Those who challenge Miss Hunnicutt to remove her hat soon find that she is aware of their own individual quirks and preferences. Amidst the chaos, the queen stops in a beautiful limousine. The delightful story results not only in the queen trading her live turkey hat for Miss Hunnicutt's live chicken hat but also in other townspeople beginning to wear chicken hats. Of course, now that Miss Hunnicutt has discovered her individuality, she is no longer content with a chicken hat. The last page of the book shows Miss Hunnicutt wearing a new hat, complete with a porcupine.

READ-ALOUD AND BOOK DISCUSSION IDEAS

Several features make this book a delight for sharing as a read-aloud during whole-group time and for explorations during individual or small-group work.

Before reading the book, invite students to notice all the details in the book jacket illustration that might help them predict what the story is about. Open the book so students can easily see the front and back of the book jacket simultaneously. Invite students to identify all the creatures that are in the garden with Miss Hunnicutt. Ask them to talk about which of the animals are alive and which are not. Tell students that they will be listening to a story about the day that Miss Hunnicutt decided to be different—more different than she had ever been before. Tell them that they will be learning about what happened because Miss Hunnicutt dared to be different.

During reading, invite students to comment on the colorful details in the illustrations. Doing so will elicit rich, descriptive oral language.

After reading, ask students to guess (drawing inferences) what other types of hats with live animals Miss Hunnicutt might wear. Listing the ideas on the blackboard will help students keep track of their thoughts. Then, show students the end pages of the book so they can confirm or change their predictions. Humorous watercolor portraits show Miss Hunnicutt with a variety of creatures, including a dripping-wet green fish, posing white poodle, beribboned platypus, and tongue-flicking chameleon. Which of their predictions were correct? Ask students to describe each of the hats, pointing out the importance of descriptive words.

Display the inside of the book jacket, which boasts a bird's-eye view of the entire village in busy preparation for the queen's visit. In fact, the back inside flap of the jacket invites students to "Peek underneath for a surprise! Remove the book jacket to discover a panoramic poster of Miss Hunnicutt's town as it prepares for the Queen's Visit. Try to find: All of the townspeople who appear in the book; all the animals that Miss Hunnicutt won't wear on her hat; all twenty-seven of Miss Bisbee's cats; What else can you find?" (n.p.). This activity helps students use illustrations to review story details and recall story events.

COMPUTER ACTIVITIES

Creativity and Presentation Software Ideas

Students of all ages and reading levels (emerging, developing, and fluent) will enjoy responding creatively to Miss Hunnicutt's story by writing or drawing in a digital response journal entry with creativity and presentation software such as KidPix Studio Deluxe 3.

1. Encourage students to draw and write sentences on screen about how they think Miss Hunnicutt felt about wearing her new hat and the events that happened because she wore her hat. Talk about the notion of cause and effect by summarizing and doing a post-reading picture walk.

2. Create a word bank of descriptive emotion words. Emerging and developing readers will benefit from a list of words such as *happy, sad, scared, nervous,* and *glad.*

3. Print out and invite students to share their illustrated sentences and their feelings about the story in whole-group discussions.

Digital Language Experience Approach

Follow the steps to support students' exploration of their self-identities through a virtual hat-design activity that will allow them to step into the shoes of the main character, Miss Hunnicutt.

MATERIALS

- Blackboard
- Chalk
- Digital camera
- Internet Hat Thinking Sheet
- KidPix Studio Deluxe 3 (2000) or PowerPoint (Microsoft Office 2003, 2003) software

1. Tell students to think about or brainstorm a list (written or drawn) of the things about them that are unique. What are their hobbies, interests, sports, family, and school activities? What are their favorite foods? For emerging and developing readers, write a master list on the board. Students may refer to their brainstormed lists when completing the next steps of the activity. Remind students that Miss Hunnicutt used her love of various types of animals to design her hats in ways that let others know she was special.

2. Use a digital camera to take a portrait of each student.

3. Import photographs into creativity and presentation software such as KidPix Studio Deluxe 3 or PowerPoint.

4. Demonstrate the activity with your own photograph. Use drawing, painting, and stamp tools to design a hat that reflects your hobbies or interests. For example, if you enjoy eating fruit, design a hat of various types of fruit that sit jauntily on your hat. If you enjoy fishing, design a hat with a boat at the base that is loaded with fish and fishing poles, etc. Write one sentence below your hat photograph that explains how the hat you designed shows "the real you."

5. Schedule each student to have computer time to design his or her own hat and write or dictate a sentence.

6. Print individual copies to send home with each student, or create a class book titled "Hats About Us." Be sure to share the book as a class read-aloud and make it available in the class library.

During author's computer chair (see Appendix B), invite students to share some of the things they are doing or have done at the computer. Many students will enjoy sharing pictures of themselves wearing unique hats created during Digital Language Experience Approaches (D-LEAs). Other students will enjoy talking about the things they learned from the Internet when they filled out their Internet Hat Thinking Sheet (see Figure 21). Provide ample time for students to showcase their work.

Figure 21
Internet Hat Thinking Sheet

Names: Date:

Sign your names on your Thinking Sheet. Open the website. Talk about and then answer the questions. When you are finished, hand in your Thinking Sheet.

1. What colors do you see on the hats?

2. What types of hats do you see?

3. What is your favorite hat and why?

Computer Software Activity

MATERIALS

■ Neighborhood Map Machine (2000) software

Miss Hunnicutt's Hat (Brumbeau & de Marcken, 2003) lends itself to a social studies connection related to the skills of reading and making maps. After giving students a brief lesson on the purposes and forms of maps, tell students that they can use a computer program to create their own maps. Neighborhood Map Machine is a software program that allows primary-grade students to create maps of imaginary neighborhoods. Interactive tools invite students to spatially arrange roads, trees, and buildings.

1. After a brief demonstration of how to use the software, invite students to work with a peer or cross-age buddy to closely examine the inside cover of *Miss Hunnicutt's Hat* book jacket, which is a birds-eye view of the village.

2. Remind students that Miss Hunnicutt lived in England. Students should point out buildings that would be found in England.

3. Encourage students to use the Neighborhood Map Machine tools to create a map of Miss Hunnicutt's village or to create a map of their own town or neighborhood.

4. Print out and display students' various mapping interpretations on a bulletin board titled "Our Views of Miss Hunnicutt's Neighborhood."

5. Debrief with students the effectiveness of the computer application in facilitating their map-drawing activities. For example, it is helpful to have stamps to use in making a map. It is also easier to delete or erase on screen than it is to try to erase crayon or markers on paper.

Internet Resources and Ideas

Hathathat: www.hathathat.com
Students will enjoy a virtual tour of unusual hats ladies wear in the winter and the summer.

1. Begin the Internet activity by asking students to describe some of Miss Hunnicutt's Hats, which are displayed on the end pages of the book. What colors do they see? What textures can they imagine? What objects and animals do they see?

2. Tell students that they will be working with a cross-age computer buddy to look at hats on a webpage. Provide them with an Internet Hat Thinking Sheet (see Figure 21 on page 114).

3. During whole-group time, encourage students to refer to their Thinking Sheet notes while sharing the information they gathered about hats on the Internet. Other hyperlinks on this website connect students to winter hats, summer hats, and a hat gallery.

After students have completed their exploration of the website, invite them to talk about their favorite hat during author's computer chair (see Appendix B).

Enchanted Learning: Hat Crafts: www.enchantedlearning.com/crafts/hats
Find guidelines and templates for students to make hats. For example, clicking on a "Flower Crown" link provides directions for using a paper plate, construction paper, scissors, and glue to make a flowery hat fit for springtime. Invite students to think of other items they might add to their hat. For example, students may cut insects or birds from construction paper to include on their hats.

Book 2: Suki's Kimono

Uegaki, C. (2003). Ill. S. Jorisch. Tonawanda, NY: Kids Can Press. $17.95. 32 pp.

BOOK REVIEW

Transparently painted, lighthearted watercolor illustrations reflect the dynamic emotions of the main character in this charming story about a girl named Suki. The illustrations, which are carefully detailed, are designed to facilitate students' understanding of the Japanese words included in the text. For example, Suki's *geta* (Japanese wooden clog shoes) are rendered in exquisite detail. The story begins with Suki, who wants to wear her blue cotton kimono, yellow *obi* (sash), and geta from her *obachan* (grandmother) on the first day of school in spite of her sisters' disapproval.

Although Suki is proud of her cultural identity, she worries about sharing her Japanese cultural experiences with her classmates. Will they make fun of her? Once at school, her worst fears are realized. Later that morning, when everyone introduces themselves and shares what they had done over the summer, Suki shares her story about her blue kimono. She takes everyone on a virtual trip to the Japanese festival that she had attended with her obachan by humming and recreating the dances she had seen. Everyone applauds Suki's story. On the way home at the end of the first day of school, Suki's sisters complains that no one had noticed their new sweaters or shoes. But Suki just smiles and dances all the way home. This is a beautiful story that may help students deal with issues of self-image and identity as they relate to their ethnic heritage.

READ-ALOUD AND BOOK DISCUSSION IDEAS

Before reading the book aloud, show students the book cover and ask, "Does anyone know what the girl on the cover is wearing?" Read the title and tell students that kimonos are worn in Japan when girls want to dress in folk costumes or put on traditional dress for special occasions. Tell students there is something else that is special about the kimono. Ask them to listen as you read to find out why it was the one thing that Suki wants to wear on the very first day of school. Ask them to think about the problem Suki faces when she wears the kimono to school.

MATERIALS

- Markers
- Poster board

During reading, direct students' attention to the text and illustrations that explain Japanese terms: kimono (traditional dress), *geta* (wooden clogs), *obachan* (grandmother), *obi* (sash), *somen* (noodles), and *taiko* (Japanese drum). Write the terms on a vocabulary chart for students to refer to throughout the book activities.

After reading, ask the following questions that help students reflect on the story and develop higher order thinking skills: Why do you think Suki wanted to wear a kimono on the first day of school? How do you think Suki felt when her classmates teased her? What did she decide to do when it was her turn to share her summer experiences? How did Suki show courage? What would you do? Discussions of this type help students think about what it means to be unique.

COMPUTER ACTIVITIES

Creativity and Presentation Software Ideas

MATERIALS

- Chart paper
- Markers
- KidPix Studio Deluxe 3 (2000) or PowerPoint (Microsoft Office 2003, 2003) software

Students will learn vocabulary words by using a combination of words and stamped icons (from KidPix Studio Deluxe 3 software) or clip art (from PowerPoint software) to write rebus sentences about Suki's experiences. Rebus sentences include a combination of words and pictures. Complete the following steps to accomplish this activity.

1. Tell students that they will use a combination of Japanese words, English words, and pictures to write rebus sentences about Suki's experiences.

2. Write a list at the top one third of the chart paper of Japanese words, their English meanings from the story, and drawings (e.g., kimono, dress, drawing of a dress; geta, shoes, drawing of a pair of shoes).

3. Write sentences in the bottom two thirds of the chart paper that use a combination of the Japanese words, English words, and drawings (e.g., write, "Suki wore her kimono, or dress, [draw a picture of a dress] to school. Suki walked in her geta, or shoes, [draw a picture of shoes]."

4. Tell students to use creativity and presentation software, such as KidPix Studio Deluxe 3 or PowerPoint, to write a rebus sentence about Suki's experiences. They must follow the pattern of including one Japanese word, one English word, and one stamp or clip art picture in each sentence.

Digital Language Experience Approach

Suki's favorite thing in the whole world was her kimono because her obachan gave it to her. Send a note (see Figure 22) home to parents and caregivers announcing a very special show-and-tell of one of their child's favorite objects or toys from home.

MATERIALS

- Digital camera
- KidPix Studio Deluxe 3 (2000) or PowerPoint (Microsoft Office 2003, 2003) software

1. Take a photograph of each student holding his or her show-and-tell object.

2. Make an e-book by importing the pictures into creativity and presentation software such as KidPix Studio Deluxe 3 or PowerPoint. Above each picture, type, "This is [student's name here] favorite thing because ____." Complete the sentence under the picture by allowing students to dictate or keyboard a sentence. Help students elaborate on their sentences to increase vocabulary. For example, if a student says, "This is my favorite thing because I like it," ask, "Tell me why you like it. Where did you get it? How does it make you feel? What are some things you do with it?" Use students' elaborated sentences and more sophisticated vocabulary to complete the activity.

Figure 22
Sample Show-and-Tell Note to Parents and Caregivers

Dear Parents and Caregivers,

This week we are learning more about how each of us is unique. We are having a very special show-and-tell time. Send your child's favorite object or toy to school on Tuesday. We will take a picture of the special items and write sentences about why they are special. Thank you for helping your child!

Sincerely,
Your Child's Teacher

---

3. For the cover, take a picture of the whole class holding their favorite objects and add the title "Our Favorite Things."

4. Show the e-book as a slide show on a computer screen or connected to a larger monitor. Students may also take their printed-out D-LEA pages or book home to share with family members.

Through this activity, students will learn that everybody has different favorite things, and they will learn more about each other. They will get a sense of accepting others as unique individuals, a key insight from the storybook.

Computer Software Activity

Students will enjoy different types of activities with the IBM Crayola Magic Princess Paper Doll Maker software, which is designed to allow students to explore different eras in history through clothing and costumes. The introductory screen displays a wardrobe room in which students may link to activities related to historical Japan. Different pieces of kimono clothing and accessories are available for students to click and drag onto the paper doll. In addition, the program is multiculturally sensitive; students may use a color palette to change the hair color, skin tone, and eye color of the virtual paper doll.

MATERIALS

■ IBM Crayola Magic Princess Paper Doll Maker (1998) software

Another computer software activity option (provided by a link that is shaped like a crayon) takes students to an interactive screen that invites them to design a kimono with stamps and colors. After creating a colorful kimono, students may dress the paper doll. Help students read the final screen of each design session. Screen text explains the unique situations during which women wear kimonos. Help students understand that kimonos are not the everyday wear in modern Japan. As students display their work during author's computer chair (see Appendix B), they can relate the kimono designs to the main idea of the story. Provide time for students to display kimonos they have designed with Magic Princess software or on the website Japan Information Network (go to www.jinjapan.org/kidsweb). Ask students what colors they used in their designs. Remind students that kimonos are not everyday wear in Japan but are only worn on special occasions.

Internet Resources and Ideas

Kids Web Japan: http://web-japan.org/kidsweb/index.html
This website, which is managed by the Japan Information Network, is designed to introduce the life and culture of Japan to students who live in other countries. The site provides basic information about Japan, including nature and climate, regions of Japan, daily life, politics and the constitution, history, tradition and culture, economy and industry, international relations, protection of the environment, schools, life outside the classroom, and sports. Direct students' attention to the link "Daily Life and Schools" so that students can explore pictures about the Japanese lifestyle.

The site also boasts a "kids gallery" where students from all over the world have submitted artwork about Japan. If students create drawings or paintings of kimonos as part of their art center activities, follow directions for submitting and posting their pictures on the website.

To learn more about kimonos, go to Virtual Japanese Culture and click "Kimono" (go to http://web-japan.org/kidsweb/virtual/kimono/top.html). During whole-group time, you may show the students pictures of different types of kimonos and read aloud information for emerging or developing readers. The website, which is updated very month, also includes folk legends of Japan, games, and an annual calendar of events or holidays in Japan. For example, clicking on the link "Kendama" leads to descriptions about how to play the game as well as a history of the game.

PBS Kids: Postcards From Buster—Video Clips: http://pbskids.org/buster/videos/index.html
On this site, video clips illustrate how students celebrate different aspects of their cultural heritages. For example, clicking on a link titled "Stepping" shows youngsters in Charleston, South Carolina, USA, doing a traditional dance from their area. The link titled "Arapaho Grass Dance" shows youngsters doing a traditional Native American dance in Wyoming, USA. Guide students in a discussion about the importance of family traditions in the lives of the students they view in the video segments. Ask them to think about family traditions that they are learning about or enjoy.

Book 3:   Unique Monique

Rousaki, M. (2003). Ill. P. Papanikolaou. La Jolla, CA: Kane/Miller. $15.95. 32 pp.

BOOK REVIEW

Monique is a young girl who does not want to wear her brown-and-blue uniform to school because she wants to be different from the other students. Thus, Monique does not set out to be a trendsetter when she wears a red hat, but even after the teacher scolds her for breaking the dress code, the next day everyone at school shows up wearing a hat. The days that follow show Monique starting and getting in trouble for other fads that range from shiny red glasses to striped socks. To counter the dress code violations, the principal posts a plethora of signs banning each fashion statement Monique tries to make. One day, much to the teacher's pleasure, Monique looks ordinary until her smile reveals bright, colorful braces. At last she has found a way to be Unique Monique without breaking the rules.

READ-ALOUD AND BOOK DISCUSSION IDEAS

Before reading, build students' background knowledge about main story concepts. For example, many primary-grade students may be unfamiliar with the concept of a uniform. Turn to a page in the book that shows an illustration of students wearing blue sweaters and khaki slacks or skirts. If students attend school where uniforms are not required, ask them to think about what it would be like, and how they would feel, if everyone had to wear identical clothes every day. If students attend a school where uniforms are required, ask them if they have ever wished they could wear different clothes. Why? Tell them that they will be hearing a story about a little girl named Monique who just wanted to be unique, or different.

During reading, highlight the causes (e.g., Monique wears something new to be different) and the effects (e.g., her classmates copy her). Once students get a sense of the cause–effect sequence of events that occurs after the first incident, invite students to predict how Monique's latest fashion trend might impact the other students. Confirm students' predictions by reading the context clues, looking at extra details in the text and illustrations. For example, when Monique decides to wear striped socks, what will the other students wear the next day? Draw your students' attention to the illustration, which includes story characters wearing a range of colorful striped socks the next day.

After reading the story, ask students how Monique felt at the end of the story. Why? What other things could Monique have done to be different? Will the other students get braces, too? Why or why not?

COMPUTER ACTIVITIES

Creativity and Presentation Software Ideas

One of the episodes on this DVD presents an animated story about Angelina Ballerina's experiences with a new mousling, Anya. Anya, a migrant harvest mouse, suffers from low self-esteem when mice at her new school accuse her of stealing all of the blackberries from the local bushes. Angelina visits Anya at her camp in the woods and discovers that Anya is a talented dancer who knows a traditional folk dance. Angelina invites Anya to perform, wearing her native costume, during a school fair. Anya teaches Angelina the dance. Soon the girls are good friends, and Anya's self-esteem has improved. Direct students to identify Anya's problem and to discuss what Angelina did to help her solve the problem. These activities will reinforce students' awareness of story structure and their ability to identify problems and solutions in stories.

> **MATERIALS**
>
> ■ *Children's Favorites, Volume 2* (Gibbons et al., 2004) DVD

Digital Language Experience Approach

Students will step into the shoes of the main character, Monique, using their photographs and creativity and presentation software.

1. Import a photograph of each student into creativity and presentation software, such as KidPix Studio Deluxe 3.

2. Invite students to create new fashion trends by using stamped icons to change their appearance. Students may also draw or paint fashion trends (e.g., drawing a pair of red glasses, similar to those worn by Monique).

3. Encourage students to write a sentence and record their voices, stating why they are unique. Assemble a "We're Unique" slide show for students to enjoy during whole-group time and author's computer chair (see Appendix B).

> **MATERIALS**
>
> ■ Digital camera
> ■ KidPix Studio Deluxe 3 (2000) software

4. Invite students to share their unique D-LEA photographs of themselves. Ask them to showcase their work or explain how they created certain effects. Discuss all the things that made classmates unique in the photographs.

Computer Software Activity

Stellaluna is a delightful CD-ROM talking book about a little fruit bat that ends up living with a family of birds. Unfortunately, Stellalluna is so different from the birds that she must learn to hide all of her natural tendencies in order to fit in. Only through a series of misadventures does Stellaluna learn how to appreciate her uniqueness.

1. Before students listen to and interact with the story during computer-center time, ask them to be ready to tell at least one thing that Stellaluna did that was like her bird family and that she did not like doing. For example, on one screen page, Stellaluna eats an insect offered to her by mother bird. The animation illustrates Stellaluna shuddering.

2. Follow up by asking students to be ready to tell at least one thing that Stellaluna learned to like about being a little fruit bat. For example, when she accidentally encounters a group of other fruit bats, she enjoys hanging upside down on a tree branch and eating a mango. The other bats teach Stellaluna by singing a song about eating mangos.

3. Allow students to share their observations during whole-group time. Ask students to make text-to-text connections by comparing how Stellaluna's story is similar to or different from Monique's story.

Internet Resources and Ideas

Girlguiding UK: What Do Rainbows Do? www.girlguiding.org.uk/xq/asp/sID.346/qx/new/about/article.asp
To learn more about uniforms and young children's groups, explore the Rainbow webpage. (A Rainbow group is an organization based in England that is similar to Girl Scouts of America in the United States.) One link of particular interest allows students to find out more about Rainbow groups around the world (e.g., India, Mexico).

Boys may be interested in exploring the Boy Scouts and Cub Scouts website. In fact, students can try to beat the computer in a game of checkers at http://usscouts.org/usscouts/checkers.asp. Students may need help understanding how the checkers move or may benefit from having the help of a cross-age computer buddy as they try to play the game. Links at the website allow students to learn more about scout badges and uniforms; however, the site is heavily reliant on text.

Boy Scouts of America: www.scoutorama.com
Click on the "Activities" link in the upper right-hand corner of this site to find out more about different Boy Scout activities. For example, a treasure hunt activity involves learning how to use a compass to follow simple directions. If the directions are followed correctly, scouts finish the course exactly where they began the activity.

Unit Conclusion

During whole-group time, remind students that all of the books for the unit deal with how different characters learn to appreciate or value special things about themselves that make them unique. Set up a display of all of the books and invite students to hold a book and share something special they learned from the book. Discuss students' notions about the main idea of the stories. Reflect on how each character learned to appreciate how she was unique or different.

Explain which unit book or activity helped you learn more about why you are special. Conclude by inviting students to share why they are special. If time permits, have a final author's computer chair session (see Appendix B) to celebrate students' computer-related activities. For example, if students have created a digital portrait of themselves wearing specially designed hats (see the D-LEA on page 113), they can display the printout or show the slide while explaining how the hat reflects why they are special.

MATERIALS

■ Books from this unit

"I have one little girl from Mexico who never spoke up in class until this unit. She got a new dog and was so excited to be able to tell her story about Blanco, her white dog, in Spanish before translating it into English. I sent both versions home, and her parents sent me a thank-you card. Wow!"

—KINDERGARTEN TEACHER

Dogs—The Pets That Love Us

UNIT BOOKS

Face-to-Face With the Dog: Loyal Companion
By Valerie Tracqui
Photographs by Marie-Luce Hubert and Jean-Louis Klein

Good Night Sam
By Marie-Louise Gay

The Great Gracie Chase: Stop That Dog!
By Cynthia Rylant
Illustrated by Mark Teague

COMPUTER RESOURCES

Caillou: Caillou's Family Fun
Clifford Reading
102 Dalmatians: Puppies to the Rescue

Thematic Connection

Through the activities and books included in this unit, students will enjoy wondering and learning about dogs. In *Face-to-Face With the Dog: Loyal Companion* (Tracqui, 2002), students will learn facts about dogs. The other two books are narratives that help students explore their feelings about dogs as pets. *Good Night Sam* (Gay, 2003) displays a young boy's comfort in having a pet dog as a sleeping buddy. In *The Great Gracie Chase: Stop That Dog!* (Rylant, 2001), students will delight in following Gracie, a fun-loving canine character, through the streets of her neighborhood as she runs away from home and then returns. All the books in this unit provide unique opportunities for students to learn how to read different genres while they learn about dogs in a combination of informational text, fictional text, and multimedia resources such as CD-ROMS, DVDs, and Internet sites.

Matrix of Literacy Skills and Strategies in Unit 8

Literacy Skills and Strategies	Activities	Title of Book	Pages
Brainstorming	U	—	126–127
	C	*The Great Gracie Chase: Stop That Dog!*	133–134
Building background knowledge on the Internet*	D, I	*Face-to-Face With the Dog: Loyal Companion*	129, 130
	I	*Good Night Sam*	132
	I	*The Great Gracie Chase: Stop That Dog!*	135
Building editing skills	C	*The Great Gracie Chase: Stop That Dog!*	133–134
Building fluency	D	*Good Night Sam*	131–132
Composing in multimedia*	C, D	*Face-to-Face With the Dog: Loyal Companion*	128–129, 129
	C, D	*Good Night Sam*	131, 131–132
	C	*The Great Gracie Chase: Stop That Dog!*	133–134
Creating and using charts	U, UC	—	126–127, 136
	R, C	*Face-to-Face With the Dog: Loyal Companion*	127–128, 128–129
	R	*Good Night Sam*	130–131
	R, C	*The Great Gracie Chase: Stop That Dog!*	133, 133–134
Determining cause and effect	I	*Face-to-Face With the Dog: Loyal Companion*	130
Determining story details	UC	—	136
	R	*Face-to-Face With the Dog: Loyal Companion*	127–128
	C, D	*Good Night Sam*	131, 131–132
	R	*The Great Gracie Chase: Stop That Dog!*	133
Developing a sense of beginnings, middles, and endings	C	*The Great Gracie Chase: Stop That Dog!*	133–134
Developing and using story grammar	R	*Face-to-Face With the Dog: Loyal Companion*	127–128
	R, D	*Good Night Sam*	130–131, 131–132
	C	*The Great Gracie Chase: Stop That Dog!*	133–134
Developing comprehension	U, UC	—	126–127, 136
	R, I	*Face-to-Face With the Dog: Loyal Companion*	127–128, 130
	R, C, D	*Good Night Sam*	130–131, 131, 131–132
	R, C	*The Great Gracie Chase: Stop That Dog!*	133, 133–134
Developing creative writing	C, D	*Good Night Sam*	131, 131–132
	C	*The Great Gracie Chase: Stop That Dog!*	133–134
Developing critical reading and thinking	D	*Good Night Sam*	131–132
	S	*Face-to-Face With the Dog: Loyal Companion*	129
Developing oral language	U, UC	—	126–127, 136
	R, C, D	*Face-to-Face With the Dog: Loyal Companion*	127–128, 128–129, 129
	R, C, D, S, I	*Good Night Sam*	130–131, 131, 131–132, 132, 132
	R, C, S	*The Great Gracie Chase: Stop That Dog!*	133, 133–134, 135

(continued)

Matrix of Literacy Skills and Strategies in Unit 8 (continued)

Literacy Skills and Strategies	Activities	Title of Book	Pages
Developing vocabulary	U, UC	—	126–127, 136
	R, C, D, I	*Face-to-Face With the Dog: Loyal Companion*	127–128, 128–129, 129, 130
	R, C, D, I	*Good Night Sam*	130–131, 131, 131–132, 132
	R, C, S	*The Great Gracie Chase: Stop That Dog!*	133, 133–134, 135
Following directions	C, D	*Face-to-Face With the Dog: Loyal Companion*	128–129, 129
	R, C, D, I	*Good Night Sam*	130–131, 131, 131–132, 132
	C, S, I	*The Great Gracie Chase: Stop That Dog!*	133–134, 135, 135
Inferring	UC	—	136
	I	*Face-to-Face With the Dog: Loyal Companion*	130
	I	*Good Night Sam*	132
	R	*The Great Gracie Chase: Stop That Dog!*	133
Making predictions	I	*Good Night Sam*	132
	R	*The Great Gracie Chase: Stop That Dog!*	133
Navigating hyperlinks*	D, I	*Face-to-Face With the Dog: Loyal Companion*	129, 130
	I	*Good Night Sam*	132
	S, I	*The Great Gracie Chase: Stop That Dog!*	135
Presenting work on a computer*	C, D	*Face-to-Face With the Dog: Loyal Companion*	128–129, 129
	C, D	*Good Night Sam*	131, 131–132
	C	*The Great Gracie Chase: Stop That Dog!*	133–134
Reading aloud	R	*Face-to-Face With the Dog: Loyal Companion*	127–128
	R, C, D	*Good Night Sam*	130–131, 131, 131–132
	R	*The Great Gracie Chase: Stop That Dog!*	133
Reading and listening for a purpose	UC	—	136
	R	*Face-to-Face With the Dog: Loyal Companion*	127–128
	R, I	*Good Night Sam*	130–131, 132
	R	*The Great Gracie Chase: Stop That Dog!*	133
Reading informational text	R	*Face-to-Face With the Dog: Loyal Companion*	127–128
	I	*The Great Gracie Chase: Stop That Dog!*	135
Retelling	D	*Good Night Sam*	131–132
Sequencing	D	*Good Night Sam*	131–132
Summarizing	UC	—	136
	R, D	*Face-to-Face With the Dog: Loyal Companion*	127–128, 129
	D	*Good Night Sam*	131–132
	C	*The Great Gracie Chase: Stop That Dog!*	133–134
Understanding a main idea	U, UC	—	126–127, 136
	R, C, D, I	*Face-to-Face With the Dog: Loyal Companion*	127–128, 128–129, 129, 130
	R, C, D, I	*Good Night Sam*	130–131, 131, 131–132, 132
	S	*The Great Gracie Chase: Stop That Dog!*	135

(continued)

Literacy Skills and Strategies	Activities	Title of Book	Pages
Understanding story structure and events	UC	—	136
	R, D	*Good Night Sam*	130–131, 131–132
	R, C	*The Great Gracie Chase: Stop That Dog!*	133, 133–134
Using adjectives	U, UC	—	126–127, 136
	R, C	*Face-to-Face With the Dog: Loyal Companion*	127–128, 128–129
	C, D, I	*Good Night Sam*	131, 131–132, 132
	S	*The Great Gracie Chase: Stop That Dog!*	135
Using nouns	U, UC	—	126–127, 136
	R, C, D	*Face-to-Face With the Dog: Loyal Companion*	127–128, 128–129, 129
	R, C	*Good Night Sam*	130–131, 131
Using verbs	U, UC	—	126–127, 136
	R, C, D	*Face-to-Face With the Dog: Loyal Companion*	127–128, 128–129, 129
	R, C, D	*Good Night Sam*	130–131, 131, 131–132
Writing descriptive sentences	C, D	*Face-to-Face With the Dog: Loyal Companion*	128–129, 129
	C, D	*Good Night Sam*	131, 131–132
	C	*The Great Gracie Chase: Stop That Dog!*	133–134
Writing letters	I	*The Great Gracie Chase: Stop That Dog!*	135

* Indicates a new-literacy skill.
U = unit introduction; R = read-aloud and book discussion ideas; C = creativity and presentation software ideas; D = Digital Language Experience Approach; S = computer software activity; I = Internet resources and ideas; UC = unit conclusion

Unit Introduction

To prepare for the unit, display stuffed-animal dogs on a table and pictures of various types of dogs as a frame for a bulletin board titled "Dogs: The Pets That Love Us." Place a poster board titled "Our Favorite Words About Dogs" (see Figure 23) in the middle of the bulletin board.

Include three columns: nouns, adjectives, and verbs. Display a collection of books about dogs, including *Face-to-Face With the Dog: Loyal Companion* (Tracqui, 2002), *Good Night Sam* (Gay, 2003), and *The Great Gracie Chase: Stop That Dog!* (Rylant, 2001) on a table, open-faced bookshelf, or chalkboard rail.

As you begin the unit, during whole-group time, ask students to join you in thinking about what they know about dogs as pets. As part of the conversation, if you own or have previously owned a dog as a pet, tell students your pet's name and explain why you enjoy having a dog for a pet. Students who own dogs will be eager to share stories about their pets. Tell students that some books about dogs

---

MATERIALS

- Books about dogs, including this unit's books
- Markers
- Pictures of dogs
- Poster board
- Stuffed-animal dogs

Figure 23
Our Favorite Words About Dogs

Nouns	Adjectives	Verbs

provide information that teaches facts about dogs and how to take care of them. Other stories help show the role that dogs play as pets in our lives. Tell students that as you read the stories in this unit, you want them to be listening for words about dogs that they would like to add to the vocabulary chart. Briefly review parts of speech such as nouns, adjectives, and verbs. Before reading each book in the unit, remind students that you want them to listen for nouns, adjectives, and verbs. As an example, read a few pages of *Face-to-Face With the Dog: Loyal Companion*, and ask students to help you create a chart of nouns, adjectives, and verbs.

Book 1:   Face-to-Face With the Dog: Loyal Companion

Tracqui, V. (2002). Photos. M.-L. Hubert & J.-L. Klein. Watertown, MA: Charlesbridge. $9.95. 32 pp.

BOOK REVIEW

This informational text about dogs provides a variety of facts through a combination of brightly colored photographs, photograph captions, and one paragraph of text per page. Students can learn about the social nature of dogs, dog behavior, dog life in the city, puppies, and different breeds and jobs for dogs. They also can learn about how dogs follow commands from human companions, how humans care for dogs (e.g., taking golden retrievers for walks and swims), and how dogs play and grow up. Students will enjoy learning about how informational text is organized and how facts are depicted in illustrations and text.

READ-ALOUD AND BOOK DISCUSSION IDEAS

Before reading, create a K-W-L chart (Ogle, 1986) on chart paper. Write the topic "Dogs" across the top of the poster. Ask students to share a few things they already know about dogs under the *Know* column. Next, list questions of things they want to learn about dogs under the *Want to Know* column. Then, rather than reading the book from cover to cover, as you would a narrative fictional picture book, start on the

MATERIALS

■ Chart paper
■ K-W-L chart
■ Markers

back page. The last page of the book (page 26) has an index of questions designed to help students either take a quick quiz about dogs or locate specific answers to questions about dogs. Finish the K-W-L chart by completing the following steps:

1. Demonstrate how to locate specific information from the book. Refer students to the list of questions they asked on the *Want to Know* column of the K-W-L chart. Group the questions by the big ideas. For example, one child might ask what dogs eat for breakfast. Another student might ask about doggie treats or if puppies like to drink milk. Group these questions under "What do dogs eat?"

2. Demonstrate how you refer to the index, scan the list of questions, locate the question "What does a dog eat?" and follow the line of dots that connected the topic (eating) to the page number (page 8).

3. Turn to page 8 and locate the picture that shows a dog eating. Read the caption "Dog food combines meat, vegetables and minerals." Return to the index and locate the question about puppies drinking milk. Continue this process for a few topics listed in the index and information available on specific pages. Tell students that some books are used to help find specific answers to questions: These are nonfiction, informational books.

4. After targeting a few questions and answers, refer to the *Want to Know* column again. Place a check mark by all questions that students answered and summarize the answers under the *Learned* column.

5. Determine what questions remain to be answered. Do a picture walk of the book, stopping to read pages that might contain information students still wish to learn.

6. Read the book, complete the *Learned* column of the chart, and discuss what students believe are the most important things they learned about dogs from this book.

7. Invite students to contribute favorite words to the vocabulary chart.

COMPUTER ACTIVITIES

Creativity and Presentation Software Ideas

Begin a class log sheet in the KidPix Studio Deluxe 3 or PowerPoint creativity and presentation software by typing the title "Things We've Learned About Dogs" on an empty screen. Whenever students learn a new fact, they may go to the computer and enter it by dictating to a cross-age computer buddy, a classroom volunteer, the teacher, or by using invented spelling or stamped icons to record their own thoughts. Remind students to type in their names and the date after each entry. At the end of the unit, print out the master list and share facts with the class.

As another option, students can also design a dog. Using tools in creativity and presentation software, such as KidPix Studio Deluxe 3, to draw or paint, instruct students to create a picture of a dog they would like to own. Dogs may be realistically constructed or fantasy

MATERIALS

■ KidPix Studio Deluxe 3 (2000) or PowerPoint (Microsoft Office 2003, 2003) software

related. Be sure each student types his or her name and the name of the dog on the pictures. Students type a description of the dog using adjectives and verbs. Print out and display the dog pictures or present in a digital slide show to enjoy during whole-group time.

Digital Language Experience Approach

Emerging or developing readers will benefit from changing the sociodramatic play center into a pet store, dog grooming shop, or a veterinarian's office. Conduct research online (use keywords on a kid-friendly site, such as Yahooligans! at http://yahooligans.yahoo.com, to initiate the search) or invite a veterinarian or pet store owner to visit to provide background information. Complete the following steps to accomplish this activity.

> **MATERIALS**
>
> - Bill-of-sale notepads
> - Cardboard boxes
> - Digital camera
> - KidPix Studio Deluxe 3 (2000) or PowerPoint (Microsoft Office 2003, 2003) software
> - Pencils
> - Pet dishes
> - Pet food
> - Pet store sign
> - Stuffed-animal dogs

1. After gathering information online or through a field trip to a pet store or veterinarian's office, place props (e.g., stuffed-animal dogs, pet dishes, pet food, cardboard boxes, pet store sign, bill-of-sale pads, pencils) for dramatic play in the center and take digital photos of students playing out the various roles related to caring for or adopting a dog.

2. Use the digital photos in creativity and presentation software, such as KidPix Studio Deluxe 3 or PowerPoint, to create a photo essay of students' playful experiences.

3. Ask students to dictate or type sentences to explain and describe their playful encounters.

During author's computer chair (see Appendix B), ask students to help you present a slide show or printed version of a bound book of their D-LEA during author's computer chair. Help students elaborate on their comments by gently asking probing questions or seeking clarification.

Computer Software Activity

Caillou, a beloved animated character from the PBS Kids series of the same name, explores different situations about pets. Use the remote control for the DVD player to interact with the resources and information provided on screen. Four of the eight episodes focus on dog-related adventures. For example, in "Lost Puppy," after Caillou and his father find a lost puppy at the park, they do their best to find the

> **MATERIALS**
>
> - *Caillou: Caillou's Family Fun* (2005) DVD

dog's owner. Ask students to talk about what they would do to find a lost pet. In "Dogs With Jobs" Calliou finds out about the training and work of a Seeing Eye dog. After viewing, discuss how dogs help people accomplish tasks. Before viewing the episode "Rescuing Gilbert and the Fire Truck," tell students to pay attention to the work that a dog at a fire station does. Before viewing the episode "Gilbert Goes to the Vet," ask students to think about why people take dogs to see the veterinarian. The DVD includes interactive games and special features, such as coloring pages, and information for parents.

Internet Resources and Ideas

Virtual Puppy: www.virtualpuppy.com

Individual students, small groups, or the whole class can adopt a virtual puppy online at www.virtualpuppy.com. Following a few simple steps will help students have a positive online experience and will support their ability to learn about caring for puppies:

1. Invite students to care for the computer puppy by first adopting and then naming a puppy.

2. Encourage students to visit the puppy to make sure that it is well fed and kept clean and healthy. Students earn number scores that reflect how well they are taking care of their virtual pet.

3. A few clicks of the button will result in pet feedings, time for play, and cleaning up. Pets sleep when the pet owners are not able to visit.

4. Ask students how their Internet activities connect to the books they are reading. What are they learning about caring for pets by caring for a virtual puppy?

Enchanted Learning: Dog Printouts: www.enchantedlearning.com/subjects/mammals/dog/index.shtml

Learn facts about dogs, read dog jokes, or print activity books that are appropriate for early readers from this Enchanted Learning website. Other resources include pictures of dogs for coloring and counting, shapes of dogs to cut, and a short sentence about dogs for children to copy by writing the sentence on their papers. Additional links at this website connect with facts about specific breeds, such as Airedale terriers, the Alaskan malamute, and the bulldog.

Book 2:   Good Night Sam

Gay, M.-L. (2003). Toronto, ON: Groundwood Books. $14.95. 24 pp.

BOOK REVIEW

One night Stella's little brother, Sam, just cannot get to sleep without his beloved puppy dog, Fred. Where could Fred be? He is not in Sam's room. Ever helpful, Stella helps Sam search the house for Fred—or rather, she tries to help. Sam is afraid of monsters in the closet, giant toads living under overstuffed chairs, and eerie shadows cast by the moon. Unhappily returning to bed and resolving to find Fred tomorrow, Sam is surprised to discover that Fred has been asleep under the quilt all along. Unfortunately, Sam still cannot get to sleep because Fred is snoring loudly. Watercolors rendered in delicate colors add charm, expression, and humor to the tale of the role of pets in overcoming nighttime fears.

READ-ALOUD AND BOOK DISCUSSION IDEAS

MATERIALS

- Markers
- Vocabulary chart

Before reading, ask younger students if they have any pets or stuffed animals that they sleep with. Ask older students if they used to have a stuffed animal or pet that they slept with. How does snuggling up next to a sleep-time companion feel? What happens if a sleep-time companion is missing?

During reading, ask students to think about Sam's problems and how his sister tries to help him solve them. These types of interactions help students learn story structure. When students understand story structure, which consists of characters, setting, problem, attempts to solve the problem, and the solution, they are better equipped to comprehend stories. After the story, ask students to think about how Sam might solve his new problem.

After reading, invite students to contribute words that they have learned about people's feelings about dogs to the vocabulary chart.

COMPUTER ACTIVITIES

Creativity and Presentation Software Ideas

Ask students to think more about how Sam can solve his new problem—he cannot go to sleep because Fred is snoring. Students can brainstorm possible solutions. The following steps outline a simple procedure for this activity.

> **MATERIALS**
>
> - KidPix Studio Deluxe 3 (2000) or PowerPoint (Microsoft Office 2003, 2003) software

1. Provide students with opportunities to learn more about the main idea by encouraging them to innovate on a story as they compose one-page sentences and illustrations of how they would solve the new problem using creativity and presentation software such as KidPix Studio Deluxe 3 or PowerPoint. For example, a student might draw a picture of Sam in bed with a large pillow over each ear. Another student might draw a picture of Sam listening to music in bed with headphones. Could Fred go into a clear, soundproof box?

2. Import students' creativity pages into a slide show or make printouts for a hard copy of the book.

3. Share the show, titled "How to Stop Fred's Snoring So Sam Can Sleep," during whole-group time. Ask each student author to explain his or her illustration and read the sentence during author's computer chair (see Appendix B).

Digital Language Experience Approach

Invite small groups of students to reenact the story in the sociodramatic play center.

> **MATERIALS**
>
> - Digital camera
> - KidPix Studio Deluxe 3 (2000) or PowerPoint (Microsoft Office 2003, 2003) software
> - Story props

1. Ask students to help you gather props to retell the story. Refer to the book to help students summarize the story and recall sequence of events, main characters, plot resolution, and details.

2. Provide story props (e.g., bedding, stuffed-animal dog).

3. Take digital photographs of students as they reenact the story.

4. Import photographs into creativity and presentation software such as KidPix Studio Deluxe 3 or PowerPoint. Allow students to place photographs in sequence and dictate or keyboard sentences for each page of the story. Remind students that their sentences should tell a new version of the story.

5. Print out students' versions of the story or compile a slide show that they can share during author's computer chair (see Appendix B). Encourage students to read aloud the pages of the slide show or book. As students take turns rereading the story, they become more fluent.

6. Encourage students to add new vocabulary words to the vocabulary chart.

Computer Software Activity

MATERIALS

■ Clifford Reading (2004) CD-ROM

The Clifford Reading CD-ROM includes 12 reading games, guided by Clifford the Big Red Dog and his friends. The setting, a carnival, creates a colorful background for learning about phonics, vocabulary, and spelling. For example, students can write stories by using words and pictures provided on screen. Another game involves matching letters to make the Ferris wheel move. The pack includes six books designed to help early readers practice and apply phonics skills.

Internet Resources and Ideas

HandsNpaws: www.handsnpaws.com/category/petpajamasloungewear
Students will likely enjoy viewing pictures of dogs in doggie pajamas, pet loungewear, doggie denim, bathrobes, beachwear, and other fun pet clothing that is available on this website. Before viewing the website during whole-group or small-group time, ask students what Sam might have done to help his dog, Fred, get ready for bed. Tell them that you are going to look at a website where people can buy pajamas and other types of clothing for dogs. Ask what other types of clothing they think might be represented on the website. As you view the photographs, ask students to describe the clothes they see. Ask them which set of pajamas, or bathrobes, they would purchase for Sam's dog.

NOVA: Dogs and More Dogs: www.pbs.org/wgbh/nova/dogs
This Public Broadcasting Service website links to slide shows or interactive games about dogs. For example, one link, titled "Working Dogs," presents a slide show that could be shared during whole-group time. Tell students they will be learning about special tasks some dogs are trained to do. For example, the slide show explains how dogs sniff out termites or use their keen sense of smell during search-and-rescue missions. Another hyperlink, titled "Dogs Around the World," invites students to match 14 different breeds of dogs to their natural environment by clicking on locations displayed on a world map. Emerging or developing readers will require an adult or cross-age computer buddy to read text that provides clues about each dog breed.

Book 3:   The Great Gracie Chase: Stop That Dog!

Rylant, C. (2001). Ill. M. Teague. New York: Blue Sky Press. $15.95. 40 pp.

BOOK REVIEW

Gracie, author Cynthia Rylant's real-life dog, becomes the main canine character of *The Great Gracie Chase: Stop That Dog!* Gracie loves her quiet house because she can help the big dog guard the house, sing to the goldfish when it gets lonely, and keep the cat company. But Gracie's quiet house is suddenly disrupted by the arrival of two noisy house painters that put the little dog in the yard when they arrive. An opportunity to take a walk, all by herself, arrives when Gracie notices the gate has been left open. Thus begins the great Gracie chase. Everyone in the neighborhood gets involved in running after Gracie. A string of good-hearted folks—the garbage man, a neighbor, a delivery woman, the paperboy, the painters, the hot dog man, and others—try to catch Gracie as she runs a zigzag course through the neighborhood. Of course, once the people have to stop to rest and catch their breath, Gracie decides it is safe to go home. Mark Teague's stylistic illustrations complement this rollicking story.

READ-ALOUD AND BOOK DISCUSSION IDEAS

Before reading, ask students if dogs usually take themselves for a walk, or if they usually go with their human companions. Tell students that in many cities, dogs can go for a walk only if they are on a leash and accompanied by their owners. Show students the book cover, read the title, and ask them what they think this story will be about.

During reading, ask students to speculate why Gracie does not just stop running. Why does she run through the fountain? Up the hill? Through the schoolyard?

After reading the story, ask students to think about what might happen the next day when the painters return to the house once again. Ask students to suggest vocabulary words from the story to add to the vocabulary chart.

MATERIALS

- Markers
- Vocabulary chart

COMPUTER ACTIVITIES

Creativity and Presentation Software Ideas

Invite students to write a group story or individual short stories about places Gracie would run through and the people she would see if she ran through your school.

1. Begin by brainstorming a list of people who might run after Gracie, trying to catch her, if she came in the front door. Where would Gracie go next? Who would follow Gracie? What would happen if Gracie ran through your classroom, out the window, and onto the playground?

2. List the new characters and locations (see Figure 24) on the blackboard as an easy reference for students to craft their own stories.

3. Decide the story will end when all the characters get tired of chasing Gracie and begin playing on the playground or another final location. For example, in the cafeteria, people might get tired of chasing Gracie and begin eating lunch, or in the library, people might get tired and start reading books.

MATERIALS

- Blackboard
- Chalk
- Crayons
- KidPix Studio Deluxe (1998) or PowerPoint (Microsoft 2003, 2003) software
- Paper
- Pencils

Figure 24
People and Places Gracie Would See at Our School

Character	Location
Bus driver	Front porch
Principal	Front door
Secretary	Front hallway
Cafeteria worker	Cafeteria
Media specialist	Library
Janitor	Hallway
Teacher	Your classroom
Children	Your classroom
All children	Playground

4. If you are writing a group story, ask different students to dictate sentences for each line of the story. Type their dictation into creativity and presentation software such as KidPix Studio Deluxe or PowerPoint. Demonstrate for students the ease of editing and revising on screen while you are typing.

5. Print out copies of the story and invite different students to draw and color illustrations for the story.

6. Bind pages into a class book to share during whole-group time. Provide a title and add the book to your class library.

Digital Language Experience Approach

Invite small groups of students to reenact the story on the playground by completing the following steps.

> **MATERIALS**
>
> - Digital camera
> - KidPix Studio Deluxe 3 (2000) or PowerPoint (Microsoft 2003, 2003) software

1. Refer to the book to help students summarize the story and recall sequence of events, main characters, plot resolution, and details.

2. Ask students to discuss which parts of the playground provide good settings for the retelling.

3. Take digital photographs of students as they reenact the story.

4. Import photographs into creativity and presentation software such as KidPix Studio Deluxe 3 or PowerPoint. Allow students to place photographs in sequence and dictate or type sentences for each page of the story. Remind students that their sentences should tell a new version of the story.

5. Print out students' versions of the story or compile a slide show that they can share during author's computer chair (see Appendix B). Encourage students to read aloud the pages of the slide show or book. As students take turns rereading the story, they become more fluent.

6. Encourage students to add new words to the vocabulary chart.

Computer Software Activity

102 Dalmatians: Puppies to the Rescue is an interactive CD-ROM that includes one game that primary-grade students will enjoy. After you install the software and sign in, a screen map of London will appear. Clicking on the building in the center of the map will present students with a doggie adoption center. The following steps with this software program support students' learning.

1. Instruct students to choose from several different dog breeds by clicking on the dog picture and selecting a name for the dog they choose.

2. Have students click on a picture of London Bridge, which will take them to a park where they can get to know their dog by virtually playing catch and feeding the dog.

3. To relate the activity to language arts skills, such as learning about adjectives and verbs, ask students to describe the things they are learning to do with their new virtual pet. Use the details of the screen to elicit rich oral language descriptions.

Internet Resources and Ideas

About Children's Books: http://childrensbooks.about.com/cs/authorsillustrato/a/cynthiarylant.htm
View the website with your students and learn more about Rylant's growing-up years, the influence of living in Appalachia on her writing, and her favorite characters. You also can see a list of her books.

Clifford Play and Learn: Peek-A-Boo Puppy: www.scholastic.com/clifford/play/peekaboo/index.htm
Peek-A-Boo Puppy is an interactive game emerging readers can plan independently. A narrated voice reads aloud text and invites students to look for Clifford the puppy in one of three different house locations: a bedroom, laundry room, or living room.

PBS Nature: Dogs: The Early Years: www.pbs.org/wnet/nature/puppies
During whole-group time, click on a "Photo Essay" link to view a slide show about the earliest days of a puppy's life. Read aloud the text that accompanies each photograph to learn facts about puppies. For example, the first slide shows a photograph of newborn puppies with their mother. The text tells students that puppies are born blind and deaf. Another photograph that is labeled as a video offers a two-minute video about a family visiting border collies and talking with a breeder about selecting a puppy. Students learn about how important it is to understand the characteristics of a breed before selecting a puppy.

Unit Conclusion

During a final whole-group meeting, display students' work and the collection of books read in the unit. Review the words on the vocabulary chart and discuss how the adjectives describe and provide a visual image of dogs, how verbs describe dogs' actions, and how nouns tell about different types of dogs. Ask students to select and talk about their favorite unit activity. Which books helped them learn more facts about dogs? Which books helped them learn more about how people feel about the dogs in their lives?

MATERIALS

- Students' work from the unit
- This unit's books
- Vocabulary chart

Dealing With Emotional Issues at Home and School

UNIT BOOKS

The Brand New Kid
By Katie Couric
Illustrated by Marjorie Priceman

A Place to Grow
By Soyung Pak
Illustrated by Marcelino Truong

What Baby Needs
By William and Martha Sears and Christie Watts Kelly
Illustrated by Renée Andriani

COMPUTER RESOURCES

Living Books: Mercer Mayer's Little Monster at School
Orly's Draw a Story
The Bread That Grew

Thematic Connection

Students' lives often are defined by their roles at school and within their families. Unfortunately, the lessons of childhood are sometimes difficult. Situations and events can be hard for students to understand and talk about. Exploring these circumstances at school can make such experiences accessible, improving students' ability to cope with complex issues. The purpose of this unit is to guide primary-grade students to use literature as a springboard for exploring, writing about, discussing, and thinking about handling difficult situations. As students engage in activities connected to ideas they can relate to, they also have occasions to learn literacy skills and strategies. Teachers can use *The Brand New Kid* (Couric, 2000) to facilitate discussions about students who feel excluded at school and what others can do to make everyone feel welcome. This book models how one courageous girl befriends the new boy in her class, which in turn opens opportunities for others to get to know him, too. *A Place to Grow* (Pak, 2002) is a multicultural story that uses a garden metaphor to explain why a family decides to move from another country to the United States. In *What Baby Needs* (Sears, Sears, & Kelly, 2001), students get a clear but sensitive first look at having a new baby in the family. They can see how their role in the family will change and get a glimpse into the changes that will occur in the household.

Matrix of Literacy Skills and Strategies in Unit 9

Literacy Skills and Strategies	Activities	Title of Book	Pages
Brainstorming	D	*The Brand New Kid*	143–144
	R, C	*A Place to Grow*	146, 147
	D	*What Baby Needs*	150–151
Building background knowledge on the Internet*	I	*A Place to Grow*	148–149
	I	*What Baby Needs*	151–152
Building editing skills	D	*The Brand New Kid*	143–144
	C, D	*A Place to Grow*	147, 147–148
Building fluency	D, S	*The Brand New Kid*	143–144, 144–145
	S	*What Baby Needs*	151
Comparing and contrasting	UC	—	152–153
	R, C	*The Brand New Kid*	142, 142–143
	D	*What Baby Needs*	150–151
Composing in multimedia*	C, D, I	*The Brand New Kid*	142–143, 143–144, 145
	C, D, I	*A Place to Grow*	147, 147–148, 148–149
	D	*What Baby Needs*	150–151
Creating and using charts	C	*The Brand New Kid*	142–143
	R	*A Place to Grow*	146
Creating concept maps and graphic organizers	C	*The Brand New Kid*	142–143
	D	*What Baby Needs*	150–151
Determining cause and effect	UC	—	152–153
	R, S, I	*The Brand New Kid*	142, 144–145, 145
Determining story details	R, D, S, I	*The Brand New Kid*	142, 143–144, 144–145, 145
	R, C, D, S	*A Place to Grow*	146, 147, 147–148, 148
	S	*What Baby Needs*	151
Developing a sense of beginnings, middles, and endings	D, I	*The Brand New Kid*	143–144, 145
	C, D, S	*A Place to Grow*	147, 147–148, 148
	R, S, I	*What Baby Needs*	149–150, 151, 151–152
Developing and using story grammar	UC	—	152–153
	R	*The Brand New Kid*	142
	R, S, I	*A Place to Grow*	146, 148, 148–149
	R, S, I	*What Baby Needs*	149–150, 151, 151–152
Developing choral reading	S	*The Brand New Kid*	144–145
	S	*What Baby Needs*	151

(continued)

Matrix of Literacy Skills and Strategies in Unit 9 (continued)

Literacy Skills and Strategies	Activities	Title of Book	Pages
Developing comprehension	U, UC	—	140–141, 152–153
	R, S	*The Brand New Kid*	142, 144–145
	R, C, D, S, I	*A Place to Grow*	146, 147, 147–148, 148, 148–149
	R, D, S, I	*What Baby Needs*	149–150, 150–151, 151, 151–152
Developing creative writing	D, I	*The Brand New Kid*	143–144, 145
	C, D, I	*A Place to Grow*	147, 147–148, 148–149
	D	*What Baby Needs*	150–151
Developing critical reading and thinking	I	*The Brand New Kid*	145
Developing oral language	U, UC	—	140–141, 152–153
	R, C, D	*The Brand New Kid*	142, 142–143, 143–144
	R, C, D	*A Place to Grow*	146, 147, 147–148
	R, D	*What Baby Needs*	149–150, 150–151
Developing phonemic awareness	C	*The Brand New Kid*	142–143
	D	*What Baby Needs*	150–151
Developing vocabulary	UC	—	152–153
	R, C, D, S, I	*The Brand New Kid*	142, 142–143, 143–144, 144–145, 145
	R, D, S, I	*A Place to Grow*	146, 147–148, 148, 148–149
	D	*What Baby Needs*	150–151
Distinguishing sounds	I	*What Baby Needs*	151–152
Drawing conclusions	C	*The Brand New Kid*	142–143
	R, I	*A Place to Grow*	146, 148–149
	R	*What Baby Needs*	149–150
Following directions	C, D, I	*The Brand New Kid*	142–143, 143–144, 145
	C, D, S, I	*A Place to Grow*	147, 147–148, 148, 148–149
	D, S, I	*What Baby Needs*	150–151, 151, 151–152
Identifying letters	I	*The Brand New Kid*	145
	S, I	*What Baby Needs*	151, 151–152
Making multicultural connections	R, C, D, I	*The Brand New Kid*	142, 142–143, 143–144, 145
	R, D, S	*A Place to Grow*	146, 147–148, 148
Making predictions	U, UC	—	140–141, 152–153
	R	*A Place to Grow*	146
	R	*What Baby Needs*	149–150
Navigating hyperlinks*	S, I	*The Brand New Kid*	144–145, 145
	I	*A Place to Grow*	148–149
	S, I	*What Baby Needs*	151, 151–152
Presenting work on a computer*	C	*The Brand New Kid*	142–143
	C, D, I	*A Place to Grow*	147, 147–148, 148–149
	C, D	*What Baby Needs*	150, 150–151
Reading aloud	R	*The Brand New Kid*	142
	R	*A Place to Grow*	146
	R, S	*What Baby Needs*	149–150, 151

(continued)

Matrix of Literacy Skills and Strategies in Unit 9 (continued)

Literacy Skills and Strategies	Activities	Title of Book	Pages
Reading and listening for a purpose	U, UC	—	140–141, 152–153
	R, S, I	*The Brand New Kid*	142, 144–145, 145
	R, S	*A Place to Grow*	146, 148
	R, S, I	*What Baby Needs*	149–150, 151, 151–152
Reading informational text	I	*What Baby Needs*	151–152
Sequencing	D, I	*The Brand New Kid*	143–144, 145
Summarizing	D, S	*The Brand New Kid*	143–144, 144–145
Understanding a main idea	U, UC	—	140–141, 152–153
	R, C, D, S	*The Brand New Kid*	142, 142–143, 143–144, 144–145
	R, C, D, S, I	*A Place to Grow*	146, 147, 147–148, 148, 148–149
	R, D, S, I	*What Baby Needs*	149–150, 150–151, 151, 151–152
Understanding concepts about print	D, S	*The Brand New Kid*	143–144, 144–145
	S	*A Place to Grow*	148
	S	*What Baby Needs*	151
Using English as a second language	S	*The Brand New Kid*	144–145
Using letter–sound correspondence	S	*The Brand New Kid*	144–145
	I	*What Baby Needs*	151–152
Using phonics: Onsets and rimes	S, I	*What Baby Needs*	151, 151–152
Using phonics: Rhyming words	S	*What Baby Needs*	151
Using verbs	D	*A Place to Grow*	147–148
	D	*What Baby Needs*	150–151
Writing descriptive sentences	UC	—	152–153
	D, I	*The Brand New Kid*	143–144, 145
	C, D, I	*A Place to Grow*	147, 147–148, 148–149
	D	*What Baby Needs*	150–151

* Indicates a new-literacy skill.
U = unit introduction; R = read-aloud and book discussion ideas; C = creativity and presentation software ideas; D = Digital Language Experience Approach; S = computer software activity; I = Internet resources and ideas; UC = unit conclusion

Unit Introduction

MATERIALS

- Chart paper
- This unit's books
- Markers

Tell students you are going to look at changes and difficulties people experience at school and at home. Share a time in your own life when you felt confused by some change in your family or at school. Perhaps it was the birth of a new brother or sister that made you feel less important. However, in time you realized you had a new place in the family. You became the older sister or brother, which meant you

Figure 25
Story Predictions

What changes or difficulties should we expect to find in the stories?

The Brand New Kid (Couric, 2000)	A Place to Grow (Pak, 2002)	What Baby Needs (Sears, Sears, & Kelly, 2001)

had special privileges and responsibilities. You learned that change could be good, too. Although we may at first think change is scary, we often find it is not. Quite often, it simply means we are growing up. Show students the covers of the three books in the unit. Ask them to predict what the books might be about. Write on chart paper students' predictions in a chart that includes each book (see Figure 25).

Tell students that the books you will be reading in this unit all help us understand how different characters handle changes and difficulties they experience at home and at school. Ask students as they listen to the stories to think about a time in their lives when things changed or were difficult and what they did to solve the problem.

Book 1: The Brand New Kid

Couric, K. (2000). Ill. M. Priceman. New York: Scholastic. $15.95. 32 pp.

BOOK REVIEW

Lazlo S. Gasky's first day of school in the United States may not be what he expected. His Hungarian features and accent draw ridicule from the other students, who perceive his differences negatively. Their teasing and humiliating tricks, such as tripping him in the cafeteria, draw concern from Ellie, a classmate who takes a courageous step toward befriending Lazlo. When the other students ask her, "Are you sick in the head?" Ellie tells them, "Now I know him you see. He isn't that different from you and from me" (n.p.). Katie Couric, NBC's coanchor on the *Today Show*, writes in her introduction that as a journalist she is concerned about the "frightening incidents of school violence that can arise from feeling alienated and ostracized" (n.p.). Her purpose for writing *The Brand New Kid* was to inspire others to reach out and help someone feel "a little less scared and a little less lonely" (n.p.). Classrooms—where such feelings begin and grow—seem a good place to start. Caldecott Honor artist Marjorie Priceman's pen and watercolor art portrays the emotions of the characters with sensitive facial expressions and colorful hues, giving Couric's message dramatic punch.

READ-ALOUD AND BOOK DISCUSSION IDEAS

Before reading the book, show students the cover and ask them what they see. What sort of expression does Lazlo have on his face? Why? What might be happening in this story? Either share a time with students when you have felt disliked or ask them to think of a similar example when they felt disliked. Most of us have experienced situations when we just did not feel accepted. Tell students that the boy in the story is a newcomer and you want them to listen to find out the story's problem.

MATERIALS

- Markers
- Poster board

During reading, point out key vocabulary words that help students understand the story (e.g., *squealed, strudel, checkmate*). Remind students to help you figure out how the young girl helps others understand that people have more in common than they might think.

After reading the book, ask the class what sorts of things they can do to help new students feel welcome. Add interesting vocabulary to a vocabulary chart on poster board titled "Words About Change at School and Home."

COMPUTER ACTIVITIES

Creativity and Presentation Software Ideas

MATERIALS

- KidPix Studio Deluxe (1998) or Kidspiration 2.1 (2005) software

Integrate social studies and math concepts using a Venn diagram labeled "About Us" (see Figure 26) to help students describe similarities and differences about themselves. Briefly explain the process and purpose of creating a Venn diagram to use as a graphic organizer to help students think about differences and similarities.

1. Create a template with KidPix Studio Deluxe or Kidspiration 2.1 creativity and presentation software that asks students to describe and make a list of what they want to be when they grow up, the color of their eyes, and a few of their personal favorites (e.g., sports, pets, music, books, movies). Students may dictate, stamp icons, draw on screen, or type simple answers to these questions. Emerging or developing readers can stamp or drag icons that depict similarities and differences within the Venn diagram template. For developing readers, you can provide a word bank or let them use inventive spelling, in which students spell words phonetically when they are unsure of the exact spelling. Inventive spelling encourages learners to experiment with letters and creative writing without being expected to follow conventional rules.

2. Ask two students to work at the computer center to create the Venn diagram using the template. Instruct one student to fill in the left circle and another student to fill in the right circle with stamped icons that represent their lists. Focus on the central section of the Venn

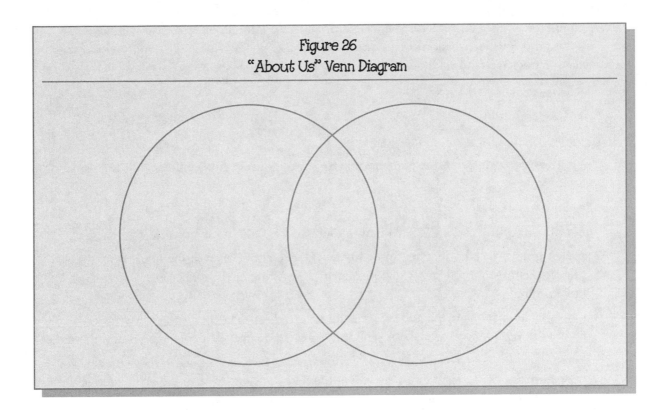

Figure 26
"About Us" Venn Diagram

diagram that indicates all of the things that students share in common. Highlight adjectives that help describe who they are. Emerging or developing readers may need the help of a cross-age computer buddy, teaching assistant, or parent volunteer.

3. Encourage students to share their Venn diagrams during whole-group time and relate how knowing all of the ways that they are similar might help if a new student joins the class. Remind students how creating a Venn diagram and graphic organizer on screen helped support their thinking processes.

4. For author's computer chair (see Appendix B), ask students to refer to the "About Us" Venn Diagram to compare their lists (see Figure 26). Students can answer the following questions: What is the same? What is different? What would the world be like if everyone was the same?

Digital Language Experience Approach

Tell students you are going to be making a book to help any new students or visitors to your classroom feel welcome, become acquainted, and feel comfortable with classroom routines and events. Arrange students in teams, assigning a task to each team.

1. During whole-group time, brainstorm with students the things they think would be important for a new student to know. Generate a list of useful information on the blackboard or on the

MATERIALS

■ Blackboard
■ Chalk
■ Digital camera
■ Microsoft Paint (1981–2001) or PowerPoint (Microsoft Office 2003, 2003) software

computer (with a monitor large enough for all to see). In either case, you will want to record the finished version on the computer for use as new students are enrolled in your class. Some things to include are

- school rules,

- classroom rules,

- map of the classroom and school,

- pictures and descriptions of the room (e.g., whole-group rug, centers, cubbies, desks or table),

- daily routines, and

- a picture of the class. (When a new student arrives, take a new picture.)

2. Assign groups to take pictures and write a sentence about each of the items from the list. Import pictures into creativity and presentation software such as Microsoft Paint or PowerPoint.

3. On separate screens or pages, ask each student to dictate, keyboard, or draw his or her favorite thing about your class or school. Be sure to include students' names and the date.

4. Encourage students to make suggestions for what to include in a welcome statement for new students. Write a summary statement of welcome to include in the last pages of the book. As you reread the text, invite students to point to words they recognize. Revise and edit by cutting and pasting using creativity and presentation software tools. This activity models for students how to revise their compositions easily.

5. Print out the book pages, design a book cover, decide on the appropriate sequence of pages, and bind the book. Ask a student to volunteer to look at the book with new students or visitors to help them become acquainted with the class. When new students or parents arrive, share the book with them.

6. Other groups of students will enjoy sharing the book they created for new students during author's computer chair (see Appendix B).

Computer Software Activity

MATERIALS

■ Living Books: Mercer Mayer's Little Monster at School (1996) software

In the Living Books: Mercer Mayer's Little Monster at School software, students can spend a virtual day with Little Monster and his friends at school, learning about ABCs, mathematics, music, and science. Little Monster also models making friends. Exploring this living book and listening to the story will help emerging readers learn concepts about print as they notice left-to-right directionality while they highlight the text. Emerging and developing readers also will benefit from echo reading in response to the story narrator. Fluent readers will enjoy practicing reading along with the story narrator. This living book offers students many entertaining learning adventures. Students can read the interactive text in English or Spanish. Support English as a second language students by allowing them to read or listen to the story in Spanish first.

1. Tell students they can repeat any part of the text or skip back to a previous page by just pointing and clicking. Students will enjoy exploring the environment and characters because it is entertaining and there are many humorous things to learn. Ask developing readers to first listen to the story and then go through the story again, clicking on any word that they do not know so that they can hear the word read by the program.

2. Ask students to be prepared to tell you how Little Monster made friends just like Ellie made friends in the book you read aloud.

Internet Resources and Ideas

Starfall.com—It's Fun to Read: All About Me! www.starfall.com/n/level-b/me/load.htm?f
Click on the ear in the lower left corner to hear the text read aloud, or have students click on the individual words they do not know. There are options for girls or boys to explore (i.e., students can follow gender-specific paths and create a boy or girl that represents themselves). Each student can create a picture of himself or herself from a template of choices. Once created, the animated self will follow him or her through creating pets, toys, and rooms in virtual homes. This interactive book is easy for even the youngest students to complete. After students create a picture of themselves, have them print it out. Assign students in pairs and ask them to compare the selves they have created to find the similarities and differences. Tie these comparisons to what students learned in the story you read aloud.

Starfall.com—I'm Reading, Chinese Fables: One Rice Thousand Gold: www.starfall.com/n/chinese-fables/one-rice/load.htm?f
Fluent readers will enjoy reading the text, while developing readers may want to highlight the unfamiliar words to hear them read. Emerging readers can be paired with cross-age buddies who are fluent readers. This fable offers an additional opportunity to teach students that people of different lands share many of the same feelings and values as people in the United States.

Book 2:   A Place to Grow

Pak, S. (2002). Ill. M. Truong. New York: Arthur A. Levine Books. $16.95. 32 pp.

BOOK REVIEW

A Place to Grow is a multicultural book about a Korean father and his daughter. The father explains to his daughter why he immigrated to a new land by making comparisons between a family's growing needs and a seed's search for the right soil, sun, and rain to grow. For example, he tells her, "Good land is warm and safe, like a cozy home. It protects the seed and helps it to grow" (n.p.). A place with too little or too much rain is similar to "when there are too many workers and not enough work. A place like that is no place to grow a flower" (n.p.). The story ends with the daughter asking her father, "Will I fly with the wind?" (n.p.) and his response, "Even if you fly across the tallest mountains, the longest roads, and the widest seas, there will always be a garden in my heart for you" (n.p.). Beautiful opaque watercolors chronicle the seed's search for a garden to grow in. Repeated lines will engage students in chanting, "So the seed flew with the wind' I ask. 'It flew with the wind' he says" (n.p.).

READ-ALOUD AND BOOK DISCUSSION IDEAS

MATERIALS

- Chart paper
- Markers

Before reading, display the book cover and ask students to make predictions about the story's characters, setting, problem, and solution. Write predictions on chart paper and encourage students to explain their predictions by pointing out picture details or by making connections to their own background experiences. Then complete a picture walk, examining all pictures, and adjust or add to the previous predictions.

During reading, tell students that as you read the story you want them to listen for three things that the seed and people need in order to grow.

After reading, list students' observations on a chart titled "What Seeds and People Need to Grow" (see Figure 27). Leave the chart posted in the room to serve as a word bank for later creative writing activities. Ask students if the story would be different if it was about a father and daughter from another country or culture. Why or why not?

Figure 27
"What Seeds and People Need to Grow" Chart

What Seeds and People Need to Grow

Seeds	People
rich soil	shelter
rain	love
sun	safety

COMPUTER ACTIVITIES

Creativity and Presentation Software Ideas

Invite students to use multimedia authoring tools in creativity and presentation software, such as KidPix Studio Deluxe, to create a picture of their "Perfect Place to Grow." Using multimedia tools that allow students to paint, stamp icons, write, import clip art, and so forth, ask students to make a picture of a place they think would be the best place to grow up. Help them recall the conditions for a healthy environment that are mentioned in the book. Teachers can ask students to work in groups to come up with a list of these conditions or request that they do another picture walk to help them remember. Students can present their multimedia slides during author's computer chair (see Appendix B).

MATERIALS

■ KidPix Studio Deluxe (1998) software

Digital Language Experience Approach

Write a letter (see Figure 28) to students' parents and caregivers explaining that the unit you are teaching focuses on discussing good places to grow.

1. Invite family members to use a disposable digital camera that you send home to take three to four photographs of their family.

MATERIALS

■ Disposable digital camera
■ Invitations
■ Kidspiration 2.1 (2005) software

Figure 28
"All About Families" Letter to Parents and Caregivers

Dear Parents and Caregivers,

We are learning about good places to grow. Recently we have studied the books *A Place to Grow, The Brand New Kid*, and *What Baby Needs*. To enrich this learning experience, we want to learn more about how families are alike and different. We especially want to learn about how families from different cultures create unique and wonderful places for students to grow.

We will be sending home a digital disposable camera for you to help your child take three or four pictures of a family activity (e.g., eating a meal, reading together, playing outside together, or any other activity that your family shares). Your child will also want to interview you with a few simple questions regarding a move your family may have made at some time in your life.

Please send the camera, after you have taken the pictures, to school with your child on [day and date]. Your child will prepare an "All About Families" computer presentation with those pictures, so please do not have the pictures developed.

To celebrate this experience, your child will send home invitations for you to attend this event.

Sincerely,
Your Child's Teacher

2. Encourage them to photograph things that make their families a good place to grow (e.g., eating a meal; sharing time together; playing outside; if appropriate, going to church; having a place to sleep).

3. Encourage students to interview their parents by asking if they have ever moved from one place to another. Why did they move to another location? What good things happened because they moved?

4. Develop and import the photographs and arrange them on a screen page of Kidspiration 2.1 or other creativity and presentation software, and leave room for the students to type a sentence or two explaining the pictures they took. Invite students to talk about their family and explain the pictures they chose. Be sure to discuss how families are the same and how they are different. Highlight the ways that families from different cultures create unique and wonderful places for children to grow.

5. During author's computer chair (see Appendix B), invite students to share their "Perfect Place to Grow" pictures and to demonstrate and explain how they created the pictures using the drawing tools. Some students will enjoy sharing the stories they created online.

6. Invite family members to attend a special "All About Families" event. Instruct students to make invitations. Post special family photographs on a bulletin board, and share family stories during whole-group time. Thank parents for attending and sharing their stories with the class.

Computer Software Activity

MATERIALS

■ Orly's Draw-a-Story (1996) software

Students can virtually experience what it might be like to move to a new place and have adventures in a new cultural setting. Orly's Draw-a-Story, set in Jamaica, invites students to enter into a story world as Orly, the main character, introduces a story premise. A drawing pad appears, as well as basic drawing tools. Students can choose from premade drawings. As Orly tells stories (four stories are available), students are invited to make pictures that accompany various story parts. Students will be motivated to continue participating when they see that the characters they have created are included in the next sections of the animated story. Students continue through several screens of the story until a sequence of pictures culminates in a completed story that can be saved and viewed repeatedly. Drawings can also be printed out for story extension activities such as sharing how they created their stories during author's computer chair (see Appendix B).

Internet Resources and Ideas

British Broadcasting Corporation: Science Clips: www.bbc.co.uk/schools/scienceclips/ages/ 5_6/science_5_6.shtml
On this interactive BBC website, click on the picture titled "Growing Plants" to add sunlight and water to help the plant grow. Audio directions walk students through each step. Students use on-screen tools to provide the perfect growing environment. Younger students may need the help of a cross-age computer buddy.

Play! Scholastic: Root Race: www.scholastic.com/play/root.htm

This website provides a Scholastic interactive game activity in which students select a vegetable and—according to its animated, emotional face—decide if it needs water, food, or air to grow.

Starfall.com: Download: Reading and Writing Journal, Level I: www.starfall.com/ni/download/level-1b/wk201.pdf

This is a free downloadable PDF file. Scroll down to page 90 and print out the page. Students can draw a picture and write a story about their families. This printable document includes writing prompts about family. Students identify their family members and write about something they enjoy doing together that makes home a perfect place to grow.

Book 3:   What Baby Needs

Sears, W., Sears, M., & Kelly, C.W. (2001). Ill. R. Andriani. New York: Little, Brown. $12.99. 32 pp.

BOOK REVIEW

William and Martha Sears, parents of eight children, inform siblings-to-be what it is going to be like as an older sister or brother. The authors are pediatric specialists (a doctor–nurse team) who approach this topic from an attachment parenting perspective. Attachment parenting subscribes to the notion that dependency on parents is a natural aspect of childhood and that parents should trust their instincts to meet the child's needs. The 5 Bs—baby bonding, breastfeeding, baby wearing (i.e., keeping the baby close to the parent's body via a sling or baby carrier), being flexible, and belief in the language value of a baby's cry—are covered in simple terms. The message is clear that meeting students' needs in a developmentally appropriate way will establish connected relationships based on love and trust. A special feature of this book is the writing style. Written in the second person, text such as "your family's new baby" and "you are growing up, becoming an older brother or sister," conveys the special role older siblings will play as part of the family. Callouts throughout the text highlight the needs older siblings have and provide an opportunity for students to express those feelings constructively.

READ-ALOUD AND BOOK DISCUSSION IDEAS

Most books introduce having a new baby to the only child in a family. *What Baby Needs* (Sears, Sears, & Kelly, 2001) introduces life with a new baby for the benefit of the existing children in the family (i.e., a growing family with two or more existing siblings). Many kindergartners through second graders may have new babies arriving in their families. It is important for them to understand that families change all the time, but the one thing that remains constant is that families love each other. Some families merge when parents divorce and remarry. Children in these blended families need to learn how to get along with older or younger siblings and stepsiblings. Thus, this book is appropriate for exploring the nature of family changes.

Before reading, show the book cover to students and ask them to consider the sorts of changes they might expect with a new baby (e.g., parents may have less time to help with homework, students may have to take on new chores, older siblings will be role models). Ask students to predict what they would look forward to and what sorts of things they might have concerns about. During reading, confirm or change students' predictions, asking students to explain their reasoning. After reading, ask students to discuss what they think the author wanted them to learn about family changes when a new baby arrives. Highlight vocabulary words about families and change that students enjoyed.

COMPUTER ACTIVITIES

Creativity and Presentation Software Ideas

MATERIALS

- KidPix Studio Deluxe (1998) software

1. Discuss cause and effect by summarizing the ideas presented in the book and doing a picture walk through the book.

2. Using KidPix Studio Deluxe creativity and presentation software, ask students to draw, stamp pictures, and write on screen about what they would expect with a new baby in the family. (This exercise could be adapted to include new family members in blended families.)

3. Print out and ask students to share their illustrated sentences in whole-group discussions about the story or during author's computer chair (see Appendix B).

4. Develop a word bank for new vocabulary words encountered. Display on the wall in the classroom for students to use in subsequent writing activities.

Digital Language Experience Approach

MATERIALS

- 8 1/2 x 11" paper
- Digital camera
- KidPix Studio Deluxe (1998) software

To help students understand how much they have grown and their families have changed since they were babies, follow these steps:

1. Prepare a simple template with creativity and presentation software, such as KidPix Studio Deluxe, that reads, "The three things I liked as a baby were _____, but the three things I like now that I'm bigger are _____."

2. Take a picture of each student with a digital camera and print it out. The picture should be no bigger than two or three inches and should be placed at the top of an 8 1/2 x 11" sheet of paper.

3. Prepare sample questions for students to think about (e.g., How have your family members changed since you were a baby? How have your favorites things changed since you were a baby?) Other questions might focus on vacations, sports, or hobbies.

4. Encourage emerging and developing readers to use inventive spelling and fluent readers to use conventional spelling. Students can also dictate their lists. For example, one student might write, "The three things I liked as a baby were crying, crawling, and sleeping a lot, but the three things I like now are laughing, walking, and eating pizza."

5. Save for a slide show and make printouts to send home for students to read to their parents.

Computer Software Activity

What would it be like not just to have a new baby in the family but at work, too? "The Bread That Grew" e-book gives students a glimpse into what might happen in that situation. Emerging and developing readers will enjoy listening and reading along with Baby Beth when she confuses words that sound alike and creates havoc in a bakery. Reading this e-book will reinforce concepts about print for emerging readers and help developing and fluent readers build background knowledge as they relate the story and puzzles to their real-life experiences.

> **MATERIALS**
>
> ■ The Bread That Grew (2002–2003) CD-ROM

1. The first screen enables users to access and create multiple activities with puzzles, letter–sound relationships, and simple movies. After students have listened to the story, invite them to read it again, drawing their attention to concepts about print, such as directionality (e.g., reading left to right), and sight words they recognize.

2. Fluent readers will enjoy listening to the story first and then trying to read expressively in the style of the narrator.

3. This interactive storybook can be read independently, or students can click on the words to have them read.

Internet Resources and Ideas

KidsHealth for Kids: Dealing With Feelings: www.kidshealth.org/kid/feeling
This website has multiple references for teachers' use. Particularly useful are the My Home & Family and My School sections. The My Home & Family section has information about sibling rivalry and the addition of a new baby in the family. Once you click on the article, be sure to look on the tabs on the right side of the page for more information. Some articles have film clips of children discussing the topics.

EdHelper.com: www.edhelper.com/clipart/teachers/org-famtree.pdf and www.edhelper.com/clipart/teachers/org-coatofarms.pdf
Print these templates to help students learn about family. The first is a template for a family tree. Students can add their parents, grandparents, siblings, and other family members. The second website suggests creating a coat of arms representing family. Students draw an icon in each quadrant. The icons can represent family interests, traditions, or activities.

Starfall.com—Learn to Read, Y Can Be a Vowel: www.starfall.com/n/y-as-e/y-as-e/load.html
This website offers a clever interactive e-book on a change to a family—a new baby sister. After listening to a brief animated song about the letter *y*, which is sometimes identified as a vowel, a hand points toward a green arrow to get to the first page of the book. Students can click on each word and hear it read aloud. They will also see a pop-up screen that shows the word, stretches the sounds, and pronounces the word. Each page has an interesting camera and film icon. Clicking on the icon results in a pop-up screen of a snapshot. Students will enjoy seeing the changes that occur in the family when the little green creature becomes the older sibling. When students finish the book, they can rate the story. At the end of the story, there is an extensive list of other interactive books and games that will help students practice phonic elements such as word families.

Unit Conclusion

Build a class time capsule out of a shoe box to help students practice their abilities to make logical predictions, analyze artifacts to seek evidence of change, and reflect on how changes they have experienced over time may have been difficult but resulted in positive outcomes. Explain that a time capsule is a container people or communities use to express what life was like during a particular time period. Tell students that you will be making a time capsule that is intended to represent how things are today. Explain that the class will revisit the time capsule in two months to see how their lives (or interests or activities) have changed.

MATERIALS

- Calendar
- Chart paper
- Markers
- Shoe box
- Tape
- Wrapping paper

1. Review how things changed for each of the characters in the stories you read during the unit from the beginning to the ending of the books. Ask students if they think that the main characters could have predicted what those changes would entail. Why or why not?

2. Invite students to include information about themselves to put in a time capsule shoe box. Students can

   - provide a dated piece of paper that shows how they write their names today,

   - put in a dated sample of schoolwork, and

   - draw a self-portrait or a picture of their families.

3. On chart paper, list students' predictions about how things might be different for them or the class in two months. Include this information in the time capsule shoe box.

4. Wrap the box in paper, tape the ends, write today's date and the name of the teacher's class on the box, and place it in a secure place.

5. Write on a calendar the exact day when the capsule will be opened during whole-group time.

6. Open the time capsule shoe box in two months to examine how students have changed and grown during the school year.

When you reopen the capsule, update the information and make comparisons. Ask students to talk about their observations and write about the changes they see in themselves and in the class. What has changed? What is the same? Revisit some of the students' favorite books from the unit. What are their new favorite books and why?

"While we were reading the books and doing the activities in this unit, we were able to have several in-depth, meaningful discussions about how we are each different. I think the most important moments occurred when we thought about how our differences make us special—and interesting."

—SECOND-GRADE TEACHER

Appreciating Differences

UNIT BOOKS

Nadia's Hands
By Karen English
Illustrated by Jonathan Weiner

The Hickory Chair
By Lisa Rowe Fraustino
Illustrated by Benny Andrews

Sidney Won't Swim
By Hilde Schuurmans

COMPUTER RESOURCES

My First Incredible Amazing Dictionary
Reader Rabbit's Toddler
Sheila Rae, the Brave

Thematic Connection

Students bring to school rich and subtle differences in home language, cultural heritage, religious beliefs, holiday celebrations, and even food preferences. Becoming aware of how people are alike and how they are unique can be a fascinating journey for students to develop an appreciation of differences. In addition, when a student learns to celebrate differences in others, he or she is likely to learn how to recognize and enjoy his or her individuality. Reading, discussing, and responding to the books in this unit may help students feel more compassion for classmates who have different customs, abilities, or even fears. The first book, *Nadia's Hands* (English, 1999), is a tale about the conflict a young girl feels about participating in a cultural tradition that she feels may separate her from her friends and the mainstream culture. *The Hickory Chair* (Fraustino, 2001) offers an opportunity for encouraging students' empathy toward others with physical limitations and underscores the importance of recognizing the unique abilities embodied by a young boy with limited vision. *Sidney Won't Swim* (Schuurmans, 2002) encourages students' empathy for a child who fears being in the water. The activities in this unit are designed to help students learn that being different does not mean being less valued. Learning to appreciate differences in others is often a process of demystification, which happens when students have the opportunity to ask questions about those differences and have their questions answered.

Matrix of Literacy Skills and Strategies in Unit 10

Literacy Skills and Strategies	Activities	Title of Book	Pages
Brainstorming	U	—	157
	I	*Nadia's Hands*	161
	C	*Sidney Won't Swim*	165
Building background knowledge on the Internet*	R, I	*Nadia's Hands*	158–159, 161
	R, I	*The Hickory Chair*	162, 164
	I	*Sidney Won't Swim*	166–167
Building fluency	S	*Sidney Won't Swim*	166
Comparing and contrasting	UC	—	167–168
	D, I	*Nadia's Hands*	159–160, 161
	D	*Sidney Won't Swim*	166
Composing in multimedia*	C, D	*Nadia's Hands*	159, 159–160
	C, D	*The Hickory Chair*	162–163, 163–164
	C, D	*Sidney Won't Swim*	165, 166
Determining chronological order	R	*Nadia's Hands*	158–159
Determining story details	R	*Nadia's Hands*	158–159
Developing a sense of beginnings, middles, and endings	R	*Nadia's Hands*	158–159
	D	*Sidney Won't Swim*	166
Developing and using story grammar	R	*Nadia's Hands*	158–159
	R	*The Hickory Chair*	162
	R, S	*Sidney Won't Swim*	165, 166
Developing choral reading	R, S	*Sidney Won't Swim*	165, 166
Developing comprehension	U	—	157
	R	*Nadia's Hands*	158–159
	R	*The Hickory Chair*	162
	R, S	*Sidney Won't Swim*	165, 166
Developing context clues	R	*The Hickory Chair*	162
	R	*Sidney Won't Swim*	165
Developing creative writing	C	*Nadia's Hands*	159
	C	*Sidney Won't Swim*	165
Developing critical reading and thinking	R	*Sidney Won't Swim*	165

(continued)

Matrix of Literacy Skills and Strategies in Unit 10 (continued)

Literacy Skills and Strategies	Activities	Title of Book	Pages
Developing oral language	U, UC	—	157, 167–168
	R, C, D	*Nadia's Hands*	158–159, 159, 159–160
	R, C, D, I	*The Hickory Chair*	162, 162–163, 163–164, 164
	R, D, I	*Sidney Won't Swim*	165, 166, 166–167
Developing vocabulary	U, UC	—	157, 167–168
	R, S	*Nadia's Hands*	158–159, 160
	R, C, D	*The Hickory Chair*	162, 162–163, 163–164
	C	*Sidney Won't Swim*	165
Distinguishing sounds	S	*The Hickory Chair*	164
Drawing conclusions	R	*Sidney Won't Swim*	165
E-mailing*	I	*Nadia's Hands*	161
	I	*The Hickory Chair*	164
Following directions	UC	—	167–168
	C, D, I	*Nadia's Hands*	159, 159–160, 161
	C, D, S	*The Hickory Chair*	162–163, 163–164, 164
	C, D, S, I	*Sidney Won't Swim*	165, 166, 166, 166–167
Inferring	R, S	*The Hickory Chair*	162, 164
	I	*Sidney Won't Swim*	166–167
Making multicultural connections	UC	—	167–168
	R, C, D, I	*Nadia's Hands*	158–159, 159, 159–160, 161
	I	*The Hickory Chair*	164
Making predictions	R	*Nadia's Hands*	158–159
Navigating hyperlinks*	R, S, I	*Nadia's Hands*	158–159, 160, 161
	S, I	*The Hickory Chair*	164
	S, I	*Sidney Won't Swim*	166, 166–167
Presenting work on a computer*	D	*Nadia's Hands*	159–160
	C, D, I	*The Hickory Chair*	162–163, 163–164, 164
	D	*Sidney Won't Swim*	166
Reading aloud	UC	—	167–168
	R	*Nadia's Hands*	158–159
	R	*The Hickory Chair*	162
	R, S	*Sidney Won't Swim*	165, 166
Reading and listening for a purpose	U	—	157
	R, I	*Nadia's Hands*	158–159, 161
	R, D, S	*The Hickory Chair*	162, 163–164, 164
	R, S	*Sidney Won't Swim*	165, 166
Reading and using map skills	S	*Sidney Won't Swim*	166
Reading informational text	S, I	*Nadia's Hands*	160, 161
	I	*The Hickory Chair*	164
Retelling	R, D	*Sidney Won't Swim*	165, 166
Selecting parts of speech	D	*The Hickory Chair*	163–164

(continued)

Literacy Skills and Strategies	Activities	Title of Book	Pages
Sequencing	C, D	*Nadia's Hands*	159, 159–160
	C	*Sidney Won't Swim*	165
Summarizing	UC	—	167–168
Understanding a main idea	R, C, D	*Nadia's Hands*	158–159, 159, 159–160
	R, C, D	*The Hickory Chair*	162, 162–163, 163–164
	S, I	*Sidney Won't Swim*	166, 166–167
Understanding story structure and events	R	*Nadia's Hands*	158–159
	D, S	*Sidney Won't Swim*	166
Using adjectives	UC	—	167–168
	I	*Nadia's Hands*	161
	D	*The Hickory Chair*	163–164
Using English as a second language	UC	—	167–168
	S	*Sidney Won't Swim*	166
Using nouns	D	*The Hickory Chair*	163–164
Using verbs	D	*The Hickory Chair*	163–164
Visualizing	R	*The Hickory Chair*	162
Writing descriptive sentences	UC	—	167–168
	C, D, I	*Nadia's Hands*	159, 159–160, 161

* Indicates a new-literacy skill.

U = unit introduction; R = read-aloud and book discussion ideas; C = creativity and presentation software ideas; D = Digital Language Experience Approach; S = computer software activity; I = Internet resources and ideas; UC = unit conclusion

Unit Introduction

Display a closed box of eight crayons and ask students to brainstorm by naming their favorite colors. List the colors on the board. Tell students that your favorite color is blue. Open the box and show that there are eight blue crayons in the box, instead of the expected variety. Draw a line through the list of colors students have mentioned. Show a picture that has been colored with only blue. Ask them how they would feel if they could only use blue crayons at school? How would our world look colored only in blue?

Tell students that the books you will be reading in this unit help us understand better how to recognize and celebrate how people are different and how their differences add color to our world. Characters in these stories, who are different in some way from their friends, learn valuable lessons about their strengths.

MATERIALS

- Blackboard
- Box of eight crayons
- Chalk
- Picture colored only with blue

English, K. (1999). Ill. J. Weiner. Honesdale, PA: Boyds Mills Press. $16.95. 32 pp.

BOOK REVIEW

Nadia, a Pakistani American girl, is chosen to be the flower girl in her aunt's wedding. Nadia's cousins recount some difficulties they experienced as flower girls in previous family weddings. Traditional wedding preparations include painting designs with a rich henna paste (*mehndi*) on the hands of the women in the wedding party. Although Nadia is honored to be chosen, she knows the paste is indelible and will not wear off before she returns to school on Monday. Nadia is torn between a sense of responsibility to her family and her need for acceptance within her peer group—a group of students she fears is likely to tease her for being different. After the wedding, Nadia comforts herself when she decides to explain how her "Pakistani hands" will look to her classmates at school during sharing time. The rich oil pastel artwork rendered in jewel tones of green, pink, and brilliant blue conveys Nadia's fears and portrays the significance of cultural heritage and tradition in Nadia's large and loving family.

READ-ALOUD AND BOOK DISCUSSION IDEAS

Before reading, display a picture of a traditional Western wedding, complete with a bride in white, a groom in a tuxedo, and a flower girl. Photographs of students in weddings are available free online at www.ruscelli.com/weddings_kids_photos.htm. As you scroll down the webpage, you will find photographs of flower girls, junior bridesmaids, and ring bearers of all ages. The same website offers photographs of complete wedding parties. Tell your students that it is a very special family event when students are asked to participate in a wedding. Tell them that you are going to read a book about a young girl who was asked to be in a wedding. Although this girl felt honored to be in her aunt's wedding, she also felt very worried about being part of this special event. Why would someone feel worried about being in a family wedding?

MATERIALS

■ Photograph of a traditional Western wedding

During reading, tell students that as you read the book, you want them to listen for why Nadia was not sure that she wanted to be in the family wedding. Next, display the book cover, drawing attention to the illustration of painted hands. Ask students to predict what a picture of painted hands might have to do with a wedding celebration. While reading the book, use author notes included after the title page to explain special vocabulary terms.

After reading, talk about what happened at the beginning, middle, and end of the story to help students gain a sense of basic chronological order in stories. Ask students to consider what they would say or do if a Pakistani classmate came to school with *mehndi*. Focus on ways classmates can be supportive of one another's traditions. There is a sense in this book that Nadia's invitation to participate in the wedding is a rite of passage. In order to point out that all people have special cultural traditions, give examples of similar rites of passage or traditions with which students from your local communities are familiar.

COMPUTER ACTIVITIES

Creativity and Presentation Software Ideas

MATERIALS

- Construction paper
- Glue
- KidPix Studio Deluxe (1998) software
- Markers
- Paper
- Scissors
- Tag board or stiff paper

1. To support students' appreciation of the artistry involved in the painted hand designs, ask them to fill a computer screen with a pattern of shapes or stamped icons using creativity and presentation software (e.g., KidPix Studio Deluxe).

2. Print out the patterns on the tag board or stiff paper.

3. Trace each student's hand on the tag board or stiff paper with the printed designs and cut it out.

4. Paste the cut-out hand shape on a brightly colored piece of construction paper to capture the vibrancy of the illustrations from the book.

5. Instruct students to sign their name on their illustration and write or dictate a sentence of advice they would give to Nadia about being in the wedding. How would they have helped her feel good about participating?

6. Display the work on a bulletin board or bind in a class book titled "Our Advice to Nadia."

Digital Language Experience Approach

MATERIALS

- Chart paper
- Disposable digital camera
- Glue
- Letter to parents
- Markers
- Microsoft Paint (1981–2001) or PowerPoint (Microsoft Office 2003, 2003) software
- Poster board

Reinforce home–school and multicultural connections by inviting students to use a disposable digital camera to work together to create a collage of family traditions snapshots. Remind students that Nadia's family had unique customs that they enjoyed, especially in relation to celebrating a wedding. All families have traditions, habits, or events that they value and enjoy. This activity is designed to help students celebrate and learn more about how each of their families is different and special.

1. Send home a letter to parents and caregivers that explains the activity and provides some examples. For example, a sports-minded family could take digital photographs of sporting events, practice sessions, and spectatorship. Other families might want to document a love for pets, religious events, or various types of family gatherings.

2. Import digital photographs into creativity and presentation software such as Microsoft Paint or PowerPoint. Instruct each student to select three to five photographs to include either on a computer screen for a slide show or on poster board as a printout.

3. Instruct each student to arrange and assemble the photographs on chart paper or on screen.

4. Discuss each family poster as students assemble it. Talk about what makes each family's interests and traditions special. Students dictate key phrases or sentences about their valued cultural and family traditions that make them different and special.

5. Display family posters around the room or down the hallways or have a slide show celebration. Guide a discussion on comparisons for the things that families have in common and the things that make families unique (e.g., some families have one parent, some have four, with stepparents; some families enjoy going to church, but most go to different types of churches; some families enjoy meals cooked at home, while other families enjoy eating at restaurants for special events). With parental permission, the teacher can add collages to the class webpage.

6. One group of students may want to share their D-LEA family collage pictures. For that group, discuss how the family photographs express each family's unique experiences and traditions.

⟋ Computer Software Activity

Reinforce computer skills and build vocabulary by asking students to further explore the meaning of words introduced in the story *Nadia's Hands* (English, 1999). Students can make real-life connections by suggesting words they know that could be related to the story. After reading the book aloud to students, ask them to suggest five vocabulary words related to the story for further word study.

1. Model how to use the My First Incredible Amazing Dictionary CD-ROM.

2. Post a list of students' chosen five words on a chart in the computer center with the reminder "Look up one of these words and tell [teacher's name here] about it."

3. During computer-center time, ask students to use the My First Incredible Amazing Dictionary CD-ROM to look up the meaning of at least one word. If they have time or are working with a computer buddy, they may look up and write definitions for more than one.

4. Invite students to share the words they have learned more about during author's computer chair (see Appendix B). Other students may want to explain how they created designs for their hands as an extension of the story or explain words they learned with My First Incredible Amazing Dictionary (1995). Be sure to load the CD-ROM and cue to the appropriate section so students easily can display and discuss what they learned and discuss which software tools they used. If time permits, discuss keypal exchanges. Always relate students' comments back to the stories they have read or listened to by explaining the relationship or asking the student to explain the relationship between real-life experiences and the characters' experiences.

ZAWAJ.COM: Wedding Customs Around the Muslim World: www.zawaj.com/weddingways/ three_days.html

Take a virtual field trip as a guest to a Muslim wedding that has traditional garb, customs, and an example of *mehndi* being applied to the bride. The text may be too difficult for younger emerging readers. Teachers either can read the text to students or just let them scroll through the prenuptial and ceremonial pictures. The colorful pictures give a chronological account of the ceremony. What adjectives would students use to describe the clothing and events? After viewing, ask students to compare what they have seen on this website to the wedding depicted in the featured story or to a traditional U.S. wedding ceremony or any other traditional weddings they have experienced.

Busy Teacher's Cafe Pen Pal Exchange: www.busyteacherscafe.com/penpals.htm

This website provides a list of contact information for teachers who are looking for pen pal classes. Students can choose a keypal (which is called a keyboard pal on this website) and exchange e-mail messages to learn about other people and places. Students will practice writing and keyboarding skills while increasing multicultural awareness by communicating with students in other regions and from other cultures.

1. Ask students to exchange information about their cultures and traditions and facts about their homeland.

2. Encourage students to exchange a series of two or three messages that are simple and to the point.

3. Brainstorm with students what they would like to learn. List questions on a chart posted by the computer that is connected to the Internet. Questions may consist of the following: What do you wear? What is your favorite holiday? What do you like to eat?

4. Read aloud the answers that students receive during author's computer chair (see Appendix B).

5. Print and post the messages on a bulletin board by the computer, or make and discuss daily a master list of things students have learned about their keypals. Highlight the similarities and differences among students and their keypals individually and during whole-group discussions.

Book 2:   The Hickory Chair

Fraustino, L.R. (2001). Ill. B. Andrews. New York: Scholastic. $15.95. 32 pp.

BOOK REVIEW

Louis is a young African American student with a special gift. The bond between Louis and his grandmother began when Louis was a baby. Blind since birth, Louis experiences his grandmother's love with his other senses, unhampered by his lack of vision. He is a boy, like any other—except that he has "blind-sight," as his grandmother so often tells him. When she dies, Louis helps family members discover the treasures she left hidden for each of them. When Louis is unable to find the treasure she left for him, it is blind-sight that sustains his faith in the knowledge that she loved him. His faith is rewarded years later when he is sharing the same hickory chair with his grandchild. Simple oil and fabric collages by acclaimed artist Benny Andrews portray the sense of a supportive family and the courage of a boy who knows he is loved.

READ-ALOUD AND BOOK DISCUSSION IDEAS

Before reading the book, ask students to close their eyes tightly and keep them closed. Hold up a fruit and then ask students, with their eyes still tightly closed, if they can tell you the color of fruit you are holding up. Tell them to open their eyes and look at a tray of fruit. What colors do they see now? Ask them if there is another way they can learn about the fruit if they cannot see. Prompt students to think about their other senses of smelling, feeling, and tasting. Tell them that you will be reading a story about a little boy who could not see but learned about things in many special ways.

> ### MATERIALS
> - Fruit
> - Tray

During reading, ask students to think about blind-sight. Write the words *blind-sight* on the blackboard. Encourage students to listen for examples of the things Louis knew without seeing. Discuss with students how Louis must have felt when his grandmother died. For many primary-grade students, this may be the first story they have heard in which someone dies. Teachers may want to consider if it is appropriate to sensitively answer any questions the story might raise.

After reading, ask students what the words *blind-sight* meant in the story. Ask them to talk about how Louis's family treated him. It may be necessary to mention that Louis's family treated him as a normal boy who had to deal with the inconvenience of learning about his world without the benefit of sight. Ask students to recall what senses Louis used to learn. By using examples from the story, students will learn to support their conclusions with evidence. If time allows, ask students to close their eyes and play a game of identify the fruit either by tasting, feeling, or smelling.

COMPUTER ACTIVITIES

Creativity and Presentation Software Ideas

Using Kidspiration 2.1 software, create a five-column table—one for each of the five senses—to reinforce categorization skills, identification skills, and collaborative learning. Demonstrate during whole-group time how students can use Kidspiration 2.1 to drag icons into the teacher-created template to categorize items by the sense used for that item (e.g., musical instruments would be categorized as hearing, food as tasting).

> ### MATERIALS
> - Kidspiration 2.1 (2005) software

1. Tell each student to locate at least two picture icons for each sense and drag them into a column. Remind students that the program will "speak" the names of the objects they are considering placing in a column as they drag the cursor over the items.

2. If time permits during computer-center time, encourage them to add more icons. Invite a cross-age computer buddy, parent volunteer, or teaching assistant to help the youngest students accomplish this task.

3. If one student becomes an expert in this activity, allow him or her to serve as a cross-age computer buddy who helps other students when asked to do so by the teacher.

4. Encourage students to explain during author's computer chair (see Appendix B) why they think the items belong under individual categories.

Digital Language Experience Approach

Create a "My Senses Book" for the classroom library.

MATERIALS

■ Digital camera
■ Kidspiration 2.1 (2005) software

1. Using a digital camera or an inexpensive disposable camera, take an exploratory walk around the school. If you have four other helpers (e.g., parent volunteers, teaching assistant, cross-age computer buddies), divide the class into five groups and assign each a sense to take a picture of. For example, the group assigned the sense of smell might take pictures of flowers on the desk or food in the cafeteria. If you do not have helpers to guide small groups, take the walk as a class and point out objects for each sense.

2. Ask students to point silently to their nose if the object relates to the sense of smell. They should do the same for the other senses, using their fingers for touch, their ears for sound, their mouths for taste, and their eyes for sight.

3. Take a series of five pictures of the class pointing to their eyes for sight, ears for hearing, and so forth.

4. Import the pictures into creativity and presentation software such as Kidspiration 2.1.

5. Print photographs and display them in the classroom on the computer monitor for all to view.

6. Ask students to help you categorize each picture by the sense it goes with. Arrange the pictures by categories behind the class picture for that sense (e.g., the first category is the photograph of the class pointing to their eyes followed by photographs of colorful objects; the next category is the class photograph of students pointing to their mouths, followed by photographs of things to taste; and so on).

7. Assemble these arrangements into a book with each sense or category beginning with a photograph of students pointing to that sense. Laminate printouts and bind into a book. An example of photographs representing each sense (suitable as a book cover) is available on the ReadWriteThink website (www.readwritethink.org/lesson_images/lesson73/senses.pdf). Be sure to include the authors' names on a title page. The teacher can also upload this activity to the class webpage for parents and other students to see.

8. Encourage students to work on identifying parts of speech in subsequent readings of the photo essay. Ask them to point out all of the nouns (i.e., person, place, or thing), verbs (i.e., actions such as seeing, hearing, tasting), and adjectives (e.g., colors, sizes) they see.

9. Set aside time for an author's computer chair (see Appendix B). Students will enjoy sharing their five-senses books and slide shows and recalling their exploratory walk. Relate their discussion to how Louis, the main character in *The Hickory Chair* (Fraustino, 2001), learned things about his world. For example, ask students to remember how they identified the different fruits earlier in the unit and to guess how Louis might learn about foods or other objects. Students also may enjoy viewing and discussing what they learned about Braille on the Internet (addressed in the Internet Resources and Ideas section below).

Computer Software Activity

Students must rely on their sense of hearing to play a game that pairs baby animals with their mothers.

MATERIALS

■ Reader Rabbit's Toddler (1999) software

---

1. Click on the elephant on the main menu of the Reader Rabbit's Toddler software.

2. Follow simple directions to play the game. The baby animal is hiding in a basket with only his or her eyes showing. The animal makes a sound, and the student has to distinguish the sound in order to click on the appropriate mother from four choices.

3. Before students play the game, tell them that they will be using their sense of hearing to match the categories of mother and baby animals.

Internet Resources and Ideas

American Foundation for the Blind: What Is Braille? www.afb.org/braillebug/braille.asp
Before students go to the computer center, remind them that the main character in *The Hickory Chair* (Fraustino, 2001) used Braille as an alternative to seeing. Tell students that activities on this website will help them learn more about Braille and will even let them see what their name looks like when written in Braille.

Emerging, developing, and fluent readers can explore the Braille alphabet. Online tools allow students to write their names. Teachers can order a free Braille Bug alphabet card for the class. Working with a cross-age computer buddy, students can click on hyperlinks to explore various concepts: "Braille: Deciphering the Code" to learn how Braille works, "Trivia" to learn interesting facts about Braille, "Braille Technology" to see how Braille is made, "Printable Braille Alphabet Key" to print their own copy of the alphabet and numbers in Braille, and "Louis Braille Biography" to learn about the young man who invented Braille.

At the bottom of the webpage, click on "Games." Here are two examples of the activities: "See Your Name in Braille!" allows you to type in your name and see how it looks in Braille. "Secret Message" lets you e-mail messages to your friends in English and the program converts it to Braille. Exploring these programs will help students understand how the character, Louis, learned to read and write without being able to use his eyes. These programs will also help students develop compassion for others with differing capabilities.

Book 3:   Sidney Won't Swim

Schuurmans, H. (2002). Watertown, MA: Charlesbridge. $6.95. 32 pp.

BOOK REVIEW

Winner of the Silver Honor and Parents' Choice Award, Hilde Schuurmans charms readers with Sidney's excuses for avoiding swimming in the water. Parents, teacher, and friends see through Sidney's fear of swimming, but does he? Does he really think swimming is stupid? Students will identify with Sidney's struggles. Inspired by her dog, Zaki, who is afraid of the water, the author helps readers reconnect with those times when they did not know how to face their fears. Schuurmans' well-drawn watercolor illustrations are comical and compassionate and are sure to attract young readers.

READ-ALOUD AND BOOK DISCUSSION IDEAS

Before reading, begin by asking students to think about a time they felt afraid to do something new. Recall a time when you were a student and felt afraid of a new experience. For example, you might have been afraid to taste a new food, such as broccoli. Before you read the story, tell students that you are going to be reading a story about a little boy who made excuses for something he did not want to do. Tell students to use story clues to figure out what Sidney's real problem is.

During reading, ask students if Sidney's parents believed he had a stomachache. This is a good opportunity to foster students' critical thinking. Ask students to support their opinion with evidence. Asking students to find details in the pictures or text that helped them figure out what Sidney's parents were thinking will help them provide supporting evidence.

After reading, ask students to retell how Sidney's friends helped him solve his problem. What would they do to solve the problem? What should Sidney do to solve his problem? Why?

COMPUTER ACTIVITIES

Creativity and Presentation Software Ideas

Use KidPix Studio Deluxe or other creativity and presentation software, and ask students to write or draw an illustration on screen of a time they felt afraid to try something new. Help students brainstorm words to express their feelings. What did they do first? Did they make excuses to avoid something new? Who helped them solve the problem in the end? How did they overcome their fears? Collect screen pages into a slide show titled "We Overcome Our Fears." Share the slide show during author's computer chair (see Appendix B).

MATERIALS

■ KidPix Studio Deluxe (1998) software

Digital Language Experience Approach

Invite small groups of students to reenact *Sydney Won't Swim* (Schuurmans, 2002).

MATERIALS

- Digital camera
- Microsoft Paint (1981–2001) or PowerPoint (Microsoft Office 2003, 2003) software
- Props

1. Let them assemble or make props for their story.

2. Help them decide which characters to use and who will play each part.

3. Help students recall the story events. As students reenact the story, take at least three photographs of the beginning, middle, and end of the story. Import photographs into creativity and presentation software such as Microsoft Paint or PowerPoint.

4. Encourage students to arrange the photographs in chronological sequence, focusing on the beginning, middle, and end.

5. Instruct students to dictate or write a sentence on the computer to retell the story for each photograph.

6. Print out copies of the photographs and bind them into class books so small groups of students can compare how their retellings are similar or different from one another's. Ask students to create a name for their books.

Computer Software Activity

Tell students that after viewing the talking e-book "Sheila Rae, the Brave," you want them to be able to tell you what Sheila Rae's problem was and how she solved it. Sometimes being afraid has its purpose—to keep us cautious and safe. Sheila Rae discovers what happens when you are not afraid of anything. Emerging and developing readers can read along with the highlighted words in this interactive book and thus reinforce concepts about print. Fluent readers will enjoy reading on their own as they discover the trouble Sheila Rae gets into when she carelessly explores a new way home and gets lost. Through repeated readings, students can develop greater fluency. To reinforce mapping skills and understand directionality (e.g., north, south, east, west), a fun and easy-to-follow map is also included of Shelia Rae's community. Students can use the map to help Sheila Rae find her way home. The text is accessible in English or Spanish.

MATERIALS

- Sheila Rae, the Brave (1996) software

Internet Resources and Ideas

KinderArt: Emotion Painting: www.kinderart.com/painting/emotion.shtml
Students can use this website to create an emotion painting online. Emotion paintings help students understand the role of feelings in art making. Talk with students about emotions. What sorts of emotions do they feel? Have students volunteer to draw different faces on the board depicting different emotions. Ask the other students to guess what emotion each face illustrates. Talk with them about how their body feels with different emotions. Tell students you feel like you have butterflies in your stomach when you are nervous. Ask them to describe the feeling in their

tummy when they are afraid. Then discuss colors. How do different colors make them feel? Which colors help them feel happy or sad? Do colors affect everyone in the same way?

The KinderArt website has explicit instructions for adapting emotion drawings to all age groups. Ask students to choose colors that represent how they are feeling and use them to draw an emotion painting. When students complete the artwork, hang each student's masterpiece in the classroom and ask the class to interpret what they see in the drawings.

Mister Rogers' Neighborhood—Parents & Teachers: Helping Children With Scary News:
http://pbskids.org/rogers/parentsteachers/special/scarynews.html
On this website, Mister Rogers's video clip explains to students how to deal with scary feelings. You will need RealPlayer to watch the clip (a link to download RealPlayer is provided on the site). Click on the hyperlink "Talking about feelings" near the bottom of the webpage. This page also lists many helpful ways and resources for adults to help students through scary situations.

KizClub—Stories Level 2, Feelings: www.kizclub.com/feelingstory/feeling1.html
Explore an e-book about feelings. Click on the arrows to hear an audio version of the text. As each feeling is introduced, a facial expression and a correlating situation are also shown. Revisiting each emotion, facial expression, and a situation under which an emotion might occur will help students better understand and identify their feelings and the emotions of others.

Mister Rogers' Neighborhood—Neighborhood of Make-Believe: How Do You Feel?
http://pbskids.org/rogers/make_believe/offlinefeel1.htm
Print two copies of the teddy bear face from this website. Students can draw a different "feeling face" on each teddy bear. Tape or paste them together over a popsicle stick to form a puppet. Use this activity as a creative way for students to express their feelings. Students can share their puppet faces and describe a situation in which they remember feeling the puppet face they are showing.

Unit Conclusion

This activity is adapted from Urbanski, E. (n.d.). *A Box of Crayons*. Retrieved January 27, 2006, from www.kinderart.com/multic/mlkjr_crayons.shtml. © Eileen Urbanski.

What would it be like to be a crayon? What color would you be? Why? Would everyone be the same color? Why or why not? Tell students that to celebrate the end of the unit, they are going to create a box of child-sized crayons to celebrate differences.

MATERIALS
■ Books from this unit
■ *A Box of Crayons* (DeRolf, 1997)
■ Butcher paper
■ Crayons
■ Digital camera
■ Glue
■ Markers
■ Poster board

1. Make a child-size pattern of a crayon out of butcher paper for each student. A printable crayon pattern can be found on the KinderArt website (go to www.kinderart.com/seasons/crayon_pattern.htm).

2. Alternately, the size of the crayon and subsequent pictures of each student can be scaled down. However, the crayon pattern needs to be large enough for students to write a list of attributes on the body of the crayon.

3. Take a digital photograph of each student, size to about 5 x 7", and print them out. Each student will cut out his or her face and shoulders from the photograph.

4. Instruct students to glue their photograph to the tip of each child-size crayon.

5. Encourage students to write or dictate some of the things they have learned to appreciate about themselves throughout the unit (e.g., what makes them different and special) on the body of the child-size crayon. What other languages besides English do they know? What family traditions are special? What physical capabilities do they have? What are their food or clothing preferences?

6. Encourage students to color the rest of the crayon their favorite color.

7. Place all of the crayons into a giant box of crayons that you can create using a large sheet of butcher paper or poster board.

8. Display the crayons on a bulletin board outside of your classroom along with a copy of the poem "A Box of Crayons." A copy of the poem can be found on the website My School Online (go to www.myschoolonline.com/page/0,1871,34898-119831-38-49158,00.html).

On the last day of the unit, have the class assemble in front of the bulletin board. If students have carpet squares, bring them to sit comfortably on the floor. As you pull each crayon out of the box, invite the student to come forward and read what he or she wrote that makes him or her special. Have on hand a display of books from the unit. Ask students to recall how the characters in the books you read during the unit were special.

"Students learned so much from this unit because they were able to make so many connections between the readings and activities with their out-of-school lives. The discussions about stories were rich, varied, and resulted in wonderful oral language development."

—KINDERGARTEN TEACHER

Bedtime

UNIT BOOKS

Bedtime!
By Ruth Freeman Swain
Illustrated by Cat Bowman Smith

Little Bunny's Sleepless Night
By Carol Roth
Illustrated by Valeri Gorbachev

Everything to Spend the Night: From A to Z
By Ann Whitford Paul
Illustrated by Maggie Smith

COMPUTER RESOURCES

Little Monster at School
Dino the Star Keeper
Stellaluna

Thematic Connection

Going to bed at the end of the day should be a time of resting, snuggling under the covers, drifting off to sleep, or hearing a favorite story from a parent or caregiver. Exploring bedtime through the books and computer-related activities in this unit allows students to learn more about the whats, whys, and hows of going to sleep at night. The nonfiction text *Bedtime!* (Swain, 1999) takes a long look at bedding and bedtime traditions across history and around the world. Students will be fascinated to learn more about how going to bed was different in past ages. They will use their imaginations to sort out what it is like to go to bed in a different country or cultural context. How does going to bed compare across time and cultures? *Little Bunny's Sleepless Night* (Roth, 1999) relates the fictional tale about a quest to sleep well and overcome feelings of loneliness. Students will have occasions to explore their feelings about bedtime and nighttime noises, seeking comfort, overcoming the difficulties of sleeping in a big bed alone, or trying to share a bedroom with another person. *Everything to Spend the Night: From A to Z* (Paul, 1999) is an alphabet concept book, which is about spending the night with a grandparent (or others). Alphabet concept books focus on words that are all related to a theme or topic. Thus, as students learn the alphabet, they also learn about a particular topic. The book provides another embedded opportunity for students to learn ABC concepts while also delving into the preparation and experiences of spending the night away from the comforts and familiar routines of home.

Matrix of Literacy Skills and Strategies in Unit 11

Literacy Skills and Strategies	Activities	Title of Book	Pages
Brainstorming	R	*Bedtime!*	173–174
	R, C	*Little Bunny's Sleepless Night*	177, 177–178
	R	*Everything to Spend the Night: From A to Z*	179–180
Building background knowledge on the Internet*	U	—	172–173
	I	*Bedtime!*	176
	I	*Little Bunny's Sleepless Night*	179
	I	*Everything to Spend the Night: From A to Z*	182
Building editing skills	C, D	*Bedtime!*	174, 175–176
Comparing and contrasting	R, D	*Bedtime!*	173–174, 175–176
Composing in multimedia*	C, D	*Bedtime!*	174, 175–176
	C, D	*Little Bunny's Sleepless Night*	177–178, 178
	C, D	*Everything to Spend the Night: From A to Z*	180, 180–182
Creating and using charts	UC	—	183–184
	R, S	*Bedtime!*	173–174, 176
Creating concept maps and graphic organizers	C	*Bedtime!*	174
Determining cause and effect	R, C	*Little Bunny's Sleepless Night*	177, 177–178
Determining chronological order	D	*Bedtime!*	175–176
Determining story details	S	*Bedtime!*	176
	R, S	*Little Bunny's Sleepless Night*	177, 178
	R, C, S	*Everything to Spend the Night: From A to Z*	179–180, 180, 182
Developing a sense of beginnings, middles, and endings	R	*Little Bunny's Sleepless Night*	177
Developing and using story grammar	R	*Everything to Spend the Night: From A to Z*	179–180
Developing choral reading	R, S	*Bedtime!*	173–174, 176
	S	*Little Bunny's Sleepless Night*	178
Developing comprehension	U, UC	—	172–173, 183–184
	R, S	*Bedtime!*	173–174, 176
	R	*Little Bunny's Sleepless Night*	177
	R, S, I	*Everything to Spend the Night: From A to Z*	179–180, 182, 182

(continued)

170

Matrix of Literacy Skills and Strategies in Unit 11 (continued)

Literacy Skills and Strategies	Activities	Title of Book	Pages
Developing creative writing	C, D	*Bedtime!*	174, 175–176
	C, D	*Little Bunny's Sleepless Night*	177–178, 178
	D	*Everything to Spend the Night: From A to Z*	180–182
Developing critical reading and thinking	UC	—	183–184
	R	*Bedtime!*	173–174
Developing oral language	U, UC	—	172–173, 183–184
	R, D, S, I	*Bedtime!*	173–174, 175–176, 176, 176
	R, C, D, I	*Little Bunny's Sleepless Night*	177, 177–178, 178, 179
	R, C, D	*Everything to Spend the Night: From A to Z*	179–180, 180, 180–182
Developing vocabulary	UC	—	183–184
	R, C, D, S	*Bedtime!*	173–174, 174, 175–176, 176
	C, D	*Little Bunny's Sleepless Night*	177–178, 178
Drawing conclusions	U	—	172–173
	R	*Little Bunny's Sleepless Night*	177
	D	*Everything to Spend the Night: From A to Z*	180–182
Following directions	U, UC	—	172–173, 183–184
	C, D	*Bedtime!*	174, 175–176
	C, D, S	*Little Bunny's Sleepless Night*	177–178, 178, 178
	C, D, S	*Everything to Spend the Night: From A to Z*	180, 180–182, 182
Identifying letters	UC	—	183–184
	R, C	*Everything to Spend the Night: From A to Z*	179–180, 180
Making multicultural connections	U, UC	—	172–173, 183–184
	R, D	*Bedtime!*	173–174, 175–176
Making predictions	R	*Bedtime!*	173–174
	R	*Little Bunny's Sleepless Night*	177
	R	*Everything to Spend the Night: From A to Z*	179–180
Navigating hyperlinks*	U	—	172–173
	S, I	*Bedtime!*	176
	S, I	*Little Bunny's Sleepless Night*	178, 179
	I	*Everything to Spend the Night: From A to Z*	182
Presenting work on a computer*	C, D	*Bedtime!*	174, 175–176
	C	*Little Bunny's Sleepless Night*	177–178
Reading aloud	R, D	*Bedtime!*	173–174, 175–176
Reading and listening for a purpose	U, UC	—	172–173, 183–184
	R	*Bedtime!*	173–174
	R	*Little Bunny's Sleepless Night*	177
	R, S, I	*Everything to Spend the Night: From A to Z*	179–180, 182, 182
Reading and using map skills	C	*Bedtime!*	174

(continued)

Matrix of Literacy Skills and Strategies in Unit 11 (continued)

Literacy Skills and Strategies	Activities	Title of Book	Pages
Reading informational text	R	*Bedtime!*	173–174
	I	*Everything to Spend the Night: From A to Z*	182
Recognizing ABC order	R, C	*Everything to Spend the Night: From A to Z*	179–180, 180
Summarizing	D	*Bedtime!*	175–176
Understanding a main idea	UC	—	183–184
	C	*Little Bunny's Sleepless Night*	177–178
Understanding concepts about print	D	*Bedtime!*	175–176
	S	*Little Bunny's Sleepless Night*	178
Understanding story structure and events	R, S	*Everything to Spend the Night: From A to Z*	179–180, 182
Using adjectives	C, S	*Bedtime!*	174, 176
	C	*Little Bunny's Sleepless Night*	177–178
Using English as a second language	S	*Bedtime!*	176
Using phonics: Letter–sound correspondence	R, C	*Everything to Spend the Night: From A to Z*	179–180, 180
Visualizing	UC	—	183–184
	C	*Bedtime!*	174
Writing descriptive sentences	UC	—	183–184
	C, D	*Bedtime!*	174, 175–176
	D	*Little Bunny's Sleepless Night*	178
	D	*Everything to Spend the Night: From A to Z*	180–182
Writing letters	UC	—	183–184
	D	*Bedtime!*	175–176

* Indicates a new-literacy skill.
U = unit introduction; R = read-aloud and book discussion ideas; C = creativity and presentation software ideas; D = Digital Language Experience Approach; S = computer software activity; I = Internet resources and ideas; UC = unit conclusion

Unit Introduction

MATERIALS

- Books from this unit
- Candle
- Cup
- Lullaby CD or tape
- Pillow
- Small blanket
- Toothbrush
- Toothpaste

As students assemble for whole-group time, set the mood by turning the lights low, lighting a candle to set right by your chair on a small table, and playing a lullaby softly in the background. From a large bag, pull out and display a pillow, a cup for water, a toothbrush and toothpaste, a book, and a small blanket. Yawn and stretch. Ask students to yawn and stretch with you. Ask them to quietly identify each item. What do they think all these things have in common? Why do they think so? Tell students that these are items that they use at a particular time of day every day. Ask them to make a good guess about the time of day they use the items. Would they use the items in the morning? For naptime? For bedtime? Guide a discussion and show

how each object is used for bedtime. Tell students that the books in this unit all have to do with learning more about how stories from authors, Internet resources, and computer activities help us understand facts and feelings about bedtime. For example, to highlight how the Internet can provide a framework for exploring knowledge and feelings, go to www.talesandlullabies.com a website that displays various songs, lullabies, and poems about bedtime. Select one song or poem to read aloud. Demonstrate how you make hyperlink connections. Discuss how reading the poem helps us think about our own bedtime experiences. For example, click on the hyperlink titled "Lullabies/Songs" and click on the displayed singer's name to hear a lullaby sung aloud. Click on the hyperlink titled "Bedtime Stories" and click on the displayed reader's name to hear the story read aloud. Display the book covers from this unit and introduce the first book you will read aloud.

Book 1: Bedtime!

Swain, R.F. (1999). Ill. C.B. Smith. New York: Holiday House. $15.95. 32 pp.

BOOK REVIEW

This delightful book, a history of bedtime, begins with illustrations of a cot, a mat, a canopy bed, a mound of straw, a sleeper couch, and animal skins on the floor of a cave and an intriguing first line of text: "When we go to bed, we are doing something that people have done for thousands of years.... We all need to rest." (p. 1). Thus begins a fascinating book, written by a preschool teacher, about various types of beds and bedtime rituals. Learn about bedding used in ancient Egypt, ancient China, and in the Middle Ages and by people in Central and South America, Louis XIV (who had 413 beds), train travelers, truckers, astronauts, and more. The book concludes with the notion that a bed is for resting, reading, feeling better, and sleeping. Final pages include facts about sleep and helpful resources for learning more about sleep habits around the world.

READ-ALOUD AND BOOK DISCUSSION IDEAS

Before reading, ask students what people need and actions they might take to go to bed at night. As students brainstorm, write a list of their words on a chart. Chorally read over the list of words with students and briefly discuss the meanings of each word. Tell students that *Bedtime!* (Swain, 1999) is a book about how people throughout history, people from other places, and even some people who have unique jobs go to bed. Could the ways people go to bed have been different long ago? Why or why not? Could the way people go to bed in other countries be different from the ways the students go to bed? Guide an oral discussion that leads to predictions about the text.

> **MATERIALS**
>
> ■ Chart paper
> ■ Markers

During reading, point out how words in text are depicted in the illustrations. For example, after reading the text on ancient China, say, "Children's pillows were covered with fabric and were sometimes in the shapes of animals who would keep watch at night," and point to the illustration of the child sleeping on a mat with his head resting on a soft pillow in the shape of a kitten. To support students' ability to compare and contrast information, consistently ask them to think and talk about how this new information is the same or different from the ways they sleep.

After reading, discuss some of the new insights students have gained from the book. Highlight the multicultural aspects of the information. Remind students that reading informational text allows them to learn many facts about a topic. Turn to the last pages of the book and select a fact to reread to demonstrate how to use features of informational text.

COMPUTER ACTIVITIES

Creativity and Presentation Software Ideas

Demonstrate for students how to use creativity and presentation software tools using KidPix Studio Deluxe or PowerPoint to create a picture map of their bedroom. Explain that a picture map is a birds-eye view of the room. Guide students to complete the following steps.

MATERIALS

■ KidPix Studio Deluxe (1998) or PowerPoint (Microsoft Office 2003, 2003) software

---

1. Recall and visualize the things that are in your bedroom and where everything is placed.

2. Create a rough draft on screen as you think about where things are located.

3. Model how to cut and paste and correct mistakes.

4. Write one simple sentence that describes the bedroom, for example, "My bedroom has one bed, one dresser, one chest of drawers, and a television." Discuss the role that adjectives play in making our thoughts as writers more descriptive to readers. Revise by adding adjectives to the sentence, for example, "My bedroom has one queen-sized bed with a blue quilt, one white dresser, one brown pine chest of drawers, and a color flat-screen television." Ask students which sentence gives them a better idea of what the room looks like.

5. Tell students to create a picture map of the place where they sleep and write one sentence that uses adjectives to describe their rooms. Sign and date the screen pages and assemble them into a slide show or printed book for sharing during whole-group time. Add a title for the composition, such as "Descriptions of our Bedrooms."

As an option, some students may prefer to create their "dream bedroom." How would they design a special bedroom? Would there be a special theme? Special pieces of furniture? Unique appliances (e.g., their own refrigerator or pizza parlor)? Encourage students to write one descriptive sentence with adjectives about their dream bedrooms. Sign and date the screen pages and assemble them into a slide show or a class book. Be sure to include a title page for the book with a title such as "Our Dream Bedrooms."

Digital Language Experience Approach

Send home a disposable digital camera and a note explaining the assignment (see Figure 29). Students take the cameras home and take photographs of the beds they sleep in at night, or they may bring in snapshots from home. Parents and caregivers and students write a brief paragraph about bedtime. This activity can highlight multicultural connections of different families and cultures that may have different bedroom configurations and routines, which will lead to comparison discussions.

<table>
<tr><td>

MATERIALS

- Disposable digital camera
- KidPix Studio Deluxe (1998) or PowerPoint (Microsoft Office 2003, 2003) software
- Note to parents

</td></tr>
</table>

1. After the cameras have been returned, which may take a week or so with each student taking a camera for one night and returning it the next day for another student's use, import digital photographs into creativity and presentation software such as KidPix Studio Deluxe or PowerPoint.

2. Instruct each student to keyboard or dictate while a cross-age computer buddy keyboards a descriptive sentence or paragraph about bedtime. What does he or she do at bedtime? What time is bedtime?

3. What stuffed animals sleep with the student? Is there a story time first? Prayers? How does the student feel about bedtime? Place students' dictated sentences and photographs in chronological order.

4. Save into a slide show or print and bind into a class book. Be sure to add a title page and title, such as "How We Go To Bed."

5. Encourage students to read pages aloud or explain computer screens. Guide a discussion about similarities and differences. Help students summarize all of the things that are the same or different. Remind students that a summary statement is short and does not give all of the details, just the most important information. Relate the discussion back to the key information about sleeping in different households and cultures that they learned from the

---

Figure 29
Sample Sleeping-Area Letter to Parents and Caregivers

Dear Parents and Caregivers,

We are currently reading books about bedtime. As part of our unit, we would like to compare our different types of beds and bedtime routines. Please take a minute to use the disposable digital camera to take a photograph of your child's sleeping area. Just turn on the camera, snap the shot, and turn off the camera. Write a few sentences about the things you and your child do as he or she goes to bed. Sign your names on the back of your paragraph. Return the camera and paragraph to me, [name of child's teacher], by [insert date]. Thank you for supporting your child's learning activities.

Sincerely,
Your Child's Teacher

book *Bedtime!* (Swain, 1999). For example, a student might notice that she sleeps with a stuffed kitten animal in the same way that one of the children in the book slept on a kitten-shaped pillow.

Computer Software Activity

Little Monster's story, which gives an account of his day at school, begins when he is sound asleep in bed. After students have viewed and read the Little Monster at School CD-ROM talking book, click the options button; then click "OK" for page 1. This allows students to hear the page read aloud again, chorally read along, and interact with screen objects available through links. To foster oral language development, ask students to notice and be ready to describe the things they see in Little Monster's bedroom. Review adjectives as describing words.

> **MATERIALS**
>
> ■ Chart paper
> ■ Little Monster at School (2002) CD-ROM
> ■ Markers

Post a list of the following questions on a chart in the computer center. A cross-age computer buddy, fluent peer, teaching assistant, or adult volunteer can help emerging and developing readers answer the following questions as they interact with the program.

- What kind of bed does Little Monster have?

- What colors are things in his bedroom?

- Does he sleep alone?

- Where is his bed located?

- What do you think happens when Little Monster goes to bed at night? Why?

- What is Little Monster wearing when he goes to bed?

During author's computer chair (see Appendix B), each student should have an opportunity to tell at least one object in the room they can describe. Collectively, students should be able to answer the questions from the chart in the computer center.

Internet Resources and Ideas

Bedtime-Story: www.the-office.com/bedtime-story
Click on the "Enter" and "Story Index" hyperlink to see a list of bedtime stories that are available on this website. Click on the link "What's It About?" to read a summary of the story. Click on the link "Tell me the story" to see illustrations and text. An adult or cross-age computer buddy can help read the story aloud for emerging or developing readers. Ask students to decide if the story would help them fall asleep at night. Ask why or why not?

Storynory: www.storynory.com
This website offers bedtime story downloads. Select a story title from a list and click on a link titled "Download the audio here." Stories may be downloaded to an iPod, MP3 player, or computer. Emerging and developing readers will enjoy listening to professionally narrated stories. Ask students to talk about the difference between reading a bedtime story and listening to a bedtime story read aloud.

Book 2:   Little Bunny's Sleepless Night

Roth, C. (1999). Ill. V. Gorbachev. Honesdale, PA: Boyds Mills Press. $15.95. 40 pp.

BOOK REVIEW

Little Bunny is an "only bunny" that gets very lonely sleeping all alone in his bedroom. One night he is inspired to sleep over with a friend so he will not be lonely. Unfortunately, every animal he tries to spend the night with presents a problem that keeps Little Bunny awake and sleepless. Finally, Little Bunny is eager to return home to his own comfortable bed and a good night's sleep. Students will enjoy learning about the different ways Little Bunny tries to solve his problem.

READ-ALOUD AND BOOK DISCUSSION IDEAS

Before reading, talk about the word *sleepless*. Ask students to brainstorm some things that might make someone have a sleepless night. List their ideas on chart paper as predictions to confirm or change during reading. Tell students that as you read the story about Little Bunny's nighttime experience, you will ask them to guess whether Little Bunny will finally be able to get a good night's sleep.

> **MATERIALS**
> ■ Chart paper
> ■ Markers

During reading, stop after Little Bunny goes to multiple friends' rooms to sleep. Ask students to think about characteristics of each animal. Then ask them to predict if Little Bunny will be able to get a good night's sleep by sharing a bedroom with each animal: Why or why not? Read aloud the result so students can confirm or change their predictions immediately. Students who learn to make and confirm or change predictions while reading are better comprehenders.

After reading, discuss why Little Bunny changes his mind about sleeping alone in his own bedroom.

COMPUTER ACTIVITIES

Creativity and Presentation Software Ideas

Students learn more about the main idea of the story by using creativity and presentation software such as KidPix Studio Deluxe or PowerPoint to create a Noisy Nighttime Noisemaker Screen of all of the things that make noise that might keep them awake at night.

> **MATERIALS**
> ■ Chart paper
> ■ KidPix Studio Deluxe (1998) or PowerPoint (Microsoft Office 2003, 2003) software
> ■ Markers

1. Brainstorm possible noisemakers (e.g., a dripping faucet, a barking dog, a snoring family member, loud music from a neighbor's house, a loudly ticking clock, crickets chirping, cars driving by, thunder, a radio, television). List a few of the items on chart paper.

2. Using the stamps toolbar in KidPix Studio Deluxe or clip art available in PowerPoint, encourage students to select and place at least five object stamps on the screen of what might keep them awake and to label the objects.

3. Ask students to state what noise each object makes. Highlight students' use of descriptive words as they talk about the objects to reinforce the use of adjectives.

4. Instruct students to write or dictate a sentence that explains how they would stop the noise from at least one object so they could go to sleep. For example, during this unit, one student said, "The clock was ticking too loudly so I put it under a fat pillow. I got a good night's sleep until it rang the next morning." Name their computer screens "Noisy Nighttime Noisemaker Screens."

5. Encourage students to present and discuss their Noisy Nighttime Noisemaker Screens during author's computer chair (see Appendix B).

Digital Language Experience Approach

Tell students that on nights when Little Bunny can sleep, he has wonderful dreams. Talk about dreaming and the type of fantasy worlds the mind creates while people rest at night. If possible, guide a shared viewing of Dino the Star Keeper (1998; see the computer software activity below for this book).

MATERIALS

- Digital camera
- KidPix Studio Deluxe (1998) or PowerPoint (Microsoft Office 2003, 2003) software

1. Take a digital photograph of each student and import into creativity and presentation software such as KidPix Studio Deluxe or PowerPoint.

2. As students see the photograph on the screen, tell them to use drawing or painting tools to create a dream scene. What might they be dreaming about? Where will the dream take place? What things or objects are in the dream?

3. Instruct students to write a story or a sentence about their dreams. What descriptive words might help a reader understand how the dream made them feel? Which words might help a reader understand what they were doing in the dream?

4. Print out hard copies to post on a class bulletin board titled "Our Dream Worlds."

5. Encourage students to share and explain computer screens of their work during author's computer chair (see Appendix B).

Computer Software Activity

MATERIALS

- Dino the Star Keeper (1998) software

Join a young boy's nighttime journey through the interactive screen pages of the Dino the Star Keeper software. Tell students that as they listen to the story, they should try to figure out where Dino the Star Keeper lives. Of course, the answer is in the little boy's dream. Emerging readers who reread or relisten to the story can point to the text as it is read aloud and chorally or echo read to support their knowledge of concepts about print. Ask students to be ready to talk about where Dino the Star Keeper lives and how they know where he lives.

Spaghetti Book Club: Book Reviews by Kids for Kids: www.spaghettibookclub.org/title.php3
Students will enjoy reading book reviews about books that focus on bedtime. In addition, they will learn how to write a book review by reading reviews written by students at different grade levels. For example, click on the letter "g" listed among alphabet letters that link to book titles that begin with a certain letter. Clicking on the letter *g* takes you to a list of over 100 books that are reviewed. Click on the hyperlink titled "Good Night Moon" and see five book reviews by children ages 5–8. Each review includes an illustration and book review. During whole-group time, point out the way the illustrations include important parts of the story. Point out how the book reviews follow a pattern: (a) What the story is mostly about; (b) how the reviewer felt about the story; and (c) who the reviewer thinks would enjoy reading the book. Students may enjoy writing their own reviews of books they have read in this unit.

HarperChildrens.com: www.harperchildrens.com/hch/havesomefun/gnmoon.asp
Many students enjoy reading Margaret Wise Brown's classic story, *Goodnight Moon* (Brown, 1947). Place a copy of the story in the art center, along with a printout of one of the illustrations from the book available at HarperChildrens.com website. Students may either follow the same color scheme found in the book's illustrations, or they may select new colors. Talk with students about how illustrations enhance our understanding of stories and, in this case, help us understand our feelings about going to bed in a familiar room.

Book 3:   Everything to Spend the Night: From A to Z

Paul, A.W. (1999). Ill. M. Smith. New York: DK Publishing. $14.95. 27 pp.

BOOK REVIEW

This alphabet concept book, written in rhyming verse, illustrates the items that a young girl has packed in her bag to spend the night with her grandpa. A large bag is filled with items that are produced in alphabetical order. However, the little girl doesn't know what to do about her missing pajamas until Grandpa saves the day. Students will enjoy reading how an elder family member helps the little girl feel more comfortable at bedtime.

READ-ALOUD AND BOOK DISCUSSION IDEAS

Before reading, bring in a small suitcase and tell students that sometimes people use suitcases if they are going to spend the night somewhere. Ask students to suggest what items they might need in a suitcase in order to be ready to spend the night. Display the cover of the book and tell them that the little girl in the story brought something for every letter in the alphabet to her grandpa's house when she spent the night there. Review ABC order by referring to a class chart of the alphabet. Tell students that the little girl

---

MATERIALS

■ Small suitcase

---

discovers she has a problem and that grandpa helps her figure out a solution. Ask students to listen for grandpa's solution.

During reading, ask students to predict what item the girl has brought with her for each letter. After students guess for each book spread, show the illustrations so they can confirm or change their predictions. Remind students that each letter has an object that begins with that letter and sound. Stress the beginning sounds of each letter to reinforce sound–symbol relationships and phonics instruction.

After reading, ask students what they would do to solve the problem. Ask them to explain how grandpa solved the little girl's problem. How could the little girl avoid the same problem in the future?

COMPUTER ACTIVITIES

Creativity and Presentation Software Ideas

Students who have spent the night with a relative or a friend will enjoy retelling and illustrating the experience. Other students will enjoy packing a virtual suitcase with their own selected alphabet letter items for spending the night away from home. Where will they go? What will they need? Will they need warm clothes? Will they need to pack food and water? Follow the following five steps to complete this activity.

MATERIALS

■ Chart paper
■ KidPix Studio Deluxe (1998) or PowerPoint (Microsoft Office 2003, 2003) software
■ Markers

1. Draw a large, empty suitcase on the computer screen or import a clip art picture.

2. Instruct students to stamp item icons or clip art available in creativity and presentation software, such as KidPix Studio Deluxe or PowerPoint, around the suitcase that they would take to spend the night somewhere.

3. Instruct students to add stamps of the alphabet letter that goes with each item. For example, students can add the letter *p* to go beside a pair of pajamas. Emerging and developing readers may need support to make graphophonemic connections, which are connections between letters and sounds that go with specific words.

MATERIALS

■ Beach towel
■ Boots
■ Digital camera
■ KidPix Studio Deluxe (1998) or PowerPoint (Microsoft Office 2003, 2003) software
■ Map
■ Picture of a beach
■ Socks
■ Suitcase
■ Sunglasses
■ Suntan lotion
■ Sweater

4. As an adaptation, instruct small groups of students to work together on the task or to select one letter and fill their virtual suitcases with items that match that letter.

5. During whole-group time, give each student a hard copy of his or her work and ask him or her to orally share items that go with each letter of the alphabet. Reinforce the letter–sound relationships and letter identification as students share.

Digital Language Experience Approach

Complete the following steps to accomplish this activity.

1. Take digital photographs of three to four students opening a suitcase you brought and unpacking things you have provided

for a pretend trip. For example, one suitcase might have the following items: heavy socks, a sweater, boots, and a map. Another suitcase might have the following items: a picture of a beach, sunglasses, suntan lotion, and a beach towel.

2. Instruct students to take turns holding up one object and stating what it is.

3. Once students have unloaded all the objects, instruct them to draw conclusions to figure out where you intended to go.

4. Import photographs into creativity and presentation software such as KidPix Studio Deluxe or PowerPoint. Instruct students to dictate or write captions for each photograph (see Figure 30 for examples). Students learn about comprehension skills, such as drawing conclusions, and writing details that include clues that enable other readers to draw conclusions.

Figure 30
Sample Pretend-Trip Photograph Captions

Page 1 photograph: "We opened the suitcase."

Page 2 photograph: "We unpacked some socks. *Socks* starts with an *S*."

Page 3 photograph: "We unpacked a sweater. *Sweater* starts with an *S*."

Page 4 photograph: "We unpacked boots. *Boots* starts with a *B*."

Page 5 photograph: "We unpacked a map. *Map* starts with an *M*."

Page 6 photograph: "We closed the suitcase."

"We guessed that [insert teacher's name here] was going to a cold place in the winter, like Alaska."

During author's computer chair (see Appendix B), print out D-LEA photograph essays to make class books so students can read the essay and try to figure out what the teacher has packed.

Computer Software Activity

Stellaluna was a little fruit bat who unexpectedly found herself spending the night with a family of birds. Ask students to listen to the story in the Stellaluna CD-ROM and be prepared to talk about how Stellaluna felt about being away from her mom at an unexpected sleepover. What did Stellaluna do? What happened during the night? How was the problem solved? Guiding students to think about the story as it is told with multimedia effects, such as sound effects, music, and animation, will help them gain new-literacy skills such as comprehending multimedia effects. Encourage students to point out different multimedia features (e.g., sad music, scary sound effects, the sound of mother's voice hurriedly calling Stellaluna's name, the animated shivers when Stellaluna first caught on a branch) that helped them understand how the lost little fruit bat felt. This will help students learn how understanding the main character's emotional state helps them enjoy and understand the story better.

MATERIALS

■ Stellaluna (2004) CD-ROM

Internet Resources and Ideas

She Knows: Sleep Over Parties: http://sheknows.com/about/look/2099.htm
This website includes everything adults want to know about planning a sleepover party but are afraid to ask. Post this URL and a brief explanation on your class website. Parents and caregivers will appreciate having advice to help prepare a great environment for primary-grade students' first group sleepover experiences. Visiting this website will help students build background knowledge about different bedtime experiences.

San Diego Zoo.org Roar & Snore Sleepovers: www.sandiegozoo.org/calendar/wap_roar_and_snore.html
Visit the San Diego Zoo website that explains what to pack if you want to "roar and snore," a phrase that refers to the roaring of animals and the snoring of people who are sleeping in close proximity. The zoo offers families a unique experience for students from ages 8 to 17 to spend the night overlooking the wild animal park. Students may have fun guessing what sleepover participants need to pack and then reading the required list, which is much longer than many students will anticipate. An itinerary for the days also is provided. For example, the activities for the first day are as follows: Arrive at 4:00 p.m., take a tour at 10:00 p.m., and go to bed at 11:00 p.m. Students can get a sense of the excitement of a zoo sleepover by accessing some of the video cameras live at www.sandiegozoo.org. They can see panda bear, polar bear, ape, and elephant cameras as well as animal videos. Photographs of wild animals are also available. Visiting this website helps students understand the different ways animals sleep through the night. It also invites them to think about nighttime adventures. Broadening students' conceptual base will make them better able to comprehend stories in the unit.

Unit Conclusion

To celebrate the conclusion of the unit and to give students an occasion to enter into the spirit of the unit goals (understanding and expressing ideas about bedtime), have a pretend sleepover.

After you get permission from the school administration, students help you write a friendly letter to caregivers and parents (see Figure 31 for an example) telling them that on the last day of the unit you will be having a pretend sleepover. Prepare chart paper with the key elements of a friendly letter: date, salutation, closing, and signature. Learning the parts of a friendly letter within an authentic context will make the experience and content more meaningful for students. Discuss with students the key information to include in the letter, and ask students to suggest sentences orally. Decide which information to use, and model writing the letter. Be sure to note in the invitation that students should bring a sleeping mat (e.g., blanket, beach towel, mat), a favorite stuffed animal or sleeping pal, and a pillow. Make a copy of the letter for parents and caregivers and send it home with the students. After the requested materials have arrived at school, complete the following steps to guide the culminating activity for the unit.

MATERIALS

- Alarm clock
- Bedtime chart
- Books and work from the unit
- Chart paper
- Cookies
- Markers
- Milk
- Note to parents
- Pillow
- Sleeping mats
- Stuffed animals

---

1. During the last 30 to 40 minutes of the last day of the unit, ask students to find a place for their mats and pillows. Go through the bedtime chart you created during the unit and ask students to visualize doing each step. Remind students that during the unit, they learned that many people have different bedtime routines, based on their home cultures and preferences. Remind students, for example, that one student listens to a story told by a grandmother before bedtime, whereas in another home, a student's older sibling or mother reads the student a bedtime story.

Figure 31
Sample Sleepover Letter to Parents and Caregivers

Dear Parents and Caregivers,

We are reading books this week about bedtime. After we learn about facts and feelings related to going to bed, we will end the unit with a pretend sleepover. Please help your child select, pack, and bring to school on [date here] the following items:
- a sleeping mat (a blanket, beach towel, or mat),
- a favorite stuffed animal, and
- a pillow.

Thank you for helping your child have a wonderful experience learning about bedtime.

Sincerely,
Your Child's Teacher

2. Pantomime with the students doing each of the bedtime activities (e.g., brushing teeth, changing into pajamas, taking off shoes).

3. Tell students to snuggle down on their "beds" and pillows while you talk to them and then read them a bedtime story. If possible, share a small carton or glass of bedtime milk and a cookie with each student. While they are eating their bedtime snack, reread one of the books from the unit or another book you have on nighttime issues, problems, or events as the bedtime story.

4. Set an alarm clock for two to three minutes. Tell students "good night, sleep tight" and ask them to pretend to sleep and not to wake up until the alarm clock goes off. Tell them that when the alarm clock goes off they need to be ready to raise their hands and tell one of their favorite activities or knowledge gained or to describe how they felt during the "pretend" bedtime experiences. Discussing how their pretend experiences reflect information they learned during the unit will help them summarize information and make connections between their experiences and information they have learned in books.

5. Display some of the work students have done in the unit so they may refer to it during the discussion.

PART 3

Content Areas and Multidisciplinary Connections

"Parents were wonderful. They came in and shared some of their jobs during a career fair that my grade level decided to have to accompany this unit. We all learned so much, and families felt so valued!"

—FIRST-GRADE TEACHER

Jobs and Careers

UNIT BOOKS

At Work in the Neighborhood
By Leslie A. Rotsky

Next Stop!
By Sarah Ellis
Illustrated by Ruth Ohi

Policeman Lou and Policewoman Sue
By Lisa Desimini

COMPUTER RESOURCES

Busy Town
I Spy: School Days

Thematic Connection

What do you want to be when you grow up? Who are the helpers who live and work in our neighborhoods? What do people who have different jobs do? These questions frequently surface in primary-grade classrooms because students are keenly interested in learning more about jobs and careers. Books in this unit provide basic information about various jobs and careers, including being a doctor, baker, teacher, florist, mail carrier, bus driver, and police officer. Through this unit, students will learn more about how to read, study, and respond to informational text. *At Work in the Neighborhood* (Rotsky, 2003) presents factual information about various jobs through an informational text question–answer format. *Next Stop!* (Ellis, 2000) follows a bus driver and his special helper throughout the daily stops on a bus route. *Policeman Lou and Policewoman Sue* (Desimini, 2003) is a narrative account of a day in the life of police partners as they carry out various routine and not-so-routine tasks.

Matrix of Literacy Skills and Strategies in Unit 12

Literacy Skills and Strategies	Activities	Title of Book	Pages
Brainstorming	C	*At Work in the Neighborhood*	190
	D	*Policeman Lou and Policewoman Sue*	196
Building background knowledge on the Internet*	U	—	188–189
	I	*At Work in the Neighborhood*	191–192
	I	*Next Stop!*	194
Building editing skills	C, D	*At Work in the Neighborhood*	190, 190–191
	C	*Policeman Lou and Policewoman Sue*	195–196
Building fluency	D	*At Work in the Neighborhood*	190–191
Comparing and contrasting	I	*At Work in the Neighborhood*	191–192
	R	*Policeman Lou and Policewoman Sue*	195
Composing in multimedia*	C, D, S	*At Work in the Neighborhood*	190, 190–191, 191
	C	*Next Stop!*	193
	C, D	*Policeman Lou and Policewoman Sue*	195–196, 196
Determining cause and effect	S	*At Work in the Neighborhood*	191
	R	*Next Stop!*	192–193
	S	*Policeman Lou and Policewoman Sue*	196
Determining story details	R	*Next Stop!*	192–193
Developing choral reading	D	*At Work in the Neighborhood*	190–191
Developing comprehension	U	—	188–189
	R, S	*At Work in the Neighborhood*	189, 191
	R, S	*Next Stop!*	192–193, 194
	R, S	*Policeman Lou and Policewoman Sue*	195, 196
Developing creative writing	D	*At Work in the Neighborhood*	190–191
Developing oral language	U, UC	—	188–189, 197
	R, D, I	*At Work in the Neighborhood*	189, 190–191, 191–192
	R, C, D	*Next Stop!*	192–193, 193, 193–194
	D, S	*Policeman Lou and Policewoman Sue*	196
Developing vocabulary	U	—	188–189
	R, D, S	*At Work in the Neighborhood*	189, 190–191, 191
	R, C, D, S, I	*Next Stop!*	192–193, 193, 193–194, 194, 194
	C, D	*Policeman Lou and Policewoman Sue*	195–196, 196
Drawing conclusions	R	*At Work in the Neighborhood*	189
	R	*Next Stop!*	192–193
E-mailing*	C	*Policeman Lou and Policewoman Sue*	195–196
Exploring critical reading and thinking	UC	—	197
	R	*Policeman Lou and Policewoman Sue*	195
Following directions	C, D, S	*At Work in the Neighborhood*	190, 190–191, 191
	C, S, I	*Next Stop!*	193, 194, 194
	C, D	*Policeman Lou and Policewoman Sue*	195–196, 196
Identifying letters	D	*At Work in the Neighborhood*	190–191
Making predictions	R	*Policeman Lou and Policewoman Sue*	195

(continued)

Literacy Skills and Strategies	Activities	Title of Book	Pages
Navigating hyperlinks*	U	—	188–189
	S, I	*At Work in the Neighborhood*	191, 191–192
	S, I	*Next Stop!*	194
	C, S, I	*Policeman Lou and Policewoman Sue*	195–196, 196, 197
Presenting work on a computer*	D	*At Work in the Neighborhood*	190–191
	D	*Next Stop!*	193–194
	D	*Policeman Lou and Policewoman Sue*	196
Reading aloud	R	*At Work in the Neighborhood*	189
	R	*Next Stop!*	192–193
	R	*Policeman Lou and Policewoman Sue*	195
Reading and listening for a purpose	U	—	188–189
	R, D	*At Work in the Neighborhood*	189, 190–191
	R	*Next Stop!*	192–193
	R, D, S	*Policeman Lou and Policewoman Sue*	195, 196, 196
Reading and using map skills	R	*At Work in the Neighborhood*	189
Reading informational text	U	—	188–189
	I	*At Work in the Neighborhood*	191–192
Sequencing	D, S	*At Work in the Neighborhood*	190–191, 191
Summarizing	UC	—	197
	R	*Next Stop!*	192–193
Understanding a main idea	C, S	*At Work in the Neighborhood*	190, 191
	R, C	*Next Stop!*	192–193, 193
Using adjectives	D	*At Work in the Neighborhood*	190–191
	D	*Next Stop!*	193–194
	S	*Policeman Lou and Policewoman Sue*	196
Using English as a second language	I	*Policeman Lou and Policewoman Sue*	197
Writing descriptive sentences	C	*At Work in the Neighborhood*	190
	D	*Next Stop!*	193–194
	C, D	*Policeman Lou and Policewoman Sue*	195–196, 196

* Indicates a new-literacy skill.
U = unit introduction; R = read-aloud and book discussion ideas; C = creativity and presentation software ideas; D = Digital Language Experience Approach; S = computer software activity; I = Internet resources and ideas; UC = unit conclusion

Unit Introduction

MATERIALS

■ This unit's books

Display the covers of the books and ask students to guess what all the books have in common. Guide students to explore what they already know about jobs and careers. Have they been thinking about what they want to be when they grow up? Many students will want to discuss the jobs of their caregivers. Visit Kids Work! (go to www.knowitall.org/kidswork/index.html) to explore interesting jobs in a virtual workplace community. Clicking on a hospital, television station, park, or information center on a pictorial map of a virtual community takes you to a menu of activities that include history, real people, job play, and work zone. Click on the "Real People" hyperlink to view videos of workers. Model how to navigate hyperlinks by clicking on at least three videos for different professions. Paraphrase the information and ask students to talk about at least one new thing they learned. Tell students they will be reading books and learning more about different jobs and careers in this unit.

Book 1:   At Work in the Neighborhood

Rotsky, L.A. (2003). New York: Blue Sky Press. $9.95. 8 pp.

BOOK REVIEW

This informational text includes a table of contents and index that consists of a series of questions and answers that are sure to hold the attention of even the youngest readers. The left side of each spread displays a bird's-eye view pictorial map of a neighborhood. The right page asks a question and invites students to turn the page with an arrow pointing the way to find the answer. For example, a photograph of a doctor examining a child tells the reader that doctors help sick people but asks a question about where doctors work. Students use map skills to locate the hospital. Turning the page reveals the map with the hospital circled in red so students can confirm or change their answers. Questions continue about bakers, teachers, florists, and mail carriers. Suggestions are included for a social studies–related project. The alphabetical index displays pages for each topic.

READ-ALOUD AND BOOK DISCUSSION IDEAS

The format of this book invites interactivity and shared reading. Before reading, display a reproduced copy of the map on page 4 of the book on chart paper. Explain how a pictorial map is intended to show where buildings and streets are located from the point of view of a bird flying overhead. Point to the names of the streets. Explain that by reading the map, you can tell that the gas station is on Beech Street. Explain that by reading the signs, you can tell the purpose of the buildings. Ask students to help you identify each building.

MATERIALS

- Chart paper map

During reading, tell them that as you read the book together, they will be looking at the map and figuring out where each person works. Tell them you will also talk about the type of work each person does. Follow the format of the book by asking questions and looking for answers. Draw attention to the tasks each person is performing in photographs.

After reading, ask students to elaborate on what each person does in the community. Doing so provides students with opportunities to summarize information and will help them build background knowledge about jobs and careers.

COMPUTER ACTIVITIES

Creativity and Presentation Software Ideas

After reading the book, ask students to brainstorm other jobs, careers, and businesses where people who were not mentioned in the book (e.g., police officer, shopkeeper) work. Invite pairs of students to select a type of job from the brainstormed list. Direct them to create a three-screen or three-page book in the format of *At Work in the Neighborhood* (Rotsky, 2003) by completing the following steps. Instruct students to use tools in creativity and presentation software, such as KidPix Studio Deluxe or PowerPoint, to design a picture on page 1 of the place where the people work and of a place the people do not work.

MATERIALS

- KidPix Studio Deluxe (1998) or PowerPoint (Microsoft Office 2003, 2003) software

1. Instruct students to perform the following three tasks on page 2:

   (a) Create an illustration (e.g., drawing, painting, clip art, imported photograph) of the person at work. For example, students could draw a chef cooking in the kitchen of a restaurant.

   (b) Write a sentence about what the person does, and ask a question about where he or she works.

   (c) Copy and paste the first page onto page 2, and draw a red circle around the correct building.

2. Collect students' work for a class book titled "Other People at Work in the Neighborhood."

3. Print out and bind for a class book or save as a multimedia slide show.

Digital Language Experience Approach

To reinforce the information from the book *At Work in the Neighborhood* (Rotsky, 2003) about places where people work, take a class neighborhood walk to help students make connections between locations and the people who work there. During the walk, take digital photographs of various business and job locations. Discuss the type of work people do who work in those locations. If possible, invite workers to answer one or two questions about their jobs. This activity will help students make connections between the texts that they read and their real-life experiences.

MATERIALS

- Digital camera
- KidPix Studio Deluxe (1998) or PowerPoint (Microsoft Office 2003, 2003) software

1. Note the addresses of where these people work.

2. Import the photographs into creativity and presentation software such as KidPix Studio Deluxe or PowerPoint, print out copies, and ask students during whole-group time to help you put the pictures in sequence. What did they see first? Second? This activity helps students use sequencing skills.

3. Under each photograph, instruct students to type information that workers provided: the name of the business, who works there, at least one job description for each location, and the address taken from the notes. Demonstrate how to edit text while composing.

4. Help and instruct a small group of students to assemble the screen pages into a slide show to share during whole-group time. To support students' awareness of concepts about print and to support fluency, instruct students to chorally read the information on screen as you point to the words. In addition, during rereadings, ask emerging readers to point to letters or words they recognize in the text.

5. Post the slide show project on a class webpage so parents can view students' collaborative work.

6. Instruct students to share what they have learned. Encourage students to make connections to the focus text, their lives, and computer activities. Remind students who are listening to a peer explain his or her work during author's computer chair (see Appendix B) to ask clarifying questions or comment on which part of the computer activity they like the most and why.

Computer Software Activity

Tell students that by visiting different places on the streets in Busy Town, they will learn about different jobs. At Bruno's Deli, students help Huckle Cat serve food and drinks. Games also offer students practice in color and shape recognition, matching words to pictures, and visual discrimination. At Building a House, Huckle builds a house for the Stitches family. Activities such as shingling the roof and furnishing the house involve directionality, orientation on screen, part–whole relationships, problem solving, observing details, and sequencing. After students help Huckle build the house, students click on a lamp to read or hear a nursery rhyme. Dr. Diane's hospital involves students in helping to bandage Norbert the Elephant. Students increase their vocabulary by listening for a body part or reading the word in the box and moving a bandage to the correct body part.

> **MATERIALS**
>
> ■ Busy Town (1993) software

Internet Resources and Ideas

Sadlier-Oxford Educational Publishing from PreK–12+: www.sadlier-oxford.com
Visit this website for interactive games on jobs and careers. Click on the "Student" hyperlink at the top of the homepage to access online games and activities. Click on the hyperlink under the Content Area Readers section of the page to go to social studies interactive games. When students click on the "Social Studies" hyperlink titled "Who Works Here?" they will see a pop-up window game page for mixing, matching, and printing out uniforms worn by firefighters, nurses, and police officers. Students will enjoy clicking through arrows that instantly change clothing items, such as hats, shirts, and pants, that they see on a person. This interactive game reinforces the concept that people wear different types of clothing to work. To increase students' vocabulary knowledge, invite them to turn their printouts into diagrams by labeling the different parts of the uniform they have selected. This interactive game is appropriate for emerging readers who cannot yet read independently and who will benefit from working with visual images.

Fluent readers may explore the website independently by clicking on the "Early Reader" hyperlink. Next, students can click on the "Social Studies" hyperlink titled "At Work in the Neighborhood." The game board presents a column of workers on the left side of the screen that includes a firefighter, policeman, baker, and gas station worker. Students can click on a worker and drag the mouse to connect the worker with the building they work in. Students who need support with reading directions may click on a speaker icon to hear directions read aloud.

Role Models on the Web: www.rolemodel.net

Students can visit this website to conduct a virtual field trip to learn more about people who have inspiring careers. Students can learn about people who excel in their chosen careers by clicking on a hyperlink about role models such as golfer Tiger Woods, actor Christopher Reeve, tennis pro Monica Seles, news anchor Diane Sawyer, and others. Emerging and developing readers will need a cross-age computer buddy to complete a webquest, an activity that is an online scavenger hunt. Provide a list of three to four questions so students can follow hyperlinks to learn more about people from various careers who are role models. For example, students can answer the following questions: How does Tiger Woods, pro golfer, help disadvantaged kids? How did Tiger Woods learn to play golf? What tournaments has Tiger Woods won? Who was news anchor Diane Sawyer's role model? What hobbies did Christopher Reeve have as a little boy? How did those hobbies help prepare him for his job as an actor? Students can record one or two facts they learned on paper or on KidPix Studio Deluxe (1998) and share what they learned during author's computer chair (see Appendix B).

Book 2:   Next Stop!

Ellis, S. (2000). Ill. R. Ohi. Toronto, ON: Fitzhenry & Whiteside. $13.95. 32 pp.

BOOK REVIEW

On Saturday, Claire rides the bus home. She sits right at the front of the bus and helps the driver. Right after the driver announces the street name for each stop (e.g., "Next stop, Moss Road"), she adds more detailed information about a site of interest at the stop (e.g., the museum stop). At each stop, she observes the people getting on and off the bus—a bald man, a woman with many bags, a girl with red hair, three big kids, and so on. Then, Claire sees a smiling woman who gives her a kiss. She is Claire's mom, who also kisses the driver, who is her mom's husband and Claire's dad. When the bus driver announces the name of the next stop, Claire and the bus driver announce that the next stop is home. This simple story is enhanced by detailed ink-and-watercolor illustrations and provides a small child's viewpoint on a bus ride around the city. The detailed illustrations highlight the variety of interests and activities of the riders whose lives briefly intersect with others on the bus. The repetition of the text suits the stop–start structure of a bus ride.

READ-ALOUD AND BOOK DISCUSSION IDEAS

Before reading, display a city bus schedule or a school bus schedule for the class. Read aloud some of the schedules and ask their purpose. Tell students they will learn about the job of a bus driver.

MATERIALS

■ Bus schedule

During reading, students will enjoy discussing what each person is doing in the story until he or she arrives at his or her destination. There are many cause–effect experiences for students to identify. For example, when a woman with many bags drops one with a puppy in it, the puppy runs away, causing the woman to drop her other bags.

The effect is that toys from the woman's other bags scatter everywhere. The result is also a chain reaction when Claire spills her drink, and papers fall from a busy woman's hand. Help students understand how all these events are related. So many things are happening at once.

Ask students who they think the smiling woman is. Why did she kiss Claire? After the smiling woman kisses the bus driver, who do students think he is? Why do they think so? After reading, ask students to comment on all the places the bus stopped. Why did the bus not take each person directly to his or her house or to a particular store? Discuss the purpose of a bus route and help students summarize what they have learned about a bus driver's duties.

COMPUTER ACTIVITIES

Creativity and Presentation Software Ideas

Using KidPix Studio Deluxe creativity and presentation software, students use the animation feature to create a busy street scene, complete with a bus selected from transportation stamps. Complete this activity by following these steps:

> **MATERIALS**
>
> ■ KidPix Studio Deluxe (1998) software

1. Instruct students to click and drag the stamp of the bus in starts and stops across the screen to simulate the stops on a bus route.

2. Encourage students to use at least two other stamps to simulate traffic, pedestrians, and objects in the street along a bus route.

3. Ask students to pretend they are driving the bus and to talk about the things they see on their bus route.

Encourage students to share bus-route animations and describe people, events, and purposes of the bus ride during author's computer chair (see Appendix B). Through this activity, students learn to use their imagination as they create their own version of this book's story. They learn more about adjectives and verbs as they construct meaningful animations of vocabulary terms.

Digital Language Experience Approach

Invite students to recreate a bus route in the block center, which is a location where children play with blocks and toy cars, so they may playfully explore how bus drivers work in the city.

> **MATERIALS**
>
> ■ Blocks
> ■ Digital camera
> ■ Index cards
> ■ KidPix Studio Deluxe (1998) or PowerPoint (Microsoft Office 2003, 2003) software
> ■ Toy bus
> ■ Toy cars

1. Take digital photographs of small groups of students setting up a bus route in a pretend city using blocks to create buildings, sidewalks, and streets.

2. Tell students to make signs from index cards for all the stores and bus stops along the bus route.

3. Encourage students to move the toy bus and cars as they play along the route in the streets of the city.

4. Import photographs into creativity and presentation software, such as KidPix Studio Deluxe or PowerPoint, and allow students to talk about and describe pictures and then dictate a story about the bus route.

5. Print out photographs and bind them into a class book or use them to create a slide show. Use a title such as "Our Block Center Bus Routes." Students have occasions to learn more about vocabulary and build richer background knowledge about jobs by doing this activity.

6. Invite students to share their computer work in progress to get feedback from students or showcase completed work. Encourage classmates to talk about what they like best about the work and to ask questions about the computer-related aspects of the activity. Students also can discuss how the activity relates to the unit's theme and the focus book, *Next Stop!* (Ellis, 2000).

Computer Software Activity

> ### MATERIALS
>
> ■ I Spy: School Days (1995) software

Using I Spy: School Days, enter Wood Block City, a community built out of wooden blocks. Students view six scenes related to a community event such as a festival, circus, or bike race. Students listen to a riddle and hunt for objects listed. An additional tool allows students to view each scene from three different perspectives. As students hunt for objects related to occupations and community events, they gain vocabulary knowledge.

Internet Resources and Ideas

Kids and Community: www.planning.org/kidsandcommunity
The Kids and Community website is designed to help students learn about cities and city planning. There are several activities that allow students to upload their own work, such as drawings or stories about cities. Emerging and developing readers will need the support of a cross-age computer buddy to interact with this website.

The hyperlink "Crazy City Stories" encourages students to write and submit their own town stories. The hyperlink "Scavenger Hunt Scrapbook" invites students to explore their town by collecting artifacts and writing unique stories. Students learn how to follow directions, manipulate the computer mouse, express oral language, problem solve, read a 3-D map, and learn vocabulary. In addition, the website provides guidelines for students to construct scrapbooks.

Book 3:   Policeman Lou and Policewoman Sue

Desimini, L. (2003). New York: Blue Sky Press. $15.95. 40 pp.

BOOK REVIEW

Join this policeman and policewoman team as they go about their daily experiences of their job. The oil and acrylic illustrations realistically depict the start of Policeman Lou and Policewoman Sue's day—sharing a cup of coffee and a muffin at a sidewalk café. Policeman Lou says hello and watches other workers go about their daily tasks. Policewoman Sue helps children cross the street to go to school. Other activities include taking care of a stray dog, writing a parking ticket, eating lunch at a diner, catching a purse thief, writing a police report, and sharing supper.

READ-ALOUD AND BOOK DISCUSSION IDEAS

Before reading, display the front cover of the book, which shows the first part of the title, *Policeman Lou*, and an illustration of a male police officer. Ask students to talk about the job of a policeman. Then turn the book over and show the back cover, which shows the second part of the title, *Policewoman Sue*, and an illustration of a female officer. Ask students to talk about the job of a policewoman. Would duties be any different for policewomen or would they be the same for them? Should policemen and policewomen have the same duties? Why or why not? Write down students' predictions about police officers' work.

During reading, make a list of a police officer's daily activities. To help students make connections to their own lives, ask them to think about activities they have observed police officers doing.

After reading, ask students to check, change, or confirm their predictions. Discuss with students gender roles in the workplace.

COMPUTER ACTIVITIES

Creativity and Presentation Software Ideas

Using creativity and presentation software, such as KidPix Studio Deluxe or PowerPoint, invite students to make a thank-you card for police officers in a local precinct or station. Discuss with students the differences between a friendly letter and a thank-you card. For example, a friendly letter includes the date and the name of the person receiving the letter. A general thank-you card may not always include the name of a specific person but may include a more general heading such as "Dear Police Officer." Friendly letters are usually very personal and include details about different types of events in the life of the sender. A thank-you card focuses on writing about different ways the sender appreciates actions or characteristics of the receiver.

> **MATERIALS**
>
> ■ Chart paper
> ■ KidPix Studio Deluxe (1998) or PowerPoint (Microsoft Office 2003, 2003) software
> ■ Markers

Complete the following steps to accomplish this activity.

1. Recall from the book the things that police officers do to help the community be a safe place.

2. Create a word bank chart of keywords and post it by the computer center. As students compose thank-you notes in KidPix Studio Deluxe for the police officers, they easily can revise their work by rereading the message to make sure it says what they want it to say, checking for spelling, and then spelling words correctly using editing tools.

3. Print out the cards, address the envelopes, and place the cards in the mail.

4. Visit CardBlast.com (go to www1.cardblast.com/apphtml/dd/showbkg-23.html) if you want students to send a thank-you e-card to a police officer. This website allows students to pick not only a background for their cards but also pictures, animations, words, and music.

5. Discuss emergency phone numbers and procedures with students to reinforce knowledge students need about safety.

6. Send home to parents and caregivers a list of emergency phone numbers, such as 911 and poison control, with a note that suggests they post the list by their telephone.

Digital Language Experience Approach

MATERIALS

- Digital camera
- KidPix Studio Deluxe (1998) or PowerPoint (Microsoft Office 2003, 2003) software
- Markers
- Paper

Invite a police officer or security guard to visit the class so students may learn background information about security personnel that will improve their comprehension. In addition, this will help students practice oral language and composing skills.

1. Instruct students to generate a list of questions to ask during the interview, such as How does someone learn to become a police officer? What are the most important skills they need to learn? What equipment do they use and why? What questions do students most want answered?

2. Take digital photographs to create a photograph essay of the visit.

3. Import photographs into creativity and presentation software, such as KidPix Studio Deluxe or PowerPoint, and invite students to dictate or write accompanying text.

4. Print out a class book after creating a title page with a title such as "Our Interview With a Police Officer." Post key photograph essay pages on a class webpage.

Students will enjoy reading photograph essays of a police officer's visit during author's computer chair (see Appendix B). Other students will want to showcase things they have learned about police officers' work in Busy Town (1993; see the following activity). Help students make connections between the computer activities and the book *Policeman Lou and Policewoman Sue* (Desimini, 2003).

Computer Software Activity

There are a lot of things to do in Busy Town. For example, the delivery truck must make deliveries of special goods to specific locations. However, when the truck drives recklessly (e.g., students manipulate a computer mouse to make a truck run over a trashcan or speed through a

MATERIALS

- Busy Town (1993) software

school zone), a policeman on a motorcycle gives the truck driver a ticket or warning. As students interact with the game, highlight the cause-and-effect relationship of the reason the truck driver received a ticket. Tell students that after playing, they should be ready to explain and describe some of the duties of a police officer in Busy Town.

Internet Resources and Ideas

The Crime Prevention Coloring Book: www.sannet.gov/police/prevention/crimeprev/cpbook.pdf
The crime prevention coloring book, a printout coloring book about safety tips provided by the
San Diego Police Department for elementary school students, is 20 pages long and written in both
English and Spanish. Spanish-speaking students will benefit from seeing vocabulary words written
in Spanish and English. Students can take printouts of the coloring-book pages home to share with
parents and caregivers the things they have learned about police officers' work during the unit.

The Police Notebook: www.ou.edu/oupd/welcome.htm
The University of Oklahoma's website consists of a virtual police notebook of helpful facts and
hyperlinks. The hyperlink titled "Kid Safety" leads to a webpage titled "Kid Safety on the Internet."
An adult or a cross-age computer buddy will be needed to help emerging and developing readers
read the important safety tips. For example, suggestions for Internet safety include reminders for
students to not give their name or address to anyone online and to be wary of strangers on the
Internet.

Unit Conclusion

Display the computer work created by students during the unit. Invite
different students to talk about their experiences and summarize what
they have learned. Ask them to discuss and vote on the computer
activity and the book they most enjoyed. Place a blue ribbon (e.g.,
made of blue construction paper ribbon pasted onto a yellow circle) on
the book cover students have chosen, and place it in a place of honor
for the day.

MATERIALS

- Blue and yellow construction
  paper
- Students' computer work from
  the unit

Transportation

UNIT BOOKS

Alphabeep: A Zipping, Zooming ABC
By Debora Pearson
Illustrated by Edward Miller

Back to School
By Maya Ajmera and John D. Ivanko

On the Move
By Sarah Fecher, Deborah Kespert, and Belinda Webster
Illustrated by Gaëtan Evrard and Jon Stuart

COMPUTER RESOURCES

Busy Town
Tonka Construction
The Airport

Thematic Connection

Bumpy school buses, red pickup trucks, family vans, grandma's big green car, speeding ambulances, and construction equipment are all forms of transportation that students find intriguing. The movement and noise of traffic on busy roads, the sounds of chugging locomotives, and the zoom of jets overhead offer sights and sounds that move at the fast pace of our busy lives. The books in this collection offer students opportunities to explore various forms of transportation that are designed to move people and things from one place to another. *Alphabeep: A Zipping, Zooming ABC* (Pearson, 2003) explores various forms of transportation, which are presented in alphabetical order. Simple illustrations provide important contextual details. *Back to School* (Ajmera & Ivanko, 2001) may seem like an unusual book to include in the collection because it deals primarily with learning about schooling around the world; however, a spread of photographs shows how different students around the world get to school. This book also functions as a springboard for discussion and activities. *On the Move* (Fecher, Kespert, & Webster, 2000), an informational book about machines that float on water, fly in the sky, or roll on the ground, serves as an excellent resource throughout the unit.

Matrix of Literacy Skills and Strategies in Unit 13

Literacy Skills and Strategies	Activities	Title of Book	Pages
Brainstorming	U	—	201–202
	C, D	*On the Move*	209
Building background knowledge on the Internet*	U	—	201–202
	I	*Alphabeep: A Zipping, Zooming ABC*	205
	I	*Back to School*	208
	I	*On the Move*	211
Comparing and contrasting	R, C	*Back to School*	206, 206–207
Composing in multimedia*	C, D, S	*Alphabeep: A Zipping, Zooming ABC*	203–204, 204, 204–205
	C, D	*Back to School*	206–207, 207
	C, D	*On the Move*	209
Creating and using charts	U, UC	—	201–202, 211
	C	*Back to School*	206–207
Creating concept maps and graphic organizers	U	—	201–202
Determining story details	D	*Alphabeep: A Zipping, Zooming ABC*	204
	R	*Back to School*	206
Developing comprehension	R, S	*Alphabeep: A Zipping, Zooming ABC*	202–203, 204–205
	R, C	*Back to School*	206, 206–207
	R	*On the Move*	208
Developing context clues	R	*Alphabeep: A Zipping, Zooming ABC*	202–203
Developing creative writing	C, D	*Alphabeep: A Zipping, Zooming ABC*	203–204, 204
	C, D	*On the Move*	209
Developing critical reading and thinking	U, UC	—	201–202, 211
	R	*Back to School*	206
Developing oral language	U, UC	—	201–202, 211
	I	*Alphabeep: A Zipping, Zooming ABC*	205
Developing vocabulary	U, UC	—	201–202, 211
	R, C, D, S, I	*Alphabeep: A Zipping, Zooming ABC*	202–203, 203–204, 204, 204–205, 205
	R, C, D	*Back to School*	206, 206–207, 207
	R, C, D, S, I	*On the Move*	208, 209, 209, 210–211, 211
Distinguishing sounds	R	*Alphabeep: A Zipping, Zooming ABC*	202–203
Following directions	C, D, S	*Alphabeep: A Zipping, Zooming ABC*	203–204, 204, 204–205
	S	*Back to School*	207
	C, S	*On the Move*	209, 210–211

(continued)

Matrix of Literacy Skills and Strategies in Unit 13 (continued)

Literacy Skills and Strategies	Activities	Title of Book	Pages
Identifying letters	C, D	*Alphabeep: A Zipping, Zooming ABC*	203–204, 204
Inferring	R	*Alphabeep: A Zipping, Zooming ABC*	202–203
Making multicultural connections	R	*Back to School*	206
	I	*On the Move*	211
Making predictions	I	*On the Move*	211
Navigating hyperlinks*	U	—	201–202
	S, I	*Alphabeep: A Zipping, Zooming ABC*	204–205, 205
	S, I	*Back to School*	207, 208
	I	*On the Move*	211
Presenting work on a computer*	UC	—	211
	D	*Alphabeep: A Zipping, Zooming ABC*	204
	C	*Back to School*	206–207
	C, D	*On the Move*	209
Reading and listening for a purpose	UC	—	211
	R, S	*Alphabeep: A Zipping, Zooming ABC*	202–203, 204–205
	R, D, I	*Back to School*	206, 207, 208
	R, S	*On the Move*	208, 210–211
Reading informational text	R, I	*Alphabeep: A Zipping, Zooming ABC*	202–203, 205
	R, I	*Back to School*	206, 208
	R	*On the Move*	208
Recognizing ABC order	C	*Alphabeep: A Zipping, Zooming ABC*	203–204
Retelling	U	—	201–202
	D	*Alphabeep: A Zipping, Zooming ABC*	204
Understanding a main idea	S	*Alphabeep: A Zipping, Zooming ABC*	204–205
	C	*Back to School*	206–207
	C, D, S	*On the Move*	209, 209, 210–211
Using phonics: Letter–sound correspondence	C, D	*Alphabeep: A Zipping, Zooming ABC*	203–204, 204
Using phonics: Onsets and rimes	I	*On the Move*	211
Using phonics: Rhyming words	I	*On the Move*	211
Using verbs	R, C, D	*Alphabeep: A Zipping, Zooming ABC*	202–203, 203–204, 204
Visualizing	R	*Alphabeep: A Zipping, Zooming ABC*	202–203
Writing descriptive sentences	C, D	*Alphabeep: A Zipping, Zooming ABC*	203–204, 204
	D	*Back to School*	207
	C	*On the Move*	209
Writing letters	D	*Back to School*	207

* Indicates a new-literacy skill.
U = unit introduction; R = read-aloud and book discussion ideas; C = creativity and presentation software ideas; D = Digital Language Experience Approach; S = computer software activity; I = Internet resources and ideas; UC = unit conclusion

Unit Introduction

The National Highway Traffic Safety Administration's homepage (go to www.nhtsa.dot.gov/kids) is an excellent resource page for teachers. In addition, the homepage also has a color graphic that illustrates various forms of transportation. Bookmark and locate the page before whole-group time so it is ready for discussion. Ask students to look at the computer monitor screen. Teachers of emerging and developing readers may need to point to each different form of transportation (e.g., airplane, bicycle, car, emergency medical services vehicle, bus) to focus students' attention. Ask students to name the different types of transportation they see.

Next, ask students to think for a minute about some of the places they have visited. Use a transportation T-chart (see Figure 32) to record the information students share. For example, as students discuss different locations (e.g., Grandma's house, the grocery store, shopping, vacation sites) write down the location and the student's name. Then, ask each student to recall how he or she got to the place he or she mentioned. Point out the different forms of transportation they used. Briefly point out why they used different types of transportation (e.g., airplanes for long distances, cars for local trips, tricycles or bicycles for neighborhood visits just down the street). Tell students that in the upcoming unit they will be learning about many different types of transportation.

Display the books from the unit: *Alphabeep: A Zipping, Zooming ABC* (Pearson, 2003), *Back to School* (Ajmera & Ivanko, 2001), and *On the Move* (Fecher, Kespert, & Webster, 2000). Ask students to look at the illustrations on the covers of the books and predict which forms of transportation they will find in each book. Introduce a Transportation Notes T-Chart (see Figure 33)

MATERIALS

- Chart paper
- Flipchart or butcher paper
- Markers
- This unit's books

Figure 32
Transportation T-Chart

A Place I Have Been	How I Got There
To my Grandma's (Jason)	airplane
To grocery store (Seth)	minivan
To my friend's house (Mary)	bicycle

Figure 33
Transportation Notes T-Chart

Form of Transportation	Where We Learned About It	Most Important Thing We Learned

that you and the students will use throughout the unit. Post it on a flipchart or on a bulletin board covered with butcher paper. At the end of each day, fill in the chart by asking students to recall (a) the forms of transportation they learned about, (b) the sources of the information (e.g., a story, an informational book, the Internet, interviews), and (c) what they think is the most important thing they learned from the unit book that was read aloud that day.

Book 1:   Alphabeep: A Zipping, Zooming ABC

Pearson, D. (2003). Ill. E. Miller. New York: Holiday House. $16.95. 32 pp.

BOOK REVIEW

The opening lines "Zipping, zooming down the street.... What's up ahead? Come on—Beep, beep!" (p. 1), which are accompanied by illustrations in vibrant colors, invite readers to travel the streets of cities, neighborhoods, and country roads to learn about various forms of transportation. A vehicle or road sign represents each letter of the alphabet. For example, the one-way sign represents the letter *o*. The newspaper truck represents the letter *n*. The sounds of vehicles in use also are included as illustrations (e.g., automobile horns honk and brakes screech).

READ-ALOUD AND BOOK DISCUSSION IDEAS

Before reading *Alphabeep: A Zipping, Zooming ABC* (Pearson, 2003), draw students' attention to the subtitle, *A Zipping, Zooming ABC*. Invite them to listen to the different types of sounds they hear as you read about different forms of transportation. Also draw attention to the end pages, which display street signs.

During reading, emerging readers will enjoy pointing to the different types of transportation they recognize. Developing readers will enjoy pointing to and reading all of the places where the word *beep* is written above the vehicles. All students are likely to enjoy an interactive experience. For example, tell them that every time you touch the word *beep* you want them to make the beep sound. After reading the 12 beeps, ask students if they think there was just a little bit of traffic on the street or a whole lot. Why was everyone beeping his or her horn? Emerging readers may also enjoy interacting by doing hand or finger motions to some of the sounds they hear for different vehicles. For example, students may first listen to the rich words of the text (including flip-flopping and gushing) about the cement mixer read aloud but on a subsequent reading may make flip-flopping and gushing motions at appropriate points in the text. For example, for the flip-flopping motion, students extend their arms and rotate their hands from left to right. For the gushing motion, students extend their hands over their heads and move them forward and downward quickly in an arching movement. Students of all ability levels also can close their eyes and visualize the movement of the vehicle based on the sound they hear.

After reading, tell students that the illustrator, Edward Miller, has a website that they will visit before the unit is over so they can learn more about him, other books that he illustrated, and activities related to *Alphabeep: A Zipping, Zooming ABC*. This is sure to be a book that young students will enjoy hearing repeatedly. It also is filled with wonderful details, sound words, action words, and vocabulary.

COMPUTER ACTIVITIES

Creativity and Presentation Software Ideas

Emerging, developing, and fluent readers will all enjoy innovating on alphabet pages of the focus book. For example, for the "A is for Ambulance" page, which shows an ambulance speeding through traffic on a busy street, ask students to illustrate the scene on a computer screen. Students use painting tools within the creativity programs (e.g., KidPix Studio Deluxe 3 or PowerPoint) for this assignment. Complete the following steps to accomplish this activity.

> **MATERIALS**
>
> ■ KidPix Studio Deluxe 3 (2000) or PowerPoint (Microsoft Office 2003, 2003) software

1. In KidPix Studio Deluxe 3, ask each student to select a page of the book and create an animation that represents the focus word depicted. For example, for the "A is for Ambulance" page, students might select an icon or stamp of an ambulance using the Stampimator tool to dynamically illustrate the way the ambulance moves and weaves through the other cars on the street. This program function is as simple as clicking on an icon or stamp, holding down the mouse, and moving the mouse (or track pad) to drag the object across the screen in different types of movements that may range from slow zigzags to quick curves. Releasing the mouse results in an instant animation. The ambulance can start, stop, weave, or race across the screen.

2. Instruct students to dictate or keyboard a sentence as text for the animation, using vibrant verbs such as *zoom, chug, dash,* and *rattle.*

3. Instruct students to help place pages in ABC order.

4. Celebrate students' work by allowing them to display and talk about their animations as an author's computer chair activity (see Appendix B).

Digital Language Experience Approach

Students will learn more about vocabulary words related to transportation by creating a digital language experience activity of the vehicles they see in the school parking lot.

MATERIALS

■ Digital camera
■ KidPix Studio Deluxe 3 (2000) or PowerPoint (Microsoft Office 2003, 2003) software

1. Take small group walks to the school parking lot and ask students to point out different forms of transportation to include in a photograph essay.

2. Take photographs of sedans, sport utility vehicles, trucks, buses, red cars, black trucks, yellow buses, and so forth that students point out and describe.

3. Import the photographs into creativity and presentation software such as KidPix Studio Deluxe 3 or PowerPoint.

4. Ask students to write descriptive sentences about each photograph. Use this opportunity to elicit and extend students' oral descriptive language and knowledge of sound–symbol relationships as you sound out and spell words together. Ask a series of questions to prompt students' thinking and support their ability to talk about what they are seeing in the photograph. A simple statement such as "I see a red truck" may be extended to a more complex statement such as "I see a long, red truck that has four big black wheels and a trailer hitch."

5. Compile the photographs and the students' accompanying statements into a class book or slide show that students will enjoy seeing and reading over and over again. Include a title such as "Transportation We Saw in Our Parking Lot" on a title page.

Computer Software Activity

Teachers should first preview the various sections of the town in the Busy Town software and then direct students to specific activities that will provide opportunities for building vocabulary concepts about transportation. Students are more likely to pay close attention and remember vocabulary if teachers tell them they will have an opportunity to show some of the things they learned about transportation during author's computer chair (see Appendix B).

MATERIALS

■ Busy Town (1993) software

This program introduces students to a main menu of a town complete with a fire station, delicatessen, hospital, gas station, warehouse, house under construction, and harbor. To move around the town and to play different games, students may manipulate various forms of transportation, such as a delivery truck to a forklift. In addition, if a student's handling of the mouse results in a car crash, the Busy Town policeman arrives on his motorcycle.

Captain Salty directs students in how to follow directions to load his ship with all the things it needs to go on a voyage. Students have opportunities to learn about the different supplies and materials required for a long voyage. Students can help two Busy Town characters, Huckle Cat and Lowly Worm, provide service for buses, cars, and motorcycles at the gas station. Students complete each task that must be done (e.g., fill the gas tank, add oil to the engine, fix a flat tire). Through these tasks, students learn how transportation vehicles receive fuel and maintenance.

Internet Resources and Ideas

Edward Miller: Children's Book Illustrator/Writer/Designer: www.edmiller.com
This website presents a biography of the illustrator and provides activities to accompany the book, such as a free bookmark, a pattern for a three-dimensional truck to color and fold, and stickers that can be printed out on labels (the website provides directions). Click on the "Book Designs" hyperlink on the homepage to get to a full screen of thumbnail sketches of Miller's work. Click on the thumbnail to see a full-screen view of an airport scene with a labeled cross-section of a commercial plane. Primary-grade students will have occasions to practice oral language skills as they talk about different parts of a plane.

EcoIQ: www.ecoiq.com
This website offers free online images of transportation. Go to http://shop.ecoiq.com/ecoiq/onlineimages/collection07TC.html for images of people walking and biking downtown. This is a great website to use as a springboard for discussing safety issues and for eliciting oral language as students are invited to point out and talk about photographs, such as bicycles, cars, trucks, and pedestrians who all share the road safely.

Bulletin Boards: www.sbcss.k12.ca.us/sbcss/specialeducation/ecthematic/trans/bbi.htm
Go to this website for transportation bulletin boards that may enhance the classroom learning environment and provide occasions for discussing various types of transportation displayed on the boards.

Book 2:   Back to School

Ajmera, M., & Ivanko, J.D. (2001). Watertown, MA: Charlesbridge; Washington, DC: Shakti for Children. $6.95. 32 pp.

BOOK REVIEW

This informational text presents colorful photographs and text that focus on school life. Photographs provide images of students around the world engaged in school-related activities such as reading various types of materials, wearing different types of clothing, and getting to school using different modes of transportation.

READ-ALOUD AND BOOK DISCUSSION IDEAS

One of the most intriguing things about this book is the collection of stunning photographs that provide glimpses into how students around the world go to school. Because young students who are emerging readers are likely forming initial impressions about school, before reading, it is important for teachers to first invite students to discuss some of the things they have learned about their own school. Where do students sit during the day? Is school held inside or outside? What do the students read? What do they wear to school? Tell students that they will be reading a book that has pictures from schools all over the world.

During reading, draw students' attention to the pages about transportation. Ask students to look over the details in the illustrations, listen to the text, and be ready to talk about what they have noticed at the end of the book.

After reading, return to the pages about transportation. Ask how students in the pictures go to school (e.g., riding a horse-drawn wagon in Bolivia, traveling by boat in Peru, using a rickshaw in the Philippines). To foster critical thinking, ask students why certain forms of transportation are better for getting to school in different parts of the world. Why would students in Peru not take a school bus to get to school?

COMPUTER ACTIVITIES

Creativity and Presentation Software Ideas

Instruct students to make a chart about how they get to school by using creativity and presentation software tools in KidPix Studio Deluxe such as stamps or clip art.

MATERIALS

■ KidPix Studio Deluxe (1998) software

---

1. Ask students to raise their hands if they ride the bus, ride in a car, ride a bicycle, walk, or use another form of transportation to get to school. Take a mental count for each form of transportation.

2. Open KidPix Studio Deluxe and type "How We Get to School" as a title for a chart.

3. Type each form of transportation in a row at the top of the chart and then draw a line under the row.

4. Ask students to have a turn at the computer to select a stamp of their form of school transportation. Type each student's name beside the form of transportation stamped in the appropriate column on the screen.

5. Follow up by asking students to view the chart and decide which are the most widely used and least used ways of getting to school.

6. Post a printed out chart on the bulletin board or an electronic copy on the class webpage, or print out copies for each student to take home and share with caregivers. Students may also ask their caregivers about how they went to and from school when they were students as a home–school activity.

For an example of a graph on how students get to school, go to www.wside.k12.il.us/pes/ Transpt/transcht1.gif. Students can compare their graph to the graph posted on the Internet. How are they the same? Different? Why are they different?

Digital Language Experience Approach

Create a photograph essay of a bus driver's work driving a form of transportation, the school bus.

MATERIALS

- Digital camera
- KidPix Studio Deluxe 3 (2000) or PowerPoint (Microsoft Office 2003, 2003) software

1. Take a photograph with a digital camera of a school bus driver.

2. Import the photograph into a creativity and presentation software program such as KidPix Studio Deluxe 3 or PowerPoint. Display the photograph on the computer monitor during whole-group time.

3. Ask students what questions they would like to ask the bus driver about his or her job. Record a list of the questions to guide an interview with the bus driver.

4. During a convenient time, interview the bus driver (e.g., after students are dropped off at school, while waiting for students to be dismissed after school). If possible, invite the bus driver to come into class for an interview.

5. Under the digital photograph of the bus driver, type information that students learned during the interview (e.g., how to drive a bus, become a bus driver, learn the route, keep everyone safe, drive the bus in traffic).

6. Print out and read the photograph essay during whole-group time. Highlight vocabulary words and key information that relate to the unit transportation theme.

7. Compose and send a classroom thank-you note or a friendly letter expressing thanks to the bus driver. Students may include illustrations about the bus driver's work on the bus.

Computer Software Activity

MATERIALS

- Tonka Construction (2001) CD-ROM

The Tonka Construction software program begins in "Tonkaland," where users can learn about 14 trucks that are used in virtual building projects. Animated workers who provide support on how to use the program are available. Construction projects include choices of (1) Truck Maintenance, for using a paint program to create trucks; (2) City Construction, for constructing various tasks at buildings (students prepare the sites by demolishing existing structures, excavating the ground, and surveying one of the sites—the task is complete when a city park is built); (3) Desert Road, for clearing rocks, grading the ground, laying asphalt, and painting lines on a paved road; (4) Snowy Mountain Rescue, for clearing an avalanche and rescuing vehicles; and (5) Quarry Exploration, for explorative play as students use a bulldozer to search for buried gold. Info Alley, a glossary section, provides details for 14 trucks and their uses. In addition, a puzzle and paint section invites students to study three trucks by repairing and painting them. Students learn about following directions and fine motor skills, such as mouse clicking and dragging objects, to accomplish tasks and solve problems.

Internet Resources and Ideas

M & O Bus Lines: www.mo-buslines.com/ie/safety/kidsafety.html
This website guides teachers and students through information on school bus safety. Students will enjoy viewing the animated features and photographs about school safety rules.

Snappy Safari With Rivera the Cheetah: www.mnsafetycouncil.org/snappy/pledge.cfm
Students learn about transportation safety and how to gather information from the Internet in this activity. The Snappy Safari hyperlink presents an animated character named Rivera the Cheetah. A menu of transportation activities includes a hyperlink in the upper right corner to take the Buckle Up Pledge online: "I will buckle up every time I ride (and I'll remind other people in the car to buckle up, too" (¶ 2). The Minnesota Safety Council will send a certificate to each student who types in his or her name indicating that he or she has taken the pledge.

Book 3:   On the Move

Fecher, S., Kespert, D., & Webster, B. (2000). Ill. G. Evrard & J. Stuart. Princeton, NJ: Two-Can. $15.25. 30 pp.

BOOK REVIEW

This informational text has detailed photographs with captions about transportation, diagrams of various parts of transportation vehicles, a table of contents, and an index. Students will enjoy learning how to use these informational text features to locate specific information about transportation. For example, students may learn about study skills by looking up a particular form of transportation, such as trucks, in the index and turning to the page that provides relevant information.

READ-ALOUD AND BOOK DISCUSSION IDEAS

On the Move (Fecher, Kespert, & Webster, 2000) is an informational text complete with a table of contents, photographs, labeled diagrams, index, and end-of-book test. Thus, it is not made to be read cover to cover.

Before reading, explain to students that some informational, nonfiction books help readers answer specific questions or teach particular types of information. Open to the table of contents and read each listing.

During reading, ask a student to select a type of transportation he or she would like to learn more about. Turn to that page and read the first paragraph. Explain what you are learning from the photographs and labeled diagram. Look at several diagrams and discuss some of the things students are learning about different vehicles.

After reading, place the book in a location where students may have access to it throughout the unit if they want to continue their research. In addition, if questions arise about different forms of transportation during whole-group time, use the book to look up the information. Finally, toward the end of the unit you may read the story "The Curious Bus Driver," which follows a man on his quest to learn about the jobs of other people (e.g., an airplane pilot, subway engineer, race car driver, ferry boat captain) who drive different types of transportation.

COMPUTER ACTIVITIES

Creativity and Presentation Software Ideas ⇢ – – – – – – – – ⇢

This activity asks students to decide what type of vehicle they would use to accomplish various tasks or arrive at various locations. Select clip art or stamps of various types of transportation from KidPix Studio Deluxe 3 software or download images from the Internet (for example, www.enchantedlearning.com/themes/transportation.shtml).

> ### MATERIALS
>
> ■ KidPix Studio Deluxe 3 (2000) software

1. As a prompt, describe a situation to the students that requires the use of a vehicle, such as "Guess what type of transportation I would need if I wanted to_____?" (see Figure 34).

   Keyboard the description and use stamped icons for an illustration of particular forms of transportation, such as cars, trucks, buses, or airplanes, on a screen or page of KidPix Studio Deluxe.

2. Ask each student what vehicle he or she would select and why. On screen page 1 type, "Guess what type of transportation I would need if I wanted to ride with many other students to get to school?" On screen page 2, import a picture of a school bus or use a stamped icon and type, "I would ride on a school bus if I wanted to go to school with many other students."

3. Arrange the prompt and responses in order, with the first page consisting of the phrases to guess the type of transportation needed for a particular type of journey. The second page should include the answer, written by each student.

4. Assemble students' work into a slide show or print out and bind hard copies of the work into a class book titled "Guess How I Would Travel?" View the book or slide show during whole-group time. Be sure to include a title page.

Digital Language Experience Approach ⇢ – – – – – – – – ⇢

Students enrich their vocabulary about transportation by creating a digital diagram of their favorite form of transportation.

> ### MATERIALS
>
> ■ Digital camera
> ■ KidPix Studio Deluxe 3 (2000) or PowerPoint (Microsoft 2003, 2003) software

1. Take a digital photograph of each student's head and shoulders.

2. Import digital photographs into creativity and presentation software such as KidPix Studio Deluxe 3 or PowerPoint.

3. Instruct students to use the software tools to draw around their photograph a picture of the form of transportation they would most like to drive (or fly).

4. Instruct students to create a diagram that labels all parts of the transportation vehicle (including the driver).

5. Assemble students' work into a slide show. Encourage students to brainstorm and select a title to include on a title page.

6. Students share their work in a slide show during author's computer chair (see Appendix B).

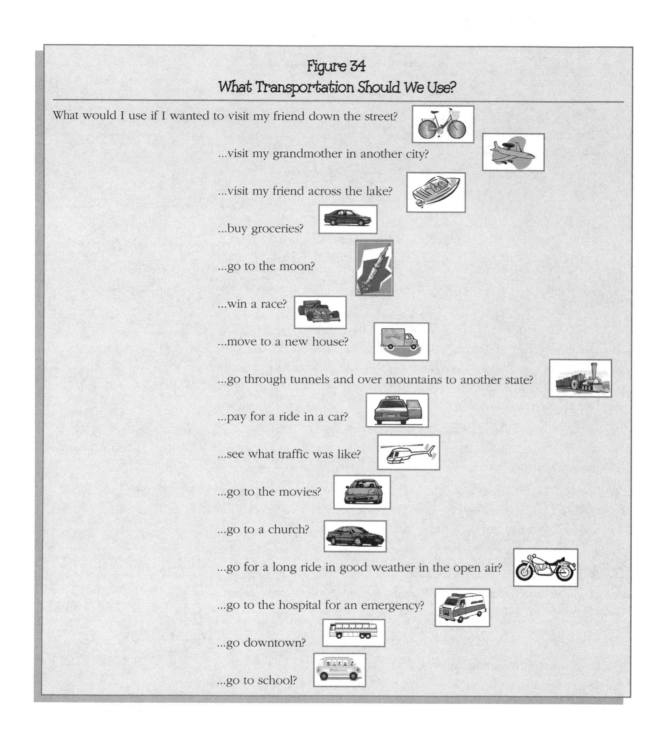

Figure 34
What Transportation Should We Use?

What would I use if I wanted to visit my friend down the street?

...visit my grandmother in another city?

...visit my friend across the lake?

...buy groceries?

...go to the moon?

...win a race?

...move to a new house?

...go through tunnels and over mountains to another state?

...pay for a ride in a car?

...see what traffic was like?

...go to the movies?

...go to a church?

...go for a long ride in good weather in the open air?

...go to the hospital for an emergency?

...go downtown?

...go to school?

Computer Software Activity

MATERIALS

■ The Airport (1996) CD-ROM

Students use The Airport CD-ROM to learn about the controls of a modern airliner, explore the control tower, and work at the ticket counter and baggage claim areas at an airport through an interactive game format. These activities help students learn vocabulary about this form of transportation. They also have opportunities to build background knowledge about how air transportation works. A cross-age computer buddy or an adult volunteer may be required to help younger students learn how to interact with the game.

Internet Resources and Ideas

Enchanted Learning: Transportation/Vehicles: www.enchantedlearning.com/themes/transportation.shtml

Go to this website to find resources about transportation and games to play. The "Make a Truck" hyperlink allows students to use the mouse to click on three different segments of trucks to change the design until all the pieces match (e.g., fire truck, garbage truck). During whole-group time, demonstrate by clicking on the first segment of a truck and ask students to predict which type of truck they will see next. This website also has printouts for transportation calendars for the current year and worksheets that include a letter of the alphabet and a form of transportation that begins with each letter for labeling the parts of a car in different languages (e.g., English, Italian, French, Spanish, German, Swedish).

Boeing Company: www.boeing.com/companyoffices/gallery/index.html

Take students on a virtual tour of Boeing airplanes. After agreeing to the website's terms of use, click on the "Virtual Tours" hyperlink to see an array of possibilities. Among other things, you can guide students on a virtual field trip of an airplane cockpit, first class and economy seating, and so forth.

Collaborative Thematic Unit: Theme: Transportation: www.libsci.sc.edu/miller/transportation2.html

This website includes finger plays and songs about transportation that will build students' vocabulary knowledge. Write and post the words on a classroom chart, or access them and view them on a computer monitor. Demonstrate each line and action of the poem or song. Ask students to join in on subsequent readings.

Unit Conclusion

For a group of mostly emerging and developing readers, celebrate students' learning about transportation by reviewing the various things they have learned and how they learned them as you reread the Transportation Notes T-Chart (see Figure 33 on page 202). This activity will support students' future abilities to be able to take notes, think about various types of resources, and create main idea or summary statements. Fluent readers may enjoy reading and discussing the various types of transportation studied in the unit as well as which particular insights or facts students drew from various resources. How did different sources of information help students assemble knowledge about this topic? If you and your students made a PowerPoint or KidPix Studio Deluxe slide show presentation or a Guess How I Would Travel book, be sure to read a hard or screen copy as part of the unit conclusion. Each student will enjoy sitting in the author's computer chair (see Appendix B) to discuss some computer-related activity he or she participated in during the unit.

MATERIALS

■ Transportation Notes T-Chart

Whales and Dolphins— Mammals of the Sea

UNIT BOOKS

Whales Passing
By Eve Bunting
Illustrated by Lambert Davis

Big Blue
By Shelley Gill
Illustrated by Ann Barrow

Whale Snow
By Debby Dahl Edwardson
Illustrated by Annie Patterson

COMPUTER RESOURCES

Imagination Express: Destination Ocean
One Small Square: Seashore
KidPix Activity Kits Volume 4

Thematic Connection

Students are understandably fascinated by one of the largest mammals on Earth, whales. They are equally fascinated by the intelligence and playful antics of dolphins. All of the books in this unit include narrative stories and informational text that explore humans' relationships with whales and dolphins. *Whales Passing* (Bunting, 2003) offers new perspectives on the lives of orcas, the largest members of the dolphin family. *Big Blue* (Gill, 2003) focuses on how a young girl's interest in whales leads to the fulfillment of her dream. *Whale Snow* (Edwardson, 2003) relates the intricate relationship among humans and animals on Earth by explaining how the Inupiat tribe in Alaska, USA, relies on whales as part of their cultural traditions. The stories are masterfully written and include beautifully illustrated graphics, which range from muted watercolor to vividly detailed paintings. The stories use narratives to relay fascinating information about some of the most interesting creatures that populate our seas and oceans.

Matrix of Literacy Skills and Strategies in Unit 14

Literacy Skills and Strategies	Activities	Title of Book	Pages
Brainstorming	U	—	215
	C	*Whale Snow*	224–225
Building background knowledge on the Internet*	C, S, I	*Whales Passing*	216, 217–218, 218–219
	I	*Big Blue*	222–223
	S, I	*Whale Snow*	225–226, 226–227
Comparing and contrasting	C	*Whales Passing*	216
	R, D, S, I	*Whale Snow*	224, 225, 225–226, 226–227
Composing in multimedia*	D	*Whales Passing*	216–217
	C, D, I	*Big Blue*	220–221, 221, 222–223
	C, D, S	*Whale Snow*	224–225, 225, 225–226
Creating and using charts	UC	—	227
	C	*Whales Passing*	216
	R	*Big Blue*	219–220
Creating concept maps and graphic organizers	S	*Whale Snow*	225–226
Determining cause and effect	R	*Big Blue*	219–220
	R	*Whale Snow*	224
Determining story details	R, D	*Big Blue*	219–220, 221
Developing and using story grammar	R, D	*Big Blue*	219–220, 221
Developing choral reading	D	*Whale Snow*	225
Developing comprehension	R, S, I	*Whales Passing*	216, 217–218, 218–219
	R, S, I	*Big Blue*	219–220, 221–222, 222–223
	R, I	*Whale Snow*	224, 226–227
Developing creative writing	C	*Big Blue*	220–221
Developing oral language	U, UC	—	215, 227
	R, C, D, I	*Whales Passing*	216, 216, 216–217, 218–219
	R, C, D, S, I	*Big Blue*	219–220, 220–221, 221, 221–222, 222–223
	R, C, D	*Whale Snow*	224, 224–225, 225
Developing vocabulary	U	—	215
	R, C	*Whales Passing*	216
	R, C, D, I	*Big Blue*	219–220, 220–221, 221, 222–223
	C, S	*Whale Snow*	224–225, 225–226
Drawing conclusions	R	*Whales Passing*	216
E-mailing*	I	*Whales Passing*	218–219
	I	*Whale Snow*	226–227

(continued)

Matrix of Literacy Skills and Strategies in Unit 14 (continued)

Literacy Skills and Strategies	Activities	Title of Book	Pages
Following directions	C, D, S	*Whales Passing*	216, 216–217, 217–218
	S, I	*Big Blue*	221–222, 222–223
	C, D, S, I	*Whale Snow*	224–225, 225, 225–226, 226–227
Inferring	R	*Big Blue*	219–220
	R	*Whale Snow*	224
Making multicultural connections	R, I	*Whale Snow*	224, 226–227
Making predictions	U	—	215
	R	*Big Blue*	219–220
Navigating hyperlinks*	S, I	*Whales Passing*	217–218, 218–219
	S, I	*Big Blue*	221–222, 222–223
	I	*Whale Snow*	226–227
Presenting work on a computer*	C, D	*Big Blue*	220–221, 221
	S	*Whale Snow*	225–226
Reading aloud	UC	—	227
	C	*Big Blue*	220–221
	R, I	*Whale Snow*	224, 226–227
Reading and listening for a purpose	R, C	*Whales Passing*	216
	R, I	*Big Blue*	219–220, 222–223
	R, S, I	*Whale Snow*	224, 225–226, 226–227
Reading and using map skills	R	*Whale Snow*	224
Reading informational text	S, I	*Whales Passing*	217–218, 218–219
	S, I	*Big Blue*	221–222, 222–223
	I	*Whale Snow*	226–227
Retelling	R, D	*Big Blue*	219–220, 221
Sequencing	D	*Big Blue*	221
Summarizing	UC	—	227
	R	*Whales Passing*	216
	I	*Big Blue*	222–223
Understanding a main idea	R, C	*Whales Passing*	216
	R, D	*Big Blue*	219–220, 221
	C	*Whale Snow*	224–225
Using adjectives	R, C, D	*Whales Passing*	216, 216, 216–217
	R, C, D	*Big Blue*	219–220, 220–221, 221
	D, S	*Whale Snow*	225, 225–226
Using nouns	C, D	*Big Blue*	220–221, 221
Visualizing	R	*Whales Passing*	216
	R	*Big Blue*	219–220
Writing descriptive sentences	D, I	*Whales Passing*	216–217, 218–219
	C, D, S	*Big Blue*	220–221, 221, 221–222
	C, D, S, I	*Whale Snow*	224–225, 225, 225–226, 226–227
Writing letters	I	*Whale Snow*	226–227

* Indicates a new-literacy skill.
U = unit introduction; R = read-aloud and book discussion ideas; C = creativity and presentation software ideas; D = Digital Language Experience Approach; S = computer software activity; I = Internet resources and ideas; UC = unit conclusion

Unit Introduction

Begin the unit by asking students to write answers to the following question posed on chart paper: What swims in the ocean but breathes air like you do? Emerging readers may draw or use invented spellings to record their guesses on the chart. Ask students to talk about their predictions. Explain that books in this unit will help them answer this question.

To create an inviting classroom learning environment that will grow as the unit unfolds, bring the color and movement of the sea into the classroom by inviting students to do an art project.

1. Cut blue and turquoise crepe paper in long strips and hang from the ceiling on one side of the room.

2. Twist the crepe paper gently to make waves and attach ends to the other side of the classroom.

3. Cut green crepe paper into shorter strips and hang from the ceiling to make seaweed and plants.

4. Direct students to draw and cut out the shape of a whale or dolphin on a folded sheet of brown kraft paper. Remind students to write their names on the tail of their sea creature.

5. Let students decide what color to paint their sea creature. Paint both sides of the brown kraft paper and then staple the two dry pieces together, leaving an opening.

6. Stuff the fish with crumpled newspaper and staple shut.

7. Tape a piece of string to the stuffed sea creature and hang it from the ceiling at different levels as though it is swimming in the sea. Continue adding sea animals to the room as students read the unit books.

MATERIALS

- Blue, turquoise, and green crepe paper
- Brown kraft paper
- Chart paper
- Markers
- Newsprint
- Paint
- Stapler
- String
- Tape

Book 1: Whales Passing

Bunting, E. (2003). Ill. L. Davis. New York: Blue Sky Press. $15.95. 32 pp.

BOOK REVIEW

On a sunny day, while taking a walk, a boy and his father stop on the edge of a seaside cliff where they see a pod of killer whales playing and swimming. They are instantly drawn into an intriguing pastime—whale watching. As the orcas surface, leap into the air, slap their tails, and dive, the boy and his father wonder if whales can talk. How do whales know where to go when they dive? In a delightful plot twist, readers soon discover that the whales are "people watching." Thus, the second part of the story is told from the orcas' perspective as the whales wonder about the strange creatures they see on the cliff. This simple story is beautifully told by award-winning author Eve Bunting. Lambert Davis, known for his ocean paintings, uses bold and vibrant colors to portray the beauty of whales in their natural habitat.

READ-ALOUD AND BOOK DISCUSSION IDEAS

Before reading, explain what it means to observe. Tell students that they will be reading about how a little boy and his father observe something occurring in the sea. One way to help students learn this concept is to arrange for them to playfully explore their powers of observation. Guide students in playing I Spy. Explain and model how to play the game. Tell students that they play the game by trying to figure out what an object is by asking questions of the person who is spying and looking around the room until they think they have figured it out. For example, for a clock, say, "I spy something that has numbers. What could it be? Look around the room at things that have numbers and then raise your hand if you have a guess." Continue providing clues until students identify the object. This game gives students the opportunity to observe, use oral language skills to ask questions, and draw conclusions.

During reading, ask them to be ready to remember what they observe about the orcas' environment.

After reading, ask students what they observed. What was the story mostly about? What did they learn about orcas?

COMPUTER ACTIVITIES

Creativity and Presentation Software Ideas

> ### MATERIALS
>
> ■ Inspiration (2005) software

Ask a computer buddy to help students describe and compare the whales' world in the sea to their own world on land.

1. Create T-charts on creativity and presentation software such as Inspiration to compare and contrast people and whales in relation to the environment they both live in, what they both eat, how they both have fun, and so forth.

2. Label one side of the T-chart "whales" and the other side "people."

3. Keyboard the characteristics that are similar in blue and those characteristics that are different in red. For example, people and whales both eat (type in blue) but they eat different things (type in red).

4. Each student can read his or her list during author's computer chair (see Appendix B).

Digital Language Experience Approach

> ### MATERIALS
>
> ■ Digital camera
> ■ KidPix Studio Deluxe (1998) software

To better understand the dual perspectives and different points of view taken in the story (i.e., the people watching the whales and the whales watching the people), arrange for students to take an in-school digital picture walk.

1. Divide students into groups of four. Tell them that each group will be walking to a different location in the school such as the library, cafeteria, gym, or school office (make prior

arrangements with willing participants such as the librarian or library aide, cafeteria worker, physical education teacher, or principal).

2. Take one group to the library. Take a digital photograph of the librarian in his or her "natural habitat." Then invite the librarian to take a photograph of the small group of students as they stand in the door looking in. Ask the librarian to write down what he or she observed when students stood in the doorway and took his or her picture.

3. Follow this routine with the other groups of students going to other school locations, such as the gymnasium, cafeteria, or principal's office.

4. When students return to the classroom, download the digital pictures and print out one copy of each picture. Review with students the place and the people their small group visited. Insert each picture on a screen page using creativity and presentation software such as KidPix Studio Deluxe.

5. Elicit and record students' language as they describe what they see in the picture their group took. For example, one group might dictate, "The librarian, Ms. Sanchez, was wearing a bright red dress and silver glasses. Her hands moved quickly as she checked in books."

6. Instruct students to look at the pictures taken by the person each group of students visited. For example, look at the picture taken by the librarian. Type the librarian's observation of students. The librarian might have written, "I saw a little boy in a blue sweater. I saw a little girl with brown hair and a big smile. I saw a boy with blond hair peeking around the library doorway. Students looked puzzled and I wondered what they were thinking."

7. Print out all of the screen pages and collect them into a book titled "Who's Looking at Whom?" Put the book into the reading center in the classroom for students to enjoy independently or with a partner when their work is finished. Students will enjoy a book about observing and being observed.

8. Ask groups of students to talk about what else they observed during their visit with the various school personnel in their natural habitats to incorporate author's computer chair (see Appendix B) with this activity. On the computer screen, display the digital photograph that was taken by the person visited of each group as students talk about where they went, whom they visited, and what they see in the picture. Guide a choral reading of each page.

Computer Software Activity

Once students log in on the opening screen of Imagination Express: Destination Ocean, instruct them to select their destination from the control panel. After selecting Destination Ocean, they click on the hyperlink "Ocean Fact Book." This talking book is divided into chapters such as The Major Oceans, Ocean Habitats, Food Chains and Webs, and Exploring Underwater. By clicking on one of the tabs on the right side of the book, a list of entries for each chapter appears. When viewing an entry from the list, students can click on a button to hear the page read aloud, view an animation, go to the next or

MATERIALS

■ Imagination Express: Destination Ocean (1995) software

the previous section of the Ocean Fact Book, go to related topics, or return to the main menu. This activity allows students to use both listening and reading skills as they engage with different factual information about oceans by listening to a page being read aloud to them, practicing reading information silently on their own, and having the opportunity to view and listen to multimedia animations.

Internet Resources and Ideas

Shamu SeaWorld: Shamu Cam: http://shamu.com/ca/shamu-cam/index.htm
This San Diego SeaWorld website gives information about killer whales. A Shamu video camera that is always focused on the killer whale's tank gives students a chance to observe Shamu. Because this is a live camera, the rate of activity varies between the hours of 10:00 a.m. and 6:00 p.m. Pacific Standard Time. This website also includes a video clip in case Shamu is not active on screen.

Invite students to keep an observation log of events in Shamu's tank (see Figure 35). At the end of this unit, ask students to discuss the different things they observed while watching Shamu in his tank via the Shamu Cam.

Shamu SeaWorld: Ask Shamu: http://shamu.com/fla/askshamu/index.htm
What would it be like to talk to a whale? What topics would students want to learn more about? Perhaps students may have questions about some of the things they have observed while watching the Shamu Cam. This webpage from SeaWorld allows students to e-mail Shamu with questions they have about whales. Replies originate from the SeaWorld Education Department. E-mails are answered seven days a week between 9:00 a.m. and 4:00 p.m. Pacific Standard Time.

For example, students might e-mail Shamu with a question about his feeding time and food (see Figure 36). Keep a list of the questions students want to ask Shamu. Send one question each day until all the questions have been sent. When "Shamu" replies, be sure to read the e-mail aloud to the class and post it on a classroom bulletin board.

To incorporate author's computer chair (see Appendix B) into this activity, check off the question that Shamu's e-mail answers from the list of questions. Reread with students the questions on the list they have not received an answer for yet. Ask students to explain how they sent their e-mail message to Shamu to reinforce the new-literacy skills of building background knowledge on the Internet and e-mailing.

Figure 35
Sample Shamu Camera Observation Log

Day of the Week	Time (If Possible)	Student	Observation
Monday	10:00 a.m.	Fred	Shamu jumps and dives.
Tuesday	10:00 a.m.	Sallie	Shamu eats buckets of fish.

Book 2:   Big Blue

Gill, S. (2003). Ill. A. Barrow. Watertown, MA: Talewinds. $15.95. 32 pp.

BOOK REVIEW

Kye has learned many facts about whales, but she wants to know more than just facts—she has a dream to swim in the ocean with a blue whale. One day, Kye tells her mother, a whale-research boat driver in Alaska, about her dream. Her mother's marine biologist friends take Kye, her mother, and their own children to Mexico to do research on whale migration. Each morning, Kye and her friends look for whales but do not find any. Then one day, while swimming, Kye sees a big blue whale. She waits to see if the whale wants to swim with her. Kye dives and swims beside the whale until she needs to come up for a breath. When she dives again the whale has disappeared. Rich watercolor illustrations show the grace and beauty of the world's largest animal—the blue whale. This story intertwines an engaging narrative about Kye's dream with interesting factual information about whales.

READ-ALOUD AND BOOK DISCUSSION IDEAS

Students will enjoy learning the wealth of information about whales this book provides. In addition, they will enjoy exploring the secondary literary theme of having a dream and wanting it to come true.

Before reading, tell students that there is a difference between the types of dreams we have when we are asleep and the type of dreams we have when we make a wish while we are awake. For example, during Christmas, one student might have dreams at night about riding on a rainbow, but while she is awake she might wish for a bicycle. Building background knowledge can help students identify with the quest of the main character. Tell students they will be reading about a little girl who had a very big dream.

During reading, point out the causes and effects that occur in the story. Because Kye shared her dream with her mother, the effect was that her dream came true. When Kye is swimming with the whale, ask

MATERIALS

■ Chart paper
■ Markers

students to visualize what it would be like to swim with the whale. As you do this, point out facts about whales that Kye learns, and record the facts on a chart. For example, you can record the fact that blue whales are the fastest swimmers in the sea or the fact that a blue whale's heart pumps 60 gallons of blood per heartbeat.

After reading, ask students what Kye's dream was. How was her dream realized? How did she feel when she was swimming with the whale? How would they feel? Ask students to share some of their own wishes. What might cause their dreams to come true? This activity gives students a chance to practice using their oral language by verbalizing what their wishes are to the others in the class. Students also can practice making predictions about how they think they might have their dreams come true.

COMPUTER ACTIVITIES

Creativity and Presentation Software Ideas

MATERIALS

■ KidPix Studio Deluxe (1998) software

The story about Kye's dream relates her emotions when her dream comes true. In KidPix Studio Deluxe creativity and presentation software, create a screen page (see Figure 37) titled [Student's Name]'s Feelings Chart. Draw a plus in the middle of the screen to make quarter sections. Write the words *Like, Don't Like, Happy,* and *Sad* in each quarter. Ask students to stamp icons or draw a picture for each section. They should also write a sentence that describes each feeling. Collect printouts and create a class book and post it on a "feelings" bulletin board, or create a slide show for viewing during computer-center time.

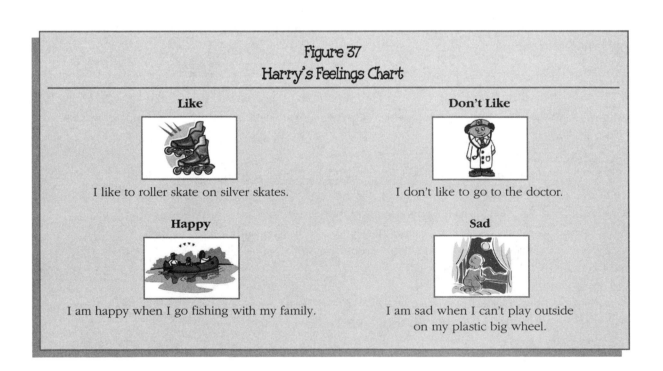

Figure 37
Harry's Feelings Chart

Like

I like to roller skate on silver skates.

Don't Like

I don't like to go to the doctor.

Happy

I am happy when I go fishing with my family.

Sad

I am sad when I can't play outside on my plastic big wheel.

To incorporate author's computer chair (see Appendix B) into this activity, display each student's page on the computer screen, and ask him or her to read his or her sentence in each section to the rest of the class. Encourage students to talk about why they chose the stamp icons they used or how and why they decided to draw the picture they drew to illustrate each emotion.

Digital Language Experience Approach

To help students gain a sense of story structure and to highlight the main idea of the story, take digital photographs of small groups of students reenacting the story.

MATERIALS

- Digital camera
- KidPix Studio Deluxe (1998) software

1. Guide students to think through the reenactment. How many different scene locations will there be? What do they need for props? Who will be which characters?

2. Download the pictures and insert each picture into a slide show using KidPix Studio Deluxe creativity and presentation software. Ask students to look at the pictures, place them in order, and explain what is happening in each picture.

3. Record retellings for each picture, or ask fluent and developing readers to write their own sentences. Emerging readers can use inventive spelling to write their sentences; however, ask them if they would like to see their words written in "grown up" or conventional spelling. Invented spelling is often used by primary-grade students for them to communicate their thoughts in writing. When introducing "grown up" writing to students, the teacher can tell students that it is alright to spell words as they hear them to get their ideas down on paper, but often there is a more "grown up" or conventional way to spell the words to make it easier for others to read what they have written. The teacher can write the words using the conventional spelling to allow students to compare it with the way they spelled the words. Encourage students to include adjectives and facts about whales in their sentences.

4. Print out for a class book titled "Big Blue" for students to enjoy.

Computer Software Activity

The One Small Square: Seashore software allows students to take a closer look at the ecosystem of the seashore or beach. Demonstrate for students the two ways to explore the 3-D Ecosystem and the Nature Guide. The 3-D Ecosystem includes representations of different types of beaches or seashores. Students can manipulate the three-dimensional models of rocky and sand shorelines as seen during the day or at night. The Nature Guide is divided into these areas: Chapter View, Pictorial Index, Activities, and Experiments. Students will benefit from a cross-age computer buddy, parent volunteer, or teaching assistant to help them explore various learning opportunities. When using the Nature Guide, students have several learning opportunities from which to choose.

MATERIALS

- One Small Square: Seashore (1996) software

- The Chapter View allows students to explore each chapter.

- The Pictorial Index allows students to learn about the creatures and plants.

- The Activities area allows students to play several interactive games.

- The Experiments area allows them to view nine different experiments that they can print out and perform.

There is also a journal in which students can insert pictures and keep a written record of their discoveries about the seashore. Students can view the journal on the computer screen or print it out on hard copy. Working with the journal allows students the opportunity to practice writing descriptive sentences about what they have discovered about the seashore or beach as they explore and participate in the learning activities. Then they can practice rereading what they have written silently on their own or read their sentences aloud to other students to share what they have learned and get feedback from their audience.

Internet Resources and Ideas

Activity & Song Book: A SeaWorld Education Department Resource: www.seaworld.org/ fun-zone/song-books/index.htm
This SeaWorld webpage contains a variety of different activities and songs. Activities include the following:

- Ocean Locomotion: Students can make the tails of a killer whale and shark move.
- Learning How to Swim Like a Whale: Students can make a whale move through the water.
- Dolphin and Me: Students can color a page that can be printed out.
- Hidden Ocean Animals: Students will find connect-the-dot pictures of two sea animals that can be printed out and completed.

Songs, many of which are sung to familiar tunes, include the following:

- "Swim Around the Sea": Students can sing to the tune of "Ring Around the Rosie."
- "Found a Mammal": Students can sing to the tune of "Found a Peanut."
- "Dolphin Family": Students can sing to the tune of "The Addams Family."
- "Whale Rap," a rap song, is also available that students can sing by creating and using a rap rhythm.

A bibliography of books that students may enjoy reading involving a connection to the sea is also included. Students can explore activities with a cross-age computer buddy. Remind students to be ready to talk and describe some of the activities they enjoyed doing most on this website during author's computer chair (see Appendix B).

Ocean Stock Footage: www.oceanstockfootage.com
This website contains short video clips about whales in their natural habitat. Watching the video clips can bring to life many of the illustrations students see while listening to and reading the books in this unit. Elicit students' oral language by asking questions such as What are the whales doing? How are they moving? How does this video clip relate to the books we have been reading?

Having students watch the video clips helps them build their background knowledge about what some species of whales look like and the habitat the whales live in. After viewing the video clips, some students will be better able to understand and connect to the illustrations seen in the books while listening to the stories being read. This activity will also help some students to develop their oral language and vocabulary because they can use words they heard while listening to the books and what they saw in the video clips to help them describe whales and answer questions about them.

Dolphin Research Center: www.dolphins.org

This website is maintained by the Dolphin Research Center, a not-for-profit education and research facility located on Grassy Key in the Florida Keys in the United States. Along with information about dolphins, this website contains a kid's page that includes the following:

- Fun Facts: By clicking on "Dolphins," students find out answers to key questions such as Do dolphins drink water? Do dolphins have fingers? Is a dolphin the same as a porpoise?

- Help Marine Mammals: This section contains suggestions for keeping the marine environment from becoming polluted.

- Games: This section contains a word search puzzle involving words associated with whales and dolphins as well as an interactive puzzle.

Dolphins Around the World: www.southwest.com.au/~kirbyhs/Dolphin.mov

This file, which contains pictures of many different kinds of dolphins, is a short movie of a dolphin swimming in the ocean and leaping into the air. Giving students an opportunity to watch this short movie helps them build their background knowledge about what one species of dolphin looks like in its natural habitat. After viewing the movie, students will be better able to understand and connect to the information about dolphins being read aloud. This activity will also help some students to practice their oral language because they can use what they saw during the movie to help them describe dolphins and talk about their behavior.

To incorporate author's computer chair (see Appendix B) with this activity, after students have had time to explore the websites with a cross-age computer buddy, ask them to talk about what they enjoyed most in this unit. What tools and strategies did they use to participate in the activities? Would they recommend this website to other students? Why or why not?

Book 3: Whale Snow

Edwardson, D.D. (2003). Ill. A. Patterson. Watertown, MA: Talewinds. $15.95. 32 pp.

BOOK REVIEW

Amiqqaq, a young Alaskan Inupiat boy, waits for his father, a whaling captain, to return home from a whaling trip. When the whaling crew successfully catches a bowhead whale, his father brings home the traditional family flag as a sign to the village to celebrate a successful whale trip. Amiqqaq begs to go along with his father to prepare the whale. The next day, everyone in the village comes to Amiqqaq's house to eat and celebrate the spirit of the whale. This book shares the traditions of the Inupiat culture and includes a short explanation about the Inupiaq language. Inupiaq words are incorporated into the story, and a pronunciation guide for these words is given.

An additional explanation about the relationship between the Inupiat tribe and whales follows the story. The watercolor illustrations show the two environments in this story. Cool colors are used to show the cold outside environment in which the Inupiat people live and work, and warm colors are used to show the warmth of their homes and closeness of the family and the community.

READ-ALOUD AND BOOK DISCUSSION IDEAS

Before reading, help students understand the story setting—the Inupiat people's home in Alaska. Display a large map of North America on the computer screen (see www.travelalaska.com/Regions/StateRegions.aspx—an interactive map of Alaska). Show students where Alaska is located. Tell students the story takes place in the winter and that they will learn about the role that whales have played in the lives of some people in Alaska. Point out to students how much of Alaska borders the ocean waters.

During reading, note how the climate where Amiqqaq lives affects all aspects of his life, from the foods he eats to the clothes he wears. Tell students to listen carefully and try to figure out what the cause–effect relationships between weather and the way of life are.

> ### MATERIALS
>
> ■ Map of North America

After reading, ask students about the role the whale played in the Inupiats' lives.

There are several literacy skills students can work on when reading this book. One skill involved is helping students determine the cause-and-effect relationship between the whales and the lives of the Inupiats and their ability to survive. Students will also infer about how much of an effect the weather and snowy environment had on the way the families of the tribe lived. A third skill students will use is comparing and contrasting and developing oral language by talking about how the Inupiat families and their own families are alike and different. Students also will listen for a purpose and recall information about the Inupiat culture that they remember after listening to the story.

COMPUTER ACTIVITIES

Creativity and Presentation Software Ideas

The main characters in the story celebrate the spirit of the whale. After all, it is the whale that provides them with so many of the things they need to live through the winter in Alaska. Remind students that the people and families did not kill the whales for sport. On the contrary, they were very thankful for the whales' provisions. Students may be familiar with the concept of Thanksgiving, a time when the United States celebrates harvests and nature's provisions. Following a general discussion about Thanksgiving and what it means to be thankful, the teacher can involve students in the following activity.

> ### MATERIALS
>
> ■ KidPix Studio Deluxe (1998) software

1. Ask students what things in nature they are happy and thankful for. What things in their lives that nature provides do their families celebrate during Thanksgiving? What foods do they typically find on a Thanksgiving celebration table?

2. Instruct students to brainstorm a list of things from nature that they are thankful for, for example, food sources (e.g., turkey, chicken, cranberries, green beans).

3. Instruct students to use a creativity and presentation software program, such as KidPix Studio Deluxe, to write about things in nature they would like to celebrate.

4. Print out and bind the pages into a book titled "We Are Thankful For..." to place in the classroom reading area.

Digital Language Experience Approach

Support students' understanding of the size of a whale through this activity. Involving students in this activity will help them visualize just how large a sperm whale is compared to themselves or objects around them.

> **MATERIALS**
>
> - Ball of string or rope 40 feet long
> - Digital camera
> - KidPix Studio Deluxe (1998) software
> - Yardstick or tape measure

1. Take a ball of string or rope at least 40 feet long to the playground.

2. Enlist the help of a cross-age computer buddy, teaching assistant, parent volunteer, or another teacher who is on the playground to take digital photographs of the activity.

3. Ask one student to hold the end of the string and walk the distance where another student will hold the end of the string. Using a yardstick or tape measure, measure out 40 feet.

4. Arrange students in a line and space them equally along the beginning and the end of the string.

5. Take a final photograph of students holding the string to show how long a sperm whale is. If possible, make sure that the school, playground equipment, or cars are in the background of the photo to provide scale to the picture.

6. Import the photograph into creativity and presentation software such as KidPix Studio Deluxe.

7. Keyboard one comment from each student about the process of measuring, the size of whales, or how large the whale is, using comparative language. Be sure to include each child's name. For example, Mary said, "A whale is bigger than a car!"

8. Post the photograph and comments on a bulletin board along with other facts you are collecting throughout the unit about whales. Follow up with choral, echo, and independent readings.

Computer Software Activity

There are four activities on the CD included in the KidPix Activity Kits Volume 4 software: Ocean Floor, Ocean Poems, Sea Animal Report, and Wonderful Whales. Each activity is presented at three levels of difficulty, which are appropriate for emerging, developing, or fluent readers; however, a cross-age computer buddy may be needed to support primary-grade students' use of this program. For each level of an activity, the instructions for completing the activity are given verbally for students in clear language.

> **MATERIALS**
>
> - KidPix Activity Kits Volume 4 (1998) software

1. Ocean Floor asks students to identify parts of the ocean floor. After students finish labeling, they can use stamps and drawing tools to illustrate an ocean floor. The teacher can print out this activity when it is completed and post it on a bulletin board for sharing.

2. Ocean Poems invites students to use descriptive words to write haiku, diamante, or cinquain poems. At Level 1, students use a template that provides the number of syllables that are necessary for each line of a haiku poem. At Level 2, students use the blank lines within the activity to write a diamante poem. At Level 3, students use blank lines to write a cinquain. The poems that students create can be imported into a slide show. Students can add their voices reading their poems to the slide show.

3. Sea Animal Report involves students in creating multimedia reports about sea animals. Divide students into groups and let each group choose the sea animal they want to learn more about. With a cross-age computer buddy or parent volunteer, have students search the Internet to find information about their sea animal. The cross-age computer buddy or parent volunteer can help students create the multimedia reports. Print out each group's report and make it into a book, which you can place in the class reading center for students to enjoy.

4. Wonderful Whales uses a Venn diagram to show similarities and differences between different types of whales. Students at each level use the drawing tools and rubber stamps to add pictures of appropriate whales. Print out the Venn diagrams that students completed, and post them on a bulletin board or compile the reports into a class book titled "Different Types of Whales."

To incorporate author's computer chair (see Appendix B) with this activity, when the slide show is completed, invite another class to view it. Display each poem on the computer screen. Instruct groups of students to read each poem aloud. Identify the topic of each poem and instruct students to explain why they chose the descriptive words they used in each one.

Another way to incorporate author's computer chair is to instruct students to share their multimedia reports on the computer. Ask them to explain what they did to find the information about their sea animal and talk about some of the websites they visited. What was their favorite website? Did they think all the websites were helpful for getting information for their report? Do they think other students in the class would like to visit the websites they used for their report? Why or why not?

Internet Resources and Ideas

Uqsruagna: www.charlesbridge.com/msp/files/id/10945
The Inupiat people have not always had a written language. Inupiat children learned by listening to the stories of the elders. In the 1880s, people outside of their culture forced the Inupiat to learn to speak English. When commercial whalers moved into northern Alaska, the schools punished Inupiat children for speaking their native language. To preserve their culture, they put their language into writing and recorded their stories. This website allows students to see the story "Whale Snow" written in the Inupiaq language. Have students compare written Inupiaq language and English. Talk about how different the two languages are by comparing how specific words from the story are spelled in Inupiaq and in English.

Whale Times: www.whaletimes.org

This website can be used by both teachers and students. It provides resource information and activities such as

- Fishin' for Facts Library: This webpage contains many links to factual information about different animals such as whales, dolphins, seals, sea lions, penguins, and sharks. This website is a good resource to use to introduce students to different whales and animals that live in or near the sea.

- Colossal Dictionary of Whale Words: This webpage contains terms related to whales. Words included in this dictionary are defined as they pertain to whales and whales' environment. These definitions may be different from the definitions for the words that are found in a standard dictionary. This section is quite extensive, with words divided alphabetically from A to Z.

- Kid's Books on the Kid's Page: This webpage includes a bibliography of students' books, young adolescent books, and nature magazines for students; these books all relate to the whale theme.

- Ask Jake, the Sea Dog: This webpage lets students e-mail Jake specific questions about ocean animals. They will receive a reply from Jake to their question within seven days. Students also review parts of a friendly letter and the content and formatting for writing e-mail messages. Read Jake's response during whole-group time.

- Whale Puzzler on the Kid's Page: In this short interactive quiz, students can answer questions about whales and get immediate feedback on their answers. Students can work in pairs to take this quiz to check their comprehension of what they read or discovered about whales.

- Whale Tale on the Kid's Page: This webpage allows students to read a never-ending whale tale with story contributions from children all over the world. This activity invites students to participate in writing this tale and gives students a chance to contribute three to five sentences to continue the story.

Unit Conclusion ⇢

During whole-group time, ask students to recall some of the computer-related activities that they have done in this unit that helped them learn more about our understanding of whales and dolphins. For example, remind students about the class book and the things they observed during their school walk. Students may share their sea poems. Some students will enjoy talking about their feelings charts. Finally, students could vote on a favorite story and explain why it was their favorite.

MATERIALS

- Crafts students created throughout the unit

Insects

UNIT BOOKS

Under One Rock: Bugs, Slugs, and Other Ughs
By Anthony D. Fredericks
Illustrated by Jennifer DiRubbio

Bumblebee at Apple Tree Lane
By Laura Gates Galvin
Illustrated by Kristin Kest

Gregory and Alexander
By William Barringer
Illustrated by Kim LaFave

COMPUTER RESOURCES

The Magic School Bus Explores Bugs
KidPix Activity Kits Volume 1
My First Science Explorer

Thematic Connection

While a formal definition of *insect* is beyond the scope of most primary-grade students, teachers will find the definition to be helpful when sorting out facts about insects. According to Merriam-Webster Online Dictionary (2005), an insect is "a: any of numerous small invertebrate animals (as spiders or centipedes) that are more or less obviously segmented b: any of a class (Insecta) of arthropods (as bugs or bees) with well-defined head, thorax, and abdomen, only three pairs of legs, and typically one or two pairs of wings" (n.p.). Many students are fascinated with insects and love to bring them from the playground to show their teachers. The books in this unit include both expository and narrative texts to help introduce primary-grade students to the world of insects. *Under One Rock: Bugs, Slugs, and Other Ughs* (Fredericks, 2001) sparks students' curiosity about bugs around them by presenting facts through poetry. *Bumblebee at Apple Tree Lane* (Galvin, 2000) offers facts about ladybugs and bumblebees. *Gregory and Alexander* (Barringer, 2003) is a picture book that helps students explore their feelings about insects by stepping into the fictional world of Gregory, a little mouse, and his friend Alexander, a little caterpillar. Tell students that the different types of books in this unit will help them learn more about insect life: facts from informational text, poetry on our feelings about insects, and a fictional tale in a story such as being friends with a mouse and a caterpillar.

Matrix of Literacy Skills and Strategies in Unit 15

Literacy Skills and Strategies	Activities	Title of Book	Pages
Brainstorming	C	*Under One Rock: Bugs, Slugs, and Other Ughs*	232
	R, C	*Bumblebee at Apple Tree Lane*	235, 236
Building background knowledge on the Internet*	I	*Under One Rock: Bugs, Slugs, and Other Ughs*	234–235
	R, C, I	*Bumblebee at Apple Tree Lane*	235, 236, 237–238
	D, I	*Gregory and Alexander*	239–240, 241
Building editing skills	D	*Under One Rock: Bugs, Slugs, and Other Ughs*	233
	C	*Gregory and Alexander*	239
Building fluency	S	*Under One Rock: Bugs, Slugs, and Other Ughs*	233–234
Comparing and contrasting	UC	—	241
Composing in multimedia*	C, D	*Under One Rock: Bugs, Slugs, and Other Ughs*	232, 233
	C, D, S	*Bumblebee at Apple Tree Lane*	236, 236, 237
	C, D	*Gregory and Alexander*	239, 239–240
Creating and using charts	R, C	*Under One Rock: Bugs, Slugs, and Other Ughs*	232
	C	*Bumblebee at Apple Tree Lane*	236
Determining story details	R, S	*Bumblebee at Apple Tree Lane*	235, 237
Developing a sense of beginnings, middles, and endings	R	*Gregory and Alexander*	238–239
Developing comprehension	R, S, I	*Under One Rock: Bugs, Slugs, and Other Ughs*	232, 233–234, 234–235
	R, C, I	*Bumblebee at Apple Tree Lane*	235, 236, 237–238
	R, D, S, I	*Gregory and Alexander*	238–239, 239–240, 240–241, 241
Developing context clues	R	*Gregory and Alexander*	238–239
Developing oral language	U, UC	—	231, 241
	R, C, D, S	*Under One Rock: Bugs, Slugs, and Other Ughs*	232, 232, 233, 233–234
	D, I	*Bumblebee at Apple Tree Lane*	236, 237–238
	R, C, D, S	*Gregory and Alexander*	238–239, 239, 239–240, 240–241
Developing vocabulary	U	—	231
	R, C, D, S, I	*Under One Rock: Bugs, Slugs, and Other Ughs*	232, 232, 233, 233–234, 234–235
	R, C, D, S, I	*Bumblebee at Apple Tree Lane*	235, 236, 236, 237, 237–238
	R, C, D, S, I	*Gregory and Alexander*	238–239, 239, 239–240, 240–241, 241

(continued)

Matrix of Literacy Skills and Strategies in Unit 15 (continued)

Literacy Skills and Strategies	Activities	Title of Book	Pages
Distinguishing between real and make-believe content	R, C, I	*Under One Rock: Bugs, Slugs, and Other Ughs*	232, 232, 234–235
Following directions	C, D, S, I	*Under One Rock: Bugs, Slugs, and Other Ughs*	232, 233, 233–234, 234–235
	C, D, S, I	*Bumblebee at Apple Tree Lane*	236, 236, 237, 237–238
	C, D, I	*Gregory and Alexander*	239, 239–240, 241
Navigating hyperlinks*	S, I	*Under One Rock: Bugs, Slugs, and Other Ughs*	233–234, 234–235
	R, I	*Bumblebee at Apple Tree Lane*	235, 237–238
	S, I	*Gregory and Alexander*	240–241, 241
Presenting work on a computer*	C, I	*Under One Rock: Bugs, Slugs, and Other Ughs*	232, 234–235
	C, I	*Bumblebee at Apple Tree Lane*	236, 237–238
	I	*Gregory and Alexander*	241
Reading aloud	R, D, S, I	*Under One Rock: Bugs, Slugs, and Other Ughs*	232, 233, 233–234, 234–235
	R, C, I	*Bumblebee at Apple Tree Lane*	235, 236, 237–238
	R, I	*Gregory and Alexander*	238–239, 241
Reading and listening for a purpose	R, I	*Under One Rock: Bugs, Slugs, and Other Ughs*	232, 234–235
	R, S, I	*Bumblebee at Apple Tree Lane*	235, 237, 237–238
	R, S, I	*Gregory and Alexander*	238–239, 240–241, 241
Reading informational text	R, S, I	*Under One Rock: Bugs, Slugs, and Other Ughs*	232, 233–234, 234–235
	R, C, S, I	*Bumblebee at Apple Tree Lane*	235, 236, 237, 237–238
	S, I	*Gregory and Alexander*	240–241, 241
Retelling	R, C	*Bumblebee at Apple Tree Lane*	235, 236
Selecting parts of speech	R, C, D	*Under One Rock: Bugs, Slugs, and Other Ughs*	232, 232, 233
Sequencing	D	*Under One Rock: Bugs, Slugs, and Other Ughs*	233
	R, C	*Bumblebee at Apple Tree Lane*	235, 236
	D	*Gregory and Alexander*	239–240
Summarizing	R, D, S	*Gregory and Alexander*	238–239, 239–240, 240–241
Understanding story structure and events	R	*Gregory and Alexander*	238–239
Using adjectives	R, C, D	*Under One Rock: Bugs, Slugs, and Other Ughs*	232, 232, 233
	S	*Bumblebee at Apple Tree Lane*	237
	D	*Gregory and Alexander*	239–240
Using English as a second language	C, I	*Under One Rock: Bugs, Slugs, and Other Ughs*	232, 234–235
Using phonics: Rhyming words	R, C	*Under One Rock: Bugs, Slugs, and Other Ughs*	232
	I	*Bumblebee at Apple Tree Lane*	237–238

(continued)

Literacy Skills and Strategies	Activities	Title of Book	Pages
Using verbs	R, C, D	*Under One Rock: Bugs, Slugs, and Other Ughs*	232, 232, 233
Writing descriptive sentences	C, D	*Under One Rock: Bugs, Slugs, and Other Ughs*	232, 233
	C, D	*Bumblebee at Apple Tree Lane*	236
	C, D	*Gregory and Alexander*	239, 239–240

* Indicates a new-literacy skill.

U = unit introduction; R = read-aloud and book discussion ideas; C = creativity and presentation software ideas; D = Digital Language Experience Approach; S = computer software activity; I = Internet resources and ideas; UC = unit conclusion

Unit Introduction

Start with asking questions about insects. For example, how many of you have ever seen an insect and where have you seen it? What is an insect? What shape? Draw this on your chart paper or the blackboard as students name characteristics, exaggerating features and colors to make a point. Ask students specific questions about their features. For example, what does the body look like? Does it have a tail? How many eyes, noses, ears, mouths, and legs? After drawing these discussed features, stand back and look at them. Ask students whether the drawing would look like an insect. Then pass around a collection of toy bugs and animals. If possible, bring real ones as well, such as ants, slugs, earthworms, and so on. Ask students to pick insects from the items, and ask them to pick animals or other bugs. Clarify these terms and discuss differences among insects, animals, and bugs. Tell students that in this unit's books, they will learn about different kinds of insects and how to distinguish insects from other bugs.

MATERIALS

- Chart paper
- Markers
- Toy bugs and animals

Book 1:   Under One Rock: Bugs, Slugs, and Other Ughs

Fredericks, A.D. (2001). Ill. J. DiRubbio. Nevada City, CA: Dawn Publications. $16.95. 32 pp.

BOOK REVIEW

A boy who is wandering in a field is curious about what could be hiding under a rock. He sees earthworms, an army of hundreds of ants, an eight-eyed spider, shiny black beetles, some tiny field crickets, a millipede, and six tiny slugs. The simple story line, which Anthony Fredericks writes as a poem, complete with repetitive text, is bound to trigger students' curiosity about insects they encounter on the playground or in the yard. Rich, earthy illustrations add considerable charm to the text. One of the best features of this book is a Field Notes section where students can find brief but interesting facts about all the creatures in the book.

READ-ALOUD AND BOOK DISCUSSION IDEAS

Before reading, ask students, "Have you ever peeked under a rock? What did you see there? If you haven't, what do you think you'd see?" Write their observations on chart paper and discuss them before reading the book. Tell them to listen to find out what the boy in the book sees under a rock.

During reading, draw attention to the rich descriptive language that includes verbs (e.g., *creep, slips, plows past*) and adjectives (e.g., *shiny and black, cool, squiggly, round*). Briefly explain to students that a verb is an action word and an adjective is a describing word. While reading aloud, point out rhyming words and enjoy the sounds of language.

After reading, review the bugs they encountered in the book and look up fascinating facts in the Field Notes section. Tell students that the book gives facts and information written in poetic form about real insect life. Draw a picture of a fantasy bug on chart paper and explain to students that you just made it up, so it is not real. Invite students to suggest special descriptive words they like from the story, and post them on a vocabulary chart on a bulletin board throughout the unit. Make note of words that rhyme in the text. Add new words to the chart as students find them in text.

COMPUTER ACTIVITIES

Creativity and Presentation Software Ideas

Choose creativity and presentation software, such as Ultimate Writing and Creative Center, Storybook Weaver, or KidPix Studio Deluxe 3, with a broad collection of background pictures and stamp icons because your students will use these backgrounds to create their own insect pictures.

1. Direct students to choose a background picture from the software—a park, rainforest, mountain, creek, or other natural scene.

2. Tell students to use stamps to populate the landscape with real insects that they might expect to find in that particular setting. Where should the insects be located? Why? Refer them to the book and to the vocabulary chart for inspiration. Students can create one fantasy bug to place in the picture.

3. Instruct students to place their name and date at the top of their picture and write a sentence couplet (i.e., at least two phrases within a sentence) using rich, descriptive words and at least two words that rhyme about how the insects move or look in their picture. First, students may brainstorm words that describe the actions in the picture. Next, they may brainstorm words that describe how things look. Third, they may identify any of the words that rhyme. Finally, they compose a sentence couplet. For example, "The bumblebees fly in a line...looking for yellow flowers that are fine." In this sentence, *line* and *fine* are the rhyming words. Students will explore rich vocabulary by brainstorming words with other students.

4. Print out pictures for a bulletin board display or collect them into a digital slide show called "My Fantastic Insect" to display during whole-group time.

Digital Language Experience Approach

After reading and discussing the book, tell students that they will make, using real food, a snack called "How to Make and Eat Worms in the Grass" (see Figure 38). During this activity, you can review the types of bugs that people can find in a field.

1. Display the written recipe on the poster board to refer easily for students and lay out all the ingredients.

2. Take pictures of your students making the recipe.

3. Take pictures of them eating the snack.

4. Import the pictures into the creativity and presentation software, such as KidPix Studio Deluxe, and discuss the order of events and the text students want to include for each picture to explain situations. For emerging readers, draw attention to how the text unfolds from left to right with a return sweep. Also invite them to point to text and reread or echo read to get a sense of speech-to-text connections.

5. Offer students the opportunity to revise the text by adding richly descriptive adjectives. Repeat this procedure for all the pictures you want to display for author's computer chair (see Appendix B).

During author's computer chair, students will enjoy reading and reviewing their recipe stories. As students reread text from the screen (choral, echo reading, or independently) ask them to highlight words they know. Ask them how they sorted the photos into a correct sequence of events.

Computer Software Activity

The Magic School Bus Explores Bugs CD-ROM teaches students about all kinds of bugs—the good, the bad, and the bizarre. For example, "What Is a Bug?" explains differences among insects and bug relatives. Books with bugs on the main screen have hyperlinks to detailed information about the specific bug. For example, there is a book with a bee on the

cover. When a student clicks this book, it leads to the next screen, which has more information about bees and wasps. Inform students that they should be ready to share what they have learned with their classmates after listening to the books on the CD-ROM.

Figure 38
"How to Make and Eat Worms in the Grass" Recipe

8 oz. cream cheese
2 boxes graham crackers
8 oz. alfalfa sprouts
16 oz. gummi worms (around 30 gummi worms or other kinds of gummi bugs)
Plastic knives and paper plates
1. Spread cream cheese on crackers.
2. Put a small handful of alfalfa sprouts on top.
3. Cover with gummi worms.

Students who are working toward fluency will benefit from practicing rereading different portions of the text. If they are working with a cross-age computer buddy, the buddy can give them feedback on how quickly and fluently they read the first time as compared to the second or third time.

In addition to the electronic books, there are many on-screen objects students can click on to reveal more information about bugs, so let students explore the entire program as time permits. Invite students to provide either an oral or written brief summary during author's computer chair (see Appendix B) of the things they learned from the CD-ROM.

Internet Resources and Ideas

Insect Images: www.insectimages.org
At this website, guide students on a website exploration to build background knowledge and demonstrate navigating hyperlinks.

MATERIALS

- Chart paper
- Markers

---

1. Click on several different hyperlinks to pictures of ants, bees, beetles, flies, and grasshoppers.

2. Ask students to think about what all the photographs have in common. How are they all alike? What are the photographs about?

3. Ask students to name some of the insects they see. List the words on chart paper. Remind students that the names they have written are nouns, a part of speech that is a person, place, or thing. As you read the words aloud, segment with the onset (first sound) and rime (ending sounds).

Let's Talk About Insects: www.urbanext.uiuc.edu/insects
"Let's Talk About Insects" is an animated and narrated 50-page e-book about insects. An index at the top of each page allows easy, instant navigation to any topic. Camponotus Pennsylvanicus Ant will guide readers throughout the book. This e-book contains information such as how many insects there are in the world; what an insect is composed of, such as a head, thorax, abdomen, rigid skin, and six legs; and so forth. The book explains how to distinguish insects from other bugs by using pictures and animations. It also shows differences among insects. The book is written and read in both English and Spanish. If you have a Spanish-speaking student who does not understand much English, he or she will benefit from listening to the text in Spanish before listening to it in English to build his or her background knowledge.

Let's Talk About Insects: Eee Gads...A New Bug: www.urbanext.uiuc.edu/insects/newbug.html
"Eee Gads...A New Bug" is also from the same website as "Let's Talk About Insects." After students read the e-book they can create their own insect by choosing antennae, wings, legs, and six color options for each body part. After creating their own insect, students can make up its name, where it lives, what it eats, what it does, and more. As students share their creations in author's computer chair (see Appendix B), highlight the differences between facts and fantasy.

Let's Talk About Insects: Am I An Insect? www.urbanext.uiuc.edu/insects/amiinsect.html
Am I An Insect? allows students to identify insects. Students must use the computer mouse to drag insects into a butterfly net. Through this activity, students will learn categorization

skills. Also, the teacher can assess students' comprehension of the book by doing this activity.

Scholastic—The Magic School Bus: Monster Bugs: www.scholastic.com/magicschoolbus/ games/bugs

Monster Bugs allows students to build their own bug by repositioning on the computer screen its body, head, legs, and wings. If a student matches all the parts correctly, the program tells them, "You've created a real bug called Butterfly. This bug is found in nature." If the student does not match all the parts correctly, it creates a monster bug and tells the student the bug is not found in nature. For the first few attempts, emerging learners may need assistance. The program also has some text, which may be most appropriate for developing readers.

Book 2:   Bumblebee at Apple Tree Lane

Galvin, L.G. (2000). Ill. K. Kest. Norwalk, CT: Soundprints. $19.95. 32 pp.

BOOK REVIEW

Bumblebee at Apple Tree Lane is a charming and informative story about the life of a queen bumblebee from the moment she awakens from a winter-long nap. After finding and cleaning a nest, she lays eight eggs and, like a hen, keeps them warm until they hatch. Laura Gates Galvin describes the bumblebee's diet and the growth of the bee colony. Students will build vocabulary and learn which eggs become worker bees and which eggs will be bumblebees. A bee's activities depend in large part on whether it develops into a worker bee or bumblebee. Handsome, realistically rendered, double-page pictures, featuring larger-than-life insects and flowers, are a special feature of this book. The author includes additional information and a glossary of important words.

READ-ALOUD AND BOOK DISCUSSION IDEAS

Before reading, bring a jar of honey to class and let your students taste it. Ask students if they know where honey comes from. Guide the conversation to what students know about bees. Look at some different photographs of bees on the Zach's Bee Photos website (go to http://photo.bees.net/gallery). Then, introduce *Bumblebee at Apple Tree Lane* and tell students that they will read a book about bumblebees.

MATERIALS
■ Jar of honey
■ Pack of plastic spoons

During reading, ensure students are following the queen bumblebee's life cycle by asking questions such as how she started her colony, how many eggs laid, and where she laid them. Review with students terminology pertaining to a bee's anatomy. Consider writing a word bank for keywords such as *nectar, larvae, cocoon,* and so forth.

After reading, discuss the most interesting details and vocabulary words students learned from the book.

COMPUTER ACTIVITIES

Creativity and Presentation Software Ideas

Ask students to think about and brainstorm the bumblebee's stages of life.

MATERIALS

- A chart showing the bumblebee's anatomy changes
- KidPix Studio Deluxe 3 (2000) software

---

1. Draw a simple chart showing how the bumblebee's anatomy changes in each stage, and place it by the computer center.

2. Using KidPix Studio Deluxe 3 creativity and presentation software, ask your students to create a slide for each stage in the life cycle of a bumblebee. If they need to, students can refer to books or other websites for more information.

3. Ask students to write one fact they learned about bumblebees. Save slides as a slide show or print out as a book called "Facts About Bumblebees" for the class library. Each student may take one printout home to share with parents or caregivers.

Digital Language Experience Approach

Students will practice descriptive vocabulary by doing this activity.

MATERIALS

- 2 packages of crackers
- 3–4 flavors of honey from a health food store (e.g., eucalyptus, clover, apple, rainforest, orange)
- Digital camera
- KidPix Studio Deluxe 3 (2000) software
- Spoons for each jar of honey

---

1. Discuss with students how honey is made, and tell them how different flavors of honey are made.

2. Show and explain to students the different flavors of honey you prepared.

3. Organize students into small groups of three or four.

4. Tell students that they will taste different flavors of honey and have to choose one favorite honey within the group.

5. Place crackers and one flavor of honey for each group of students, and tell each group to taste each flavor of honey by spreading honey onto the crackers and eating them.

6. Ask each group to describe and discuss the taste. While each group describes the taste, take pictures of group discussions and the honey the group tasted.

7. Continue taking pictures while one group tastes the honey. Move onto the next group after one group is finished tasting their honey. Repeat steps 5 and 6 until each group tastes all of their honey.

8. Import pictures into creativity and presentation software, such as KidPix Studio Deluxe 3, and discuss with students what pictures they want to include of their honey-tasting experience. After choosing the pictures, ask students to add comments about the pictures by using descriptive words that they used while they were tasting the honey. Students can share their slide show about the bee snack experience with the class during author's computer chair (see Appendix B).

Computer Software Activity

Crawling Creatures, from the KidPix Activity Kits Volume 1 software, has four activities: Create an Insect, Balanced Diet, Mystery Graph, and Ant Chants. The Create an Insect activity allows students to create their own insects by using stamps and edit insects by using drawing tools. Through this activity, students will learn new vocabulary and facts about the habitats of specific insects. It also fosters creativity by allowing students to design and name unique insects.

MATERIALS

■ KidPix Activity Kits Volume 1 (1998)

Internet Resources and Ideas

Bees at Enchanted Learning: www.enchantedlearning.com/themes/bees.shtml
This website has three bee rhymes for students to read aloud and bee printouts for students to color. Read the poems aloud and stress which words rhyme and why. One printout is appropriate for developing students because it has a more complex picture of a honeybee with names of its body parts and other more technical information. The other printout has a simpler picture without labels of body parts. A real asset of this website is the Color a Bee Online option, which allows students to color online by clicking a desired color on the left of the screen first and then placing and clicking the cursor on a part of the bee picture on the right side of the screen; this activity also provides basic information about bees. There is a cloze activity, which is a fill-in-the-blank activity that you can print out about bee anatomy and life, that is most appropriate for developing readers.

National Honey Board: Downloads: www.nhb.org/download
National Honey Board Downloads has rich resources for teachers. When you go to www.nhb.org/download/education/teachgde.pdf, there are four lesson plans to teach about honeybees: (1) Cooperation—learning the importance of cooperation among honeybees; (2) Communication—recognizing the many forms of communication and vocabulary among honeybees and extended activity about human communication; (3) Pollination—understanding the parts of a flower, the process of pollination, and the importance of the honeybee in this process; and (4) Honey I Love You—understanding the origin of honey as well as its various colors, flavors and forms.

Nature—Alien Empire: Bee Anatomy: www.pbs.org/wnet/nature/alienempire/multimedia/bee.html
This website provides the outer and inner view of a bee. When students put the mouse pointer on a body part of the bee, the body part changes to a different color to be distinguished from the rest of the body parts, and the name of the body part appears. When students click a body part, a simple explanation about the body part appears on the bottom of the screen. After a guided reading and virtual tour as a whole group, students may be able to visit the website independently.

National Honey Board: Just for Kids! www.honey.com/kids
The National Honey Board developed this website for students. It has interesting information about honeybees and why they make honey. It also provides honey-related trivia, history, vocabulary, recipes for kids, games, and materials for teachers. The pollination map is an interesting section that shows some of the fruits and vegetables pollinated by bees in the United States.

Nature—Alien Empire: Enter the Hive: www.pbs.org/wnet/nature/alienempire/multimedia/hive.html

This website is also provided by pbs.org but focuses on beehives rather than bees. This website has an interactive informational e-book about beehives and contains four different stories about honeybee hives, pollination, developing larvae, and storing honey. This webpage fits well with the storybook *Bumblebee at Apple Tree Lane* (Galvin, 2000) because it covers the similar stories such as pollination, developing larvae, and storing honey, and gives multimedia presentations of the story that provide a good visual aid for primary-grade students about bees and beehives. You may wish to turn the music off because it can be distracting. Even if you turn off the music, you can still hear the bee buzzing sound.

Buzzy Bee: www.magickeys.com/books/bee/index.html

"Buzzy Bee" by Carol Moore is an e-book for primary-grade students. It is a short and funny story with different flower names. It may be good for a quick teacher read-aloud with students, and students will learn new vocabulary about flowers such as daffodils, tulips, and hyacinths. Because it does not have a read-aloud function, some students may need extra guidance from a cross-age computer buddy.

Buzzy Bee and Friends: www.magickeys.com/books/beebf/index.html

"Buzzy Bee and Friends" by Carol Moore is an online e-book for primary-grade students. It is another short story about Buzzy Bee discussed in the previous Internet resource and idea. It provides different kinds of butterflies who share flowers with bees.

Book 3: Gregory and Alexander

Barringer, W. (2003). Ill. K. LaFave. Victoria, BC: Orca Book Publishers. $16.95. 32 pp.

BOOK REVIEW

Gregory, a young mouse, lives in a park with his best friend, Alexander (Al), a caterpillar. Gregory lives at the bottom of a very large tree, and Al lives nearby on the leaves of a milkweed plant. Gregory and Al like to watch children playing in the park, and sometimes they try to mimic at night what the children played. What they enjoy most is watching children flying all different kinds of kites. Gregory visits a local toy store to find a kite his own size, but all the kites are too big for him. One night Al tucks himself into a blanket and falls into a deep sleep. Gregory waits, and waits, and waits some more. One day, a beautiful butterfly greets Gregory by name and reveals himself to be the transformed Al. Once again they play together, but this time Gregory has a beautiful butterfly kite. With the help of a spider, they attach a long silky line from Alexander's belly to Gregory's hand. Alexander, who has to fly south for the winter, promises Gregory that Gregory will meet another caterpillar next summer. Painted in acrylics on watercolor paper, this book contains unique, pastel-toned images that make readers feel the warmth of friendship and reinforce the life cycle of butterflies in a fictional text.

READ-ALOUD AND BOOK DISCUSSION IDEAS

Before reading, discuss what it means to be best friends. For example, ask, "What makes someone a very best friend?" Show the book cover and ask students what kind of relationship the mouse and the caterpillar might have. What do students know about the life cycle of butterflies that might influence the friendship between a caterpillar and a mouse?

During reading, discuss Gregory's emotional changes and point of view, which are illustrated well with pictorial context clues. Remind students that viewing the pictures can help them learn additional information for understanding the story. Discuss with students the problem in the story and the role that the life cycle of a butterfly plays in solving the problem.

After you have finished reading, discuss the topic of friendship. For example, Gregory and Al helped each other. How did they help each other at the beginning, middle, and ending of the story? To make a text-to-life connection, ask your class when and how they have helped their friends. Also, you can incorporate science into the discussion by asking students to help you summarize the life cycle of the butterfly.

COMPUTER ACTIVITIES

Creativity and Presentation Software Ideas

Students will create their own e-book about a butterflies when using this software. It can be an informational or fictional book, such as *Gregory and Alexander* (Barringer, 2003). Before each student works at the computer, demonstrate how to use KidWorks Deluxe creativity and presentation software. By creating an e-book, students can organize their thoughts and information about butterflies and practice writing and editing skills. Students can share their work with others.

> **MATERIALS**
>
> ■ KidWorks Deluxe (1995) software

1. Ask students to type in their names to sign in and then click "yes."

2. Tell students to click on the "New Book" icon on the screen. On the next screen, "My Story" as the default title will appear, and the author will appear as "By [user's sign-in name]."

3. Ask students to change the title as they desire by clicking on the title. Students can also change the book cover image by clicking on the book with the paintbrush on the cover located on the bookshelf in the lower left-hand corner of the screen. Give students time to explore the program and learn from each other about how to use the program.

4. Instruct students to click on the arrow icon on the lower right-hand corner of the book to work on the next page. Each page has two options: (1) either a "pencil" icon to create a text page or (2) a "paint brush" icon to create a drawing page.

5. Ask students create their own stories and pictures.

6. Students can print out their book when they are finished and can either share their stories on screen or hard copy with class.

> **MATERIALS**
>
> ■ Caterpillars
> ■ Clear two-liter bottle
> ■ Digital camera
> ■ KidPix Studio Deluxe 3 (2000) software
> ■ Net
> ■ Paper towels
> ■ Rubber band
> ■ Scissors
> ■ Stick
> ■ Vegetable leaves

Digital Language Experience Approach

Go online to order caterpillars (go to www.butterflyskyfarm.com), or locate caterpillars in a local garden and raise them to the butterfly stage while studying this unit. This project will allow your students to connect their study of insects and butterflies with the real-life experience of nurturing a dozen caterpillars as they metamorphose into butterflies. While raising the caterpillars, students need to keep an observational journal that includes richly descriptive words and take pictures of each stage of the cycle. The steps to growing a caterpillar are as follows:

1. Order caterpillar habitats online or make with a clear two-liter bottle. Cut the narrow top off and place a paper towel, a stick, and fresh vegetable leaves in the bottle.

2. Change the vegetable leaves every day to feed the caterpillars.

3. Put a net over the top of the two-liter bottle, and place a rubber band over the net to hold it in place.

4. Take digital photographs of the process of making the habitat of the caterpillars on the first day of the experiment for the butterfly journal, and ask your students to keep taking pictures and notes for their journal during the experimental period. When a student takes pictures, remind him or her to write down dates and some notes such as the size and activities of the caterpillar (e.g., sleeping, eating, crawling).

5. Import pictures into KidPix Studio Deluxe 3 creativity and presentation software and ask students to write an e-journal about their observation that goes along with the imported pictures. During author's computer chair (see Appendix B), encourage students to share what they observed and discovered about butterflies, useful tips, or findings for classmates to share with each other. For example, a student might share a picture and say, "I took this picture because ____. When I took this picture, I used the flash, but the reflection of the flash blocked the caterpillar. So I found that it is better to take pictures next to the window where it is very bright."

Through this experiment, students can become experts on butterflies.

If possible, make a butterfly garden with your class. It will provide a rich field for students to explore butterflies and a good motivation for them to make a connection between science and reading more information about butterflies. You can find more information about how to make a butterfly garden at these websites: The Butterfly WebSite (go to http://butterflywebsite.com/butterflygardening.cfm) or How to Make Butterfly Gardens (go to www.uky.edu/Agriculture/Entomology/entfacts/misc/ef006.htm).

Computer Software Activity

My First Science Explorer software consistently invites students to explore scientific facts through reading aloud texts and asking questions. Students will be able to navigate the program independently based on their personal interests. Tell students that they will find out more about insects by exploring this software program. They will make their own decisions about what to learn while navigating the program. At the end, they can share what they learned through the program with class. After installing the program, there will be four windows that will take you to the place you want to explore. This software provides four settings on the main screen: Countryside, City, Kitchen, and Workshop.

MATERIALS

- My First Science Explorer (1999) software

1. Click on Countryside for this insect theme. Then click on a picture of animated flowers in the middle of the screen, which takes you to the next screen.

2. On the next screen, you will see a caterpillar, earthworm, dandelions, a snail, and a grasshopper. When you click each one of them, it will open another window that contains a paragraph of information and a picture on the right, and the website starts reading the text aloud to you.

3. Listen and read along with the text, and click on a hyperlink on the top left of the screen to collect a badge for science school. Students have to collect all the badges to win a medal. These badges and the medal motivate students to explore and listen to the informational text of the program.

4. Click on a caterpillar on the screen, and it will open a new window with a question: How do caterpillars turn into butterflies? Give students time to explore the software to find out much more information about insects.

On the initial screen page, there is a section called My Progress that shows a teacher how many prizes, stickers, and badges students have collected through the activities and listening to the program. Another section called Science Workbook may be too difficult for emerging readers and writers because it requires independent reading, and some answers require typing. Make sure that students are engaged at the appropriate level or have a computer buddy who is a fluent reader to offer support.

Internet Resources and Ideas

Beal Early Childhood Center: Exploring Butterflies in Kindergarten: www.shrewsbury-ma.gov/schools/beal/curriculum/butterfly/butterflies.html
Exploring Butterflies in Kindergarten has complete information about butterflies: the butterfly's life cycle and body, the caterpillar's and chrysalis's body, facts about butterflies, and differences between moths and butterflies. It will provide another opportunity for students to read informational text and enhance vocabulary development.

Butterflies & Bugs: www.billybear4kids.com/butterfly/flutter-fun.html
Butterflies & Bugs has beautiful photographs about butterflies. The Butterflies to Print & Play section has a butterfly maze, coloring section, flashcards, and bookmarks. The butterfly photographs in Flashcards and Bookmarks are very pretty. Also, craft ideas and online games with butterflies are available on this website. This is a good website for various activities related to butterflies, and by playing these games students will gain background knowledge and vocabulary about butterflies.

Unit Conclusion

Close the unit by having a grand conversation or show-and-tell time about what students have learned about insects. Students celebrate what they have learned by viewing unit projects, viewing slide shows, or comparing fantasy bugs they have made in the unit with real insects they studied. They may also review their informational books or slides or their favorite activity and share what they learned through this unit.

Math Is Fun

UNIT BOOKS

What's a Pair? What's a Dozen?
By Stephen R. Swinburne

Math Fables: Lessons That Count
By Greg Tang
Illustrated by Heather Cahoon

MATH-terpieces: The Art of Problem-Solving
By Greg Tang
Illustrated by Greg Paprocki

COMPUTER RESOURCES

Peter Rabbit's Math Garden
I Spy: School Days
Math Blaster, Ages 6–9

Thematic Connection

Number concepts, counting, adding, and subtracting are all basic skills students encounter in the early grades. Books in this unit offer primary-grade students unique opportunities to learn more about the connections of various mathematics concepts to everyday life, fables, and great works of art. The intent of this unit is to provide primary-grade students with an opportunity to explore basic mathematics concepts through children's literature and computer activities. The driving theme is that mathematics is fun. *What's a Pair? What's a Dozen?* (Swinburne, 2000) introduces numbers and number-related words. *Math Fables: Lessons That Count* (Tang, 2004) introduces numbers, number concepts, and groupings of numbers through rhyming fables. *MATH-terpieces* (Tang, 2003) presents visually oriented mathematics problems inspired by great works of art.

Matrix of Literacy Skills and Strategies in Unit 16

Literacy Skills and Strategies	Activities	Title of Book	Pages
Brainstorming	C	*What's a Pair? What's a Dozen?*	246
Building background knowledge on the Internet*	I	*What's a Pair? What's a Dozen?*	247
	I	*Math Fables: Lessons That Count*	250–251
	I	*MATH-terpieces: The Art of Problem-Solving*	253
Building editing skills	C	*MATH-terpieces: The Art of Problem-Solving*	252
Building fluency	D	*What's a Pair? What's a Dozen?*	246
Comparing and contrasting	U	—	244
	I	*What's a Pair? What's a Dozen?*	247
Composing in multimedia*	C, D	*What's a Pair? What's a Dozen?*	246
	C, D	*Math Fables: Lessons That Count*	248–249, 249
	C, D	*MATH-terpieces: The Art of Problem-Solving*	252
Creating and using charts	R	*What's a Pair? What's a Dozen?*	245
	S	*Math Fables: Lessons That Count*	250
Developing choral reading	U	—	244
Developing comprehension	R, S, I	*What's a Pair? What's a Dozen?*	245, 247, 247
	R, C, D, I	*Math Fables: Lessons That Count*	248, 248–249, 249, 250–251
	R, C, S, I	*MATH-terpieces: The Art of Problem-Solving*	251, 252, 253, 253
Developing context clues	I	*What's a Pair? What's a Dozen?*	247
	R	*Math Fables: Lessons That Count*	248
	R	*MATH-terpieces: The Art of Problem-Solving*	251
Developing creative writing	C	*What's a Pair? What's a Dozen?*	246
	C	*Math Fables: Lessons That Count*	248–249
	C, D	*MATH-terpieces: The Art of Problem-Solving*	252
Developing fluency	C	*What's a Pair? What's a Dozen?*	246
Developing oral language	U, UC	—	244, 253
	R, C, D	*What's a Pair? What's a Dozen?*	245, 246, 246
	R, C, D, S	*Math Fables: Lessons That Count*	248, 248–249, 249, 250
	R, D	*MATH-terpieces: The Art of Problem-Solving*	251, 252
Developing vocabulary	U	—	244
	R, C, D, S, I	*What's a Pair? What's a Dozen?*	245, 246, 246, 247, 247
	R, C, D, S, I	*Math Fables: Lessons That Count*	248, 248–249, 249, 250, 250–251
	R, C, S	*MATH-terpieces: The Art of Problem-Solving*	251, 252, 253
Drawing conclusions	R	*Math Fables: Lessons That Count*	248
Following directions	R, C, D, S	*What's a Pair? What's a Dozen?*	245, 246, 246, 247
	R, C, D, S, I	*Math Fables: Lessons That Count*	248, 248–249, 249, 250, 250–251
	C, D, S, I	*MATH-terpieces: The Art of Problem-Solving*	252, 252, 253, 253
Navigating hyperlinks*	S, I	*What's a Pair? What's a Dozen?*	247
	I	*Math Fables: Lessons That Count*	250–251
	S, I	*MATH-terpieces: The Art of Problem-Solving*	253

(continued)

Matrix of Literacy Skills and Strategies in Unit 16 (continued)

Literacy Skills and Strategies	Activities	Title of Book	Pages
Presenting work on a computer*	C	*What's a Pair? What's a Dozen?*	246
	C	*MATH-terpieces: The Art of Problem-Solving*	252
Reading aloud	C, D	*What's a Pair? What's a Dozen?*	246
	R, C, D, I	*Math Fables: Lessons That Count*	248, 248–249, 249, 250–251
Reading and listening for a purpose	R, S, I	*What's a Pair? What's a Dozen?*	245, 247, 247
	R, C, D, I	*Math Fables: Lessons That Count*	248, 248–249, 249, 250–251
	R, I	*MATH-terpieces: The Art of Problem-Solving*	251, 253
Reading informational text	R	*MATH-terpieces: The Art of Problem-Solving*	251
Sequencing	D, I	*What's a Pair? What's a Dozen?*	246, 247
Understanding a main idea	C, D, S, I	*What's a Pair? What's a Dozen?*	246, 246, 247, 247
	R	*Math Fables: Lessons That Count*	248
Using adjectives	C	*What's a Pair? What's a Dozen?*	246
	R, C	*MATH-terpieces: The Art of Problem-Solving*	251, 252
Using phonics: Rhyming words	R, C, I	*Math Fables: Lessons That Count*	248, 248–249, 250–251
	R	*MATH-terpieces: The Art of Problem-Solving*	251
Visualizing	I	*Math Fables: Lessons That Count*	250–251
	R	*MATH-terpieces: The Art of Problem-Solving*	251
Writing descriptive sentences	C, D	*What's a Pair? What's a Dozen?*	246
	C, D	*Math Fables: Lessons That Count*	248–249, 249
	C, D	*MATH-terpieces: The Art of Problem-Solving*	252

* Indicates a new-literacy skill.

U = unit introduction; R = read-aloud and book discussion ideas; C = creativity and presentation software ideas; D = Digital Language Experience Approach; S = computer software activity; I = Internet resources and ideas; UC = unit conclusion

Unit Introduction

Display a collection of cookies or pieces of fruit spaced evenly on a plate or tray. Be sure to have at least one per student. Ask students how they can figure out how many cookies or pieces of fruit are on the plate. When students suggest that the pieces can be counted, take a moment to count them. Write the number on chart paper and chorally read it as a group. Next, ask students how they can figure out if there is enough for each student to have one cookie or piece of fruit. Then count the students, write the number on chart paper, and chorally read it as a group. Compare the numbers and ask if there are enough or too many? How do they know? Tell students that they have just worked on a mathematics problem. Tell them that reading the books in this unit will help them have more fun with numbers and mathematics. Serve the cookies or pieces of fruit during a special snack time.

MATERIALS

- Chart paper
- Cookies or fruit
- Markers
- Plate or tray

Book 1: What's a Pair? What's a Dozen?

Swinburne, S.R. (2000). Honesdale, PA: Boyds Mills Press. $15.95. 32 pp.

BOOK REVIEW

This delightful book begins with "Everything starts with one" (p. 3) and then continues to explain and illustrate different ways of representing number-related words through color photographs of children involved in everyday events. For example, in the first half of the book, the number 1 is represented through words such as *single* and *first* and the prefix *uni-*; the meaning of 2 is shown through words such as *pair, couple, second,* and *double* and the prefix *bi-* in the first half of the book. The second half of the book is written in the form of a guessing game in which students use information in photographs to answer questions related to the mathematics concepts and words that were discussed in the first half of the book. For example, it asks, "Can you find the pair?" (p. 21), and the answer follows on the next page with another picture.

READ-ALOUD AND BOOK DISCUSSION IDEAS

Before reading, ask students, "If there were no numbers, what would our world be like? Could we tell what time it is? Would we know how many candles to put on a birthday cake?" Then show the book cover and read the title. Tell students they will learn all about number-related words and the importance of numbers.

During reading, use a Number Words Chart (see Figure 39), and fill it in while reading about each number.

After reading the book to students, review with them the Number Words Chart and discuss examples of each word so students can grasp a concrete concept of each word. Students who have a firm grasp of number concepts will enrich their vocabulary concepts. Others students will have occasions to build some foundational understanding about numbers and number words throughout the unit.

MATERIALS

- Markers
- Number Words Chart

Figure 39
Number Words Chart

1	2	3	4
One	Two	Three	Four
First	Second	Third	Fourth
Uni-	Bi-	Tri-	Quart-
Single	Double	Triple	Quadruple

COMPUTER ACTIVITIES

Creativity and Presentation Software Ideas

To reinforce the concepts of *single*, *double*, and *triple*, students create an ice cream cone on screen.

<table>
<tr><td>

MATERIALS

- Chart paper
- Ice cream
- Ice cream cones
- KidPix Studio Deluxe 3 (2000) software
- Markers
- Number Words Chart

</td></tr>
</table>

1. Review the concepts of *single*, *double*, and *triple* on the Number Words Chart (see Figure 39 on page 245) and tell students that they will create ice cream cones that represent these concepts by using creativity and presentation software such as KidPix Studio Deluxe 3.

2. Brainstorm about the ice cream flavors with students and write them down on chart paper for students to refer to as needed.

3. Invite students to use stamping and drawing tools to create three screen pictures for different numbers of scoops of ice cream: a single scoop (of their least favorite flavor of ice cream), a double scoop (of a flavor they like), and a triple scoop (of their favorite ice cream flavor). Discuss with students the differences among the terms *least favorite*, *like*, and *favorite*.

4. Encourage students to dictate or write labels on screen for each ice cream cone that they created. Instruct them to write sentences that use the new vocabulary terms on each screen and to remember to write their name and the date at the top of the screen. For example, they could write, "I like a single scoop of lemon custard because that's my least favorite ice cream flavor. I like a double scoop of vanilla ice cream with a cherry on top because I like vanilla. I like a triple scoop of chocolate chip ice cream because it's my favorite. I get to eat three scoops."

5. Print out their pictures and bind them into a book called "Our Single, Double, and Triple Scoop Cones," and create an on-screen slide show. Share the slide show during author's computer chair (see Appendix B). Encourage students to read and talk about the differences between the number concepts. Invite students to read aloud their screens. Prepare ice cream and cones so each student can have a single scoop to taste. Take a digital photograph of the class with their single scoops and import into KidPix Studio Deluxe 3 as the last page of the slide show.

Digital Language Experience Approach

<table>
<tr><td>

MATERIALS

- Digital camera
- KidPix Studio Deluxe 3 (2000) software

</td></tr>
</table>

Reinforce the concept of ordinal numbers with digital photography.

1. Take a digital photograph of a line of five students.

2. Make five screen copies of the same picture by using creativity and presentation software such as KidPix Studio Deluxe 3.

3. Invite the student who was first in line to draw a diagram label "first" and write a sentence using his or her name on the first picture of the screens, e.g., "[The student's name] is first in line."

4. Continue the process with the second through fourth student in line and finish with the student who is "last" in line by using each picture of the screens.

5. Print out copies for each student to take home and read to caregivers. By reading aloud to their parents and caregivers, students will develop reading fluency and vocabulary.

Computer Software Activity

MATERIALS

■ Peter Rabbit's Math Garden (2005) software

Peter Rabbit's Math Garden software has four educational games to help students develop fundamental mathematics skills. Each game has three difficulty levels. After solving the mathematics problems, students get a reward, carrots, which students can exchange for seeds for his or her personal garden. When the student earned enough carrots, he or she can go to his or her personal garden by clicking a garden icon on the bottom of the screen. When the personal garden screen opens, there are different kinds of seeds that the student can plant in his or her personal garden. To get the kind of seed the student wants, he or she has to exchange with carrots they earned from solving mathematics problems. Students will learn and practice essential mathematics concepts, counting and number relationships, memory and concentration, sorting and grouping, and adding and subtracting, which will help to improve confidence in mathematics. Students will practice comprehending and understanding a main idea to solve problems correctly.

Internet Resources and Ideas

Even & Odd: www.primarygames.com/storybooks/even_odd/start.htm
This website contains an interactive story, "Even & Odd" by Susan Beasley. This interactive book reinforces the concepts of even, odd, and pairs from *What's a Pair? What's a Dozen?* (Swinburne, 2000). Fluent readers will be able to read this book independently. Emerging and developing readers will reinforce vocabulary words.

Primary Games: Squigly's Apples: www.primarygames.com/squigly/start.htm
Squigly's Apples is a mathematics game that deals with ordinal numbers. Students will be able to recognize how to spell ordinal numbers. For example, it is written *fifth* rather than *5th*. This website is appropriate for emerging readers who will learn background knowledge and vocabulary words about mathematical concepts.

The Counting Story: A Story by Rolando Merino for His Son Tommy: www.magickeys.com/books/count/index.html
This e-book "The Counting Story" by Rolando Merino is a story about numbers 1 to 11. It is an animated book, and each page starts with the same sentence except for the number that is on the specific page.

Book 2:   Math Fables: Lessons That Count

Tang, G. (2004). Ill. H. Cahoon. New York: Scholastic. $16.95. 40 pp.

BOOK REVIEW

This book helps students develop early number concepts including grouping and rhyming words. Poems in fable form about one spider, two birds, three turtles, four squirrels, and so forth mix numbers and literature to introduce students to the notion that numbers are made of combinations and sets of other numbers. Poems with catchy titles, such as "Going Nuts," "Midnight Snack," and

"Gone With the Wind," are short, descriptive, and excellent for the exploration of numbers 1 to 10. Bright, cartoon-like illustrations depict animals grouped in different ways. The last words of every second and fourth verse rhyme. A final page offers ideas to help more accelerated learners combine groups of numbers in new ways. Greg Tang intertwines the primary mathematics theme of number combinations with the secondary literary theme of the moral of a fable. The following morals are found in the book: Good things will come to those who wait; sometimes the most important thing in life is just to try; it is wise to plan ahead and always be prepared; appreciate having enough food; do not procrastinate; and cooperate with each other.

READ-ALOUD AND BOOK DISCUSSION IDEAS

Before reading, tell students a brief fable, such as Aesop's The Ant and the Grasshopper, and explain to them the concept of the moral of a story. Because each poem has its own moral, there are plenty of topics to discuss while reading the book. Because mathematics stories are written in fable format, it is appropriate to discuss both mathematics and language arts concepts such as poetry and fable genres.

MATERIALS

- Blocks
- Paper bags
- Tray

During reading, you might need to point to a picture that relates to the text and, to ensure comprehension, ask students questions about the picture and text.

After reading, to reinforce number combinations, prepare nine mystery paper bags filled and labeled with 2 to 10 blocks. Bag 2 has 2 blocks; bag 3 has 3 blocks, and so forth. Invite pairs of students to dump the contents of one bag onto a tray (e.g., the bag that has 4 blocks). Tell each student to take some of the blocks in their hands until they are holding all the blocks (e.g., one student has 1 block and the other has 3 blocks). Direct the class to count how many blocks each student has and state the number in sentence (e.g., "Israel has 1 red block and Jennifer has 3 red blocks."). Then ask the class to suggest another combination of blocks that would combine to make 4 blocks (e.g., 2 and 2; 0 and 4). Demonstrate the groupings in number sentence format.

COMPUTER ACTIVITIES

Creativity and Presentation Software Ideas

Students innovate on a fable they enjoyed from the focus book *Math Fables: Lessons That Count* (Tang, 2004) by substituting a different set of animals for a fable story involving number sentences.

MATERIALS

- KidPix Studio Deluxe 3 (2000) software

1. Demonstrate, for example, by selecting "Going Nuts" (p. 10) as the stimulus poem.

2. Keyboard a new title, "Going Bananas," using creativity and presentation software such as KidPix Studio Deluxe 3.

3. Innovate in the software on the text as follows. If the original reads

> 4 squirrels frolicked in the leaves
> one brisk fall afternoon,
> when suddenly it dawned on them
> that snow was coming soon (p. 10)

then the innovated text can read

> 4 monkeys frolicked in the trees
> one brisk fall afternoon at the zoo,
> when suddenly it dawned on them
> that snow was coming soon.

4. Encourage small groups of students to work with an adult to innovate on other mathematics poem fables, following the same original format.

5. Remind students to write their name and date at the bottom of the screen page.

6. Print out and display new fables on a bulletin board to read and discuss during whole-group time. Students can take home copies of their work to share with caregivers and to reinforce number concepts at home.

Digital Language Experience Approach

MATERIALS

- Digital camera
- KidPix Studio Deluxe 3 (2000) software
- Two hula hoops or two segments of rope

1. Use a digital camera to capture moments when students group themselves in different ways to represent a target number. For example, tell a group of five students to stand in front of the class. Then ask them to sort themselves out in at least two combinations that make five (such as one standing alone and the other four standing together). Guide students through this activity.

2. Place two hula hoops or make large circles out of rope. Direct two students to stand in one circle and three students in the other.

3. Ask students to suggest other ways to combine sets of students to make a group of five. Take photographs of students standing in different combinations.

4. Import those pictures into creativity and presentation software such as KidPix Studio Deluxe 3.

5. Make a slide show called "Combinations of Numbers Book" of the pictures. You can create a book as a whole group with emerging or developing readers or as a small-group activity with fluent readers.

6. Save the book as a slide show as well so students can watch the presentation during author's computer chair (see Appendix B). Invite students to read aloud their screen. Ask students to share their experiences about the grouping activity and what they have learned.

7. Ask students to explain the groupings they were in, if the creativity and presentation software has a voice-recording function, to make the activity accessible to emerging readers who can view the slide show independently during computer-center time.

Computer Software Activity

Instruct students to use the program tools to make an I Spy riddle game that involves combining numbers of objects in different groupings. For example, demonstrate how to use the Venn diagram function to place two objects in one circle (e.g., a dog and a cat), two objects in another circle (e.g., a car and a bicycle), and one object in the middle of the two circles (e.g., a monkey on a skateboard) (see Figure 40).

Write clues on the blackboard that help students locate items on screen. Create another Venn diagram and ask small groups of students how they would group different combinations of items to make a total of five objects. Younger students will need a cross-age computer buddy to accomplish this assignment. Encourage cross-age computer buddies to talk with students about their decisions.

MATERIALS

■ I Spy: School Days (1995) software

Internet Resources and Ideas

The Little Animals Activity Centre: www.bbc.co.uk/schools/laac/music/fdi.shtml
A fox at this website asks viewers to choose whether they want to play a dance game or listen to a rhyme. Clicking the "Animal rhyme" doorbell will allow students to listen to a rhyming e-book. The e-book stimulates students' imaginations by allowing them to visualize words. Students also can practice comprehension and find what words rhyme in the book.

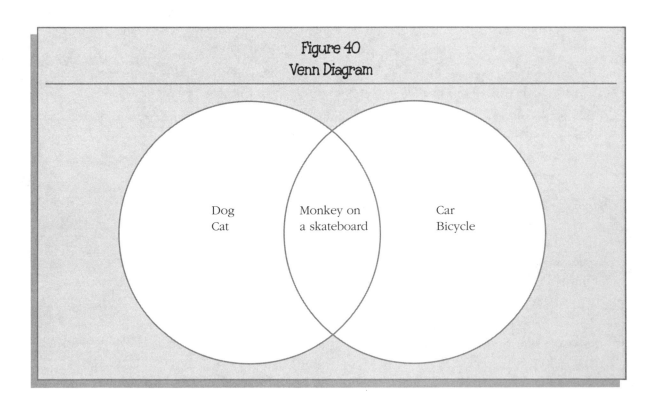

Figure 40
Venn Diagram

Dog
Cat

Monkey on
a skateboard

Car
Bicycle

The Little Animals Activity Centre: www.bbc.co.uk/schools/laac/numbers/chi.shtml
There are three kinds of games with three ability levels related to the unit: addition, subtraction, and combined addition and subtraction. These simple mathematics games reinforce basic skills for students with minimal mathematics education. Macromedia Shockwave Player installation is required for most of the games.

Number Circus: www.lil-fingers.com/circus/index.php
"Number Circus" by David Lumerman is an animated counting e-book about basic number concepts for emerging readers. It requires Macromedia Flash for sound and graphics. Students will learn how to spell numbers 1 through 9.

Book 3:   MATH-terpieces: The Art of Problem-Solving

Tang, G. (2003). Ill. G. Paprocki. New York: Scholastic. $16.95. 32 pp.

BOOK REVIEW

MATH-terpieces combines art masterpieces with mathematics concepts in an unexpectedly delightful way. Visually presented problems draw inspiration from artworks by 12 artists including Edgar Degas, Paul Cézanne, Pablo Picasso, and Andy Warhol. The overall mathematics focus is to practice adding by understanding that different combinations of objects taken from paintings add up to a targeted number. For example, van Gogh's "The Starry Night" inspired an activity, Star Power. The left page of the spread displays the masterpiece, and the text presents the problem. The right page displays groups of four by using one and three stars and two and two stars. Students determine which groupings combine to make a group of seven.

This book is written in a form of poetry with rhyming words. Teachers can use this book not only for mathematics concepts but also for language arts.

READ-ALOUD AND BOOK DISCUSSION IDEAS

Before reading, do a picture walk and talk about the great works of art included in the book. Draw attention to how Greg Tang selected one object to highlight in a problem. Tell students that you will be reading and solving the problems together as you read the book.

During reading, interact with students and help them sort out the problems. For some problems, read the descriptive statements and ask students to visualize, or make a mental picture. Instruct students to check their imaginative masterpieces with the illustrations and enjoy viewing the masterpieces.

During reading, also emphasize rhyming words of each poem. You can select target rhyming words to enhance students' word-recognition skills.

After reading, ask students to discuss their favorite paintings and review the target rhyming words.

COMPUTER ACTIVITIES

Creativity and Presentation Software Ideas

Tell students that they will create a math-masterpiece problem by innovating on the focus book *MATH-terpieces: The Art of Problem-Solving* (Tang, 2003). Discuss the format the author used to incorporate fine arts throughout the book. If necessary, reread several poems from the book and emphasize last two verses. For example, in van Gogh's poem on page 12, the first verse is about the first impression of the art and the second verse is about the author. Then, last two verses ask mathematics questions. Emphasize the last two verses for this project. Tell students that they will create a math-masterpiece problem for themselves like the book they just read.

MATERIALS

■ KidPix Studio Deluxe 3 (2000) software

---

1. Instruct students to create a computer illustration of a masterpiece by using creativity and presentation software, such as KidPix Studio Deluxe 3, or by downloading a picture from a museum website, such as the Museum of Fine Arts in Boston, Massachusetts, USA (go to www.mfa.org/collections/index.asp).

2. Encourage students to select one object from the illustration and cut and paste it onto another portion of the screen to create their own art-inspired problem to solve.

3. Instruct students to write descriptive word-problem sentences beneath the illustrations that use adjectives.

4. Ask a cross-age computer buddy to help emerging and developing readers to accomplish this task.

5. Save students' work in a slide show called "My Math-Masterpiece" and invite students to figure out the answer to the problem during author's computer chair (see Appendix B).

Digital Language Experience Approach

To make connections between art and mathematics, ask students to walk around the school, find art, and to try to create a mathematics problem using the art they found.

MATERIALS

■ Digital camera
■ KidPix Studio Deluxe 3 (2000) software

---

1. Take digital photographs of framed art displayed in the hallways of your school.

2. Import photos into creativity and presentation software such as KidPix Studio Deluxe 3.

3. Ask students to select one of the pictures and ask a number question about the contents. For example, in a picture of a team who won a trophy, students might ask, "How many trophies do you see?" In a picture of a flower garden, students might ask, "How many red flowers do you see? How many red and pink flowers do you see?" Students also may want to try painting pictures in the styles of different artists from the focus book and add questions on screen. Send printouts home for students to share with caregivers.

4. Print out and display the pictures on a "Can you figure it out?" bulletin board.

Computer Software Activity

The Math Blaster, Ages 6–9 software is full of interesting games that are played in a galactic setting. With six difficulty levels in ten different subject areas, students can select to work on addition, subtraction, multiplication, division, fractions, decimals, percentages, estimation, number patterns, or problem solving. Students can play at their own ability level and focus area.

MATERIALS

■ Math Blaster, Ages 6–9 (1997) software

Internet Resources and Ideas

Math Brain on Funbrain: www.funbrain.com/brain/MathBrain/MathBrain.html
Math Brain provides excellent online mathematics games for grades 1 through 8. The website has 25 games with beautiful animations. To play each game, students need to be able to read and follow directions.

Count Us In: www.abc.net.au/countusin
This website is designed to help children understand basic mathematics concepts. The many interactive animated mathematics games cover basic mathematics skills such as counting; adding; subtracting; representing numbers 1–10; and understanding ordinal numbers, volume, chance, data, halves, and length. Students can choose from two ability levels for each game: easy and hard. For example, for the easy level in game 3, students are asked to count objects and put the numeral in the blank at the bottom of screen. For the hard level, students are asked to spell out the number word after filling in the numeral. Each game is downloadable. To play the games and solve the problems, students have to be able to read text and follow directions.

Unit Conclusion

MATERIALS

■ Books from this unit

Display the books read in the unit. Ask students to talk about the things they learned from each book. Remind students of the key concepts and exhibit examples of students' computer-related activities. Play some of the students' favorite mathematics CD-ROM games or revisit websites to reinforce the notion that mathematics is indeed fun.

Dinosaurs With a Twist

UNIT BOOKS

Dinosaurumpus!
By Tony Mitton
Illustrated by Guy Parker-Rees

The Field Mouse and the Dinosaur Named Sue
By Jan Wahl
Illustrated by Bob Doucet

The Dinosaurs of Waterhouse Hawkins:
An Illuminating History of Mr. Waterhouse Hawkins, Artist and Lecturer
By Barbara Kerley
Illustrated by Brian Selznick

COMPUTER RESOURCES

Dinosaurs: Giant Reptiles
The Magic School Bus Explores the Age of Dinosaurs
Dinosaur Adventure 3-D

Thematic Connection

Many primary-grade students have questions about dinosaurs, the large creatures that once walked the Earth. What did dinosaurs look like? What do fossils tell us about dinosaurs? What are the names of dinosaurs? Were any dinosaurs small? The books in this unit help students answer these and other questions in both fiction and nonfiction texts. In *Dinosaurumpus!* (Mitton, 2003), emerging and developing readers can participate in choral responses, move to the rhythmic beat of the text, and learn the names of different dinosaurs. Fluent readers will enjoy reading this on their own but may need assistance with some dinosaur names. *The Field Mouse and the Dinosaur Named Sue* (Wahl, 2000) relates the true story about the journey of a dinosaur named Sue; however, it is told from a mouse's-eye view by a fictional character that made his home under one of the dinosaur's bones. The fictional text allows students to learn about dinosaurs in a playful manner. *The Dinosaurs of Waterhouse Hawkins* (Kerley, 2001) deals with one man's quest to understand how dinosaurs looked when they roamed the earth.

Matrix of Literacy Skills and Strategies in Unit 17

Literacy Skills and Strategies	Activities	Title of Book	Pages
Building background knowledge on the Internet*	C, I	*Dinosaurumpus!*	259, 260
	C, I	*The Field Mouse and the Dinosaur Named Sue*	261–262, 263–264
	C, D, I	*The Dinosaurs of Waterhouse Hawkins: An Illuminating History of Mr. Waterhouse Hawkins, Artist and Lecturer*	266, 266–267, 267–268
Building fluency	S	*Dinosaurumpus!*	260
Comparing and contrasting	C	*Dinosaurumpus!*	259
	D	*The Field Mouse and the Dinosaur Named Sue*	262–263
Composing in multimedia*	C, D	*Dinosaurumpus!*	259, 259–260
	C, D	*The Field Mouse and the Dinosaur Named Sue*	261–262, 262–263
	C, D	*The Dinosaurs of Waterhouse Hawkins: An Illuminating History of Mr. Waterhouse Hawkins, Artist and Lecturer*	266, 266–267
Counting numbers	I	*Dinosaurumpus!*	260
Creating concept maps and graphic organizers	C	*Dinosaurumpus!*	259
Determining cause and effect	R	*The Dinosaurs of Waterhouse Hawkins: An Illuminating History of Mr. Waterhouse Hawkins, Artist and Lecturer*	264–266
Determining chronological order	C	*Dinosaurumpus!*	259
Determining story details	I	*The Field Mouse and the Dinosaur Named Sue*	263–264
	I	*The Dinosaurs of Waterhouse Hawkins: An Illuminating History of Mr. Waterhouse Hawkins, Artist and Lecturer*	267–268
Developing a sense of beginnings, middles, and endings	R	*The Dinosaurs of Waterhouse Hawkins: An Illuminating History of Mr. Waterhouse Hawkins, Artist and Lecturer*	264–266
Developing choral reading	U	—	258
	C, UC	*Dinosaurumpus!*	259, 268
Developing comprehension	R, S, UC	*Dinosaurumpus!*	258, 260, 268
	R, S	*The Field Mouse and the Dinosaur Named Sue*	261, 263
	R, S, I	*The Dinosaurs of Waterhouse Hawkins: An Illuminating History of Mr. Waterhouse Hawkins, Artist and Lecturer*	264–266, 267, 267–268
Developing creative writing	D, I	*Dinosaurumpus!*	259–260, 260
	C	*The Field Mouse and the Dinosaur Named Sue*	261–262
Developing critical reading and thinking	R	*The Dinosaurs of Waterhouse Hawkins: An Illuminating History of Mr. Waterhouse Hawkins, Artist and Lecturer*	264–266

(continued)

Literacy Skills and Strategies	Activities	Title of Book	Pages
Developing oral language	U	—	258
	S, UC	*Dinosaurumpus!*	260, 268
	C, D	*The Field Mouse and the Dinosaur Named Sue*	261–262, 262–263
	R, D, I	*The Dinosaurs of Waterhouse Hawkins: An Illuminating History of Mr. Waterhouse Hawkins, Artist and Lecturer*	264–266, 266–267, 267–268
Developing vocabulary	U	—	258
	C, D, S	*Dinosaurumpus!*	259, 259–260, 260
	R, C, D, I	*The Field Mouse and the Dinosaur Named Sue*	261, 261–262, 262–263, 263–264
	R, S	*The Dinosaurs of Waterhouse Hawkins: An Illuminating History of Mr. Waterhouse Hawkins, Artist and Lecturer*	264–266, 267
Distinguishing between real and make-believe content	U	—	258
Drawing conclusions	R	*The Dinosaurs of Waterhouse Hawkins: An Illuminating History of Mr. Waterhouse Hawkins, Artist and Lecturer*	264–266
Following directions	C, D, I	*Dinosaurumpus!*	259, 259–260, 260
	C, D, S	*The Dinosaurs of Waterhouse Hawkins: An Illuminating History of Mr. Waterhouse Hawkins, Artist and Lecturer*	266, 266–267, 267
Identifying letters	C	*Dinosaurumpus!*	259
Inferring	C, I	*The Dinosaurs of Waterhouse Hawkins: An Illuminating History of Mr. Waterhouse Hawkins, Artist and Lecturer*	266, 267–268
Navigating hyperlinks*	C, D, S, I, UC	*Dinosaurumpus!*	259, 259–260, 260, 260, 268
	C, S, I	*The Field Mouse and the Dinosaur Named Sue*	261–262, 263, 263–264
	C, S, I	*The Dinosaurs of Waterhouse Hawkins: An Illuminating History of Mr. Waterhouse Hawkins, Artist and Lecturer*	266, 267, 267–268
Presenting work on a computer*	C, D	*Dinosaurumpus!*	259, 259–260
	D	*The Field Mouse and the Dinosaur Named Sue*	262–263
	C, D	*The Dinosaurs of Waterhouse Hawkins: An Illuminating History of Mr. Waterhouse Hawkins, Artist and Lecturer*	266, 266–267
Reading aloud	R	*Dinosaurumpus!*	258
	R	*The Field Mouse and the Dinosaur Named Sue*	261
	R	*The Dinosaurs of Waterhouse Hawkins: An Illuminating History of Mr. Waterhouse Hawkins, Artist and Lecturer*	264–266

(continued)

Literacy Skills and Strategies	Activities	Title of Book	Pages
Reading and listening for a purpose	C	*Dinosaurumpus!*	259
	R	*The Field Mouse and the Dinosaur Named Sue*	261
	R	*The Dinosaurs of Waterhouse Hawkins: An Illuminating History of Mr. Waterhouse Hawkins, Artist and Lecturer*	264–266
Reading informational text	C, S	*Dinosaurumpus!*	259, 260
	S, I	*The Field Mouse and the Dinosaur Named Sue*	263, 263–264
	R, S	*The Dinosaurs of Waterhouse Hawkins: An Illuminating History of Mr. Waterhouse Hawkins, Artist and Lecturer*	264–266, 267
Retelling	UC	*Dinosaurumpus!*	268
	R, C, D	*The Field Mouse and the Dinosaur Named Sue*	261, 261–262, 262–263
	I	*The Dinosaurs of Waterhouse Hawkins: An Illuminating History of Mr. Waterhouse Hawkins, Artist and Lecturer*	267–268
Sequencing	C	*Dinosaurumpus!*	259
	R	*The Dinosaurs of Waterhouse Hawkins: An Illuminating History of Mr. Waterhouse Hawkins, Artist and Lecturer*	264–266
Summarizing	R	*The Dinosaurs of Waterhouse Hawkins: An Illuminating History of Mr. Waterhouse Hawkins, Artist and Lecturer*	264–266
Understanding a main idea	I	*The Field Mouse and the Dinosaur Named Sue*	263–264
	I	*The Dinosaurs of Waterhouse Hawkins: An Illuminating History of Mr. Waterhouse Hawkins, Artist and Lecturer*	267–268
Using adjectives	D	*Dinosaurumpus!*	259–260
	C	*The Field Mouse and the Dinosaur Named Sue*	261–262
Using phonics: Letter–sound correspondence	R	*Dinosaurumpus!*	258
Using phonics: Onsets and rimes	R, UC	*Dinosaurumpus!*	258, 268
Using phonics: Rhyming words	R, I, UC	*Dinosaurumpus!*	258, 260, 268
Using verbs	C	*The Field Mouse and the Dinosaur Named Sue*	261–262
Visualizing	U	—	258
	R	*Dinosaurumpus!*	258
Writing descriptive sentences	I	*The Dinosaurs of Waterhouse Hawkins: An Illuminating History of Mr. Waterhouse Hawkins, Artist and Lecturer*	267–268
	C	*Dinosaurumpus!*	259
	C	*The Field Mouse and the Dinosaur Named Sue*	261–262

* Indicates a new-literacy skill.
U = unit introduction; R = read-aloud and book discussion ideas; C = creativity and presentation software ideas; D = Digital Language Experience Approach; S = computer software activity; I = Internet resources and ideas; UC = unit conclusion

Unit Introduction

Display for students this unit's book covers and point to the illustrations, which include a dinosaur skeleton, a dinosaur model, and a cartoon-like painting of a dinosaur. Note to students the different ways that illustrators depict the dinosaurs and the dinosaur skeleton. Ask students which illustrations they think are most realistic and which might be fantasy. Tell them that the books in this unit will help them learn about dinosaur names, a dinosaur who went to a museum, and a man who made big models of dinosaurs a long time ago. Some students will be eager to share the names of dinosaurs that they already know. Tell students that dinosaurs ranged in size from that of a chicken to more than 100 feet long. You might want to show them a graph or picture of a 4-foot-tall child compared to multiple sizes of dinosaurs in order to help them visualize size and scale.

MATERIALS

- Books from this unit
- Graph or picture of a 4-foot-tall child

Book 1:   Dinosaurumpus!

Mitton, T. (2003). Ill. G. Parker-Rees. New York: Orchard Books. $15.95. 32 pp.

BOOK REVIEW

Brightly colored prehistoric dinosaurs and boldly printed rhymes invite students to join the Dinosaurumpus!: "Shake, shake, shudder...near the sludgy old swamp. The dinosaurs are coming. Get ready to romp" (p. 3). Students will want to repeat the chorus as teachers read about the dancing dinosaurs and their tail-thwacking playmates. Even the typically grumpy T-Rex is a happy fellow, stomping, bomping, and romping. So pick up the beat and create a rumpus of your own.

READ-ALOUD AND BOOK DISCUSSION IDEAS

Before reading to students, ask them to imagine what a Dinosaurumpus! might look like. Ask them to be ready to remember the names of different dinosaurs in the book.

During reading, emphasize the rhyming words and cadence of the text. In addition, point out to students the words with onsets that repeat a sound (e.g., *quake/quiver, shake/shudder, big/bony, snip/snap*). You might also point out instances of onomatopoeia (words that imitate the sound they denote). For example, Stegosaurus moves with a "clatter, clatter, clatter" (p. 9) of her bony plates; Brontosaurus swings his tail with a "thwack, thwack, and thwack" (p. 7).

After reading, reinforce comprehension by asking students to recall names of the dinosaurs.

COMPUTER ACTIVITIES

Creativity and Presentation Software Ideas - - - - - - - - - - - - ▸

MATERIALS

- Butcher paper
- KidPix Studio Deluxe (1998) software
- Markers

For emerging readers, use creativity and presentation software, such as KidPix Studio Deluxe, to create a "Scales and Tales" alphabet book, classifying animals into those that have either tails or scales, or assemble an online version by building a class webpage of dinosaur names and fun facts. Students will gain practice categorizing and presenting their ideas on the computer. These activities will help students build research skills and learn to provide evidence to support their ideas. There are dinosaur names for every letter of the alphabet. The website Enchanted Learning: Zoom Dinosaurs (go to www.enchantedlearning.com/subjects/ dinosaurs) has information on names and facts about dinosaurs. The site includes an alphabetical listing of the dinosaurs with a picture and description of each dinosaur. Creating the following projects will help students learn more about life sciences while exploring interesting facts about prehistoric times.

- Each student (or pair of students) could be responsible for one letter of the alphabet. Assign letters to students and have them select a dinosaur whose name begins with that letter.

- Reinforce social studies concepts by asking fluent readers to create a life-size prehistoric timeline to position around the room. Pictures can be copied from the website or drawn. Emerging readers can place the pictures or drawings of dinosaurs on the timeline for the appropriate era.

- Ask students to write descriptive sentences by adding a few fun facts about each era or dinosaur from the Enchanted Learning website (www.enchantedlearning.com/subjects/ dinosaurs). The site has pictures and information to assist you in this project. An example timeline is available also under "Evolution of Dinosaurs" on the same website, located below the title "All About Dinosaurs."

Digital Language Experience Approach - - - - - - - - - - - - - - ▸

MATERIALS

- Digital camera
- PowerPoint (Microsoft Office 2003, 2003) software

Encourage students' creativity and written communication skills by creating a class slide show about dinosaurs titled "What We Have Learned About Dinosaurs."

1. Take a digital photograph of each student to be used later on the title page of each student's creation. Import the photographs into creativity and presentation software such as PowerPoint.

2. Instruct emerging readers to use inventive spelling (spelling words phonically, using one letter for each sound) to write descriptive sentences about their favorite dinosaur on screen. Developing and fluent readers can create a one-page story about their favorite dinosaur. Students' individual creations can also be poems, stories, scanned drawings, or a log sheet

of interesting facts about dinosaurs or dinosaur myths. Ask students to share their creations with the class during author's computer chair (see Appendix B).

3. Create the slide show using creativity and presentation software such as PowerPoint, and display it for parent night so that each parent can see the on-screen example of their child's work. Ask students to help come up with a title for your screen show.

Alternately, your might want to build a class webpage to display what the class learned about dinosaurs in this unit. Tips on building a teacher-created website are available on the following websites: Education World (go to www.education-world.com/a_tech/tech161.shtml), Web Reference (go to www.webreference.com/greatsite.html), and World's Worst Website (go to www.angelfire.com/super/badwebs), which has several examples of what not to do when creating a website.

Computer Software Activity

Students can read or click on an icon to listen to each line of text in this interactive nonfiction book about dinosaurs. Pictures are realistic and show the dinosaurs in a natural habitat. Emerging readers should listen to the text and be ready to tell at least two things they learned about dinosaurs. Developing and fluent readers should echo read for fluency practice and be ready to tell two things they learned about dinosaurs.

Internet Resources and Ideas

Enchanted Learning: Zoom Dinosaurs—Classroom Activities: How to Write a Funny Dinosaur Poem: www.enchantedlearning.com/subjects/dinosaurs/classroom/Poem.shtml
This website aligns well with *Dinosaurumpus!* (Mitton, 2003) because it provides students with ideas for writing a funny dinosaur poem. Step-by-step instructions and prompts are easy to follow. However, teachers may want to simplify the activity for emerging and developing readers by pairing them with fluent readers or a parent volunteer to help them read the instructions. A sample poem and steps for creating the poem are included on the site. Following the instructions on the website, start by creating a poem with students so they can see, hear, and participate in the creation. There is also an especially helpful webpage of word families at www.enchantedlearning.com/rhymes/wordfamilies that students can print out to help them find rhyming words.

Students also can practice counting numbers by completing an online dot-to-dot outline of a dinosaur. Correctly completing the dot-to-dot puzzle yields a well-known dinosaur picture at the Enchanted Learning webpage: www.enchantedlearning.com/cgi-bin/Dots.cgi/Trex.

Discovery Channel When Dinos Roamed America: Dino Lookup: http://dsc.discovery.com/convergence/dinos/lookup.html
What prehistoric beasts lived in your neighborhood? Help students build research skills and background knowledge by asking them to look up their zip codes to find out which dinosaurs lived where they now live. Try a few zip codes of family and friends around the United States.

Book 2: The Field Mouse and the Dinosaur Named Sue

Wahl, J. (2000). Ill. B. Doucet. New York: Scholastic. $12.95. 32 pp.
(out of print, available from resellers)

BOOK REVIEW

Field Mouse lives peacefully in a South Dakota, USA, burrow under a big, old bone. His peaceful life is noisily interrupted by thunderous bangs when a strange group of people turns the ground upside down. Archaeologists uncover his old bone, which is part of the largest, most completely found tyrannosaurus rex, a dinosaur named Sue. The fossilized bone that was once Field Mouse's roof is now missing. In search of his bone, Field Mouse journeys from his burrow in South Dakota to the Field Museum of Natural History in Chicago, Illinois, USA, where he eventually finds his bone and makes his new home. Jan Wahl, who has written more than 100 children's books, offers children a mouse's-eye view of a true story involving archaeologists and paleontologists digging, cleaning, and reassembling the fossilized dinosaur. Muted earth-tone drawings by Bob Doucet convey realistic perspectives of Sue's size and scale. Do not miss the end pages, where Wahl presents a photograph of Sue's skull with an account of the importance of this discovery.

READ-ALOUD AND BOOK DISCUSSION IDEAS

Before reading, show students a map of the United States and trace the trail from South Dakota to Chicago. Tell them that the story about a little mouse that makes the long journey from South Dakota to Chicago is also the story about a dinosaur named Sue and the people who found her. Tell students that after reading, they should be able to explain how the little mouse traveled so far, what type of dinosaur Sue was, and how old she was.

> **MATERIALS**
>
> ■ Map of the United States

During reading, briefly explain vocabulary, discussing the work of archaeologists, paleontologists, and museum curators. As you introduce each worker, give a brief description of the job each one does. The book has numerous illustrations of these professionals at work. Show students these workers in the pictures to help them better visualize the tasks they perform.

After reading, check comprehension by encouraging students to recall events and answer questions about Field Mouse's journey and Sue's age and what type of dinosaur Sue was.

COMPUTER ACTIVITIES

Creativity and Presentation Software Ideas

Using creativity and presentation software such as KidPix Studio Deluxe 3, ask students to create a story about finding dinosaur fossils in their backyard. This activity will help develop students' oral and written language as they practice using verbs and writing descriptions. In addition, students will enjoy creative expression.

> **MATERIALS**
>
> ■ Chart paper or a large tablet
> ■ KidPix Studio Deluxe 3 (2000) software
> ■ Markers

1. Remind students about the dinosaur that lived in their neighborhood activity from the previous section (see page 260). If necessary, students can return to that website (go to http://dsc.discovery.com/convergence/dinos/lookup.html) to look up the dinosaur that lived in their zip code. Once students have identified the dinosaur that inhabited their neighborhood in prehistoric times, encourage them to write about that discovery.

2. Ask emerging and developing readers to use the drawing tools in KidPix Studio Deluxe or other creativity and presentation software to recreate the dinosaur and draw its habitat to reinforce scientific facts they have learned. Students can use Stampinator in the software to stamp dinosaurs or dinosaur footprints across the screen. Students can easily animate these footprints by controlling the mouse. Students also can add sound.

3. Emerging readers can write verbs (e.g., *thud, boom, bam,* and *thunder*) on screen describing the sounds and motion of the footprints.

4. Encourage developing and fluent readers to write a paragraph or short story about finding the fossils of their dinosaur in their backyard. Ask these students to include science facts about their dinosaur (e.g., "My dinosaur is a carnivore or herbivore. My dinosaur could walk or fly.").

5. Encourage students to talk about how they created their stories and pictures during author's computer chair (see Appendix B). Be sure to ask students to listen for details introduced in the unit. You may also want to create a list of vocabulary words for students to use in future writings. Write these on a large tablet and display them on a bulletin board or chart paper for reference.

Digital Language Experience Approach

Write a photo essay that compares Sue's size to a field mouse (approximately two to five inches long, excluding the tail) and to the sizes of students. After the activity, assemble the pictures on a poster board and ask students to add comments or observations about what they see and have learned.

MATERIALS

- Digital camera
- Poster board
- PowerPoint (Microsoft Office 2003, 2003) software
- Tape measure
- Thick yellow yarn
- Two markers

1. Access Sue's vital statistics (go to www.fieldmuseum.org/sue/vital.html).

2. Use a long tape measure and lengths of thick yellow yarn to begin the comparison.

3. Go to the playground or the gym and place a marker to represent the tip of Sue's nose. Measure a straight line until the distance reaches the end of her tail. Place the second marker there.

4. Place yellow yarn between the two markers.

5. Prepare a tiny field mouse out of poster board (2.5 inches long) and place it approximately where Sue's foot would be. Talk to students about the things they notice about the size comparison. Which is bigger? Which is smaller?

6. Instruct students to determine their size in comparison to Sue's and the field mouse's size.

7. Encourage students to take turns lying down near the mouse so other students can compare the size of a student. Take photographs of how many students lying end to end it takes to reach Sue's size.

8. Import the photographs into creativity and presentation software such as PowerPoint.

9. Use PowerPoint to record students' voices reciting interesting facts they learned about Sue. View the slide show during author's computer chair (see Appendix B).

Computer Software Activity

Using The Magic School Bus Explores the Age of Dinosaurs software, students can take a virtual trip on the Magic School Bus to visit the three periods of the Mesozoic Era (Triassic, Jurassic, and Cretaceous) and the inhabitants and habitats of those periods. While there, students can also explore dinosaurs, continents, and time periods as they help the teacher, Ms. Frizzle, find missing creatures and solve puzzles, such as using the "dino-sizer" to match dinosaur sizes to everyday items, such as a five-story building to a brontosaurus. These puzzles will reinforce earlier lessons on size and scale comparisons. Emerging, developing, and young fluent readers will benefit from the support of a cross-age computer buddy to interact with this CD-ROM. During author's computer chair (see Appendix B), students can also demonstrate how they accessed information with the software.

> **MATERIALS**
>
> - The Magic School Bus Explores the Age of Dinosaurs (2003) software

Internet Resources and Ideas

Sue at the Field Museum: www.fieldmuseum.org/sue
Show students Sue's website. Students will learn what it is like to go to a museum and get an idea of the behind-the-scenes activities that take place there after hours. In addition, students will learn many facts to supplement the things they learned from the book. For example, they can step into the story by going on a virtual tour of Sue's arrival and preparations at the museum (see www.fieldmuseum.org/sue/image_frame3.html). The Digital Library Project of the Chicago Public Schools/University of Chicago Internet Project webpage gives students a good idea of what paleontologists do as students scroll through the images. During author's computer chair (see Appendix B), ask students to discuss the information they accessed.

> **MATERIALS**
>
> - Chocolate chip cookies
> - Toothpicks

Digging for Dinosaurs: Prospecting: www.lib.uchicago.edu/ecuip//diglib/science/dinodig/scrapbook/photos/paleo/jpsite/prospecting/index.html
Reinforce background knowledge about the jobs scientists perform. Remind students about the earlier discussions you had about paleontologists and archeologists. Students can view junior paleontologists digging for fossils. Enlarge slides 11, 12, and 13 for a better view of their finds; then look at the tools that paleontologists use.

Digging for Dinosaurs: Brushes: www.lib.uchicago.edu/ecuip//diglib/science/dinodig/scrapbook/tools/brushes.html
Students can learn how to clean and prepare dinosaur bones. Be sure to see both slides of the tools archeologists use to prepare fossils. Imitate cleaning rare fossils. Give students chocolate

chip cookies and a toothpick (and a small paintbrush if available). They can "dig" out the chocolate chip with the toothpick and brush away the crumbs with the paintbrush. Let them excavate the chocolate chips without damaging either the chip or the cookie. Of course, students can eat their "fossils." Students will gain insight into the real life experiences of scientists as they go through the steps of uncovering their "fossils."

Jeff Poling Images: www.dinosauria.com/gallery/jeff/jeff.html

What can people learn from old bones and fossils? View actual pictures of a fossil taken of Sue's skull in The Field Museum of Natural History in Chicago, Illinois, USA. Students will gain background knowledge about science explorations and may feel motivated to seek more information about the world and its history. Interactions with this website can also increase students' vocabulary.

Book 3: The Dinosaurs of Waterhouse Hawkins: An Illuminating History of Mr. Waterhouse Hawkins, Artist and Lecturer

Kerley, B. (2001). Ill. B. Selznick. New York: Scholastic. $16.95. 48 pp.

BOOK REVIEW

In the mid-19th century, no one knew what a dinosaur looked like. No one, that is, except Waterhouse Hawkins, a Victorian artist and sculptor who thought he could figure out what dinosaurs looked like by studying fossils. With the help of one scientist, Hawkins built the life-sized replicas he envisioned from fossils and similar animals. Determined to educate the world about these magnificent creatures, Hawkins introduced his creations to the scientific community at a formal dinner party held *inside* one of his dinosaur models. Reproductions of his dinosaurs were commissioned by Queen Victoria and Prince Albert and displayed in the Crystal Palace in Sydenham, England. Although more recent research has revised his conceptions of prehistoric life, many of his dinosaurs are still exhibited in England. The inside cover pages in this well-researched nonfiction work display a copy of the invitations he sent to British scientists in 1853. The author's notes, included after the story, chronicle the history of the book, information about the Crystal Palace in England, further information about Hawkins's experiences in the United States, the author's reasons for writing, and the illustrator's experiences researching Hawkins's work in England.

MATERIALS

- Blackboard or chart paper
- Boxes or sacks
- Chalk
- Flashlight
- Markers
- Tray

READ-ALOUD AND BOOK DISCUSSION IDEAS

Before meeting in whole-group time, take apart a flashlight and place the pieces in several different boxes or sacks. When you meet with students during whole-group time, open one of the bags and place the contents (e.g., the flashlight lens and one battery) on a tray. Ask students if they can figure out what the object is. What are the pieces? What color do they think the object might be and why? Draw the two pieces (e.g., the lens and the battery; see Figure 41) on chart paper or the blackboard. Then tell students you are going to use your imagination to try to draw a complete picture of what you think the object might look like. Start with the lens and draw a large square around it, saying, "I think that this plastic piece might be a window-like object that goes on a large square box so people can look inside." Then draw a little drawer as a battery storage compartment. Next, open another bag and show students the contents (e.g., a flashlight casing and another battery). Tell students that now that you have more pieces of the puzzle, you need to change the drawing (e.g., draw the flashlight). What would change? Why? Quickly do a revised sketch.

Tell students that although people know a lot about dinosaurs, they still do not *really* know the dinosaurs' colors. Remind students that there are some things that we know, for example, the size and shape of some dinosaurs because imaginative people in the past used clues from nature to begin reconstructing parts and wholes of dinosaurs. Remind students how scientists assembled Sue in the book *The Field Mouse and the Dinosaur Named Sue* (Wahl, 2000). Tell students that this book is about a man who tried to figure out over a hundred years ago what dinosaurs looked like. Say that the story is about how Waterhouse Hawkins did something amazing to help people get excited and learn about dinosaurs. Before reading, conduct a picture walk and ask students to predict what will happen in the first part of the story. What sort of person is Mr. Hawkins? Why did someone write a book about him?

Teachers may want to preread the text so that when they read to students they can paraphrase some sections that Barbara Kerley wrote in complex language. During reading, focus students' attention on the beautifully rendered illustrations, the sequence of events, and causes and effects in the book (such as how Mr. Hawkins helped others learn more about dinosaurs). Asking students to listen for a purpose will enhance their comprehension and help them provide evidence to support their opinions.

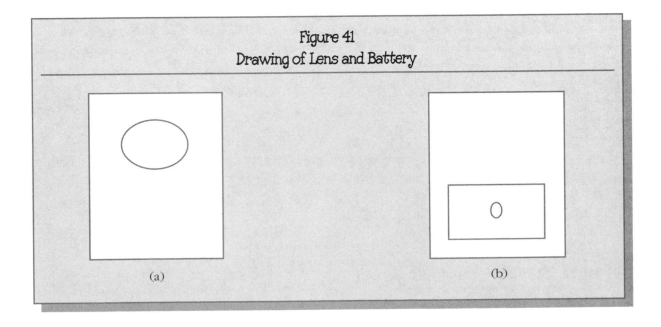

Figure 41
Drawing of Lens and Battery

(a)

(b)

After reading, ask students to talk about how Mr. Hawkins helped people learn more about dinosaurs. What impact do they think Mr. Hawkins's work had on other scientists and on the public? Why?

COMPUTER ACTIVITIES

Creativity and Presentation Software Ideas

MATERIALS

- Microsoft Paint (1981–2001) software

1. Instruct students to use creativity and presentation software, such as Microsoft Paint, to first design and then create a dinosaur and dinosaur name from their imaginations. Reinforce phonemic awareness by encouraging students to use inventive spelling (spelling phonically) for their dinosaur name.

2. Instruct students to copy the picture of the dinosaur onto another screen. They will open a new screen to do this.

3. Tell students to erase most of the dinosaur on the second screen, leaving only the head, tail, or legs showing.

4. Name the second dinosaur parts picture "Can you guess what [insert name of dinosaur] looks like?"

5. Assemble the two pages into a slide show.

6. Students place names and dates on their screen pages.

7. Import the pages into a class slide show titled "Use the Clues and Guess What Our Dinosaurs Look Like."

Remind students that Mr. Hawkins envisioned dinosaurs from just a few clues. Ask fluent readers to add to the slide show a written story about the dinosaur they would like to discover. Encourage them to answer these questions: Where does it live? What does it eat? Draw or import a picture of students' chosen dinosaurs into the slide show.

Digital Language Experience Approach

Students will engage in authentic expressions of experience by creating multimedia examples of their favorite book about dinosaurs.

MATERIALS

- Digital camera
- Dinosaur books from school library
- PowerPoint (Microsoft Office 2003, 2003) software

1. Tell students to choose their favorite dinosaur book. It can be a book from their personal collection or from the library.

2. Take a digital picture of each student holding his or her favorite dinosaur book.

3. Import this picture into the computer using creativity and presentation software such as PowerPoint.

4. Tell students they are going to create a representation of their favorite book. Their creation can be a poem, story, picture, or a combination of these.

5. Create a slide show of each student holding his or her book and a copy of the creation representing the book. Alternately, you can print these out and display on a bulletin board.

6. During author's computer chair (see Appendix B), ask students to explain their creation and tell why it represents their favorite book.

Computer Software Activity

> **MATERIALS**
>
> ■ Dinosaur Adventure 3-D (1995) software

Students can use the Dinosaur Adventure 3-D software to explore Paleo Island and collect information about dinosaurs and prehistoric times that will help them solve problems, build fossils, and rescue baby dinosaurs from the Triassic tar pits. But, to get to the tar pit, students will have to answer questions about dinosaurs. For example, which dinosaurs are meat eaters? Three levels are included, ranging from easy to more difficult. Students have to jump from object to object in the tar pit to save the baby dinosaur and go to another part of the island, which shows a different era. This interactive program allows students to apply what they have learned about dinosaurs. It is also easy to navigate and will reinforce science concepts about dinosaurs and their habitats.

Internet Resources and Ideas

Search 4Dinosaurs: Prehistoric Postcards: www.search4dinosaurs.com/postcard.html
This website has beautiful pictures and an extensive list of prehistoric creatures and habitats. Emerging and developing readers will enjoy exploring the scenes and images. Students also can send a postcard to a friend or classmate.

The Dinosaurs of Waterhouse Hawkins: Creating Giants: www.suzyred.com/4waterhouse sample110.pdf
This questionnaire asks students to determine the main ideas and supporting details in *The Dinosaurs of Waterhouse Hawkins: An Illuminating History of Mr. Waterhouse Hawkins, Artist and Lecturer* (Kerley, 2001). Fluent readers might be able to work independently. Beginning and emerging readers will need support from a cross-age computer buddy or parent volunteer reading the questions. Students may need to refer to the story to support their answers with evidence from the text.

Enchanted Learning: Zoom Dinosaurs: Dinosaur Fun: www.enchantedlearning.com/painting/ dinosaurs.shtml
Click on "Dinosaur Online Coloring Book" located on the color band beneath the title. Scroll through the alphabetical listing of the dinosaurs to choose one to color online from the provided palette. Each picture has a few more interesting facts about that dinosaur's habitat, size, and habits. Ask students to write or explain why they think dinosaurs were particular colors. What have they learned about dinosaurs' environments that make them believe this? For example, the shape of the dinosaur's mouth and head indicates whether he was an herbivore or carnivore. Students can classify dinosaurs based on the habitat of the dinosaur or the creature's diet.

Enchanted Learning: Zoom Dinosaurs: www.enchantedlearning.com/subjects/dinosaurs/index. html

To name your dinosaur, click on the hyperlink "How Dinosaurs Are Named" under the "All About Dinosaurs" hyperlink. Then click on the Greek and Latin root names used for dinosaurs to name your creations. Learning roots of words will help students decode new words.

Unit Conclusion

Conduct your own Dinosaurumpus (i.e., dancing and singing with the dinosaurs). Prepare a chart with the verse "Shake, shake, shudder...Get ready to romp!"

Remind students which words in the poem rhyme. As you reread aloud the book *Dinosaurumpus!* (Mitton, 2003), point to the chart for choral reading. Add the following verse:

MATERIALS

- Chart paper
- Markers

> We better watch out
> Here comes [name of another dinosaur
>   learned from the reading],
> And he weighs a ton!
> So do not shout
> Just run, run, run!

Ask students which words rhyme in the new verse you have created. As you read the first and second verses, insert one of the dinosaur names (i.e., the names of the dinosaurs students learned from the unit) written on the board by pointing to it while students read and complete the verse.

For a nice twist on this activity, add the syllable *-osaur* to the end of students' names. For example, *Jason* would become *Jason-osaur*. Chorally read the aforementioned verses you made up as a class, and when you come to the student's dinosaur name, he or she states either a favorite dinosaur or something learned during the unit.

Students can also discuss what and how they learned from the Dinosaur Adventure 3-D software. Some students will enjoy sharing what they learned from the Internet by conducting an Internet website walk, an activity that allows them to navigate through hyperlinks and talk about what they learned at each one. Fluent readers or those with cross-age computer buddies may also talk about the decisions they made during navigation. Most students will enjoy relating what they learned about dinosaurs and their habitats to the real-life experiences they had in the classroom as they applied this knowledge in active learning endeavors.

"I've started incorporating the weather website into my daily calendar routine. My students are learning to get information from the Internet, and we update the weather forecast every day. It's a great addition to my routines."

—KINDERGARTEN TEACHER

What Season Is It?

UNIT BOOKS

Seasons
By Patricia Ryon Quiri

It Feels Like Snow
By Nancy Cote

Night Rabbits
By Lee Posey
Illustrated by Michael G. Montgomery

COMPUTER RESOURCES

A Tree Through the Seasons
Mercer Mayer's Just Grandma and Me

Thematic Connection

Every time students go outside, they directly experience the effects of the seasons; however, few primary-grade students understand the forces at work that make the changes happen. Seasons change, and the beauty of nature changes along with the seasons. The types of clothes children wear change. And, along with changes in clothing, children's seasonal activities also change. The purpose of this unit is to celebrate the unique types of weather and experiences that occur during different seasons. Books in this unit help students explore more deeply the everyday observations and experiences they have in regard to the seasons. Informational texts on the pages of a book and on a computer screen provide students with facts about the seasons. The fictional stories help students understand how authors and illustrators help readers experience seasons. The first book, *Seasons* (Quiri, 2000), is an informational text that focuses on questions primary-grade students ask about why the seasons change and how those weather changes affect people's lives. The second book, *It Feels Like Snow* (Cote, 2003), a fictional account about a woman who can predict snow storms, helps students learn about how to prepare for winter and the value of friendships in difficult times. The third book, *Night Rabbits* (Posey, 1999), is a fictional narrative that examines a father and daughter's unique summer experiences when a group of rabbits visits the yard of their family cabin.

Matrix of Literacy Skills and Strategies in Unit 18

Literacy Skills and Strategies	Activities	Title of Book	Pages
Brainstorming	U, D, S	*Seasons*	272, 274–275, 275
	R	*It Feels Like Snow*	277
Building background knowledge on the Internet*	U, I	*Seasons*	272, 275–276
	R, UC	*It Feels Like Snow*	277, 283
	I	*Night Rabbits*	282–283
Building fluency	U	*Seasons*	272
	C, I	*Night Rabbits*	281, 282–283
Comparing and contrasting	C, S	*Seasons*	273–274, 275
Composing in multimedia*	D, S	*Seasons*	274–275, 275
	D, I	*It Feels Like Snow*	278–279, 279–280
	C, D	*Night Rabbits*	281, 282
Creating and using charts	D, S	*Seasons*	274–275, 275
	R, C, S	*It Feels Like Snow*	277, 277–278, 279
	U, R, D, UC	*Night Rabbits*	272, 281, 282, 283
Creating concept maps and graphic organizers	S	*Seasons*	275
	C	*Night Rabbits*	281
Determining story details	I	*It Feels Like Snow*	279–280
Developing choral reading	S	*Seasons*	275
	C	*It Feels Like Snow*	277–278
	U, I	*Night Rabbits*	272, 282–283
Developing comprehension	R, S	*Seasons*	273, 275
	R, D, S, I	*It Feels Like Snow*	277, 278–279, 279, 279–280
	R, S, UC	*Night Rabbits*	281, 282, 283
Developing context clues	R	*It Feels Like Snow*	277
Developing creative writing	C	*It Feels Like Snow*	277–278
	I	*Night Rabbits*	282–283
Developing oral language	R, D	*Seasons*	273, 274–275
	R, D	*It Feels Like Snow*	277, 278–279
	R, C, D, S, UC	*Night Rabbits*	281, 281, 282, 282, 283
Developing vocabulary	U, R, D, S, I	*Seasons*	272, 273, 274–275, 275, 275–276
	R, I	*It Feels Like Snow*	277, 279–280
	R, C, D, I, UC	*Night Rabbits*	281, 281, 282, 282–283, 283
Drawing conclusions	C, S	*Seasons*	273–274, 275
	R	*Night Rabbits*	281
Following directions	D, S, I	*Seasons*	274–275, 275, 275–276
	I	*It Feels Like Snow*	279–280
Making predictions	R	*Night Rabbits*	281

(continued)

Literacy Skills and Strategies	Activities	Title of Book	Pages
Navigating hyperlinks*	S, I	*Seasons*	275, 275–276
	R, I	*It Feels Like Snow*	277, 279–280
	I, UC	*Night Rabbits*	282–283, 283
Presenting work on a computer*	D	*Seasons*	274–275
	D	*It Feels Like Snow*	278–279
	C	*Night Rabbits*	281
Reading aloud	U, R, S, I	*Seasons*	272, 273, 275, 275–276
	R	*It Feels Like Snow*	277
	R, S	*Night Rabbits*	281, 282
Reading and listening for a purpose	U, R, S, I	*Seasons*	272, 273, 275, 275–276
	R	*It Feels Like Snow*	277
	R	*Night Rabbits*	281
Reading informational text	R, S, I	*Seasons*	273, 275, 275–276
	I	*Night Rabbits*	282–283
Retelling	S	*Seasons*	275
	R, D, S, I	*It Feels Like Snow*	277, 278–279, 279, 279–280
	C, D, UC	*Night Rabbits*	281, 282, 283
Sequencing	R, D	*Seasons*	273, 274–275
	D	*It Feels Like Snow*	278–279
	D	*Night Rabbits*	282
Understanding a main idea	C, UC	*It Feels Like Snow*	277–278, 283
	S	*Night Rabbits*	282
Understanding concepts about print	U, S	*Seasons*	272, 275
Understanding story structure and events	R	*It Feels Like Snow*	277
Using adjectives	D	*Seasons*	274–275
	I	*It Feels Like Snow*	279–280
	R, C	*Night Rabbits*	281
Using phonics: Rhyming words	U, I	*Night Rabbits*	272, 282–283
Visualizing	I	*Seasons*	275–276
Writing descriptive sentences	D	*Seasons*	274–275
	C, D, I	*It Feels Like Snow*	277–278, 278–279, 279–280
	C, UC	*Night Rabbits*	281, 283
Writing letters	I	*It Feels Like Snow*	279–280

* Indicates a new-literacy skill.
U = unit introduction; R = read-aloud and book discussion ideas; C = creativity and presentation software ideas; D = Digital Language Experience Approach; S = computer software activity; I = Internet resources and ideas; UC = unit conclusion

Unit Introduction

Before meeting as a group, go to the website CanTeach (go to www.canteach.ca/elementary/songs poems64.html) to locate poems and songs about the seasons. Copy a poem on chart paper and point to the words as you read the poem aloud to students. Becoming familiar with poetry through repetition, choral readings, echo readings, and finger pointing (pointing to each word as it is read) helps students create memory links for recalling the four seasons and gaining literacy skills such as concepts about print. This reinforces the concept of a word to students as they read along with the teacher. Students begin to make the connection between what they are saying and the word as it is read. Repeated readings will foster students' fluency.

Next, display a 12-month calendar that has photographs of different seasonal times of the year and ask students to read the names of the months with you as you turn the pages. Ask students why the pictures for different months show people wearing different types of clothing or why the trees look different throughout the year. Guide students to the notion of the changing seasons. For example, for the month of August, the calendar might show a person swimming or playing in the sand. Talk with students about what the person is wearing. Talk about why it is appropriate to wear a swimming suit in August. Ask what the trees look like in August and what color the leaves on the trees are. Then turn to the month of October. The calendar might show a person raking leaves. Ask students what kinds of clothing this person is wearing, such as a sweater or jacket. Ask why someone wears this type of clothing in October. Why is this person raking the leaves? What color are the leaves? Why are there so many leaves on the ground? What do the trees look like in October? Through discussing the calendar pictures representative of each season, help students draw the conclusion that the weather changes in a cycle as the seasons change.

Create a K-W-L chart (Ogle, 1986) about the seasons (see Figure 9 on page 48 for an example of a K-W-L chart): What do students already know about the seasons? What do they want to know? What have they learned? Tell them that at the end of the unit, you will fill out the chart with things they have learned about the seasons from books and computer resources. Tell students that one of the books, *Seasons* (Quiri, 2000), will help them learn facts about the seasons. The other two books, *It Feels Like Snow* (Cote, 2003) and *Night Rabbits* (Posey, 1999), are fictional stories that will help them explore their feelings about things that happen during winter and summer.

MATERIALS

- Chart paper
- K-W-L chart
- Markers
- Photograph calendar of the seasons
- Poem or song

Book 1: Seasons

Quiri, P.R. (2000). Minneapolis, MN: Compass Point Books. $21.26. 32 pp.

BOOK REVIEW

This expository text offers an excellent introduction to the concept of the seasons. Colorful photographs and carefully drawn illustrations provide graphic details for information included in eight short chapters. Chapters 1 through 3 give information about the Earth and explain how the position of the Earth affects the different seasons throughout the year. As you read through this book before reading it aloud to students, note that some concepts may be difficult for some emerging or developing readers to grasp, so think about places in the text where you might need to paraphrase or point out graphic details. Chapters 4 through 8 include information about how changing weather affects living things. Questions are posed at various points in the book to give students opportunities to think about and discuss what they know and what they have learned about the seasons. The final pages include a glossary, index, and list of additional resources that teachers will find helpful.

READ-ALOUD AND BOOK DISCUSSION IDEAS

Before reading, refer to the K-W-L chart (Ogle, 1986) from the beginning of the unit. Highlight the questions that students wanted to find answers to about the seasons. Tell students that you are going to read an informational book. Tell them to listen carefully to see if they can find the answers to their questions. Do a picture and text walk of the book. To conduct a text walk, go through the book and point out examples of words or phrases that students will hear in the text before the book is read aloud. Explain briefly the different parts of the book to help students gain knowledge that will help them distinguish between nonfiction and fiction text structures and purposes.

MATERIALS

■ K-W-L chart

During reading, use the chapter titles to demonstrate which chapters are likely to answer specific questions, such as "During what season do people wear mittens?" This question could be answered after listening to the chapter that depicts how people's clothing needs to change seasonally. In addition, point out new vocabulary words that are of interest to students and helpful in filling out the *L* part of the K-W-L chart.

After reading, fill in the K-W-L chart and discuss what students learned. Summarize the sequence of the seasons. Recap features of informational text (e.g., index, glossary) and how those features help readers target specific information.

COMPUTER ACTIVITIES

Creativity and Presentation Software Ideas

This idea was adapted from the KidPix Activity Kit: Volume 1 (1998) software Favorite Season Graph activity. The adaptation involves using creativity and presentation software such as KidPix Studio Deluxe to complete the activity. First, instruct students to find out which season is the most popular among their classmates, using the Favorite Season Graph activity. The objective of this activity is to demonstrate one-to-one correspondence, counting, and displaying seasonal preferences on a pictorial bar graph. Tell students that they will be creating several graphs about the seasons in this activity. Explain to students that in order to complete the graphs, they must follow several steps.

MATERIALS

■ Four labeled containers (one for each season)
■ KidPix Studio Deluxe (1998) software
■ Slips of paper

1. Demonstrate how to make a pictograph with KidPix Studio Deluxe during whole-group time. For example, list three types of ice cream at the top of the computer screen:

chocolate, vanilla, and strawberry. Tell students to think about their favorite flavor. Ask each student to use the X stamp provided in the software to stamp an X under the corresponding column. Add your own X at the end of the activity and explain to students that you have created a bar graph. Help them notice the column that seems to have the most Xs. Count the number of Xs in each column and announce the class favorite.

2. Explain that there are other ways to create a graph. For the second graph, instruct students to sign a slip of paper and place it in one of four containers labeled with the name of the season they like the most. Place the containers in the computer center so students can count the slips for each season and use that information to make a pictograph of their favorite season. Have pairs of students complete a pictograph that represents the class seasonal preferences by counting the slips in the season containers. Be sure that students place their names and the date at the top of the screen.

3. After finishing the activity, print out the graphs.

4. During whole-group time, display one of the graphs and guide the class to read the graph to compare and contrast the seasonal information shown in the graph to answer questions such as "Which season is the most popular in our class?" "Which season is the least popular in our class?" "How many more students in the class like spring more than fall?" "How many more students like winter more than summer?"

Digital Language Experience Approach

After reading about the seasons, allow students to show their artistic creativity by painting a seasonal mural. Use the following steps to complete the activity.

1. Divide the class into four groups.

2. Measure off four 4-foot-long pieces of paper from a roll of butcher paper, and give each group one of the pieces. Tell each group of students they will create a mural for one of the seasons. Group 1 will create a summer mural, group 2 will create a fall mural, group 3 will create a winter mural, and group 4 will create a spring mural. Before students begin painting, review the information about the seasons from the K-W-L chart (Ogle, 1986) that was filled out during the unit. Brainstorm with each small group the details they will include in their pictures. In addition, display the pictures of the seasons from the photograph calendar.

MATERIALS

- Butcher paper
- Crayons or markers
- Digital camera
- KidPix Studio Deluxe (1998) software
- K-W-L chart
- Photograph calendar

3. Take photographs of students as they create their murals.

4. Display the murals in the classroom or on a hallway wall.

5. Take a photograph of each group of students with their completed mural.

6. Using creativity and presentation software such as KidPix Studio Deluxe, ask small groups of students to keyboard or dictate sentences about the items they included on each mural. Through this activity, students develop their oral language and vocabulary and practice writing descriptive sentences about what they included in their seasonal mural.

7. Print photographs of the process. Ask students to place the photographs in chronological order. Ask them to talk about the sequence of events.

8. Print and bind the photographs into a class book titled "Our Seasons Murals," or collect the photographs into a digital slide show for the whole class to enjoy and discuss.

The presentations created with KidPix Studio Deluxe can be used for an author's computer chair activity (see Appendix B). Have the small groups of students present their slide shows to the rest of the class. As they do this, ask the other students to read their sentences. Allow students to explain how they decided what to include in the seasonal murals. Encourage students to elaborate on what their group did to create their slide show and their mural. Through making a presentation about their slide shows, students are practicing oral language skills and learning to speak clearly about how they went about accomplishing a task. They also are practicing their sequencing skills by talking about the order in which they did things as they worked on the mural.

Computer Software Activity

A Tree Through the Seasons CD-ROM contains an electronic storybook about an apple tree. The story follows the life of an apple tree throughout the year as the seasons change. Colorful photographs and drawings accompany the text of the story. As the story is read aloud by the computer, the text is highlighted in phrases. Emerging readers will

---

MATERIALS

■ A Tree Through the Seasons (1993) CD-ROM

---

have opportunities to learn concepts about print if they practice tracking the text in left-to-right directionality as they echo read or chorally read. The story is read at a pace that can be followed easily by emerging and developing readers. After students have viewed the CD-ROM, invite them to explain what happens to an apple tree through the seasons. Ask them to add any relevant information to the K-W-L chart (Ogle, 1986) you began at the onset of the unit. Also ask, "What did you learn about the apple tree during each season? How does the tree change as the seasons change?" Encourage students to retell what they learned about the life of the apple tree during each season of the year.

Internet Resources and Ideas

BrainPop: Seasons: www.brainpop.com/science/weatherandclimate/seasons (website requires subscription after 14-day free trial)
This website includes a short, animated video about the seasons. Emerging and beginning readers may need a cross-age computer buddy for support. After watching the movie, students can take a short multiple-choice quiz about the seasons and get immediate feedback for each answer given. Students or the teacher can print out an activity page found by clicking on the Activity Page link, which students complete after viewing the movie to reinforce the information that they learned about the seasons. Clicking on the "Experiment With Bob, the Ex-Lab Rat" hyperlink takes students to an interactive experiment that demonstrates how the tilt of the Earth affects the changing of the seasons. After visiting this link and engaging with the interactive experiment, students can use what they learned to explain why the seasons change. The literacy skills related to this activity include building background knowledge on the Internet, developing vocabulary

related to the seasons, comprehension of the information learned through the interactive experiment, and navigating hyperlinks.

NASA Kids: http://kids.msfc.nasa.gov
Clicking on the film icon on the opening page of the site takes students to the NASA toons page, where there are several short animations. Students can view a short animation—a visual and audio explanation of what causes the Earth's seasons and how they are affected by the position of the Earth during its orbit of the sun. Clicking on the closed-captioning button displays the text for the animation narration on the screen. This activity involves facts about the first day of spring. Students must use their comprehension skills as they read the text or as the text is read to them to learn about the changing seasons. This site is useful for building background knowledge on the Internet about the seasons and practicing navigating hyperlinks as students move between webpages.

Rainbow Magic: www.rainbow-magic.com/holidays
Selecting the hyperlinks for each of the seasons on the homepage of this website takes students to webpages with interactive activities; libraries of stories and poems; audio files of music and songs related to the seasons; interactive jigsaw puzzles, "create a pic" puzzles, and slide puzzles in which students can move the pieces of the puzzles on the computer screen; and links to other websites to extend and expand students' learning about each season. Primary-grade students can work on some of the online activities individually, but many tasks require working with a peer or a cross-age computer buddy. Links to webpages containing holiday activities are available only during specific times of the year, so students can work on holiday activities that are associated with the current season.

Author's computer chair (see Appendix B) can be easily incorporated with the use of this activity. Allow students to explore the various activities on their own, with a peer, or with a cross-age computer buddy. After they have had several opportunities to visit the site, have students talk about what they did when they visited it. What was their favorite activity? What did they learn about the seasons or seasonal holidays from participating at this site? Do they think other students would enjoy visiting this site and doing some of the things they did?

Book 2:   It Feels Like Snow

Cote, N. (2003). Honesdale, PA: Boyds Mills Press. $15.95. 32 pp.

BOOK REVIEW

Alice has unique ways of forecasting when it will snow. She can just feel it in various parts of her body. For example, as Alice sweeps leaves, her big toe begins to throb. Alice tries to warn her friends and neighbors about the upcoming snow, but no one listens because they think she is just a silly old woman. The falling snow catches her friends and neighbors unprepared. Additional incidents leave Alice's friends unprepared for the weather changes. Finally, Alice warns her friends of a blizzard because she felt her elbows click, but they ignore her. The next morning when a blizzard leaves waist-deep snow, Alice invites all of her unprepared friends over to share her supplies. Each guest brings a gift and apologizes. Alice is never thought of again as a silly old woman. This delightful story is told in easy-to-understand language. The vibrant illustrations include details that complement and extend the story. For example, the farm animals take Alice's warnings to heart by watching for weather changes and even joining her inside her house during the blizzard. After reading this story, ask students if they or someone in their family has ever been able to predict that something was going to happen before it happened. Talk about how sometimes people get feelings about something before it occurs. Another topic to discuss is how everyone has unique gifts and talents and people should embrace people's differences and uniqueness, not ridicule other people. Also talk about why it is important to listen to what others have to say so they are not caught unprepared.

READ-ALOUD AND BOOK DISCUSSION IDEAS

Before reading, ask students to think about what they know about weather forecasts. Go to the USA Today Weather website (go to http://asp.usatoday.com/weather/weatherfront.aspx), and use hyperlinks to get a local weather forecast as well as maps that display radar, temperature, precipitation, and so forth. Tell students that predicting the weather is a science and that weather predictions are especially important in the winter and explain why. Ask students to talk about the type of weather conditions that people might need to be aware of in the winter. Tell students that they will be listening to a story about a woman who had an unusual way to predict winter weather. Be sure students understand that this book is different than the previous book in the unit. This book is a fictional or make-believe story.

MATERIALS

■ Vocabulary chart

During reading, discuss how the author's style helps readers understand more about people's feelings about the winter season. Highlight key vocabulary, such as *blizzard*, and help students identify the problem in the story. Scaffold students' learning by asking questions. What happened to Alice's friends when it snowed? Why did Alice's friends come to her house? What did Alice do for her friends after the blizzard? Point out to students that the illustrations provide additional information, or context clues, that help them understand the story.

After reading, ask students what lesson Alice's friends learned by the end of the story. Why did Alice want them to believe her predictions about the weather? How did her friends help one another during the winter? In addition, after reading the story, build vocabulary by asking students to recall words for a Winter Words vocabulary chart. If necessary, do an after-reading picture walk and ask students to name the things that are associated with winter (e.g., coats, snow shovels, snowflakes, snow, blizzard, heaters, scarves). Post the chart so students may refer to it when writing about the winter season.

MATERIALS

■ KidPix Studio Deluxe (1998) software
■ K-W-L chart
■ Photograph calendar
■ Poster
■ Wall murals from this unit

COMPUTER ACTIVITIES

Creativity and Presentation Software Ideas

Ask small groups of three to four students to work with a cross-age computer buddy or parent volunteer in creativity and presentation software such as KidPix Studio Deluxe to write a new story called "It

Feels Like Spring" about Alice's ability to predict the weather during a different season—spring. Discuss the type of weather that occurs in spring. Refer to the K-W-L chart (Ogle, 1986) created during this unit's introduction (see page 272 for the unit introduction and Figure 9 on page 48 for an example of a K-W-L chart). Refer students to the wall murals and photograph calendar used earlier in the unit to remind them about the season of spring. Place a poster in the computer center that reminds cross-age buddies or parent volunteers and students about the details of the task.

1. Describe and illustrate in KidPix Studio Deluxe three things about spring that Alice can predict (e.g., a wind storm in March, a rain storm in April, a sunny day in May).

2. Include what might happen to Alice's friends if they do not follow her warnings (e.g., the wind blows clothes off the clothes line, the rain ruins a new hairdo, a friend gets too hot when she insists on wearing a winter coat on the sunny day).

3. Answer how Alice can help her friends on the hot, sunny day (e.g., having a garage sale of springtime clothes, or setting up a lemonade stand).

4. Print and bind copies of the small-group "It Feels Like Spring" stories to place in the class library or import them into a slide show.

To involve author's computer chair (see Appendix B) with this activity, have each group of students do a choral reading of their "It Feels Like Spring" stories on the computer screen to the rest of the class. After they read their story, ask them to talk about how they created it. Have them explain why they selected the three things that Alice could predict for their story and how they knew those things happen in spring.

Digital Language Experience Approach

Before starting this activity, the teacher or a parent volunteer needs to record the story "It Feels Like Snow" on a tape. Explain to students that people often read the same story more than once because they enjoy it. Tell students that in this activity they are going to use the story "It Feels Like Snow" again, but this time they will do something different.

1. Invite students to act out the story as they listen to it.

2. Take photographs of students as they act out the story.

3. Download the pictures and insert them into slide show using creativity and presentation software such as KidPix Studio Deluxe.

4. Show the slides to the class and have students retell the part of the story they were acting out in each picture.

MATERIALS

- Digital camera
- KidPix Studio Deluxe (1998) software
- Tape recorder

---

5. Invite students who appear in each picture to write a sentence about themselves and what they are doing in the photograph on each slide. This step reinforces the reading–writing connection. Writing about their involvement in acting out the story gives students practice writing descriptive sentences about the picture they appear in.

6. For author's computer chair (see Appendix B), show the slide show and ask each student appearing in the picture to read the sentence on their slide. When the slide show is over, ask

students to talk about what they like to do during the winter. Help students make connections between what the people in the story did and what students do during snowy weather. Also talk about what they learned about being prepared for emergencies such as when there is a blizzard.

Computer Software Activity

MATERIALS

■ A Tree Through the Seasons (1993) CD-ROM

A Tree Through the Seasons CD-ROM storybook follows the life of the apple tree throughout the year as the seasons change. In this activity, students focus on the tree during only one season. The activity expands students' scientific knowledge about trees and how they survive during the winter. Often students think that trees are not alive or die during the winter, so this activity allows them to understand that the cycle of life a tree continues during the year.

1. Ask students to reread or re-view the CD-ROM and focus more closely on what happens to the tree during winter.

2. Invite students to tell what they learned about the tree in winter. Does the tree die? Why does it not have leaves?

3. Invite students to add any additional information to the K-W-L chart (Ogle, 1986) you began at the onset of the unit.

4. To incorporate author's computer chair (see Appendix B) with this activity, remind students about the electronic storybook about the apple tree. Ask them to think about what they learned about the apple tree during each season. What did the tree look like in the spring, summer, autumn? Then ask them retell what they learned about the apple tree during the winter months.

Internet Resources and Ideas

Snow Days: www.popularfront.com/seasonsgreetings
Visitors to this interactive website are able to create a unique snowflake online. The teacher should explain that each snowflake is different. After watching the teacher demonstrate how to create a snowflake on the screen, students can make and submit their snowflakes online. For inspiration, encourage students to view snowflakes that have been made by other visitors to the website and read their attached messages. This is a simple yet engaging activity to encourage creativity and visual self-expression in students. During this activity, students will have to follow directions for creating their unique snowflakes. After their snowflakes are finished, students have the opportunity to write a message. This message can be attached to the snowflakes they made. They are able to submit their snowflakes for others to view online. As a class, view several of the snowflakes on the website that have been made by others. They can practice sending and receiving e-mail when they select snowflakes they like and respond to other snowflake creators about their work or read messages from others who respond to their snowflake creations.

Billy Bear's Playground: www.billybear4kids.com/holidays/winter/fun.htm
This child-friendly website includes a wide range of winter activities. Some activities are completed online, while others can be printed out. One activity that uses online tools allows students to create

personalized stationery. Once they have made stationery, they can print it out with an envelope that they can assemble. Students may enjoy writing a letter to their family members about what they have learned about the winter season during this unit. There are other activities available for students to print out and use such as mazes, dressing a snowman, and interactive jigsaw puzzles.

To incorporate author's computer chair (see Appendix B) with this website, instruct students to talk about the activities they chose to do from the website. Have them describe what the activity was that they chose as their favorite and retell what they did during that activity. Encourage them to use descriptive words when talking about the activity. If they worked on a printable activity, have them share their work with the class and talk about what they did to complete the activity.

Skills students can work on with the activities from this website include creative writing, writing letters, navigating hyperlinks, following directions, and using oral language.

There are also resources for the teacher available on this website. One resource is a bingo card. The cards have different holiday or themed pictures for the center free spot and different five-letter words across the top. For example, the Flake-Snowman card has a snowman in the free square and the word "flake" across the top of the card. Teachers can make a word bingo game by printing out the decorated bingo cards and writing words students have learned or need to practice in the squares. There are several different themes to choose from. Making personalized certificates is another teacher resource. Teachers can choose from a rather extensive list of certificates such as the Outstanding Reader Award or Reading Achievement Award. They can fill in students' names online and print out the certificates. Teachers instead can choose blank Achievement Award certificates, fill in the student's name and what the certificate is for, and then print them out. Teachers also can print out ribbon awards and fill in the student's name and what the special ribbon award is for.

Book 3:   Night Rabbits

Posey, L. (1999). Ill. M.G. Montgomery. Atlanta, GA: Peachtree. $15.95. 32 pp.

BOOK REVIEW

Elizabeth's father worked very hard to make the lawn look great all year, but now uninvited rabbits are eating the grass during the night. Elizabeth loves to watch the rabbits as they leap and play on the lawn, but her father is upset. After thinking hard, she comes up with an idea for what to do about the rabbits. Her father appreciates Elizabeth's efforts, but he worries that the rabbits may still eat the grass. In the end, Elizabeth's efforts pay off when her father decides to share the lawn with the rabbit friends. Lee Posey's story, written from Elizabeth's point of view, uses simple, descriptive language that helps bring the story to life. This story is set during the summer and uses Michael Montgomery's beautiful, soft-edged watercolor illustrations to add to the feeling of gentleness and serenity. The underlying theme in this book, how people and animals can share the same environment peacefully, should encourage young readers to appreciate nature and work to protect it.

READ-ALOUD AND BOOK DISCUSSION IDEAS

Before reading, take students on a picture walk and invite them to tell you what time of year it is. What clues help them make a logical prediction? Tell students you want them to learn how one little girl, Elizabeth, helped her father solve a big problem.

During reading, note details provided in the illustrations, such as beautiful flowers in the garden, that let the reader know the story takes place during the summer.

MATERIALS

■ Vocabulary chart

After reading, ask if Elizabeth and her father could have done other things to solve their problem. Discuss how the story would have been different if it had been set during the winter. Finally, to encourage vocabulary development, invite students to list summer words they remember from the story on a vocabulary chart.

COMPUTER ACTIVITIES

Creativity and Presentation Software Ideas

Ask students to think about an experience during their last summer vacation. Using creativity and presentation software, such as Kidspiration 2.1, ask each student to create a concept web about what he or she did.

MATERIALS

■ Kidspiration 2.1 (2005) software

1. Tell students to type their names in the center of the screen.

2. Ask students to tell you about what they did during vacation. Type in the different activities that students were involved in and link them to the center circle. Encourage students to elaborate on what they did, and keep adding information links as they get more descriptive about their activities.

3. See how many layers of details students can develop. Gather different types of information under specific links (e.g., food, sightseeing, family members, mode of travel). The literacy skills students use in this step include using adjectives to describe activities, creating concept webs and graphic organizers, presenting work on the computer, and practicing using oral language to talk about what they did.

4. Title the concept web "[Student Name's] Vacation Fun." Print out each student's inspiration concept web to share during whole-group time.

5. For an author's computer chair activity (see Appendix B), display each student's concept web on the computer. Ask the student to point to one activity on the web, trace the link with his or her finger to the description of the activity, and read the description on the screen. Encourage the student to then elaborate about the activity beyond what is on the screen.

This activity helps students learn how to construct a concept web. It shows them how to start with a general concept and get more detailed and descriptive with each successive level they add to the web. Students also practice oral language and using descriptive words as they talk about their activities.

Digital Language Experience Approach

Instruct students to act out *Night Rabbits* (Posey, 1999).

MATERIALS

■ Digital camera

1. Assign one student to be Elizabeth, one student to be Father, and four students to be the rabbits.

2. As students act out the story, take photographs.

3. Upload the pictures and print them out.

4. Instruct students put the pictures in the correct order on the board.

5. Ask students to retell the story using the pictures for help as needed.

6. Record their retelling on chart paper.

7. Insert the pictures at the appropriate places in the story.

This activity can be used for work on sequencing and retelling. Students get practice in sequencing when they put the photographs in the order the events happened. They also practice retelling the events in the story by connecting those events with the pictures.

Computer Software Activity

MATERIALS

■ Mercer Mayer's Just Grandma and Me (1993) software

Ask students to read along with the story in this software about a grandmother and grandson's day at the beach. Tell students to be ready to explain all the summertime activities they view in the story. How did the grandmother and grandson get to the beach? What did they see? What did they do? How would the story have been different in the winter? Skills used in this activity include comprehending the story, reading and listening for a purpose, and using oral language to answer the questions.

For author's computer chair (see Appendix B), invite students to talk about the things they learned about the summer from the story about virtually going to the beach with a grandparent.

Internet Resources and Ideas

CanTeach—Elementary Resources: Songs & Poems: www.canteach.ca/elementary/songs poems.html

CanTeach is a website with resources that many elementary teachers will find useful. The website has two main areas: Elementary Resources and Thousands of Links. The Elementary Resources section includes lesson plans and songs and poems for areas such as English language arts, social studies, science, and math. For example, within the English language arts area are lessons plans for beginning reading and writing, creative writing, listening and speaking, and novel and picture book activities. This area also contains themed book lists. The Thousands of Links section contains links for the areas such as English language arts, fine arts, English as a second language, and technical education. Within the English language arts area are links for reading and writing resources; authors and illustrators and their creations; and online books, stories, and other writings. The Songs & Poems webpage includes a collection of poems in categories such as the seasons, animals, special days, vegetation, food, family and friends, language arts, math, at home, and poetry collections. Emerging and developing readers can read the seasonal poems chorally from the computer screen, and fluent readers can read from a printed-out version. Skills involved with this website include building background knowledge on the Internet, choral reading, and building fluency.

Seasons of the Year: www.viterbo.edu/academic/ug/education/edu250/korth/web%20Quest%20 Project%202.html

The main webpage, Seasons of the Year, contains the names of the four seasons. Each season name links to a webpage that tells the months of the year that are in each season, holidays that are celebrated during the season, vocabulary words for objects related to the season, and several informational sentences about the season. A Teacher Materials link leads to an activity that teachers can have their students complete. The activity page includes a link to a rubric for evaluating students' performance.

This website can be used to encourage students to develop their vocabulary and use those seasonal words as they engage in creative writing. Have students choose one season and write a creative story using the vocabulary words found on their chosen season's page. They can also practice navigating hyperlinks to move from webpage to webpage to learn about the seasons. The skills that can be worked on by visiting this website include developing vocabulary, creative writing, navigating hyperlinks, and building background knowledge on the Internet.

Revisit the seasonal pages and read aloud the information on each page with students. After reading a page, invite students who chose to write about that season to share their creative writing for an author's computer chair activity (see Appendix B).

Unit Conclusion

Review with students the information used to fill out the K-W-L chart (Ogle, 1986) at the beginning of the unit. Revisit favorite websites such as CanTeach (go to www.canteach.ca/elementary/songspoems64.html) to enjoy poems and NASA Kids (go to http://kids.msfc.nasa.gov) to view animations about the seasons. Instruct students to write a group report about the things they have learned about the current season. Take a walk outside, weather permitting, to foster students' ability to make observations to include in the group story. For example, ask, "What other activities are there to enjoy during the season?" Send a copy of the group story home with students so they can share their work with their caregivers.

MATERIALS

- Chart paper
- Copies of the group report
- K-W-L chart
- Markers

"My students and I felt like space explorers as we navigated through the pictures, text, and video clips on the websites suggested in this unit. With every click of the mouse, we felt as if we were on the verge of a new discovery."

—FIRST-GRADE TEACHER

Blasting Off to Explore Space

UNIT BOOKS

The Solar System
By Dana Meachen Rau

The Life of an Astronaut
By Niki Walker

Space Exploration
By Dana Meachen Rau

COMPUTER RESOURCES

The Magic School Bus Explores the Solar System
KidPix Activity Kits: Volume 4
Bailey's Book House

Thematic Connection

As the sun goes down and the stars and moon appear in the dark nighttime sky, children make wishes on the first stars they see. What could be more exciting to students than learning about what lies beyond the stars? Indeed, humans' desire to learn more about the unknown has been the driving force behind exploration. The nonfiction books in this unit deal with one of the last frontiers for exploration—space. The first book, *The Solar System* (Rau, 2000), gives a general overview of the sun, planets, moons, asteroids, and comets. The second book, *The Life of an Astronaut* (Walker, 2001), examines astronauts' training and space missions. The third book, *Space Exploration* (Rau, 2003), gives students a chance to learn about how people historically have perceived the sun, moon, stars, and planets and begins by briefly discussing early astronomers. The book concludes by addressing various topics related to space exploration—the use of telescopes by scientists, various types of space missions, and the future of space exploration. The books included in this unit clearly present factual information about space and incorporate colorful photographs that support and enhance the text. By working through this unit, students will begin to develop an appreciation of the courage that astronauts demonstrate and better understand how space agencies around the world are working cooperatively to build and operate an international space station. Through their involvement with this unit, students will have the opportunity to read and work with expository text. The books in this unit present factual information that will allow students to practice reading nonfiction text with an efferent purpose of learning about the solar system, astronauts, and exploring space.

Matrix of Literacy Skills and Strategies in Unit 19

Literacy Skills and Strategies	Activities	Title of Book	Pages
Brainstorming	U, UC	—	287, 298
	C, D	*The Solar System*	288–289, 289–290
	D	*The Life of an Astronaut*	293
	C	*Space Exploration*	295–296
Building background knowledge on the Internet*	R, I	*The Solar System*	288, 291
	I	*The Life of an Astronaut*	294
	I	*Space Exploration*	297
Building fluency	C	*The Life of an Astronaut*	292
Comparing and contrasting	UC	—	298
	R	*The Solar System*	288
	R	*The Life of an Astronaut*	292
Composing in multimedia*	C, D	*The Solar System*	288–289, 289–290
	C, S	*The Life of an Astronaut*	292, 293–294
	C, D, S	*Space Exploration*	295–296, 296, 297
Creating and using charts	U	—	287
	I	*The Solar System*	291
	C	*Space Exploration*	295–296
Developing comprehension	R	*The Solar System*	288
	R, C, S	*The Life of an Astronaut*	292, 292, 293–294
	R, C, I	*Space Exploration*	295, 295–296, 297
Developing creative writing	I	*The Life of an Astronaut*	294
	C	*Space Exploration*	295–296
Developing critical reading and thinking	I	*The Solar System*	291
Developing oral language	U, UC	—	287, 298
	R, C, D, S	*The Solar System*	288, 288–289, 289–290, 290
	R, C	*The Life of an Astronaut*	292
	R, C, D, S	*Space Exploration*	295, 295–296, 296, 297
Developing vocabulary	U, UC	—	287, 298
	R, C, S, I	*The Solar System*	288, 288–289, 290, 291
	R, C, D, S	*The Life of an Astronaut*	292, 292, 293, 293–294
	R, D, I	*Space Exploration*	295, 296, 297
Distinguishing between real and make-believe content	C	*Space Exploration*	295–296

(continued)

Literacy Skills and Strategies	Activities	Title of Book	Pages
Drawing conclusions	S	*The Solar System*	290
E-mailing*	R	*The Solar System*	288
Following directions	U, UC	—	287, 298
	C, S, I	*The Solar System*	288–289, 290, 291
	C, D, S, I	*The Life of an Astronaut*	292, 293, 293–294, 294
	C, S, I	*Space Exploration*	295–296, 297, 297
Making predictions	R	*The Life of an Astronaut*	292
Navigating hyperlinks*	R, I	*The Solar System*	288, 291
	S, I	*The Life of an Astronaut*	293–294, 294
	C, S, I	*Space Exploration*	295–296, 297, 297
Presenting work on a computer*	D	*The Solar System*	289–290
	C, S	*The Life of an Astronaut*	292, 293–294
	D	*Space Exploration*	296
Reading aloud	R, I	*The Solar System*	288, 291
	R	*The Life of an Astronaut*	292
	R	*Space Exploration*	295
Reading and listening for a purpose	R, S	*The Solar System*	288, 290
	R, S, I	*The Life of an Astronaut*	292, 293–294, 294
	R, I	*Space Exploration*	295, 297
Reading and using map skills	I	*The Solar System*	291
Reading informational text	R, S, I	*The Solar System*	288, 290, 291
	R, S, I	*The Life of an Astronaut*	292, 293–294, 294
	R, I	*Space Exploration*	295, 297
Retelling	R, C, S	*The Solar System*	288, 288–289, 290
	R, D	*The Life of an Astronaut*	292, 293
	R, C, D, I	*Space Exploration*	295, 295–296, 296, 297
Sequencing	D	*The Solar System*	289–290
	D, S	*The Life of an Astronaut*	293, 293–294
Summarizing	R, S	*The Solar System*	288, 290
	R	*The Life of an Astronaut*	292
Understanding a main idea	C	*The Life of an Astronaut*	292
	C	*Space Exploration*	295–296
Using adjectives	R, C, D	*The Solar System*	288, 288–289, 289–290
	C	*The Life of an Astronaut*	292
	S, I	*Space Exploration*	297
Visualizing	R, D	*The Life of an Astronaut*	292, 293
Writing descriptive sentences	U	—	287
	R, C	*The Solar System*	288, 288–289
	C, D, S	*The Life of an Astronaut*	292, 293, 293–294
Writing letters	R, I	*The Solar System*	288, 291

* Indicates a new-literacy skill.
U = unit introduction; R = read-aloud and book discussion ideas; C = creativity and presentation software ideas; D = Digital Language Experience Approach; S = computer software activity; I = Internet resources and ideas; UC = unit conclusion

Unit Introduction

Post pictures of space and planets around the room to create a learning environment that focuses on the unit theme—space exploration. Write the following questions on chart paper: When you look at the sky during the day, what do you see? At night, what do you see in the sky? Create a T-chart using creativity and presentation software, such as KidPix Studio Deluxe, with the left column heading "During the Daytime" and the right column heading "During the Nighttime." Have students type their responses under each question on the T-chart on the computer (see Figure 42).

MATERIALS

- Chart paper
- File folders
- KidPix Deluxe (1998) software
- Markers
- Pictures of space and planets

Tell students that they are going to learn about things in the sky that people have wondered about for many, many years. Tell them that they are going to be explorers who learn about space from this unit's books and computer activities. Give students a "Space Explorer" file folder and ask them to draw a picture on the front of the folder about what they think space looks like. Tell students to sign and date their pictures. Use the folders as a portfolio, a place to keep their assignments as they learn about space. Print out a copy of the introductory T-chart for students to put in their individual folders.

Book 1:   The Solar System

Rau, D.M. (2000). Minneapolis, MN: Compass Point Books. $15.95. 32 pp.

BOOK REVIEW

This simply written expository text provides an excellent introduction to the solar system and objects that can be found in space. Beginning with characteristics of the sun, the nine planets, moons, asteroids, and comets, this book uses bold black type to highlight space-related vocabulary words. Next, the book goes into a brief description of how people have learned about space throughout history—from Copernicus, to the first unmanned space crafts, to the Apollo 11 moon landing. The book concludes with the idea that people still have much to learn through

---

Figure 42
Things We See in the Sky T-Chart

During the Daytime	During the Nighttime
•	•
•	•

---

space exploration. Colorful photographs throughout the book augment the text with visual details. Other helpful features include a glossary of the words highlighted throughout the text, a short list of interesting space facts, and a list of both print-based and Internet resources.

READ-ALOUD AND BOOK DISCUSSION IDEAS

Before starting this lesson, print out the Solar System lithograph set available for free from the National Aeronautics and Space Administration educational materials website (go to www.nasa.gov/pdf/58275main_Solar.System.Lithograph.Set.pdf) for teachers to use. This is a set of 15 color lithographs of the planets, the sun, asteroids, comets, and other orbiting bodies. Before reading, show students the lithograph of the solar system. Tell them that we live on a planet in the solar system. Ask students what the name is of the planet we live on. Point to the planet Earth. Then point to and read the names of the planets in the picture. Go to the website Astronomy For Kids (go to www.frontiernet.net/~kidpower/astronomy.html). This website contains information about the solar system, planets, sun, and other objects in space. Click on the Solar System hyperlink and read the information to students. Show the picture of the sun. Click on the Sun hyperlink and read the information about the sun. Next show the picture of Mercury. Click on the Planets hyperlink, select the planet's name, and read the information about Mercury. Continue showing the pictures of each planet in order. Select each planet name and read the information about it. When you have finished visiting each planet, tell students that reading books in this unit will help them learn more about space, including the solar system.

During reading, encourage students to talk about the pictures and practice using adjectives as they describe what they see.

After reading, ask students to recall information they learned from their Internet visit and the book. The literacy skills involved in this activity include using adjectives, building background knowledge on the Internet, retelling information learned and developing vocabulary related to the solar system.

COMPUTER ACTIVITIES

Creativity and Presentation Software Ideas

Before beginning this activity, the teacher should create a computer page titled "Where Do You Live?" and type in 10 sentence beginnings (see Figure 43) using creativity and presentation software such as KidPix Studio Deluxe. Explain to students that there are many ways to describe where they live and that when they complete this activity they will have described it 10 different ways, including where they live in the solar system.

Tell students they will complete the first sentence during computer-center time.

MATERIALS

■ KidPix Studio Deluxe (1998) software

1. Skip the first sentence on the computer page and complete sentences 2–10 as a whole group on the computer. Give prompts to guide students as they complete each of the sentences. For example, for the second sentence, ask students to name the city

---
Figure 43
"Where Do You Live?" Sentence Beginnings

Where Do You Live?
1. I live at [leave blank for student's address].
2. I live in [the city].
3. I live in [the state].
4. I live in [the country].
5. I live on [the continent].
6. I live in [the hemisphere].
7. I live on [the planet].
8. I live in [the Solar System].
9. I live in [the Milky Way Galaxy].
10. I live in [the Universe].

they live in. Save this computer page as a file for use during computer-center time.

2. During computer center time, open the computer file that the whole group completed, and use this file to complete the first sentence to create an individual page for each child. Working with one student at a time, ask the student if they know their home address. If the student knows his or her address, then ask him or her to recite it while you type in the information on the "Where Do You Live?" page. If the student does not know his or her address, then read the address to him or her, and ask the student to repeat it several times. After you have typed the address into the first sentence on the "Where Do You Live?" page, practice reading the address with the student.

3. Print out each child's "Where Do You Live?" page as you finish it. Send the printout home with each student. Encourage students to practice reading the sentences with their parents or caregivers.

The purpose of this activity is to encourage students to expand their thinking and help them realize that there is more than one way to describe something such as where they live.

Digital Language Experience Approach

Engage students in role-playing an interview to practice their oral language development.

1. Ask students to brainstorm questions they would like to ask an expert on the solar system. List the questions on chart paper.

2. Select three questions that the teacher can answer after reading the book, *The Solar System* (Rau, 2000).

MATERIALS

- Chart paper
- Digital camera
- KidPix Studio Deluxe (1998) software
- Markers

3. Tell students that three students will role-play as reporters, and each one will ask the teacher—the expert—one question. Explain that role-playing means that people have a conversation, but they pretend to have another job or to be someone else, and that you will pretend to be the expert.

4. Invite a cross-age computer buddy, a parent volunteer, a teaching assistant, or another adult at the school to take photographs of students conducting the interview.

5. Import the pictures into a creativity and presentation program such as KidPix Studio Deluxe. As a whole group, let students decide what order to put the pictures in to create a slide show.

6. Show each picture and invite students to describe each photograph.

7. Record students' sentences about the photographs.

8. Print and bind the photographs into a class book titled "Our Interview With a Solar System Expert."

Computer Software Activity

Emerging and developing readers will need the help of a cross-age computer buddy to interact with The Magic School Bus Explores the Solar System CD-ROM, which encourages students to learn about the solar system through a fact-finding mission. The scenario begins in Ms. Frizzle's classroom, which displays pictures of the nine planets, the moon, and the solar system. Ms. Frizzle and each of the children in her class have written reports. Each planet or moon report includes the following information: "[Planet name] At a Glance," "Why I Want To Go to [the planet]," and "Cool Facts About [the planet]."

MATERIALS

■ The Magic School Bus Explores the Solar System (2001) CD-ROM

One activity students using this software can work on is to find Ms. Frizzle in the Solar System. Ms. Frizzle and the members of her class are supposed to take a trip to the planetarium, but instead the magic school bus they are on turns into a rocket and blasts into outer space. During the trip, the class discovers that Ms. Frizzle has disappeared, but she left a message to the class so they can try to find her on one of the planets or the moon.

To find Ms. Frizzle, students using this CD-ROM must visit the planets in the solar system. While on a planet, students have the opportunity to learn about that particular planet and to play a game and try to collect a token that will help find Ms. Frizzle. One clue to help find Ms. Frizzle is revealed when students successfully complete the game. Students can use up to three clues to help them figure out where Ms. Frizzle is. Another activity students can do with this CD-ROM is to create a passport booklet to show which planets they visited. In their passport, students can draw a picture of each planet and write something they learned about the planet after their visit.

For author's computer chair (see Appendix B), ask students to talk about which planet they visited was their favorite and why they liked it. Ask them to look through their passport booklet and select one planet that they visited. Invite them to share the picture they drew of that planet and what they wrote about the planet in their passport booklet with the rest of the class.

StarChild: http://starchild.gsfc.nasa.gov/docs/StarChild/StarChild.html

This is an excellent website produced as a service of the High Energy Astrophysics Science Archive Research Center within the Laboratory for High Energy Astrophysics at the National Aeronautic and Space Administration. This website provides factual information about the solar system, the sun, the planets, the moon, comets, asteroids, the universe, galaxies, stars, The Milky Way, and black holes.

The information on this website is presented at a beginning or a more advanced level. By selecting the beginning level (Level 1), students can listen to the information about the solar system, the sun, the planets, and other space objects and topics read aloud by the computer. Selecting the more advanced level (Level 2) requires students to read information on their own on those topics written in more advanced language.

There are also space-related activities that students participate in. Activities are also presented at the beginning and more advanced levels. For example, in Level 1, there is an interactive solar system map in which students decide what planet goes into each orbit. Another Level 1 activity is Planet Tac Toe, an interactive Tic Tac Toe quiz about information students listened to as they visited different webpages. During the quiz, an *X* appears in the Tic Tac Toe square if the answer is correct. If the answer is incorrect, the computer shows the correct response. A third activity at this level is a game in which students must match pictures of objects found in the solar system that are the same. Examples of Level 2 activities include completing a chart by calculating the student's weight on various planets and putting the phases of the moon in correct sequence.

When working with younger students, Level 1, the beginning level, should be used, and students should work with a cross-age computer buddy to complete the activities because some of the activities require reading directions or typing answers.

Book 2:   The Life of an Astronaut

Walker, N. (2001). New York: Crabtree Publishing. $23.92. 32 pp.

BOOK REVIEW

This expository text is written in easy-to-understand language and supported by colorful photographs of astronaut candidates as they go through their training in hopes of becoming a NASA astronaut. This book is organized around 15 different topics relevant to the life of an astronaut. Each topic involves two pages of text and photographs. The topics in this book can be grouped generally under five headings that include background information, training, living in space, missions, and the future of space exploration. The topics in this book can be read as stand-alone readings or be used in any order that the teacher deems useful. The first group of topics addresses background information and includes a description of what an astronaut and a mission is, gives a brief history of astronauts, and explains who the members of a space mission are both in the spacecraft and as a part of the ground crew. The next group of topics addresses how astronauts are trained and includes information on how they practice in simulators and learn about weightlessness. The third group of topics addresses living in space and includes information on spacesuits and how astronauts move around inside the spacecraft, work in space, eat and sleep in space, and stay clean and healthy in space. The fourth group of topics addresses space missions and includes information about how astronauts return to Earth, the lengths of space missions, and the dangers of being an astronaut. The last topic addresses the requirements for future astronauts and includes information about Space Camp where children can learn and train on various types of equipment to prepare them for life in space. Space-related vocabulary words used in the text are defined in a glossary found on the last page of the book.

READ-ALOUD AND BOOK DISCUSSION IDEAS

Before reading, ask students to close their eyes and imagine being an astronaut who is about to blast off into space on a manned mission to the moon. Ask them to imagine and predict what tasks they will have to do in space after blastoff as well as what it will be like to work and live in space during their mission. Allow time for students to describe and talk about what they imagine.

During reading, make note of which of the students' predictions were accurate and which information in the text was new.

After reading, discuss the work done by astronauts. Ask students to name some of the jobs astronauts do while in space. Discuss why working in space takes a long time. Talk about how difficult it is for the astronauts to do their work outside the spacecraft because of the spacesuits they must wear. Have students compare how the astronauts do a job such as tightening a bolt in space and how different it is for someone on Earth to do that same job.

COMPUTER ACTIVITIES

Creativity and Presentation Software Ideas

Students create an animation of a walk in space. Students will learn to use the animation feature of creativity and presentation software such as KidPix Studio Deluxe by creating a space-related slide for a class slide show.

MATERIALS

■ KidPix Studio Deluxe (1998) software

---

1. Instruct students to create a space background (e.g., paint the background black, add yellow star stamps) using the KidPix Studio Deluxe animation feature.

2. Instruct students to create an animation of an astronaut doing a space walk using the space-related stamps. To use the animation tools, click on a stamp, drag it across the screen, and release. The animation is automatic and can be saved by the teacher for a class slide show.

3. Tell students to type a sentence that describes their animated pictures.

4. Collect the animated pictures and create a slide show to share during author's computer chair (see Appendix B).

Digital Language Experience Approach

Students make space helmets out of empty gallon water bottles and aluminum foil. Set up materials in the art center.

1. Empty gallon water bottles with the handle and spout cut off so the remainder of it will fit comfortably over a child's head.

2. Cut out a section from the front of the water bottle so students will be able to see.

3. Write each child's name inside the back edge of the water bottle with a permanent black marker.

4. Tell each small group of students that you will be taking digital photographs of how to make a space helmet that they will turn into a how-to essay.

5. Take digital photographs of students as they follow the steps to make their space helmet. After they have made their helmets, they will write a group how-to essay explaining and describing the steps they followed to accomplish this task.

6. Make a poster listing the following steps for making a space helmet using creativity and presentation software such as KidPix Studio Deluxe. Place the poster in the art center.

7. Read the steps for making their space helmets with students before they begin. Students will follow these steps students to make a space helmet:

   a. Choose a plastic water bottle and help students cover it with aluminum foil. Use glue to hold the aluminum in place.

   b. Instruct students to glue an index card with their astronaut name (e.g., "Commander Kylie") on the front of the bottle.

   c. Instruct students to place their helmet in the hallway to dry.

Students can use the helmets in sociodramatic play to reenact what they have learned about astronaut life.

MATERIALS
■ Aluminum foil
■ Digital camera
■ Empty gallon water bottles
■ Glue
■ Index card
■ KidPix Studio Deluxe (1998) software
■ Permanent marker
■ Poster board
■ Shoe box

Computer Software Activity

Explain to students that they are going to write a report, which contains factual information. A developmentally appropriate report will involve finding and recording just a few facts. Working with a cross-age computer buddy, students gather, interpret, and use data about the planets in the solar system and create a report or a presentation. For primary-grade students, use the lowest software level for this activity.

In this activity, students use clues to identify planets, draw pictures of planets using the drawing tool, and answer questions using KidPix Activity Kits Volume 4 software. Students read a clue at the top of the screen to determine which planet to draw and use the typewriter tool to

MATERIALS
■ KidPix Activity Kits Volume 4 (1998) software
■ KidPix Studio Deluxe (1998) software

write the name of the planet on the blank line. Using the information from the How To page and Data page, students complete the page about the first planet. They repeat these steps for each of the remaining planets and save each page. They can use the drawing tools and rubber stamps to create a cover page for their report and print it out to make a book. Students can also create a presentation by importing the pages into a slide show. The teacher helps students upload their saved pages in the order of the distance of each planet from the sun. Students can record their voices and use other prerecorded sounds to create multimedia presentations about the planets in creativity and presentation software such as KidPix Studio Deluxe.

Internet Resources and Ideas

NASA Space Place: www.spaceplace.nasa.gov/en/kids
This website first appeared as an educational outreach project of NASA. Targeted for primary-grade students, this website is designed to teach students that science, technology, and learning about space can be fun and understandable. This website includes games, projects, animations, cool subjects, amazing facts, and a friends share area.

Activities that students can become involved in include making a robot puzzle, creating a model Saturn decoration, building a galactic mobile, making and using a star finder, finding their way through a tiny space maze, playing a space trivia game, and finding comet-related words in a word search. The Friends Share webpage allows students to see what other students have done while learning about space and includes materials that other students have submitted to the website.

Billy Bear's Personalized Storybooks: www.billybear4kids.com/story/personalized/storybooks2.html
This website allows students to create a personalized storybook about the planets in the solar system. The student becomes the main character of the storybook. After the teacher downloads the file titled Our Planets, the student opens the file, types his or her name, and clicks the hyperlink to personalize the story. Students will enjoy practicing their reading with their storybooks on the computer screen. Within the storybook pages are hidden hotspots. As students read their stories, by moving the mouse on the page, the cursor arrow turns red when there is a hidden hotspot. Hidden hotspots include animations, pictures, or sounds when the student clicks on them. Students can save the storybooks to access or print out for reading later.

Other storybooks that students can create online include an alphabet book, a baby animals book, a book about the first day of school, and a book about the rainforest. Teachers will find lots of ideas and activities at this website.

DLTK's Crafts for Kids: Outer Space Section: www.dltk-kids.com/crafts/space/space.html
This website features a variety of printable craft projects and coloring pages that are suitable for students at the emerging, developing, and fluent reader levels. The coloring pages include pictures of a space shuttle, other spacecrafts, and strange space aliens. The craft project ideas include activities such as an orbiting object paper plate craft, an astronaut paper roll craft, and a magic stars craft. Each project idea identifies the appropriate age level of students for the project and contains complete directions and a materials list that teachers can print out. Some crafts also include printable templates to use for completing the projects. Teachers will find this a good resource for craft projects suitable for primary-grade students to work on.

Rau, D.M. (2003). Minneapolis, MN: Compass Point Books. $22.60. 32 pp.

BOOK REVIEW

Human beings are curious creatures. People have explored the Earth by walking across the land and sailing on the oceans. Even today, there are still parts of Earth that are left to be explored, but the Earth is small compared to the universe. The book begins with a brief description of the solar system. The second chapter gives a brief background explanation of the history of discoveries that have been made by exploring the sky by astronomers such as Ptolemy and Carl Sagan. The third chapter discusses how telescopes are important tools of astronomers and how the telescopes developed from the first telescope used by Galileo to the Hubble Space Telescope. The fourth chapter explains unmanned missions and discusses unmanned spacecrafts that have been launched to extend the exploration of outer space. The fifth chapter explains the manned missions to the moon in the 1960s and then moves to space shuttle missions. The last chapter discusses the future of space exploration and the building of the International Space Station.

Students and teachers can use the excellent two-page color chart at the end of the book to review the planets and other objects in the solar system. A glossary defines space-related vocabulary words that appear throughout the text in color. Following the glossary is a list of "Did You Know?" space information. The last helpful feature of this book is a listing of excellent print-based texts and websites that teachers can use as resources to extend classroom teaching and student learning about space exploration.

READ-ALOUD AND BOOK DISCUSSION IDEAS

Before reading the book, bring a telescope (or a paper towel tube covered with aluminum foil) into the classroom, and talk about the use of telescopes. Briefly explain to students how a telescope allows someone to see things that are far away more clearly.

During reading, point out to students facts about telescopes and how they have been used in scientific inquiry.

After reading about different ways of exploring, ask students to retell what they learned about using a telescope to explore Earth and space.

MATERIALS

- Telescope or paper towel tube covered in aluminum foil

COMPUTER ACTIVITIES

Creativity and Presentation Software Ideas

Invite students to create a fantasy story about outer space travel. Discuss the difference between real and make-believe, or fact and fantasy. Tell them to use their imaginations to create a fantasy tale. What type of things might they see on a space adventure? For students to create their fantasy story with the Bailey's Book House software, the teacher needs to explain the following procedure:

MATERIALS

- Bailey's Book House (1994) software

1. Direct students to click on the books on the bookshelf from the main menu, a living room setting. This connects students to an interactive, fill-in-the-blank story, complete with animations and sound effects.

2. Instruct students to select a main character on the first page and click on the spaceship on the second page. The remaining four pages allow students to choose their own space adventure. Options allow students to listen to the story again (text is highlighted as it is read aloud), or to print out a copy of their story.

Students can share their stories by reading them aloud or retelling their stories during author's computer chair (see Appendix B).

Digital Language Experience Approach

The sociodramatic center is a place where primary-grade students can use their imaginations and pretend to be someone else. During time spent in this center, they not only have a chance to be creative, but they can also develop and practice their oral language. They will also benefit from the socializing and learning to play cooperatively with others. Many different scenarios can be acted out by turning the sociodramatic play center into different types of environments.

MATERIALS

- Blocks
- Digital camera
- Helmets
- Job chart
- KidPix Studio Deluxe (1998) software
- Paper towel tubes
- Rope
- Silver oven mitts

---

1. Turn the sociodramatic play center into a space station, complete with telescopes (i.e., paper towel tubes), helmets (made previously in the art center during this unit [see page 293]), big gloves (i.e., silver oven mitts), a tether for space walks (i.e., a rope), cargo and supplies (i.e., blocks), and a job chart (i.e., a list of things for students to do, such as viewing planets with the telescope, conducting a space walk, eating space food, and moving cargo).

2. Document students' creative play with digital photographs.

3. Import the photographs into creativity and presentation software, such as KidPix Studio Deluxe, and invite students to create a story about what they did while the were playing.

4. Display the digital photographs on the computer and invite students in each picture to dictate a sentence about what they were doing in the picture. Type their responses under the pictures.

5. Print out photographs and bind them into a class book, or create a slide show for students to view during author's computer chair (see Appendix B).

6. During author's computer chair, show the slide show of pictures and instruct students to read their sentences to the rest of the class. Ask them to elaborate beyond what they dictated when they were playing in the sociodramatic play center.

Computer Software Activity ---------------->

Students will enjoy creating a fantasy space monster by using software tools in Bailey's Book House and following directions. In this activity, a space monster standing on a platform changes immediately in response to students' mouse clicks. When students have finished making their space monster, the teacher can print it out. During author's computer chair (see Appendix B), instruct students to share the space monster they created and tell a story about it or describe it using rich adjectives.

MATERIALS

■ Bailey's Book House (1994) software

Internet Resources and Ideas

HubbleSite: http://hubblesite.org/discoveries

This website contains a lot of information about the Hubble Space Telescope and includes hyperlinks to a News page, Gallery of pictures page, Discoveries page, SciTech page, Fun page, and Reference page. The Discoveries webpage provides students with an excellent introduction to the Hubble Space Telescope. They can watch a multimedia presentation about the Hubble Space Telescope and how telescopes have been used to explore space. Another multimedia presentation available is about the Milky Way Galaxy. Teachers should preview the presentations on this website before using them with younger students. Teachers deciding to use the presentations can scaffold younger students' learning by reading aloud the books in this unit, involving students in other activities about space included in this unit, bringing in information and pictures of the space telescope and galaxies, and talking about the Hubble Space Telescope and the Milky Way Galaxy to acquaint students with these topics before showing the presentations. Tell students to listen carefully and be ready to talk about the space telescope and the Milky Way Galaxy after watching the presentations. Ask students these questions: Who can tell me something they remember about the Hubble Space Telescope? Who can tell me something they remember about our Milky Way Galaxy? Encourage students to practice using adjectives as they use their oral language to talk about what they saw in the presentations.

KidsAstronomy.com: www.kidsastronomy.com/index.htm

This website, designed for students to learn about space and astronomy, contains hyperlinks to webpages about the Solar System, Deep Space, Space Exploration, and a Fun With Astronomy zone of space-themed activities. The webpage about the Solar System provides hyperlinks to information for students to learn about the sun, planets, moons of the solar system, asteroids, and comets. The Deep Space webpage contains hyperlinks to information about the universe, black holes, galaxies, stars, nebulas, and quasars. The Space Exploration webpage contains hyperlinks to information about the space shuttle, future spacecraft, and exploring Mars. The Fun With Astronomy Zone webpage contains hyperlinks to different space-themed activities such as a memory game, shape matching game, word search game, and make-a-solar-system activity where students can add the planets to the solar system one at a time and watch the planets orbit the Sun.

Unit Conclusion

Ask students to turn their Space Explorer portfolio folders over and draw a picture on the back of the folder of what they think space looks like now that they have finished the unit. When students are finished, by opening their folders, they can compare and contrast what they knew before the unit to what they have learned during the unit. Make available the books that students read aloud during the unit so they may refer to them as they participate in a grand conversation about the unit and all the things they have learned. To start the discussion, ask each student to name one fact about space he or she learned during the unit. For example, if a student learned that the moon orbits the Earth, ask the student to elaborate on what else they know about the moon, such as what the surface of the moon looks like or what the environment of the moon is like. To continue in the spirit of explorers, ask students to brainstorm what other things are yet to be known about space.

MATERIALS

■ Markers

Steps for Conducting a Digital Language Experience Approach

1. Set up a unit-related activity that involves small groups of students in physical activity.

2. Take digital photographs (or video) of students' experiences as they engage in the activity.

3. View digital photographs to elicit students' talk, dictation, or composing about the sequence of events. Elicit rich language from students that expresses the experience.

4. Import the digital photographs or video into creativity and presentation software with the purpose of preparing a presentation that best tells the story for an audience of peers.

5. Sort photographs into a sequence of events and type in with a keyboard students' dictation to accompany the digital photographs.

6. Present the digital language experience approach to students in printed form or on a computer screen with creativity and presentation software.

7. Use small-group rereadings, choral readings, or multimedia readings as a springboard for literacy learning in follow-up activities (e.g., fluency practice, word sorts, vocabulary, decoding).

Steps for Conducting Author's Computer Chair

1. Create a social atmosphere and learning environment that fosters peer collaboration and a sense of community where it is safe for students to share their ideas and receive appropriate feedback from their peers.

2. Begin by conducting minilessons to demonstrate and model author's computer chair components.

3. Schedule time and space in the weekly schedule to accommodate author's computer chair.

4. Invite students to share different types of computer-related work that are in different stages of completion.

5. Establish initial discussion routines in which students are seeking feedback by reminding students to (a) state the purpose of their time in author's computer chair, (b) show what progress they have made, (c) ask for help in how to move forward, (d) discuss how to use peers' ideas, and (e) state the next steps.

Adams, M.J. (1990). *Beginning to read: Thinking and learning about print*. Cambridge, MA: The MIT Press.

Ansell, S.E., & Park, J. (2003). Tracking tech trends: Student computer use grows, but teachers need training. *Education Week's Technology Counts, 22*(35), 43–44, 48.

Clements, D.H., & Nastasi, B.K. (1993). Electronic media and early childhood education. In B. Spodek (Ed.), *Handbook of research on the education of young children* (pp. 251–271). New York: Macmillan.

Cochran-Smith, M., Paris, C.L., & Kahn, J.L. (1991). *Learning to write differently*. Norwood, NJ: Ablex.

Cullinan, B.E. (1989). *Literature and the child* (2nd ed.). San Diego, CA: Harcourt.

de Jong, M.T., & Bus, A.G. (2002). Quality of book-reading matters for emergent readers: An experiment with the same book in a regular or electronic format. *Journal of Educational Psychology, 94*, 145–155.

Eeds, M., & Wells, D. (1989). Grand conversations: An exploration of meaning construction in literature study groups. *Research in the Teaching of English, 23*(1), 4–29.

Flood, J., & Lapp, D. (1997–1998). Broadening conceptualizations of literacy: The visual and communicative arts. *The Reading Teacher, 51*(4), 342–344.

Galda, J., & Cullinan, B.E. (1991). Literature for literacy: What research says about the benefits of using trade books in the classroom. In J. Flood, J.M. Jenson, D. Lapp, & J.S. Squire (Eds.), *Handbook of research on teaching the English language arts* (pp. 529–535). New York: Macmillan.

Gilster, P. (1997). *Digital literacy*. New York: Wiley.

Hall, T. (2002). *Differentiated instruction*. Retrieved December 7, 2005, from http://www.cast.org/publications/ncac/ncac_diffinstruc.html

Hoffman, J.V., Roser, N.L., & Battle, J. (1993). Reading aloud in classrooms: From a model toward a "model." *The Reading Teacher, 46*(6), 496–503.

International Reading Association (IRA). (2001). *Integrating literacy and technology in the curriculum* (Position statement). Newark, DE: Author. Retrieved January 17, 2006, from http://www.reading.org/resources/issues/positions_technology.html

International Society for Technology in Education (ISTE). (2002). *ISTE/NCATE standards for educational technology programs*. Retrieved December 14, 2005, from http://cnets.iste.org/ncate

Labbo, L.D. (1996). A semiotic analysis of young children's symbol making in a classroom computer center. *Reading Research Quarterly, 31*(4), 356–385.

Labbo, L.D. (2000, April). 12 things young children can do with a talking book in a classroom computer center. *The Reading Teacher, 53*(7), 542–546.

Labbo, L.D. (2004, April). Author's computer chair. *The Reading Teacher, 57*(7), 688–691. *Reading Online*. Retrieved December 14, 2005, from http://www.readingonline.org/electronic/rt/4-04_column

Labbo, L.D., Eakle, A.J., & Montero, K.M. (2002). Digital Language Experience Approach (D-LEA): Using digital photographs and creativity software as a Language Experience Approach innovation. *Reading Online*. Retrieved December 14, 2005, from http://www.readingonline.org/electronic/elec_index.asp?HREF=labbo2/index.html

Labbo, L.D., Kinzer, C.K., Leu, D.L., & Teale, W.H. (2003, May). *Kids, computers, and literacy learning: Stepping into K–3 classrooms*. Paper presented at the 48th Annual Convention of the International Reading Association, Orlando, FL.

Labbo, L.D., Love, M., Park, M., & Hubbard, B. (2004, May). *Language, literature, and technology—Enhancing young children's literacy development*. Paper presented at the 49th Annual Convention of the International Reading Association, Reno, NV.

Labbo, L.D., & Reinking, D. (2003). Computers and early literacy education. In N. Hall, J. Larson, & J. Marsh (Eds.), *Handbook of early childhood literacy research* (pp. 338–354). Thousand Oaks, CA: Sage.

Labbo, L.D., & Teale, W. (2001, April). *Figuring out how computers fit in: Practical classroom applications for K–3 computer-related literacy instruction.* Paper presented at the 46th Annual Convention of International Reading Association, New Orleans, LA.

Leu, D.J., & Kinzer, C.K. (2003). *Effective literacy instruction: K–8* (5th ed.). Columbus, OH: Merrill.

Leu, D.J., & Leu, D.D. (with Leu, K.R.). (1999). *Teaching with the Internet: Lessons from the classroom.* Norwood, MA: Christopher-Gordon.

Lincoln, Y.S., & Guba, E.G. (1985). *Naturalistic inquiry.* Thousand Oaks, CA: Sage.

Lomangino, A.G., Nicholson, J., & Sulzby, E. (1999). The influence of power relations and social goals on children's collaborative interactions while composing on the computer. *Early Childhood Research Quarterly, 14,* 197–228.

McKenna, M.C. (1998). Electronic texts and the transformation of beginning reading. In D. Reinking, M.C. McKenna, L.D. Labbo, & R.D. Kieffer (Eds.), *Handbook of literacy and technology: Transformations in a post-typographic world* (pp. 45–59). Mahwah, NJ: Erlbaum.

McKenna, M.C., Reinking, D., & Bradley, B.A. (2001, November). *The effects of electronic trade books on the decoding growth of beginning readers.* Paper presented at NATO Advanced Study Institute, Il Cioco, Italy.

Merriam-Webster online. (2005). Springfield, MA: Merriam-Webster. Available: http://www.m-w.com

Morrow, L.M. (1989). *Literacy development in the early years: Helping children read and write.* Englewood Cliffs, NJ: Prentice-Hall.

Moss, J.F. (1984). *Focus units in literature: A handbook for elementary school teachers.* Urbana, IL: National Council of Teachers of English.

National Association for the Education of Young Children (NAEYC). (1998). *Technology and young children—Ages 3 through 8* (Position statement). Washington, DC: Author. Retrieved December 14, 2005, from http://www.naeyc.org/about/positions/PSTECH98.asp

National Center for Educational Statistics. (1999). *Internet access in public schools and classrooms: 1994–1998.* Retrieved December 14, 2005, from http://nces.ed.gov/surveys/frss/publications/1999017

Ogle, D. (1986). K-W-L: A teaching model that develops active reading of expository text. *The Reading Teacher, 39*(6), 564–570.

Spiegel, D.L., & Fitzgerald, J. (1986). Improving reading comprehension through instruction about story parts. *The Reading Teacher, 39*(7), 676–682.

Stauffer, R.G. (1970). *The language-experience approach to the teaching of reading.* New York: Harper & Row.

Turbill, J. (2003, March). Exploring the potential of the digital language experience approach in Australian classrooms. *Reading Online.* Retrieved December 14, 2005, from http://www.readingonline.org/international/inter_index.asp?HREF=turbill7

Vacca, J.L., Vacca, R.T., Gove, M.K., Burkey, L.B., Lenhart, L.A., & McKeon, C.A. (2003). *Reading and learning to read* (5th ed.). New York: Allyn & Bacon.

Yaden, D.G., Rowe, D., & MacGillivray, L. (2000). Emergent literacy: A matter (polyphony) of perspectives. In M.L. Kamil, P. Mosenthal, P.D. Pearson, & R. Barr (Eds.), *Handbook of reading research* (Vol. 3, pp. 425–454). Mahwah, NJ: Erlbaum.

CHILDREN'S LITERATURE CITED

Brown, M.W. (1947). *Goodnight moon.* Ill. C. Hurd. New York: Harper.

Copper, M. (2005). *Snow White.* New York: Dutton.

DeRolf, S. (1997). *A box of crayons.* New York: Random House.

Evertts-Secker, J. (2004). *Little red riding hood.* Cambridge, MA: Barefoot Books.

Galdone, P. (1981). *The three billy goats gruff.* New York: Clarion Books.

Gay, M.-L. (1997). *Rumpelstiltskin.* Toronto, ON: Groundwood Books; Vancouver, BC: Douglas & McIntyre Ltd.

Lesser, R. (1999). *Hansel and Gretel.* New York: Dutton.

Lewis, H. (2004). *Cinderella.* New York: Scholastic.

Marshall, J. (1988). *Goldilocks and the three bears*. New York: Dial Books for Young Readers.

Martin, B., Jr. (1992). *Brown bear, brown bear, what do you see?* New York: Henry Holt.

Story book: Folktales from around the world. (2006). Retrieved January 13, 2006, from http://story.lg.co.kr:3000/english/story/index.jsp

Wiesner, D. (2001). *The three pigs*. New York: Clarion Books.

Zelinsky, P.O. (1997). *Rapunzel*. New York: Dutton.

COMPUTER RESOURCES CITED

102 dalmatians: Puppies to the Rescue [CD-ROM]. (2000). Available: Burbank, CA: Disney Interactive.

The Airport [CD-ROM]. (1996). Available: Humongous Entertainment; Atari.

Alphabet: Play With the ABCs [CD-ROM]. (2002). Available: Tivola Publishing.

Arthur's Reading Games [Computer software]. (1999). Freemont, CA: The Learning Company.

ArtRageous: The Amazing World of Art [Computer software]. (1995). Cambridge, MA: Softkey Multimedia.

Bailey's Book House [Computer software]. (1994). San Francisco: Edmark/Riverdeep.

Blue's Clues ABC Time Activities [Computer software]. (1998). New York: Humongous Entertainment.

The Bread That Grew [CD-ROM]. (2002–2003). Available: Maestro Learning Company.

Busy Town [Computer software]. (1993). New York: Simon & Schuster.

Cinderella: The Original Fairy Tale [CD-ROM]. (1990). Available: Buffalo, NY: Discis Knowledge Research.

Clifford's Musical Memory Games [Computer software]. (2002). New York: Scholastic.

Clifford Reading [CD-ROM]. (2004). Available: Scholastic.

Crayola Magic 3-D Coloring Book Cool Critters [Computer software]. (2000). White Plains, NY: IBM; Shelton, CT: Crayola.

Crayola Magic Princess Paper Doll Maker [Computer software]. (1998). White Plains, NY: IBM.

Curious George Downtown Adventure [CD-ROM]. (2002). Available: Knowledge Adventure.

Dino the Star Keeper [Computer software]. (1998). Bridgeport, CT: Greene Bark Press Inc.

Dinosaur Adventure 3-D (Version 4.0) [Computer software]. (1995). Torrance, CA: Knowledge Adventure.

Dinosaurs: Giant Reptiles (Version 1.71) [Computer software]. (1993). Washington, DC: National Geographic Society.

Dr. Seuss's ABC [CD-ROM]. (1999). Available: The Learning Company.

IBM Crayola Magic 3-D Coloring Book Cool Critters [Computer software]. (2004). White Plains, NY: IBM

IBM Crayola Magic Princess Paper Doll Maker [Computer software]. (1998). White Plains, NY: IBM.

Imagination Express: Destination Ocean (Version 2.0) [Computer software]. (1995). Elgin, IL: Sunburst Technology.

Inspiration (Version 7.6) [Computer software]. (2005) Portland, OR: Inspiration Software. Available: http://www.inspiration.com/companyinfo/index.cfm

I Spy: School Days [Computer software]. (1995). New York: Scholastic.

The Jolly Postman's Party [Computer software]. (1997). New York: Dorling Kindersley Multimedia.

JumpStart Artist [Computer software]. (2000). Torrance, CA: Knowledge Adventure.

JumpStart First Grade [Computer software]. (1995). Torrance, CA : Knowledge Adventure.

JumpStart Music [Computer software]. (1998). Torrance, CA: Knowledge Adventure.

Just Grandma and Me [Computer software]. (1999). Fremont, CA: The Learning Company.

KidPix Activity Kits Volume 1 [Computer software]. (1998). Cedar Rapids, IA: Riverdeep.

KidPix Activity Kits Volume 4 [Computer software]. (1998). Cedar Rapids, IA: Riverdeep.

KidPix Studio Deluxe (Version 1.0) [Computer software]. (1998). Navato, CA: Broderbund.

KidPix Studio Deluxe (Version 3.0) [Computer software]. (2000). Cedar Rapids, IA: Riverdeep.

Kidspiration (Version 2.1) [Computer software]. (2005). Portland, OR: Inspiration Software.

KidWorks Deluxe (Version 1.0) [Computer software]. (1995). Torrance, CA: Knowledge Adventure.

Living Books: Mercer Mayer's Little Monster at School [Computer software]. (1996). Novato, CA: The Learning Company.

The Magic School Bus Explores the Age of Dinosaurs [Computer software]. (2003). New York: Scholastic.

The Magic School Bus Explores Bugs [CD-ROM]. (2001). Available: Scholastic.

The Magic School Bus Explores the Solar System [Computer software]. (2001). New York: Scholastic.

Math Blaster, Ages 6–9 [Computer software]. (1997). Torrance, CA: Davidson Associates.

Mercer Mayer's Just Grandma and Me [Computer software]. (1993). Novato, CA: Living Books.

Microsoft Office 2003 [Computer software]. (2003). Redmond, WA: Microsoft Corporation.

Microsoft Paint (Version 5.1) [Computer software]. (1981–2001). Redmond, WA: Microsoft Corporation.

Music Ace: Makes Learning Music Fun (Version 1.5) [Computer software]. (2000). Chicago: Harmonic Vision.

Music Ace 2 [Computer software]. (2003). Chicago: Harmonic Vision.

My First Incredible Amazing Dictionary [CD-ROM]. (1995). New York: Dorling Kindersley Multimedia.

My First Science Explorer [Computer software]. (1999). New York: Dorling Kindersley Multimedia.

Neighborhood Map Machine (Version 2.0) [Computer software]. (2000). Watertown, MA: Tom Snyder Productions.

One Small Square: Seashore [Computer software]. (1996). Los Angeles: Virgin Sounds and Vision.

Orly's Draw-a-Story [Computer software]. (1996). Novato, CA: Broderbund.

Peter Rabbit's Math Garden [Computer software]. (2005). Fremont, CA: The Learning Company.

Reader Rabbit's Toddler [Computer software]. (1999). Fremont, CA: The Learning Company.

Sheila Rae, the Brave [Computer software]. (1996). Novato, CA: Broderbund.

Snow White and the Seven Hansels [Computer software]. (2000). New York: Viva Media.

Stellaluna [CD-ROM]. (2004). Available: The Learning Company.

Storybook Weaver Deluxe [Computer software]. (1994). Fremont, CA: The Learning Company.

Tonka Construction [CD-ROM]. (2001). New York: Infogrames Interactive; Atari.

A Tree Through the Seasons [CD-ROM]. (1993). Available: Discis Knowledge Research/Harmony Interactive.

Ultimate Writing and Creative Center [Computer software]. (1996). Freemont, CA: The Learning Company.

DVDs CITED

Gagne, P.R. (Producer), & McDonald, R. (Producer/Director). (2004). Flossie and the Fox. In *Curious George rides a bike (and more tales of mischief)* [DVD]. New York: Scholastic.

Gibbons, G. (Producer), Mason J. (Writer), Slade, B. (Writer), Lever, S.-A. (Writer), Page, J. (Writer), McIntosh, R. (Director), & Taylor, K. (Director). (2004). *Children's favorites, volume 2* [DVD]. London: HIT Entertainment.

Pilotte, J. (Director), Bouchard, J.E. (Writer), Duffy, H. (Writer), Mauffette, J. (Producer), Moss, P. (Producer), & Taylor, L. (Producer). (2005). *Caillou: Caillou's family fun* [DVD]. Hollywood, CA: PBS: Cookie Jar Entertainment/Chouette.

SUGGESTED READINGS

Binder, S., & Ledger, B. (1985). *Preschool computer project report*. Oakville, ON: Sheridan College.

Cuban, L. (2001). *Oversold and underused: Computers in the classroom*. Cambridge, MA: Harvard University Press.

Leu, D.J. (1997). Caity's question: Literacy as deixis on the Internet (Exploring literacy on the Internet). *The Reading Teacher, 51*(1), 62–67.

AUTHOR AND SUBJECT INDEX

Note: Page numbers followed by *t* or *f* indicate tables or figures, respectively.

CHILDREN'S LITERATURE AND COMPUTER RESOURCES INDEX

LITERACY SKILLS AND STRATEGIES INDEX

ENGLISH AS A SECOND LANGUAGE, USING: with bedtime stories, 176; with difference stories, 166, 167–168; with emotional issues, 144–145; with fairy tales, 79–81, 83–84; with insect stories, 232, 234–235; with job stories, 197; with writing, 69–70

F

FLUENCY, BUILDING: with art, 96, 97–98, 104–105; with difference stories, 166; with dinosaur stories, 260; with dog stories, 131–132; with emotional issues, 143–144, 144–145, 151; with fairy tales, 79–81, 83–84, 84; with insect stories, 233–234; with job stories, 190–191; with math, 246; with season stories, 272, 281, 282–283; with space stories, 292; with writing, 62–63, 66–67

FLUENCY, DEVELOPING: with math, 246

FOLLOWING DIRECTIONS: with art, 96, 97–98, 99–100, 100, 102–103, 103; with bedtime stories, 172–173, 174, 175–176, 177–178, 178, 180–182, 182, 183–184; with difference stories, 159–160, 161, 162–163, 163–164, 164, 165, 166–167, 167–168; with dinosaur stories, 259–260, 260, 266–267, 267; with dog stories, 128–129, 129, 130–131, 131–132, 132, 133–134, 135; with emotional issues, 142–143, 143–144, 145, 147–148, 148–149, 150–151, 151–152; with fairy tales, 78–79, 79–81, 82–83, 83–84, 84–85, 86–87, 88–89; with insect stories, 232, 233–234, 234–235, 236, 237–238, 239–240, 241; with job stories, 190–191, 191, 193, 194, 195–196, 196; with math, 245, 246, 247, 248–249, 250–251, 252, 253; with music, 50–51, 52, 53, 55–56, 56–57; with poetry, 39–40, 41–42, 44; with sea mammal stories, 216–217, 217–218, 221–222, 222–223, 224–225, 225–226, 226–227; with season stories, 274–275, 275–276, 279–280; with self-concept, 112–113, 113–114, 114–115, 115, 116–117, 117–118, 118–119, 120–121, 121; with space stories, 287, 288–289, 290, 291, 292, 293–294, 294, 295–296, 297, 298; with transportation stories, 203–204, 204–205, 207, 209, 210–211; with writing, 63, 66–67, 68–69, 69

FRIENDLY LETTERS, WRITING, 64–65, 66–67

G

GRAPHIC ORGANIZERS. *See* concept maps and graphic organizers, creating

H

HYPERLINKS, NAVIGATING: with ABC books, 19–20; with art, 97, 99–100, 101, 104; with bedtime stories, 172–173, 176, 178, 179, 182; with difference stories, 158–159, 160, 161, 164, 166–167; with dinosaur stories, 259–260, 260, 261–262, 263–264, 266, 267–268, 268; with dog stories, 129, 130, 132, 135;

with emotional issues, 144–145, 145, 148–149, 151–152; with fairy tales, 79–81, 82–83, 84–85, 88; with insect stories, 233–234, 234–235, 235, 237–238, 240–241, 241; with job stories, 188–189, 191–192, 194, 195–196, 196, 197; with math, 247, 250–251, 253; with music, 50–51, 54, 56–57; with poetry, 36; with sea mammal stories, 217–218, 218–219, 221–222, 222–223, 226–227; with season stories, 275–276, 277, 279–280, 282–283; with self-concept, 115, 118–119, 121; with space stories, 288, 291, 293–294, 294, 295–296, 297; with transportation stories, 201–202, 204–205, 205, 207, 208, 211

I

INFERRING: with difference stories, 162, 164, 166–167; with dinosaur stories, 266, 267–268; with dog stories, 130, 132, 133, 136; with music, 48–49, 50; with sea mammal stories, 219–220, 224; with self-concept, 112, 119–120, 122; with transportation stories, 202–203

INFORMATIONAL TEXT, READING: with art, 97–98, 99, 104; with bedtime stories, 173–174, 182; with difference stories, 160, 161, 164; with dinosaur stories, 259, 260, 263–264, 264–266, 267; with dog stories, 127–128, 135; with emotional issues, 151–152; with fairy tales, 79–81; with insects, 232, 233–234, 234–235, 236, 237–238, 240–241; with job stories, 188–189, 191–192; with math, 251; with sea mammal stories, 217–218, 218–219, 221–222, 222–223, 226–227; with season stories, 273, 275–276, 282–283; with self-concept, 114–115, 115, 118–119, 121; with space stories, 288, 290, 291, 292, 293–294, 294, 295, 297; with transportation stories, 202–203, 205, 206, 208; with writing, 66

L

LETTERS, IDENTIFYING: with ABC books, 16, 17, 18, 19, 21, 23–24, 24, 26, 27–28; with bedtime stories, 179–180, 180, 183–184; with dinosaur stories, 259; with emotional issues, 145, 151–152; with job stories, 190–191; with poetry, 43; with transportation stories, 203–204, 204

LETTERS, WRITING: with bedtime stories, 175–176, 183–184

LETTER–SOUND CORRESPONDENCE: with art, 96, 97–98; with emotional issues, 144–145, 151–152; with poetry, 31–32, 33, 38–39, 39–40, 43, 44; with transportation stories, 211

M

MAIN IDEA, UNDERSTANDING: with art, 95–96, 100–101, 103; with bedtime stories, 177–178, 183–184; with difference stories, 158–159, 159–160, 162–163,

163–164, 166–167; with dinosaur stories, 263–264, 267–268; with dog stories, 126–127, 127–128, 128–129, 129, 130–131, 131–132, 132, 135, 136; with emotional issues, 140–141, 142–143, 143–144, 144–145, 146, 147–148, 148–149, 149–150, 150–151, 151–152, 152–153; with job stories, 190, 191, 192–193, 193; with math, 246, 247, 248; with sea mammal stories, 216, 219–220, 221, 224–225; with season stories, 277–278, 282, 283; with self-concept, 112, 113–114, 114–115, 116–117, 117–118, 118–119, 119–120, 120–121, 121, 122; with space stories, 292, 295–296; with transportation stories, 204–205, 206–207, 209, 210–211; with writing, 63

MAP SKILLS, READING AND USING: with bedtime stories, 174; with difference stories, 166; with job stories, 189; with sea mammal stories, 224; with self-concept, 114–115; with space stories, 291

MULTICULTURAL CONNECTIONS, MAKING: with art, 102–103, 104; with bedtime stories, 172–173, 173–174, 175–176, 183–184; with difference stories, 158–159, 159–160, 161, 164, 167–168; with emotional issues, 142–143, 143–144, 145, 146, 147–148, 148; with fairy tales, 79–81, 85–86; with sea mammal stories, 224, 226–227; with self-concept, 114–115, 116–117, 118–119, 121; with transportation stories, 206, 211

MULTIMEDIA. *See* composing in multimedia

N

NOUNS, USING: with ABC books, 17, 18–19; with difference stories, 163–164; with dog stories, 126–127, 127–128, 128–129, 129, 130–131, 131, 136; with poetry, 33; with sea mammal stories, 220–221, 221; with self-concept, 111

NUMBERS, COUNTING: with dinosaur stories, 260

O

ONSETS AND RIMES: with dinosaur stories, 268; with emotional issues, 151–152; with fairy tales, 86–87; with poetry, 33, 35–36, 36, 43, 44

ORAL LANGUAGE, DEVELOPING: with ABC books, 17, 21–22, 25, 26; with art, 96, 97, 100–101, 104–105; with bedtime stories, 172–173, 173–174, 175–176, 176, 177–178, 178, 179–180, 180–182, 183–184; with difference stories, 157, 158–159, 159–160, 162–163, 163–164, 164, 165, 166–167, 167–168; with dinosaur stories, 258, 260, 261–262, 262–263, 264–266, 266–267, 267–268, 268; with dog stories, 126–127, 127–128, 128–129, 129, 130–131, 131–132, 132, 133–134, 135, 136; with emotional issues, 140–141, 142–143, 143–144, 146, 147–148, 149–150, 150–151, 152–153; with fairy tales, 75–77, 77–78, 79, 81–82, 83–84, 85–86, 86–87, 88–89; with insect stories, 231, 232, 233–234, 236, 237–238, 238–239,

239–240, 240–241, 241; with job stories, 188–189, 189, 190–191, 191–192, 192–193, 193–194, 196, 197; with math, 244, 245, 246, 248–249, 249, 250, 251, 252, 253; with music, 47–48, 51–52, 54–55, 55–56; with sea mammal stories, 215, 216–217, 218–219, 219–220, 220–221, 221–222, 222–223, 224–225, 225, 227; with season stories, 273, 274–275, 277, 278–279, 281, 282, 283; with self-concept, 111, 112–113, 113–114, 115, 116, 118, 120–121, 122; with space stories, 287, 288–289, 289–290, 290, 292, 295–296, 296, 297, 298; with transportation stories, 201–202, 205, 211; with writing, 61, 63, 64–65, 65–66, 66–67, 68–69, 69, 70

P

PARTS OF SPEECH, SELECTING: with difference stories, 163–164; with insect stories, 232, 233

PHONEMIC AWARENESS, DEVELOPING: with emotional issues, 142–143, 150–151; with poetry, 33

PHONICS, USING: with ABC books, 25, 27; with art, 96, 97–98; with bedtime stories, 179–180, 180; with dinosaur stories, 258, 260, 268; with emotional issues, 144–145, 151–152; with fairy tales, 86–87; with insect stories, 232, 237–238; with math, 248–249, 250–251, 251; with music, 54–55, 55–56; with poetry, 31–32, 33, 35–36, 36, 38–39, 39–40, 43, 44; with season stories, 272, 282–283; with transportation stories, 211

PREDICTIONS, MAKING: with ABC books, 17; with art, 102; with bedtime stories, 173–174, 177, 179–180; with difference stories, 158–159; with dog stories, 132, 133; with emotional issues, 140–141, 146, 149–150, 152–153; with fairy tales, 75–77, 77–78, 81–82; with job stories, 195; with music, 54–55; with poetry, 33, 37; with sea mammal stories, 215, 219–220; with season stories, 281; with self-concept, 112, 119–120; with space stories, 292; with transportation stories, 211; with writing, 61–62, 66–67

PRESENTING WORK ON COMPUTER: with art, 95–96, 96, 99–100, 100, 103, 104–105; with bedtime stories, 174, 175–176, 177–178; with difference stories, 159–160, 162–163, 163–164, 164, 166; with dinosaur stories, 259–260, 262–263, 266–267; with dog stories, 128–129, 129, 131–132, 133–134; with emotional issues, 142–143, 147–148, 148–149, 150–151; with fairy tales, 79, 82–83, 83–84, 86–87, 88–89; with insect stories, 232, 234–235, 236, 237–238, 241; with job stories, 190–191, 193–194, 196; with math, 246, 252; with music, 49, 50, 52–53, 55; with poetry, 33–34, 34–35, 37–38, 38–39, 42–43; with sea mammal stories, 220–221, 221, 225–226; with season stories, 274–275, 278–279; with self-concept, 113–114, 115, 117–118, 118–119, 120–121; with space stories, 289–290, 292, 293–294,